# ORGIES OF FEELING

# ORGIES OF FEELING

## MELODRAMA AND
## THE POLITICS OF FREEDOM

## ELISABETH R. ANKER

Duke University Press  Durham and London  2014

© 2014 Duke University Press
All rights reserved
Printed in the United States of America on acid-free paper ∞
Typeset in Minion Pro by Westchester Book

Library of Congress Cataloging-in-Publication Data
Anker, Elisabeth R.
Orgies of feeling : melodrama and the politics of freedom / Elisabeth R. Anker.
pages   cm
Includes bibliographical references and index.
ISBN 978-0-8223-5697-4 (pbk : alk. paper)
ISBN 978-0-8223-5686-8 (cloth : alk. paper)
1. United States—Politics and government—2001–2009.
2. United States—Politics and government—2009–
3. Emotions—Political aspects—United States—History—21st century.
4. Political oratory—United States—History—21st century.
I. Title.
E902.A576 2014
973.93—dc23   2014001931

*Cover (top to bottom)*: Ground Zero, courtesy Getty Images News/the White House; Hillary
Rodham Clinton, courtesy of the White House/Pete Souza; waving flags, courtesy of the
George W. Bush Presidential Library/Paul Morse; secretary of defense Donald H. Rumsfeld
and commander general Tommy Franks, courtesy of the Department of Defense/Helene C.
Stikkel.

*For my parents, Carol Teig Anker and*
*the late Donald Jay Anker*

An *orgy of feeling* [is] employed as the most effective means of deadening dull, paralyzing, protracted pain. . . . To wrench the human soul from its moorings, to immerse it in terrors, ice, flames, and raptures to such an extent that it is liberated from all petty displeasure, gloom, and depression by a flash of lightning: What paths lead to *this* goal? And which of them do so most surely?

—FRIEDRICH NIETZSCHE,

*On the Genealogy of Morals*

# CONTENTS

# ACKNOWLEDGMENTS

I am a collaborative thinker, and other people's thoughts, comments, and scholarship have inextricably shaped my own. I am deeply grateful to so many people for making this work possible. My wonderful dissertation committee at UC Berkeley—Wendy Brown, Linda Williams, and Judith Butler—nourished the ideas that grew into this book. Wendy has been the most dedicated and generous advisor possible; she is a model of integrity, rigor, and compassion. Her work on politics and power opened new horizons of possibility for me. I simply would not think as I do without her. Linda's fantastic class on film theory changed the trajectory of my research. I thank Linda for introducing me to melodrama, for teaching me the pleasures of film criticism, and for encouraging me to see how political theory and film studies have so much to say to each other. Judith's intellectual daring and ethical generosity are an inspiration. I thank Judith for teaching me to think subtly about violence; to adjudicate the demands of Marx, Foucault, and Freud; and to have faith in my own work. A special thank you to Shannon Stimson for her unwavering support of my research, and to the late Michael Rogin, whose work continues to shape my understanding of American political culture.

I've had the good fortune to present earlier drafts of book chapters in lectures and colloquia. For their invitations and discussions, I thank Scott Loren and Jörg Mettelman at the Universität St. Gallen (and the support of the embassy of the United States in Switzerland); Lawrie Balfour and Stephen White at the University of Virginia; Chris Holmes and the Mellon Working Group at Brown University; Sharon Krause and John Tomasi at

Brown University's Political Philosophy Workshop; Dana Luciano and the DC Queers study group; Lori Marso at Union College; and Mort Schoolman, Peter Breiner, and Torrey Shanks at the University at Albany, SUNY.

Many people graciously read and commented on parts of this book in earlier stages, and I thank Lawrie Balfour, Mary Bellhouse, Cristina Beltran, Jane Bennett, Sam Chambers, Theo Christov, Alyson Cole, Bill Connolly, Ingrid Creppell, Jennifer Culbert, Ann Davies, Jodi Dean, Alex Dent, Shirin Deylami, Joshua Dienstag, Tom Dumm, Yaron Ezrahi, Kennan Ferguson, Jason Frank, Simona Goi, Lindsey Green-Simms, Cheryl Hall, Renee Heberlee, Chris Holmes, Dustin Howes, Sharon Krause, Joel Kuipers, Isis Leslie, Tal Lewis, Susan Liebell, Lori Marso, James Martel, Melani McAlister, Keally McBride, Bob Meister, Michael Morell, Sudarat Musikawong, Andy Murphy, Laurie Naranch, Anne Norton, Bibi Obler, Joel Olson, Davide Panagia, Samantha Pinto, Smita Rahman, Mark Reinhardt, Ruby Rich, Sara Rushing, Joel Schlosser, Mort Schoolman, John Seery, Torrey Shanks, Mike Shapiro, Lars Toender, Chip Turner, Rob Watkins, Calvin Warren, Meredith Weiss, Stephen White, Liz Wingrove, and Victor Wolfenstein. Steven Johnston and Simon Stow read the entire manuscript over in detail, and they helped me to sharpen ideas big and small; they are both wonderful critics. Leigh Jenco, Emily Nacol, and Jennifer Nash have been generous interlocutors at many stages of the book. Bonnie Honig and George Shulman helped me to see the critical potential in melodrama; thank you.

Other institutions have provided the support crucial to developing this project. I spent an incredible year at Brown University as a postdoctoral fellow in the Pembroke Center for Teaching and Research on Women. I would especially like to thank Elizabeth Weed, Suzanne Stewart-Steinberg, and Bernard Reginster for their conversations, encouragement, and good cheer. I was also very lucky to have a second home at the Political Theory Project while at Brown, and I owe a debt of gratitude for all of the faculty members associated with the PTP for including me as an official "honorary member." My year as a visitor at Johns Hopkins University was exciting and productive. I thank the many friends and colleagues there, especially Jane Bennett and Bill Connolly, whose scholarship and friendship continue to mean so much to me.

Friends and teachers at Berkeley read parts of the manuscript in early form, and I thank Robert Adcock, Diana Anders, Ivan Ascher, Jack Jackson, Martin Jay, Bob Kagan, Allison Kauffman, Sara Kendall, Robyn Marasco, Colleen Pearl, Shalini Satkunanadan, Kaja Silverman, Sharon Stanley, Annika Theim, Paul Thomas, Yves Winter, and all of the participants in Wendy

Brown's vital dissertation group. I also thank Mark Bevir for encouraging me to publish a seminar paper that formed the basis for this book. My good friends at Berkeley shared in navigating the labyrinths of Barrows and Telegraph, and their friendships were a key part of graduate school; thanks to Ryan Centner, Ralph Espach, Jane Gingrich, Jill Greenlee, Rosie Hsueh, Stephanie Mudge, Mike Nelson, Robin Stein, and Rachel VanSickle-Ward.

The George Washington University has generously supported this research in many ways, and I thank the Columbian College of Arts and Sciences in particular for two faculty grants to complete the book. The Department of American Studies has been a first-rate place to work and learn; for their collegiality and friendship, I'd like to thank Jamie Cohen-Cole, Tom Guglielmo, Chad Heap, Kip Kosek, Richard Longstreth, Jim Miller, Jen Nash, Suleiman Osman, Dara Orenstein, Phyllis Palmer, Elaine Peña, Gayle Wald, and Calvin Warren, and especially my supportive mentors, official and unofficial: Terry Murphy and Melani McAlister. I have learned a tremendous amount from our graduate students, including those in my seminars on democracy, melodrama, and critical theory. Thanks especially to Craig Allen, Megan Black, Greg Borchardt, Shannon Davies Mancus, Lindsay Davis, Emily Deitsch, Megan Drury, Emily Dufton, Ramzi Fawaz, Kara Heitz, Scott Larson, Joe Malherek, and Katie Rademacher.

My editor at Duke University Press, Courtney Berger, has offered valuable guidance and wise suggestions at every step of the process, and I am thankful for her enthusiasm and support of the book. The two reviewers for the press offered excellent suggestions for improving the manuscript, and I am grateful for their thoughtful and thorough engagement with it. Receiving their reports was a gift. Jan Williams meticulously prepared the index. I would also like to thank all of the people at Duke University Press, especially Ken Wissoker, Danielle Szulczewski, Heather Hensley, and Rebecca Fowler, for supporting and shepherding the production of the book.

My oldest friends have been with me through all the melodramas, big and small: Stephanie Goldberg Kresch, Lauren Levin Bender, Sara Lippmann, and Kim Nemirow. A very special thank you to Gina Demos for her wisdom, and for her encouragement to pursue a career in academia. My partner in crime, my amazing brother, Jon (Jawarhalal) Anker, makes me laugh like no one else, and I thank him for bringing the fabulous Dara, Elias, and Everett Anker into my life. I adore Lillian Anker, my one-hundred-year-old grandma. I thank her for her love and courage, and for reminding me at key points not to sweat the small stuff. Grandma Billie, you are a true inspiration. My family means the world to me: thank you to David, Christie, Noah, and Nathan Teig; Michele, Berkeley, Bridget, and Bella Barnett; Mark, Annie, Charlotte, and Madeline Havekost; and Pat and Oscar Scherer, my second parents and two of the kindest people on the planet. I love you all. I also thank the family members who live on in their influence and love: Ella Teig, Seymour Anker, William Teig, Moe Swartz, and my father, Donald Jay Anker, whom I miss every day.

Matthew Scherer has lived with melodrama for a decade, and his comments on this book have been invaluable to me. I continue to be amazed by his wisdom, thoughtfulness, and love. Meeting Matt has been the most fortuitous event of my life, and I am grateful beyond words for this world we've created together. Daniel Jay Anker-Scherer and Lilah Eve Anker-Scherer were born during the writing of this book, and they have brought immeasurable joy and wonder into the world. They truly make the ordinary extraordinary, every day.

My parents, Carol Sue Teig Anker and Donald Jay Anker, have supported me from my earliest moments, and they know all too well why I am compelled by melodrama. Thank you for your endless love, for showing me how to work hard, for creating a home filled with laughter, and for teaching me how to prioritize the things and people that matter most. I love you both, and I dedicate this book to you.

Parts of chapter 1 were published in earlier form in "Villains, Victims and Heroes: Melodrama, Media, and September 11" in *The Journal of Communication* 55, no. 1 (March 2005). An earlier version of chapter 5 was published as "Heroic Identifications; or, 'You Can Love Me Too—I Am So like the State,'" in *Theory and Event* 15, no. 1 (2012), and an earlier version of chapter 6 appeared as "Left Melodrama" in *Contemporary Political Theory* 11, no. 2 (May 2012).

# MELODRAMA AND THE POLITICS OF FREEDOM

## Melodramatic Political Discourse

One story line about the attacks on the World Trade Center and the Pentagon on September 11, 2001, became particularly influential in American political discourse. It went something like this: On a clear and cloudless Tuesday at the dawn of the new millennium, the United States lost its innocence in a horrifying attack. Moms and dads, friends and neighbors, black Americans and white Americans began the day going about their usual business: making breakfast, kissing loved ones good-bye, heading to work. Unbeknownst to them a small group of evil men, bent on destroying freedom, were initiating a terrible plan. They hijacked commercial airplanes and flew them into two of the most prominent symbols of American freedom and power, the World Trade Center and the Pentagon. Thousands of people died and lost loved ones. The entire nation was overwhelmed by the violence, and all Americans suffered in some way as its victims. The spectacle of destruction certified the irrationality and evil of the attackers at the same time that it confirmed the nation's virtue. After the attacks, Americans joined together with a clear moral imperative to eradicate terrorism from the world order and to fight for the nation's, indeed all of civilization's, imperiled freedom. Americans were compelled to launch a war on terror. While citizens were enjoined to go about the ordinary business of their daily lives, state agencies in partnership with contracted multinational corporations were tasked with mobilizing military interventions in key nations, expanding institutions of national security, and detaining individuals across the globe suspected of sharing terrorist proclivities. Despite the obstacles, America's victory in this global war was assured from the outset. Within this story, the triumph of freedom and virtue were foreordained.

This story was employed by many political officials, news-media outlets, ordinary citizens, and public intellectuals to depict the 9/11 attacks and their effects. The story was told as an epoch-shaping yet aberrant event in the otherwise continual spread of global freedom. And yet, despite the historical distinctiveness of the events it depicts, the story line is all too familiar: The story of 9/11 is a melodrama. This depiction of the attacks adheres to the conventions of a genre form that portrays dramatic events through moral polarities of good and evil, overwhelmed victims, heightened affects of pain and suffering, grand gestures, astonishing feats of heroism, and the redemption of virtue. Melodramas convey stories about the suffering of virtuous people overcome by nefarious forces, and they examine political and social conflict through outsized representations of unjust persecution. Literary, film, and cultural studies scholars have long understood the importance of melodramatic genre conventions to American cultural production. Melodramas have had widespread influence in theater, literature, and cinema since the nineteenth century, from mass novels to silent films to action spectacles, from *Uncle Tom's Cabin* (1852) to *The Birth of a Nation* (1915) to *The Terminator* (1984). Linda Williams and Fredric Jameson even identify melodrama as the most popular form of American mass culture.[1] Yet I argue that melodrama is more than a film, literary, or cultural genre; it is also a political genre, more precisely a genre of national political discourse. Melodramatic genre conventions are found in political rhetoric, governing processes, citizenship practices, and formations of national identity. Melodrama shapes the legitimation strategies of national politics, and the very operations of state power.

What I call *melodramatic political discourse* casts politics, policies, and practices of citizenship within a moral economy that identifies the nation-state as a virtuous and innocent victim of villainous action. It locates goodness in the suffering of the nation, evil in its antagonists, and heroism in sovereign acts of war and global control coded as expressions of virtue. By evoking intense visceral responses to wrenching injustices imposed upon the nation-state, melodramatic discourse solicits affective states of astonishment, sorrow, and pathos through the scenes it shows of persecuted citizens. It suggests that the redemption of virtue obligates state power to exercise heroic retribution on the forces responsible for national injury. Melodrama depicts the United States as both the feminized, virginal victim and the aggressive, masculinized hero in the story of freedom, as the victim-hero of geopolitics. Its national injuries morally legitimate the violence, extensions, and consolidations of state power that melodrama posits as necessary both for healing the nation's wound and for reestablishing the state's sovereign freedom. Melodramatic political discourse provides the tableaux and the legitimacy for the late-modern expansion of state power.

Melodrama is often associated with intimate affairs, personal misfortune, and domestic problems within the home, and even scholars who have written most incisively about the political effects of melodrama primarily examine how it attends to social injustices within the nation and finds redress for them in intimate relationships rather than in efforts to challenge injustice in more directly political ways.[2] Yet as a political discourse, melodrama operates in different registers: the suffering of U.S. subjects that it depicts appears to be caused by something outside the national body; an unjust injury wounds the entire nation, and this transforms melodrama to a more public, national, and state-centered register. The eradication of injustice in melodramatic political discourse is not about finding consolation in the domestic sphere, as it is in many film and literary melodramas; it is about an aggressive performance of strength in the national political sphere.[3] The agency in melodramatic political discourse focuses on global and spectacular displays of power; its sphere of action is public and usually institutional because of the villainy it aims to countermand. In melodramatic political discourse, the nation's terrible injury becomes the foundational justification for violent and expansive state power.

*Orgies of Feeling* investigates the history, political strategies, and affective pulls of melodramatic political discourses, with a focus on contemporary U.S. politics. While melodramatic cultural expressions are not limited to the United States—as the phenomena of Latin American telenovelas, Nigerian "Nollywood" videos, Soviet expressionism, and South Korean film make clear—this book focuses on American melodrama in order to map its work as a nation-building and state-legitimating discourse.[4] Melodrama became an influential political discourse after World War II, gaining popularity with the rise of the cold war and televisual political communication. It circulated throughout the second half of the twentieth century, as its conventions helped to narrate the expansion of U.S. global power and justify the growth of the national-security state. Melodramatic political discourses often legitimated anticommunist international relations and the burgeoning neoliberal political economy (though as I also show, melodrama sometimes worked in different or contradictory ways, and had unintended effects). In the twenty-first century, and especially after the 9/11 attacks, melodrama's popularity exploded in political discourse, in large part because of the nation-state's realignment against terrorism. *Orgies of Feeling* examines the rise of melodramatic political discourse after World War II, but pays special attention to melodrama's operations in the new millennium.

The melodramas that I track in this book often promote a specific type of citizenship, in which the felt experience of being an American comprises not only persecuted innocence and empathic connection with other Americans' suffering but also the express demand to legitimate state power. In these melodramas, the nation's unjust suffering proves its virtue, and virtue authorizes dramatic expressions of state action, including war and state surveillance. In contemporary politics, the intensifications of antidemocratic and often violent forms of state power—including military occupation, the exponential growth of the national-security state, the formalization of racial profiling, the narrowing of already minute points of access to political power for nonelite citizens, the criminalization of nonviolent protest, the militarization of police power, and the further abridgements of institutionalized civil liberties—are partly rooted in the melodramatic mobilization of a political subject who legitimates them as an expression of the nation's virtue.

A paradigmatic example of melodramatic political discourse is President George W. Bush's speech on the War in Afghanistan at the Pentagon on October 11, 2001. The story that the speech emplotted relied on melodramatic genre conventions—including a narrative of virtue and redemption, heightened affects of pain, detailed explanations of individual suffering, and a sense of overwhelmed victimhood that transmutes virtue into strength—to both unify national identity and authorize a war that had already begun four days prior. He stated,

> On September 11th, great sorrow came to our country. And from that sorrow has come great resolve. Today, we are a nation awakened to the evil of terrorism, and determined to destroy it. That work began the moment we were attacked; and it will continue until justice is delivered. . . . The loss was sudden, and hard, and permanent. So difficult to explain. So difficult to accept. Three schoolchildren traveling with their teacher. An Army general. A budget analyst who reported to work here for 30 years. A lieutenant commander in the Naval Reserve who left behind a wife, a four-year-old son, and another child on the way. But to all of you who lost someone here, I want to say: You are not alone. . . . We know

the loneliness you feel in your loss. The entire nation, entire nation, shares in your sadness. . . .

The hijackers were instruments of evil who died in vain. Behind them is a cult of evil which seeks to harm the innocent and thrives on human suffering. Theirs is the worst kind of cruelty, the cruelty that is fed, not weakened, by tears. . . . This week, I have called the Armed Forces into action. One by one, we are eliminating power centers of a regime that harbors al Qaeda terrorists. We gave that regime a choice: Turn over the terrorists, or face your ruin. They chose unwisely. . . . We're not afraid. Our cause is just and worthy of sacrifice. Our nation is strong of heart, firm of purpose. Inspired by all the courage that has come before, we will meet our moment and we will prevail.[5]

The speech details the events on September 11, 2001, through melodramatic conventions that emphasize the intense pain the attacks caused to ordinary individuals, and the speech uses that pain to mark the virtue of all Americans who share in the sadness of the people directly injured or killed by terrorism. Bush details the violence of the 9/11 events by specifying the people who died as moms and dads, schoolchildren, and neighbors— ordinary people, people just like his listeners. It is as if their travails could be, indeed are, our own. Melodrama confers virtue upon innocent people who unjustly suffer from dominating power, and this is part of the genre's cultural work; in this deployment of melodrama, all Americans suffer from the attack, and thus all share in the nation's virtue. The speech connects the children who lost parents with "our country": the children's innocence is a metonym for that of the nation, for what it has lost after this terrifying attack. This connection is a binding gesture that brings a nation ordinarily riven and stratified by class, race, immigration status, and sex into a shared unity that circumvents instead of represses stratification. It makes hierarchies of power and identity irrelevant to the experience of being an innocent and injured American in the wake of 9/11. The suffering that unifies the nation is suffering from terror. Other political modes of understanding also circulate in this speech to bind people together and mark the legitimacy of war: a deep sense of injustice and fear from the 9/11 attacks, American exceptionalism, and masculinist protection.[6] Yet melodramatic conventions work here to solicit the sense that war *has already been legitimated* by the felt sorrow that unifies the nation. Melodrama, in this speech, insists that the affective experience of sorrow is equivalent to the authorization of war.

This speech cultivates the heightened affects Americans were experiencing by explicating them, naming sorrow, loss, and resolve in a way that turns them into norms for proper feeling and then yokes them together into a narrative trajectory. Sorrow and loss pave the way for "great resolve," so that the determination to "destroy" evil is positioned as a foregone conclusion that grows organically out of sorrow. The move to destroy terrorism then becomes a moral requirement and a narrative expectation for addressing the nation's suffering, rather than a contestable political decision.[7] In this speech, melodramatic conventions form a nation-building discourse that distinguishes who is and is not American by demarcating proper victimhood in relation to state power: virtuous Americans identify with the suffering of grieving Americans, but they also sanction heroic state action against evil. War is promised to deliver a justice so clear and right that it is "worthy of sacrifice." The willingness to sacrifice further gestures to the goodness of the nation willing to make itself sacrificial in response to its sorrow, even as it is presupposed that real sacrifice will never be asked of the vast majority of the polity; in other speeches Bush asks Americans to sacrifice for the war effort by hugging their children, going shopping, and traveling by airplane.[8] In this melodrama the primary indicators of good citizenship, of what it means to be a real American, consist of a felt suffering from terrorism, plus the resolve to go to war. More than other genres, such as the jeremiad and the impasse (which I will discuss), melodrama offers a reassuring narrative trajectory that bestows innocence and moral authority on the United States, and then authorizes state power as an expression of the nation's virtue.[9]

Melodramatic political discourses can mark people who find its depictions unconvincing or wrong, or who actively question the legitimations it enables, as morally bankrupt, as un-American, as villainous, or even as terrorist.[10] This is not to say that deployments of melodramatic discourse eliminate dissent, but rather that their depictions cast dissent as both illegible and unbearably cruel to injured victims—to real Americans. Many people, of course, have condemned melodrama's moral injunctions or refused its legitimations of state power, even if they have not labeled these injunctions or legitimations melodramatic.[11] Since the first days after 9/11, for instance, marginalized political groups (especially but not limited to those on the left) resisted the melodramatic assumption that the attack signified American innocence or a virtuous nation, and spoke out against its moral mandate for retributive state violence. But melodrama may still have contributed to the affective responses to the events, even for people who resisted some of its terms. Upon encountering its depictions, one may hate its overt pathos yet cry at the suffering it shows. One might reject melodrama's depiction of national identity yet find welcome connection in the virtuous community it offers. One might find that melodramatic tenets unacceptably simplify politics yet want to see brutal villains duly punished. Some parts of melodrama are more compelling than others, and melodramatic conventions do not need to be totalizing to have partial effects. Individuals are often moved in inconsistent ways by its depictions. These inconsistencies are part of melodrama's affective charge. Many people have had to struggle with or against melodramatic conventions in staking their interpretations of the terrorist attacks and their aftermath, indeed in staking what kind of citizens they are or want to be. Even for those people who have responded ambivalently or antagonistically to it, melodrama has become the most powerful genre form of the war on terror.

*Orgies of Feeling* investigates different forms of melodramatic political discourse, including melodramas of neoliberalism, communism, and capitalism, with particular focus on melodramas of terrorism. Melodramatic political discourses can be found in the news media, political interviews, popular punditry, informal conversation, micropolitical registers, political theory, and organizing norms, as well as in the formal state rhetoric of presidential addresses: melodramas move through multiple vectors. The use of melodrama is not forced or coordinated across media outlets or political parties; its popularity across two centuries of cultural media make it readily available to multiple sites of power and address for depicting political life. Even though melodrama became a common rhetorical genre of the Bush administration in the first decade of the new millennium, and the administration certainly seized on melodrama's popularity to support its policies, melodrama did not originate from the administration or from any single source of authority. Its widespread use came from a much larger and contested historical trajectory that spans fields of power and political affiliation. Given the circulation of melodrama across political registers, I am thus less interested in judging whether melodrama is right or wrong in its depictions of political life—whether melodrama gives a true account or a false one—than in discerning its multiple workings and effects, its different appeals for different sites of power and subjectivity. People are not compelled by melodrama merely by coercive rhetoric or charismatic leaders. Melodramatic depictions of virtuous victimization, and predictions for the heroic overcoming of subjection, work on and through people in ways quite different from and beyond what institutional deployments of melodrama may intend. People who are drawn to melodrama's conventions, or who welcome its narrative assurances, do not necessarily respond to melodrama in predetermined ways. The processes of melodramatic subjectivity are not identical with the strategic aims of melodramatic political discourse, although they are coextensive. To presuppose that subjectivizing processes are the same as or are exhausted by discursive intent would be to assume that political discourses equal political subjects, that discourses determine psychic life, and that melodrama works the same way in different spaces, structures, and institutions.

To ascribe intent by a few elites for the pervasive use of melodrama is to ignore its appeal to a broad segment of the U.S. population, and to miss what melodrama's popularity reveals about contemporary American political life. The question of who intends for melodrama to happen, or who controls its circulation and employment, is not unimportant, but to answer it by placing responsibility for melodrama's popularity only on a few bad, powerful apples—rather than by also examining its appeal to a broad citizenry—is to mirror melodrama's strategy of claiming innocence and virtue for its victimized protagonists while displacing blame only to an all-powerful villain. The interesting question for this book is therefore not "why are citizens duped by the elite's use of melodrama into legitimating antidemocratic and violent state power?" but "what type of citizens may be compelled by melodramatic political discourse, and what do they imagine the powers it legitimates will do?"

## The Promise of Freedom

Melodramas grapple with moral questions and aim to establish "moral legibility," as Peter Brooks argues in his seminal account of the form.[12] They identify virtuous behavior and postulate that society also recognizes real virtue. In many film and television melodramas, the recognition of virtue is the endpoint of the narrative, and the climax of the story demonstrates the protagonist's moral goodness. Yet in melodramatic political discourse, moral legibility—the identification of the nation's virtue—is not the only factor motivating the widespread use of melodrama. There is another, perhaps more compelling, attraction: melodrama promises *freedom* for those who are virtuous. The moral legibility of melodramatic political discourse is in the service of an expectation that freedom is forthcoming for both injured citizens and the nation-state. The allure of melodramatic political discourse is the promise of emancipation that it offers those who unjustly suffer.

The norm of freedom that circulates in melodramatic political discourse is rooted in particularly liberal and Americanized interpretations of freedom as self-reliance, as unconstrained agency, and as unbound subjectivity. It combines these interpretations together as normative expressions of a sovereign subject, one who obeys no other authority but one's own, who can determine the future and control the vagaries of contingency through sheer strength of will. Freedom requires the capacity for final authority over the space of the nation and aims to shore up boundaries of territories and bodies to make them impermeable to the influence of others. Freedom as this form of sovereign subjectivity seems to require control or mastery over the external world for its full exercise. Freedom, in this normative definition, is often equated with both individual and state sovereignty. Indeed, melodrama provides a site at which state and individual agency are conflated, as if the achievement of state sovereignty confers personal sovereignty upon every American. The practices of freedom that melodramas depict thus often take shape through an imaginary of freedom as the performance of sovereignty through unilateral action, war, intensified national security, and even as the institutionalization of what Gilles Deleuze calls "societies of control," as all are deployed in the service of controlling the political field and taming risk.[13] This version of sovereignty implies that the state—and by extension the individual citizen—should be not only free *from* the coercions of others but also free *over* others. This latter freedom, though seldom explicitly acknowledged, is what ensures the possibility of the former.

The promise of sovereign freedom is present in melodramatic political discourse whether it shapes the cold war argument in the 1950s that the nation has a moral requirement to eradicate the evil of communism from the world order, or the neoliberal argument in the 1980s that welfare must be eliminated because it is a form of oppression that erodes individual freedom. Both melodramas, while organized around different stories and deployed for different purposes, offer the promise of future freedom through state power for virtuous Americans under siege. Neoliberal melodramas might seem to link freedom to limited state power, since economic policies grouped under the term *neoliberal* claim to facilitate individual freedom by deregulating corporations and cutting both taxes and welfare. However, they typically limit only certain types of state power, those that hamper corporate profit or provide social services, both of which come to be cast as un-American, as outside the proper national body, and as forms of individual oppression. They increase state powers that expand military might, corporate growth, and surveillance. As Sheldon Wolin notes, neoliberal policies discredit the state's ability to serve the needs of the people, but they do not weaken state power.[14] Neoliberal melodramas use the language of individual freedom not to retrench state power but to *expand* securitized and militarized forms of it.[15]

Melodrama hearkens a future in which U.S. citizens and the state exercise their rightful entitlement to unconstrained power. As in Bush's speech announcing the War in Afghanistan, melodramatic political discourses promise that U.S. military and state actions, together with the corporations that work through and as state power, can transform a sense of being overwhelmed by power into a scene of triumphant strength and sovereign control. Similarly, Bush's very first words to the nation describing the 9/11 attacks do not reflect a deep misunderstanding of the events or an empty rhetorical flourish: "Freedom itself was attacked this morning by a faceless coward. And freedom will be defended." These words are a precise expression of the promises that melodramatic political discourse offers the unjustly injured nation: virtuous victims can gain back their sovereignty from anti-American forces by feats of heroic might.[16]

A desire for sovereign freedom is thus a decisive factor in the authorization of state power as it takes shape in melodramatic political discourse. The promise of melodrama is that the American nation, once victimized, will eventually reassert its sovereign freedom through the virtuous acts of heroism it must perform against the cause of its injury. The melodramatic legitimation of violent, expansive, and constraining forms of power is thus paradoxically motivated by a desire to experience unconstrained freedom. This differs from the way that melodramatic genre expectations shape cinema, theater, and literature, when story lines can end in pathos and tragedy for injured protagonists: an innocent victim may die after his or her virtue is celebrated, as in *Uncle Tom's Cabin* or *Brokeback Mountain* (2005), or a hero will sacrifice his or her own life in order to save another or to uphold justice, as in *The Birth of a Nation* or *Saving Private Ryan* (1998). But in national politics melodramatic story lines that end without securing the universal freedom of their protagonists are generally left outside the expectations of the narrative. Freedom is frequently the stated goal of melodramatic initiatives in foreign, domestic, and military policy, and it is crucial to take these myriad and explicit claims for freedom seriously as motivating factors behind expansions of state power. It is no coincidence that the Iraq War's combat zones were called "the front lines of freedom," or that the War in Afghanistan was officially titled Operation Enduring Freedom. To be sure, freedom is not the only desire motivating the legitimation of these wars; vengeance, violence, Islamophobia, and an escape from fear coexist alongside freedom.[17] But these other motivations have gained much more scholarly attention at the expense of the study of freedom, and they have overshadowed the ways that a desire for freedom sits beside and even underwrites these more overtly insidious motivations, giving them a legitimate form of expression.

By positioning melodrama in relationship to freedom, this book emphasizes how contemporary desires for freedom are often constituted and delimited by the very forms in which they are articulated. Taking seriously Saba Mahmood's warning not to "tether the meaning of agency to a predefined teleology of emancipatory politics," this inquiry asks instead *how* a desire for sovereign freedom is cultivated out of melodramatic depictions of political events.[18] Mahmood cautions scholars against uncritically accepting that there is an ontological desire for freedom that drives individuals, especially when freedom is imagined as a settled achievement of an abstract liberal subject. She asks instead, "what sort of subject is assumed to be normative within a particular political imaginary?"[19] Rather than using Mahmood's warning to deny that desires for freedom exist in American political subjects, however, I examine how a desire for freedom is produced within and conditioned by various melodramatic political discourses. I specify the particular content of "freedom" that shapes the very political subjectivity that desires it, and use the study of melodrama to ask: How do unilateral state violence and individual license come to inhabit contemporary definitions of freedom and agency? How is a teleology of emancipation melodramatically imagined through the legitimation of war and national security? I posit that the melodramatic cultivation of a desire for freedom develops at a moment in which long-standing frustrations of political powerlessness combine with the immediate shock of terrorism to operate on national subjects already constituted by certain expectations of liberal freedom and democratic citizenship.

Melodramatic discourses are so widespread, I argue, because they revive the guarantee of sovereign freedom for both the state and the individual in a neoliberal era when both seem out of reach. This lost guarantee of sovereignty has a long and contested genealogy that I examine more in the book, but one way to unpack it here is to work backward and start from the spectacle of nonsovereignty on September 11. The 9/11 attacks were shocking not only for the violence they committed but for the story of freedom they derailed. They disclosed—in a spectacular and horrifying way—failures of both state and individual sovereignty, and melodramatic conventions promised that both types of sovereignty could be regained. Judith Butler argues that 9/11 entailed "the loss of a certain horizon of experience, a certain sense of the world itself as a national entitlement," and melodrama became appealing in the post-9/11 era because it seemed to reestablish that sense of entitlement.[20] The loss of "the world itself as a national entitlement" was a loss of unconstrained freedom for the nation-state, a loss of its seeming capacity to protect itself, monopolize the use of force, and steer geopolitics. Enacted by "faceless" cowards—inconspicuous agents whose weapons of mass destruction were ordinary objects like box cutters and commercial airplanes, and who self-destructed upon their own "victory" (doers that did not exceed the deed)—the attacks appeared to be the effect of invisible forces rather than identifiable state actors, their agents easily eluding state apparatuses of surveillance and militarized border systems. They performed, as the collective Retort argues, "the sheer visible happening of defeat."[21] In effortlessly penetrating national borders, the attackers upended two beliefs: that America was invulnerable to serious attack by foreigners and that geopolitical boundaries could demarcate state sovereignty. Indeed, if the state is defined through Max Weber's classic definition as that which has "the monopoly on the legitimate use of violence," a definition in which state power is ipso facto sovereign, then the 9/11 events challenged the very workings of the state by revealing its nonsovereignty.[22]

The loss of the world as a national entitlement traversed individual and state agency.[23] The attacks created a loss for individuals in their presumed capacity under reigning norms of liberal individualism to be self-reliant and sovereign over their own bodies. By indiscriminately murdering unknown and unsuspecting individuals, the attacks challenged the monadic premises of individual self-reliance, what Sharon Krause calls the long-standing liberal belief that "the individual is understood to be the master of her own domain."[24] The mass violence shed light on the intense social vulnerability of individual bodies, revealing how individuals are always, as Butler argues, "exposed to others, at risk of violence by virtue of that exposure."[25] The terrorist attacks thus violently upended the sovereign freedom story that entwines states and subjects. Whether sovereignty is defined as having the ultimate power or authority to make decisions about life and death (as in Carl Schmitt or Giorgio Agamben), the capacity to authoritatively reign over a defined geographic or bodily space (as in Thomas Hobbes or Jean Bodin), or the right of self-determination and self-making against the dominations of others (as in Jean-Jacques Rousseau), the 9/11 events revealed contracted possibilities of sovereign power.[26] In highlighting the vulnerabilities and dependencies of contemporary life, the attacks challenged sovereignty as the grounding presupposition of both individual agency and international relations.

Melodrama's narrative teleology of freedom responds by revitalizing norms of sovereignty for both individuals and states, and this is part of its widespread appeal. Melodrama's affective and narrative forms aim to resecure the nation's virtue and reestablish its sovereign power. Melodrama becomes more potent after 9/11's radical destabilization of national narratives about freedom and power because the genre's emplotment of a familiar narrative trajectory—injury then redemption—seems to restabilize the promise of sovereignty. Bonnie Honig writes that melodramas thematize "the sense of being overwhelmed by outside forces"; melodramas depict individual protagonists as vulnerable to and powerless against the violence and cruelty of the outside world.[27] This makes melodrama well suited for depicting situations of overwhelming vulnerability. But in political discourse melodrama goes further, as it also promises that overwhelmed subjects can overcome their vulnerability by dramatic counter-acts of force, acts that melodrama equates with the achievement of freedom. In promising that freedom is forthcoming for virtuous sufferers, melodrama implies that complex global vulnerability and interdependence can be overcome by expressions of state power reasserting U.S. global might, which will then reflect back to American individuals their own sovereignty.

In melodrama's narrative temporality, however, sovereign freedom can only be achieved *after* an overwhelming experience of vulnerability, powerlessness, and pain: this is how melodrama positions the United States as the victim and hero of world politics. In Dick Cheney's war on terror melodrama, for instance, "This is a struggle against evil, against an enemy that rejoices in the murder of innocent, unsuspecting human beings. . . . A group like Al Qaeda cannot be deterred or placated or reasoned with at a conference table. For this reason the war against terror will not end with a treaty, there will be no summit meeting or negotiations with terrorists. The conflict will only end with their complete and permanent destruction and in victory for the United States and the cause for freedom."[28] The nation's overwhelming experience of unjust victimization heralds its grandiose reclamation of sovereign power through "permanent destruction" of the evil villain that caused the nation's powerlessness. Melodrama's moral economy transmutes affectively intense experiences of unjust victimization into the anticipation of, and justification for, violence imagined as sovereign agency.

*Orgies of Feeling* thus challenges the conventional critical gloss on the post-9/11 moment by arguing that it was *freedom*, not national security, that many Americans thought they were achieving by dramatically increasing state power in the pursuit of terrorism. On most readings of millennial politics, U.S. citizens have willingly traded freedom for security: Americans have responded to terror by retreating from the burdens of individual liberty to the safety of a protector state.[29] On these readings, Americans legitimated retractions of their civil liberties as well as massive increases in national security in order to buttress their newfound exposure to violence. Yet melodrama's primary appeal for those who legitimated, even relished, intensifications of state power, and perhaps even for those who contested many of its tenets, was that it rehabilitated the promise of sovereign agency. After the 9/11 attacks spectacularly intensified felt experiences of powerless and vulnerability shaping political life at the new millennium, melodrama revived the pursuit of sovereign freedom in response. The melodramatic story of 9/11 reveals a desperate and violent attempt to pursue freedom as a morally righteous reclamation of sovereignty in a volatile, disempowering, and nonsovereign era.

## Orgies of Feeling and Unfreedom

The loss of the world as a national entitlement that drew Americans to melodrama did not only stem from the 9/11 attacks, however. It was decades in the making. Reigning U.S. norms of sovereignty and liberal self-reliance have suffered crippling blows in an era of corporate deregulation and intensified state power, as the might of the global superpower and the agency of individuals have been continually weakened by transnational capital flows and geopolitical shifts of influence. The 9/11 events were a single, albeit spectacular, example of a more long-standing condition of "waning sovereignty," what Wendy Brown calls the weakening of "the fantasy of human control over human destiny."[30] This fantasy, by no means limited to U.S. political imaginaries, takes particular form in U.S. politics through vast deployments of military and economic power paradoxically upheld by ideologies of liberal individualism, which assume that sovereign agency is the rightful entitlement of U.S. subjects. Melodrama responds to waning sovereignty by offering that dramatic performances of state power can restore heroic, sovereign agency to both the individual and the state. By promising heroic emancipation from terrorist evil, melodramatic political discourse implies that U.S. political subjects can overcome the ineffectual and devitalized political agency that saturates contemporary life beyond the singular event of terrorism.

Deployments of post-9 / 11 melodrama intensified a singular affective experience of terror with a strategic aim to displace chronic and low-grade experiences of constraint, fear, and vulnerability that are routinized in contemporary political life. This affective displacement is what Friedrich Nietzsche refers to as an "orgy of feeling." Orgies of feeling describe a counterintuitive attempt to ameliorate confusing feelings of powerlessness by imposing intense affects of victimization—including terror, pain, sorrow, helplessness, and shock—upon the self.[31] According to Nietzsche, orgies of feeling aim to rehabilitate freedom, or at least ameliorate the affects of felt powerlessness, through new experiences of intensified affect. The new and more painful affects minimize earlier and more confusing affects of helplessness in two ways: first by overwhelming the earlier ones so that they recede from experience, and second by promising that this new, more intense experience of victimization can be fought against so that it paves the way for a coming freedom. Mobilized through melodramatic political discourse, orgies of feeling drew from the horror and vulnerability brought on by terrorism to overwhelm daily experiences of fear and demobilization, and also to implicitly promise an impending emancipation from them. Orgies of feeling are a mechanism by which long-standing yet ordinary experiences of political powerlessness in the late-modern era are displaced onto the terror of 9 / 11.

I refer to daily experiences of devitalized agency throughout the book with the shorthand *unfreedom*. Unfreedom marks a set of conditions of the late-modern and neoliberal moment, which include mass political disenfranchisement, experiences of being overpowered by the agentless forces of globalization, increasing economic inequality and financial precarity across populations, tightening norms for acceptable individual behavior, and decreasing political agency for influencing collective governing decisions. Unfreedom refers to contemporary experiences in which citizens are continually demobilized and demoralized, excluded from politics, and made into consumers rather than active players in the operations of collective decision making; in which multinational corporate power promotes vast levels of exploitation while evading political accountability and public visibility; in which jobs and families have been uprooted, severed, and micromanaged while a politics of fear pervades work and home life; in which systems of support from state, family, and community structures have been financially broken and systematically destroyed; in which the nexus of capitalism and state governance pushes the goals of efficiency, subjugation, and flexibility to organize the terms of collective governance and individual flourishing at the expense of notions of equality or justice; in which mediated information exposes various horrors and subjugations from around the world yet insists that nothing can be done to change them; and in which no large-scale political collectivity offers significant societal-wide change, as significant change does not seem viable. These conditions influence people in very different ways and are differentially allocated depending on relative privilege in hierarchies of class, race, sexuality, immigration status, regional location, and gender, among other categories. The generalized and often ineffable sense of helplessness and vulnerability that these conditions produce, however, are becoming commonplace across many populations. Under these conditions, individuals seem unable to experience self-determination or effect change in the world. Experiences of unfreedom are not only frightening but also confusing, as their causes are often difficult to discern. The modes of power that produce them are often experienced as nonagentic and spatially unlocatable; they are global yet micropolitical, impinging yet intangible, "faceless" yet mobile, and replicating with alacrity. They create a widespread sense of precariousness and constraint that is not so much explicitly expressed as felt in unarticulated yet nagging affects of impotence, anxiety, constriction, and resentment.

For post-9/11 melodramatic political subjects—those individuals who find melodrama compelling, and who accept its solicitations—the affective intensity of 9/11's horror and violence may have overwhelmed more long-standing experiences of unfreedom. In the retrospective temporality of an orgy of feeling, these earlier experiences were relocated to the 9/11 events, which then become their site of origin. Melodrama orgiastically displaced a broadly shared but deeply isolating and confusing sense of powerlessness onto a clearly shared and obvious sense of being attacked and robbed of one's freedoms. Political subjects who draw upon melodrama employ its orgiastic way of making powerlessness legible by naming complex experiences of unfreedom to be the effects of a terrorist attack caused by villains. As Raymond Williams notes about melodrama, it transposes broad social conflicts onto the particular scenarios it emplots, making a particular scene stand in for and replace a larger conflict.[32] Melodramatic orgies of feeling are a form of this transposition. They alleviate daily experiences of contracted agency by displacing their confusing causes onto singular spectacles and naming Americans innocent victims of evil forces. Long-standing vulnerabilities and global dependencies are thus confronted through an orgy of feeling that predicts their eradication through masterful acts of sovereign power. The 9/11 attacks enabled the intensification of melodramatic political discourse, but the end of the twentieth century created the conditions by which it would become particularly appealing.

Through melodrama, a desire to resist prevalent forms of contemporary unfreedom is orgiastically incited by and displaced onto terrorism, which then forms a new melodramatic imaginary of sovereign freedom in response. The contemporary discourse of anti-immigration is often patterned in a similar way; it positions immigrants, rather than terrorists alone, as evil villains out to disempower Americans. As the war on terror has been unable to make good on the promise of sovereign freedom (which I discuss in detail later), one of its effects is to relocate the villainy that overwhelms America from terrorists onto immigrants, especially poor and brown ones. In a globalized era where inside versus outside territorial boundaries and us versus Other national identities are increasingly challenged and hard to define, anti-immigration and terrorism melodramas both attempt to reinstate clear markers between the United States and its Others, between the inside and outside of the nation, in order to promote national unity and reestablish the state's jurisdictional control and monopoly of violence. Melodramatic narratives of terrorism and immigration both foretell that various modalities of unilateral state power will disable villainy and consequently undo daily experiences of enervated power. They suggest that freedom from and mastery over unaccountable transnational power can be heroically (re)gained through spectacular increases in antidemocratic state power that can punish or expel foreign threats to the nation. These melodramas further reveal how norms of neoliberalism do not necessarily diminish or devalue state power in the twenty-first century; they also incite dramatic increases in its use and value. Neoliberal policies decrease state support in the name of individual freedom, yet the vulnerability these policies create also leads people to *reinvest* in securitized state power in a misplaced attempt to end their vulnerability.

Melodramatic political discourse's emphasis on the heroic reclamation of freedom places it in contrast to other genre forms that emphasize how neoliberalism's production of widespread vulnerability leads to an enervated agency, including those that Lauren Berlant identifies as the genre of "the impasse." Cultural products in the genre of the impasse depict how people adapt to crumbling fantasies of the good life and liberal democracy, fantasies that include economic security, political representation, and class mobility; even if these fantasies were never fully achievable in the first place, the impasse shows how it has become increasingly hard to sustain belief in them. The genre of the impasse, found in literature, poetry, and film, among other places, depicts individuals who do not have the energy to actively resist the tidal changes devastating ordinary life, and aim merely to survive them. For Berlant, the genre of the impasse disrupts familiar narrative trajectories that would herald the end of suffering or promise a better life, and emphasizes instead how people endure their precariously lived conditions by improvising and adjusting to them.[33] Melodramatic orgies of feeling offer a different generic response to contemporary conditions of vulnerability and unfreedom: they shore up an energizing subjectivity. Melodrama's orgies of feeling aim to cast off feelings of helplessness and paralysis. Whereas the impasse attends to an overburdened subject trying to *adapt* to precarity and the waning of sovereignty, melodrama's orgies of feeling attend to an overburdened subject trying instead to *overcome* precarity, and thus to (re)experience the sovereign freedom he or she desires.[34] Their goal is mastery over unaccountable and overwhelming powers, rather than adjustment to them.

For Berlant, the genre of the impasse reveals the waning popularity of melodrama in American culture, as melodrama's heightened affects do not accord with the population's growing sense of exhaustion by the difficult conditions of ordinary life.[35] Yet melodrama has been an increasingly popular genre of national politics throughout much of the later twentieth century, and especially after the 9/11 events, so it might be more precise to say that melodrama and the impasse coexist as different strategies for adjudicating unfreedom. Melodrama and the impasse do not cancel each other out, therefore, but circulate in distinct ways and different planes of social life. As a political discourse, melodrama is staged in a more publicly political way than the impasse, which is often experienced in "zones of labor, neighborhood, and intimacy" that respond more explicitly to the ordinary conditions of unfreedom than melodrama's displaced focus on spectacular acts of terrorism and retributive state power.[36] Unlike the impasse, which shows how individuals have not (yet) been defeated by what is overwhelming, melodramatic subjects attempt to prove their ability to overwhelm what is overwhelming, and therefore recapture their sovereign agency.[37]

The melodramatic legitimation of violent state power betrays a desperate attempt to experience the exercise of freedom as it has been promised by the norms of sovereignty and license that govern U.S. political discourse even though, as decades of daily forms of unfreedom demonstrate, they have lost their relevance as governing norms. In examining the waning of sovereignty, Brown argues that the proliferation of border walls in the contemporary era is an attempt to materially reinstate territorial sovereignty through concrete demonstrations of might and impermeability. Ironically, however, border walls further weaken the sovereignty they are deployed to buttress; she writes, "At the same time that walls dissimulate declining state sovereignty with a spectacle of its rectitude and might, walls cleave the reality of global interdependence and global disorder with stage set productions of intact nationhood, autonomy and self-sufficiency."[38] The use of melodrama is a similar attempt to revive the promise of sovereignty in an era of its collapse, though it operates in more figurative ways, in discursive registers and gestural performances. Yet similar to the promises of sovereignty that border walls aim to concretize, melodrama's discursive promises of imminent sovereignty are equally unachievable, and the terms of its promise deepen the conditions of unfreedom that they are deployed to resist. Melodrama's orgies of feeling position victimization to herald a general overcoming of unfreedom, but they authorize war, surveillance, occupation, the truncation of civil liberties, the criminalization of dissent, the militarization of domestic politics, and heightened levels of individual regulation as the mode of that overcoming. In legitimating violent and intrusive governing and corporate powers as a moral imperative for the practice of sovereign freedom, melodrama entrenches the disempowerment it is employed to overcome, and it abrogates the freedoms it promises to engender.

My concern about the deepening of unfreedom that occurs through melodramatic political discourse arises out of a broader dilemma regarding the pursuit of freedom that has vexed critical political theory since the mid-twentieth century, and is arguably critical theory's animating concern: people often seem not only to refuse to challenge experiences of subjection but also to assist them, indeed to harbor deep attachments to conditions of unfreedom. Though my argument is indebted to critical theoretical approaches to this broad dilemma, it inverts the more common mode of critique, which locates the operations of oppression in seemingly emancipatory pursuits.[39] Instead, this study poses a different dilemma. It asks: even in one of the more unliberatory eras in contemporary politics—when political subjects do not just acquiesce to but often actively support policies that sanction large-scale violence and murder, and that shrink venues for dissent, possibilities for political participation, and pursuits of justice—is there a glimmer of a desire to challenge unfreedom, an intent to undo the oppressions that individuals often seem so willing to uphold? This is not to offer an optimistic reading of a dark era in political life or to justify the complicity of American citizens who acquiesce to and actively sanction violent, inhumane, or oppressive policies. Quite the contrary. But it is to tell a different and overlooked story, a story about contemporary political subjects who do not reflexively desire unfreedom, but whose challenge to unfreedom is obstructed by the very strategies they mobilize in their efforts.

## Genres of Politics

To argue that melodrama is a genre of political discourse is to argue that political events, ideas, subjectivities, legitimating strategies, and actions are mediated by the different modalities in which they are depicted and made legible. Genres of political discourses work as a set of interpretive conventions and affective expectations for public political life. These genres provide norms and anticipations for the trajectory of political events, articulate models for civic morality and citizenship, offer possibilities for the exercise of power, employ temporal schemas for the content of political life, and solicit particular felt experiences in their participants.[40] They certainly do not do all this at once, nor do they each do all of them equally well, or well at all, but different genres resonate at different historical moments and encourage certain actions, subjectivities, and legitimations while discouraging others. The effects of these genres are never inevitable, incontestable, or even linear; as this book shows, they double back, challenge themselves, fail in their intended deployments, blend with other genres, and depict the same situation in multiple ways.

While melodrama and other genres of political discourse are at work, from official presidential speeches to informal dinner conversation, *Orgies of Feeling* primarily examines national and official political discourse because it is often what garners enough power, prestige, and nationwide audiences to define the national conversation, especially in times of crisis.[41] National political discourse is often what most powerfully legitimates the exercise of political and economic power. This legitimating work is a key component of melodramatic political discourse; hence its proliferation in these realms. My focus is televised and print news media, political speeches, and debates and interviews fashioned for mass spectators and public occasions, as well as the political theories that analyze or uphold their legitimating tasks. These sites are important for the national identities they propose, the government programs they aim to authorize, the orgies of feeling they display and generate, the types of citizenship they sustain and instigate, and the visions of collective life they imagine. Yet these sites do not develop in isolation from one another; their discourses reverberate back and forth with varying degrees of intensity. Nor are melodramatic discourses merely the calculated invention of a political or media elite. They are formed from mutable combinations of political pressures, cultural genre expectations, media practices, official state rhetoric, affective dispositions, economic structures, theological sediments, and political-theoretical ideas, as well as institutions of power that can include but are not limited to "the state." While disparate governmental functions grouped together as "state power" and elite political actors do have heightened capacity to mobilize various political discourses, these discourses often counteract or exceed what formal institutions or elite actors have intended.

Many different genres circulate at any historical moment in U.S. political discourse. In the post-9/11 era other genres have competed with melodrama or amalgamated into it to cultivate different links between the pursuit of freedom and the content of national identity. Melodrama directly competes with the jeremiad, a perennially popular genre in American culture patterned on biblical lamentations of the prophets, which offers a strident moral critique of a degraded society and prophecies that society will collapse if it continues down its wayward path.[42] Jeremiadic genres of political discourse depicting the 9/11 attacks in their immediate aftermath often inhabited the ends of the political spectrum. On the political-radical left, jeremiadic tropes depicted the attacks as a direct consequence of American imperialism and domination in the Middle East, as punishment for the pursuit of freedom through geopolitical mastery. Noam Chomsky, for instance, argued that "the U.S. is regarded as a leading terrorist state, and with good reason," and portrayed the nation as reaping what its intelligence agencies have sown in prior decades of neoimperial conquest and military expansion.[43] Chomsky's book 9-11 prophesied a world in which the United States would be mired in an unwinnable war in Afghanistan that would deplete its own economy while killing thousands of its own citizens (a prophecy that has largely come to pass).

On the evangelical religious right, and with a much looser sense of historical causality, jeremiads depicted the 9/11 events as punishment for American secularism, immorality, and liberal politics. The televangelist Jerry Falwell's claims that the attacks were "probably deserved" is an example, as when he stated, "I really believe that the pagans, and the abortionists, and the feminists, and the gays and the lesbians who are actively trying to make that an alternative lifestyle, the ACLU, People for the American Way, all of them who have tried to secularize America. I point the finger in their face and say 'you helped this happen.'"[44] While these two jeremiads are very different in their location of blame, consolidations of national identity, and suggestions for future action, both make the United States, and various populations within its borders, accountable in part for the terrorist attacks. Melodrama, by contrast, often places responsibility for injury not upon the nation—the sufferers of the attack—but upon evil villains who remain outside the wounded collective it defines. Unlike the jeremiad, then, melodrama banishes any claim that the national body it constructs bears accountability for the events, whether that accountability is real or imagined, invidious or deserved.

In melodrama responsibility for violence is located only externally, explicitly to non-American terrorists and often implicitly to Arab Muslim populations; this is part of melodrama's nation-building work. A key component of melodrama's ability to confer virtue on the nation is that it does not demand the nation's self-critique for the conditions of unfreedom in which it is enmeshed. The theater historian Robert Heilman writes of the melodramatic form: "If disaster comes from evil, it is the evil of others, not ourselves; we are innocent and do not need to look more steadily at ourselves. . . . One is untroubled by indecisiveness, by awareness of alternate courses, by weakness, or by counter imperatives."[45] The national body is not divided against itself—it is neither implicated in evil nor accountable for its own political engagements. Whereas the jeremiad proposes the national body as a split subject, one who is partly accountable for the wrongdoing it experiences, melodramatic subjects—both the national body and the individual self—are unified and defined wholly by goodness, so that the pursuit of their freedom by any means becomes an expression of virtue, and they can rest safe in the monopathy of their moral fiber.

Part of the difference between melodrama and the jeremiad is found in their temporalities: in the jeremiad the 9 / 11 narrative begins well before the specific date of September 11, 2001, and includes actions taken by American citizens in the preceding years; in melodrama the narrative begins with the destruction of the World Trade Center, and this different starting point changes the nature of accountability. In melodrama, no prior U.S. action bears upon the story, so the nation is able to become an innocent victim. This might explain why melodrama is more compelling in times of political crisis, why more people might latch on to melodrama, take pleasure or comfort in its organizing terms, or allow it to capture their imagination. Melodrama is thus often privileged over jeremiadic constructions in part because its claims of American morality and innocence rebut nationwide accountability for terrorism. Part of the appeal of melodrama is to prove the virtue of the nation to the nation—to make the nation's goodness morally legible to itself. Melodrama promises an imminent emancipation from the forces of unfreedom, as it names the nation and its citizens a force of unvarnished good in the world; this accounts for its pervasiveness and appeal.

Melodrama's political expression often intersects with and absorbs other popular conventions shaping American politics, including a masculinized self-reliance in political culture, patterns of demonology in American history, the expansionist drive of the American state, and the exceptionalist character of the politico-religious imaginary. Melodramatic political discourse also blends into the "clash of civilizations" thesis that characterized a fundamentally antagonistic geopolitics in the 1990s and gained new credence in the twenty-first century. The genre arising out of the popular deployment of Samuel Huntington's clash-of-civilizations argument postulates that the world order is organized by fundamental cultural antagonisms between developed, Christian civilizations and underdeveloped, often Muslim societies.[46] The genre works synergistically with melodrama: both streamline complex situations into a tidy world order based on "natural" antagonisms between fundamentally different religiously based societies. Both employ what Michael Rogin diagnoses as the "demonization" of evil Others in which political ideas and identities that seem to differ from mainstream U.S. liberal norms and sanctioned political identities are made monstrous and denied political legibility.[47] Yet the clash of civilizations, as Huntington originally conceived it, did not need an act of victimization to jump-start its narrative—the antagonism it posits is always preexisting, generated by long-standing religious orders that underpin civilizational differences. Like melodrama, the clash of civilizations made claims of superiority for its American protagonists, but unlike melodrama these claims were not based on the innocence or inherent virtue of the United States. The genre conventions in the clash of civilizations makes it more difficult for the United States to claim *moral* goodness over its enemies, which melodrama by contrast easily confers upon the nation.

Writing in the 1990s, Huntington argued that the clash of civilizations was a "realist" analysis, an amoral, pragmatic interpretation of long-term religious-cultural antagonisms.[48] A focus on melodrama explains how the clash-of-civilizations thesis became more explicitly moralized in post-9/11 public discourse. The *New York Times* columnist Thomas Friedman, a key liberal supporter of the wars in Afghanistan and Iraq, draws on the clash of civilizations in his "9/11 Lesson Plan" to make (even as he denies making) moral claims of superiority for the United States that ground his justification for war: "We Americans are not better than any other people, but the Western democratic system we live by is the best system on earth. Unfortunately, in the Arab-Muslim world, there is no democracy, too few women's rights and too little religious tolerance. It is the values and traditions of freedom embraced by Western civilization, and the absence of those values and traditions in the Arab-Muslim world, that explain the main differences between us."[49] After 9/11 the realpolitik veneer of the clash-of-civilizations thesis peeled off, once melodramatic conventions attached to its antagonistic worldview to reveal the moralized and racialized hierarchies underlying its argument.[50] After the 9/11 terrorist attacks, the clash was revealed as a civilizational melodrama.

## The Study of Melodramatic Political Discourse

In examining the operations of melodramatic political discourse, this book draws on a range of thinkers and disciplines. *Orgies of Feeling* frames its concerns about power, freedom, sovereignty, and the legitimation processes of state action through engagement with political theorists central to the modern and late-modern critical tradition, especially Friedrich Nietzsche, Karl Marx, Sigmund Freud, Max Weber, Walter Benjamin, and Michel Foucault. Yet the book employs the resources and approach of critical cultural analysis to examine the operations of melodrama in various source materials, including political rhetoric, news media, Hollywood film, and political theory. The analysis of melodrama is indebted to both Marxist and feminist film studies, which revalued the melodramatic form from its colloquial rendering as simplified and histrionic, appealing only to women's private concerns, and instead reclaimed it as a central genre to American culture, one that is rife with the contradictions and dominations of contemporary life.[51] Yet melodramatic genres of political discourse differ in key respects from their film-genre cousins, and this book parts ways with the insistence that melodrama is primarily oriented toward female audiences, and that its key texts are the woman's film and domestic drama. Melodramatic political discourse draws heavily on more action-oriented spectacles, and thus my study of melodrama is also informed by reception studies, theater history, film-industry scholarship, and early cinema accounts that place melodrama as an action genre and highlight its production of thrill, moral clarity, and heroism alongside its scenes of suffering, what Linda Williams calls its "cycles of pathos *and* action."[52]

*Orgies of Feeling* tracks melodramatic political discourse in multiple ways. The first three chapters of this book stake the political work of melodrama by examining its operations in news media on September 11, its historical development from French postrevolutionary theater to twentieth-century U.S. politics, and its legitimation strategies in political speeches. Chapters 4 and 5 scrutinize melodrama's varied effects on citizenship and political subjectivity. These chapters focus on the political subjects who find melodrama's solicitation of legitimacy compelling or desirable for a host of reasons that extend into the daily conditions of contemporary life far beyond spectacles of terror. Chapter 6 and the conclusion examine the alternative political forms that melodrama takes. They investigate melodramas of leftist political theory and melodramas of failed sovereignty, respectively. These chapters cull melodrama's ability to galvanize desires for freedom from sovereignty, militarism, and violence. Together they ask if melodramatic genre forms can harbor more emancipatory and less devastating possibilities for the practice of freedom than those examined in earlier chapters.

Chapter 1, "The Venomous Eye: Melodrama, Media, and National Identity after 9 / 11," delineates five primary conventions of melodramatic political discourse and examines how these conventions take shape in the media coverage on September 11, 2001. Reading the media coverage of the 9 / 11 attacks as a melodrama, I argue that various political and media sources deployed melodramatic conventions to depict the attack and its effects by vividly restaging and personalizing the events, employing a moral economy of good and evil to make them legible, using visceral language and intense emotional gestures, encouraging spectators' identification with injured victims, and placing the attacks in a narrative whereby injured goodness leads to triumphant freedom. Engaging Nietzsche's concept of "the venomous eye" to interrogate melodramatic political discourse, the chapter argues that by cultivating U.S. national identity out of injured goodness, melodramatic political discourse is saturated with ressentiment against the forces that seem to cause the nation's powerlessness. The visual spectacle of nationwide injury by terrorist villains retrospectively generates the nation's moral purity and nourishes a vengeful form of nationhood aiming to salve the nation's gaping wound by asserting U.S. freedom through acts of global violence. The news coverage is a key moment in the production of contemporary melodramatic political discourse as it relates to terror, because watching the news was the primary experience of the 9 / 11 attacks for most Americans. Throughout the coverage, the nation's virtue is made manifest by its unjust suffering, and this dynamic sets the stage for the subsequent authorization of violent state power.

Chapter 2, "The Melodramatic Style of American Politics: A Transnational History," contextualizes melodramatic political discourse by examining its history and development. While post-9/11 melodramatic political discourse is a turning point in the use of melodrama, it is part of a long lineage of moments in which melodrama shapes political discourse, and it connects to an even larger transnational lineage of melodrama on stage and screen. This chapter asks: how did a cultural genre that originates as a critique of power in postrevolutionary French theater come to serve recent expansions in U.S. state power? Challenging film and literary scholars who suggest that melodrama is a democratic genre, this chapter argues instead that melodrama is a liberal genre, and that a focus on liberalism shifts the study of melodrama's political effects. The chapter begins with melodrama's origins on the French stage at the inception of institutionalized liberal politics. It considers two of the earliest French stage melodramas, *Coelina, ou l'enfant du mystère* (*Coelina; or, The Child of Mystery*) and *Valentine, ou la séduction* (translated into English as *Adeline: Victim of Seduction*), that illustrated in visually spectacular and affectively astonishing form a liberal narrative for how certain forms of lived suffering were not caused by nature or contingency but by an unjust and hierarchical society that limited individual freedom. The chapter then follows melodrama's migration to American theater and film in the mid-nineteenth century, when melodrama is rearticulated within American norms and practices of liberal freedom, such as self-reliant individualism and American exceptionalism. *The Poor of New York*, one of the earliest and most popular American stage melodramas, is exemplary here; it heroizes the individual pursuit of self-sufficiency in a capitalist society. *The Poor of New York* plots a triumphalist ending with poor victims emancipated by spectacles of individual heroism that result in massive wealth accumulation. The chapter then moves to melodrama's uptake in post–World War II politics as a discourse about U.S. freedom and state sovereignty. Melodrama's genre conventions gain political utility both by helping to make sense of America's new role as global superpower and by smoothing its use of spectacle into the rise of televisual politics. In this part of the chapter, I begin an archive of U.S. melodramatic political discourse. I examine five key instances of melodramatic discourse in the later twentieth century, from the Truman Doctrine speech that laid the foundation for the postwar national-security state to Ronald Reagan's presidential inaugural speech that offered a national neoliberal politics of individual worker-heroes engaged in war against the debilitating forces of welfare. This archive reveals not only melodrama's influence in postwar politics but also liberal individualism's conviviality with the growth of the national-security state and unaccountable corporate power.

Chapter 3, "Felt Legitimacy: Victimization and Affect in the Expansion of State Power," returns to the contemporary era to examine how deployments of melodrama have legitimated aggressive forms of state power in the pursuit of freedom. Melodramatic political discourse legitimates state actions, such as the War in Afghanistan and the creation of the U.S. Department of Homeland Security, by depicting state action as a moral obligation upon virtuous citizens and as a narrative expectation for the achievement of freedom. Combined, these moral obligations and narrative expectations encourage the felt sense that these policies are both necessary and already legitimate. They cultivate what I call *felt legitimacy* for state action, an intensely affective state in which legitimacy is felt as righteous, true, and obligatory; felt legitimacy makes institutional decision-making processes seem irrelevant to the authorization of state action. Felt legitimacy thus works in a contrary fashion to the formal procedures and collective practices of deliberation that define legitimacy in democratic and liberal political theory (even as those practices cultivate their own affective states). Yet it is consonant with observations by Foucault and Weber on the discursive and affective production of state authority. Felt legitimacy may be the most meaningful form of consent to state power in an era defined by neoliberalism's decimation of liberal institutional politics, operating even when no formal political process has occurred to instantiate that feeling. This chapter scrutinizes key melodramatic speeches alongside theories of legitimacy in Weber and Foucault to examine how, through melodrama, state actions acquire legitimacy outside the agonistic and institutional processes that Americans, as well as political theorists, often idealize as the hallmark of democracy.

Chapters 4 and 5 emphasize the victim-hero political subjectivity formed out of the turn to melodramatic political discourse and ask what type of political subject might legitimate expansive state power in the pursuit of freedom. Melodrama's primary appeal for those who consent to its legitimations of intensified state power is that it promises to rehabilitate freedom in an era that challenges freedom at every turn. Melodrama's discursive production of felt legitimacy is therefore often effective, but not because Americans blindly follow the dictates of national political discourse or suffer from false consciousness. Instead, citizens' authorization of expansive power is an effect of a more complicated process that melodrama helps to broker. Their authorization is animated by a desire to diminish the constraints of various overwhelming powers pervading contemporary life, a desire to challenge experiences of unfreedom. Chapter 4, "Orgies of Feeling: Terror and the Failures of the (Neo)Liberal Individual," builds on Nietzsche's "orgies of feeling" to examine how melodramatic political discourse nourishes an affectively overwhelmed political subjectivity. In orgies of feeling, overwhelming affects displace ordinary experiences of vulnerability onto a dramatic story of injured freedom. The affective pull of melodramatic politics upon the subjects it interpellates—its ability to instigate pathos—solicits subjects to take on new forms of national suffering as their own, in a counterintuitive attempt to alleviate their chronic experiences of powerlessness and unfreedom. The term *orgies of feeling* articulates how melodrama might be appealing precisely because its heightened affects seem to offer the overcoming of daily unfreedoms through intense suffering.

Chapter 5, "Heroic Identifications; or, You Can Love Me Too—I Am So Like the State," turns from the work of victimization examined in chapter 4 to the work of heroism, its interrelated concept, to continue the scrutiny of melodramatic victim: hero subjects who legitimate their own unfreedom. Melodramatic political subjects do not so much desire their own subjection as reroute their desires for freedom into the orgiastic legitimation of war, securitization, and dedemocratization. The chapter argues that Americans who legitimate violent and impinging state actions may do so in a counterintuitive attempt to experience their own heroic, individual power. Engaging Freud's work on identification by historicizing his reading of it, this chapter examines how melodramatic subjects might identify with state action in a paradoxical effort to experience individual freedom. Violent unilateralism models the sovereign freedom denied to individuals who are shaped both by daily experiences of unfreedom and precarity and by expectations for individual sovereignty generated out of American liberal individualism. Liberal individualism normalizes the unencumbered and self-sufficient subject, positing a model of political subjectivity impossible for anyone to live up to, yet one to which many people still strive in their desires to experience individual freedom. Individualism makes unilateral state power seem a desirable and promising path for experiencing sovereignty otherwise unattainable in daily life. Melodramatic support of state power thus stems in part from individual identifications with state power, as if dramatic state action is an extension of individual action and an expression of individual freedom. This chapter thus reveals how, in a neoliberal era that fetishizes personal responsibility and disinvests in state support for individual welfare, individuals themselves do not necessarily disidentify with the state—they grapple with their increasing vulnerability in part by deepening their identification with state power.

Chapter 6 and the conclusion examine alternate ways that melodrama has worked as a discourse about freedom. Melodrama's cultivation of desires for sovereign power could perhaps, at first blush, seem to be only a conservative phenomenon, one tied to an antidemocratic securitizing politics aiming to justify its own power. Melodrama could also seem to be the purview mainly of lowbrow popular political discourse, with intellectual discourse and especially political theory exempt from the moral economy and affective charge of its promise for sovereignty. Challenging this view, chapter 6, "Left Melodrama," suggests that melodrama has at points also infused leftist political theory, obstructing theoretical strategies for challenging unfreedom even when it galvanizes desires for radical social transformation. This chapter moves from national politics to political theory to examine how melodrama inhabits different registers for energizing the pursuit of freedom. The chapter reexamines melodramatic desires for freedom by focusing on their instantiation not in promises of individual sovereignty but in Marxist revolutionary desire. It argues that *The Communist Manifesto* is a nineteenth-century melodrama, and that the manifesto's melodramatic conventions are imitated in the twenty-first-century texts of Giorgio Agamben, Michael Hardt, and Antonio Negri as a way to hold on to the manifesto's promise of emancipation.

What I call *left melodrama* is a form of contemporary political critique that combines thematic elements and narrative structures of the melodramatic genre with a political perspective grounded in a left theoretical tradition, fusing them to dramatically interrogate oppressive social structures and unequal relations of power. Left melodrama shares many of the attributes and effects of contemporary political discourse—moral polarization, connections between victimization and virtue, pathos for the suffering of others, and detailed spectacles of unjust persecution—though its political orientation and medium of expression are different. Namely, left melodrama is a product of what Benjamin calls "left melancholy," a critique that deadens what it examines by employing outdated and insufficient analyses to current exploitations.[53] Left melodrama is melancholic insofar as its mimicry of *The Communist Manifesto* makes the text stand in for revolutionary desire, and thus disavows its attachments to the failed promises of leftist political theory: that it could provide a means to freedom. Whereas the manifesto's melodrama promised radical political transformation, current left melodrama melancholically incorporates the manifesto's melodramatic style in an effort to revivify that promise. Its melancholic efforts can be just as self-defeating as more popular and conservative forms of melodramatic political discourse that promise the overcoming of unfreedom through sovereign state power.

"Melodramas of Failed Sovereignty: The War on Terror as a Women's Weepie" concludes *Orgies of Feeling* by arguing that melodrama's ability to vitalize desires for freedom need not lead only to sustaining fantasies of sovereignty or to effecting the continual devitalization of political agency. The conclusion examines another, less widespread but still popular, form of U.S. melodrama that tells the very story of failed pursuits of sovereign freedom within its narrative structure. This subgenre of melodrama, the *melodrama of failure*, substitutes failed freedom for the triumph of virtue. Its conventions can be found not only in films such as women's weepies but also in political discourses about the war on terror. This chapter first examines the famous women's weepie film *All That Heaven Allows*, which works within the genre conventions of melodrama to offer a critique of impoverished imaginaries of freedom. It then rereads George W. Bush's performance of "mission accomplished," examined in chapter 5 as a heroic fantasy of sovereign freedom, to show how it instead exemplifies the women's weepie scenario of obstructed agency. "Mission accomplished," a spectacle that announced the end of the Iraq War by having the president pilot a fighter plane in a visual demonstration of American heroism, does not conclude with sovereign triumph but with a failed pursuit of sovereignty.

By directly illustrating how and why sovereign freedom is unachievable in contemporary politics, melodramas of failure help to detangle freedom from sovereignty, suffering from virtue, and interdependence from domination. The melodrama of failure in "mission accomplished" reveals how freedom must be imagined and practiced on terms other than heroic individualism, sovereign action, and violent unilateralism in order to undo the systemic experiences of helplessness that freedom aims to challenge. Melodramas can thus also offer space to envision nonsovereign, interdependent, and collective practices of freedom that directly address the overbearing powers their story lines aim to challenge. The dramatization of failed sovereignty, then, may ironically be melodrama's most galvanizing contribution to the practice of freedom in contemporary politics.

# ONE

# THE VENOMOUS EYE

*Melodrama, Media, and National Identity after 9 / 11*

> You couldn't call yourself an American if you hadn't, in solidarity,
> watched your fellow Americans being pulverized, yet what kind of
> American did watching create?
> —Amy Waldman, *The Submission*

Melodramatic political discourses depict the nation-state as a virtuous and innocent victim overwhelmed by villainous action. They draw upon a moral economy that locates goodness in national suffering, and that locates heroism in unilateral state action against dominating forces. Melodramatic discourses often depict war and state surveillance as *moral* imperatives for both the amelioration of nationwide suffering and the achievement of nationwide freedom. In melodrama, the United States becomes virtuous by the very experience of being injured, as if acts of violence against the nation demonstrate the nation's exceptional virtue. This chapter first sketches the primary genre conventions that form melodramatic political discourse, sketches that will be complicated, unraveled, and challenged throughout the book.[1] While melodrama, like all genre forms, is somewhat unstable, melodramatic political discourse has a distinctive set of characteristics that give it a recognizable integrity, even as its conventions mutate across media platforms and historical events.[2] Melodramatic conventions influence one of the most heightened dramas in U.S. history, the media coverage of the 9 / 11 events. The second half of this chapter scrutinizes media coverage from September 11, 2001, to investigate the operations and effects of melodramatic political discourse in this context; it asks: How does a melodramatic narrative of victimization and retribution negotiate the ambiguities of political crisis? In what ways does melodrama rearticulate dominant ideals of U.S. nationhood through depictions of terror? What conceptions of political agency does melodrama enable, and what political practices emerge as its effect?

### Five Conventions of Melodramatic Political Discourse

The first convention of melodramatic political discourse is a moral economy of good and evil that shapes its depictions of political events and national identity. Good equates to the U.S. nation-state, evil equates to the sources of national injury, and as these moralized identities circulate they reinforce each other—so that claims of national goodness are enabled and sustained by the injuries caused by evil Others. As Peter Brooks describes melodrama more broadly, "[Melodrama's] starting point must be in evil. . . . The force of evil in melodrama derives from its personalized menace, its swift declarations of intent, its reduction of innocence to powerlessness."[3] Melodrama's moral economy originates in *evil*, and it relies on evil to identify goodness and generate a narrative trajectory. This moral economy thus aligns with what Friedrich Nietzsche has called "the venomous eye of ressentiment"—a strategy of identity production in which goodness is produced out of injury by evil, and the legitimation of reactive vengeance becomes part of that identity. Goodness is identified only after one suffers at the hands of evil. Nietzsche describes identities produced by goodness as such: "He has conceived 'the evil enemy' '*the Evil One*,' and this in fact is his basic concept, from which he then evolves, as an afterthought and pendant, a 'good one'—himself!"[4] The category of goodness arises with and through the naming of evil; in this temporal reversal, goodness is dependent on a prior identification of its opposite for its content and character. Goodness is produced by retrospectively positing a moral self that seems to exist before "the evil enemy," even as it emerges through and from the antagonistic relationship with evil.

In the melodramatic moral economy of U.S. political discourse, goodness is produced by just this type of temporal reversal, constituted through the prior act of goodness's defilement by evil. In Nietzsche's concept of the venomous eye, evil is not just the constitutive opposite of goodness; it actively aims to harm goodness. In melodramatic political discourse, the venomous eye of ressentiment works to understand good Americans as under siege by evil action. Yet the temporal reversal of melodramatic identity production occludes this retrospective process and imagines the identity of the "good" nation and "good" citizen to exist independently of the appearance of an evil antagonist who wants to maim the nation.[5] In melodrama, goodness comes to appear as a stable identity of U.S. nationhood even as the nation first requires harm by evil to establish the content of goodness. The qualities that make up goodness thus shift depending on the evil that serves as its definite opposite; so in melodramas of communism the nation's goodness is predicated on individual freedom, the free market, and capital accumulation, among other things. In melodramas of terrorism the nation's goodness is predicated on tolerance, individual freedom (again), and the judicious use of violence—violence that is deemed moral because it is democratically legitimated and state organized, among other things. In each of its iterations, the ascription of "goodness" to the nation through the venomous eye of melodrama disavows its dependence on a diagnosis of evil and proceeds as though its own goodness exists independently of an evil Other out to harm the nation.

Second, melodramatic political discourse designates political actors and agency through characters of victims, villains, and heroes. The nation's antagonists are villains—invaders foreign to the proper national body—while the nation is often at once the victim and the hero, both what suffers from villainy and what has the strength to overcome its adversary through the force of its goodness. (I examine the dynamics of heroism more in the fourth convention; here I focus more on victimization.) Melodrama's moral economy overlaps with these designations so that its depictions of victimization confer goodness on those who suffer unjustly. America becomes a virtuous nation *through* the harm it suffers. In melodrama, victimization is also equated with innocence, so that the nation's injury often retrospectively designates a previctimized nation that was innocent and pure.[6] This dynamic is part of what Brooks and Thomas Elsaesser note as melodrama's theological inheritance in Judeo-Christian worldviews that link suffering to goodness and retrospectively posits a state of innocence before villainy strikes.[7] The connection between virtue, victimization, and suffering is a grounding presupposition of melodrama's moral economy, even as it is often, though not always, divested of explicit religious references. In melodramatic political discourse, the nation's injury offers proof of its goodness.

In melodramatic political discourses only certain injuries qualify for inclusion in the construction of victimization and suffering. Whether villainy is defined as terrorism, communism, immigration, an overweening welfare state, or another designation, any harmful action or socially produced suffering that is not caused by the accepted definition of villainy is generally not viewed as a publicly recognized form of victimization. The victimized national identity this creates includes the sense that proper Americans love freedom and suffer from its injury but excludes politically produced injuries that wound Americans but are not directly related to the accepted definition of nationhood.[8] The nation's melodramatic national identity thus unifies the nation at that same time that it elides the systemic class, racial, ethnic, sexual, religious, and gendered injuries that beset a nation riven daily by structural and socially produced conflict, and this identity disavows many other forms of political injury and violence as part of the experience of nationhood it constructs.[8] As Lauren Berlant describes melodrama, it makes spectacles of injury stand in for, and thus exclude, the underlying social conflicts that contribute to the differentiated forms of suffering people endure.[9] In political discourse melodrama often elides any form of social suffering that cannot be reduced to an effect of the villain it explicitly names to be the cause of national pain. The suffering produced by common experiences of structural inequality, racism, homophobia, gun violence, corporate globalization, local governmentality, environmental degradation, military action, "collateral damage," and Islamophobia remain unmarked—and at times, calling attention to them is deemed an assault on the nation itself. The mark of a good American, in melodrama, is the capacity to suffer with others, but only in their experience as joint victims of sanctioned villainy. In other words, melodrama's moral economy generates national identity out of an attachment to a shared virtue injured by villainy, and at the same time both homogenizes and renders illegible more commonplace effects of political violence not produced by the evil that melodrama diagnoses.

Third, melodramatic political discourse traffics in *intensified affect* that relies on certain kinds of *identifications* with the suffering of others. Melodramas display gestural language and spectacles of unjust victimization that can cultivate heightened affective experiences of distress, terror, sorrow and pity, and anticipation.[10] The original invention of the term *mélodrame* by Jean-Jacques Rousseau highlights this aspect of the genre: Rousseau combined the Greek words *melos* and *drama* to describe a play in which nonverbal communication, gestural language, and heightened melos (music) conveyed emotion and ideas to the audience more powerfully than words alone.[11] While the term rapidly outgrew Rousseau's definition, it continues to account for the way that melodrama both conveys heightened emotions and solicits them in an audience. Melodramatic political discourse draws on heated gestures of suffering that encourage pathos in people who feel pain of others' victimization, who feel suffering, terror, grief, and astonishment at spectacles of horrifying villainy that afflict other Americans. Affective intensity is thus not only performed within melodramatic scenarios but also encouraged in spectators and citizens who consume these scenarios and rearticulate them according to their own fantasies, material conditions, and lived experiences.

Melodrama's ability to generate heightened emotions in its participants highlights the importance of *identification* in the work of melodramatic political discourse. Linda Williams emphasizes the role of pathos in melo- drama more broadly, and as Aristotle describes in his canonical definition of *pathos*, the term seems to require a kind of identification with the suffer- ing of others.[12] Pathos, for Aristotle, details how a scene of wounding or killing arouses great pity in spectators; pathos includes both an experience of watching the large-scale suffering of others and "being acted upon" through the emotions by this watching. Ben Singer similarly describes melodrama's affective work as a "visceral physical sensation triggered by the perception of moral injustice against an undeserving victim."[13] In feminist film theory, audience identification with victimization is one of melodrama's defining terms; identification links the performance of suffering to spectators' affec- tive experience (which does not, however, mean that the performance is mimicked in its reception or that the performance and the spectators' expe- rience are the same).[14] What makes U.S. melodramatic political discourse different from other kinds of melodrama, however, is that it often encour- ages identification not only with suffering Americans but also with the very exercise of state power. Melodrama often mobilizes identification with state action.[15] This identification with the demonstrable exercise of power also differentiates melodrama from other forms of U.S. patriotism and national identity, which cultivate identification more with shared civic traits that stand in for the nation, rather than melodrama's additional identification with the exercise of power itself.

Fourth, melodramatic political discourse diagnoses situations in which citizens are overwhelmed by forces outside their control, and this discourse puts an experience of powerlessness into a comprehensible, narrative form. Melodrama, as Martha Vicinus writes, "sides with the powerless."[16] Melodra- matic political discourse creates a narrative that makes sense of the feeling of being besieged by a dominant power, whether powerlessness seems to come from communist infiltration of U.S. institutions, from nefarious immigrants out to steal the jobs of virtuous citizens, or from the overwhelming power of capital in the countermelodrama of left political discourse that I explore in chapter 6.[17] And yet melodramatic political discourse emphasizes the experience of powerlessness in order to chart a course of action that will restore the power of the virtuous. Melodramatic political discourse illustrates the experiences of besieged and overwhelmed people, and also heralds the overcoming of that experience. Melodramatic political discourse thus goes further than filmic and literary melodramas, especially domestic melodramas, in its dramatization of overpowered individuals. It both emphasizes scenes of unjust social suffering and posits the heroic overcoming of injustice and suffering through the rapid accretion of power and the eradication of evil. Melodramatic political discourse merges the experience of victimization to that of heroism, turning the nation-state into a victim-hero so that its overwhelming experience of weakness is precisely what promises control over the antagonist that imperils it.

In melodramatic political discourse, then, the dramatization of powerlessness is a strategy of power, a way to promise that victims can reclaim global (and individual) control out of political crises of impotence and injury. Nietzsche's diagnosis of "the venomous eye of ressentiment" is again relevant, as it attends to the counterintuitive transformation of victimhood into power. Diagnoses of besieged virtue legitimate revenge against the cause of injury; they are, Nietzsche argues, "the most fundamental of all declarations of war."[18] In Nietzsche's analysis, the venomous eye is a critical strategy of power born of fear, rage, and impotence, a way to condemn conditions of unfreedom, to mark them as unfair and unjust. But the identity of the goodness it produces also legitimates and even enables retribution as a way to gain power over what it experiences as dominating.[19] The venomous eye performs a mode of critique that aims to wrest control from crises of impotence and injury by reclaiming the capacity to experience power. Melodrama's venomous eye legitimates revenge against whatever is deemed evil and aims to actualize that revenge as an expression of American strength. By harnessing moral power to the legitimation of vengeance and destruction, the venomous eye of melodramatic political discourse reclaims power out of crises of diminished agency.

Fifth, melodramatic political discourse anticipates the triumph of freedom as its conclusion. The discourse's conventions promise a climax in which the national victim-hero prevails in the quest to overthrow the evil villains who have tried to destroy the nation's freedom. Melodrama promises that dominating powers will be overthrown, victimization will be redressed, and the experience of freedom will be achieved for the virtuous:

melodrama equates the promise of overcoming villainy with the promise of freedom. Its teleology of freedom crosses with liberal interpretations of freedom and agency popular in U.S. politics to produce a normative image of sovereignty as a culminating achievement for both individual subjects and state power. Melodrama attaches to national norms and founding fantasies of sovereignty that propose that individuals determine their own fate and deserve to experience agency unbound by the demands of others. In the venomous eye of melodramatic political discourse, the narrative begins with pathos but ends with the spectacle of heroic sovereignty envisioned as freedom.

Culminating with the end of evil and the triumph of the virtuous, melodramatic political discourse often draws more from the conventions of early twentieth-century stage melodrama and its trajectory into stereotypically masculinized action melodrama than it does from the domestic drama or the woman's film. While melodramas generally end their narratives by highlighting virtuous people, domestic melodramas and "women's weepies" often stop there, and sometimes even show the failure of protagonists to overcome villainy even as they valorize the victim's goodness. In Marcia Landy's analysis, domestic melodramas show "a constant struggle for gratification and equally constant blockages to that attainment."[20] Yet in melodramatic political discourse, unconstrained freedom, not constant blockage, is typically the promised teleology for virtuous victims. Melodramatic political discourse is therefore more in tune with the spectacles of "thrills, chills, and spills" common to stage and early cinema melodramas, which often end with the success of the plucky and self-reliant hero. The discourse's narrative expectation is a happy-ending conclusion that not only makes virtue legible but also emancipates virtuous people from the overwhelming forces that aim to destroy them.[21] Even though melodrama culminates in a heroic reclamation of freedom, its heroic story line is in opposition to tragic constructions of heroism. Tragedy tarries with the inevitable losses endemic to political life and grapples with contingency as a powerful force in shaping the agency of individuals and political events.[22] Tragic heroes are unable to wrest their fate away from tragedy's predetermined path, yet they are also split subjects, riven by accountability for their own flaws and pain. Melodramatic political discourse, by contrast, disavows the hero's accountability for either its own suffering or the suffering it causes others. In linking heroism to individual citizens and state power, melodrama's narrative seems to herald the ability for virtuous Americans (and the state) to master their own fate, remain virtuous in their self-identity, and experience sovereignty.

Yet in the dynamic of melodramatic political discourse, freedom must be preceded by injury; indeed, freedom cannot be achieved without the suffering and victimization at the hands of the overwhelming powers that precede and legitimate its exercise. In melodramatic political discourse, experiences of victimization presage a future of power and sovereignty, so that victimization becomes necessary for the achievement of freedom. In melodramatic political discourse, then, neither the state nor the individual can successfully pursue freedom without first experiencing victimization. Indeed, melodramatic tactics must constantly reenact the nation's injury, a dynamic that Wendy Brown calls "wounded attachments," in order to both uphold the nation's virtuous identity and continually justify the tactics it deploys in eradicating unfreedom.[23] Melodramatic political discourse repeatedly highlights the nation's wounds in order to sustain the claim that the state actions it legitimates are virtuous pursuits of freedom.

### Melodramatic Political Discourse in the 9/11 News Media

News-media platforms, and the political discourses that filter through and generate them, are common sites for melodramatic political discourse, and melodrama is often found at the nexus of media and politics. If, as Francesco Cassetti argues, the twentieth century was the century of film, the beginning of the twenty-first may be one of news media, or at least this is the most prominent form that melodrama now takes.[24] Melodramatic political discourse gains prominence in twentieth-century politics (as I detail in the following chapter), but it achieves particular power and resonance in the twenty-first century, in part because of the way it is used to depict the crisis of the terrorist attacks on the World Trade Center and Pentagon. The national experience of the 9/11 terrorist attacks depended in large part on the news media's depictions, narrations, and interpretations, which often drew from the conventions of melodramatic political discourse. For the vast majority of Americans, the media coverage of 9/11 was *the* primary experience of the terrorist attacks. What we now refer to by the shorthand *9/11* was an experience literally mediated through the television coverage consumed across the United States and the globe.[25] Most Americans reported being mesmerized by the events of 9/11 and compulsively following news coverage for days on end.[26] The news coverage thus harbored particular power for shaping experiences of the 9/11 events, and the conventions employed in this coverage were often drawn from melodrama. This might be one of the reasons that many people described the 9/11 attacks as "like a movie."

Circulating within hours after the attacks, melodramatic genre conventions influenced news commentary, political speeches, camera editing, interviews, and even musical scoring. The frequent recourse to melodramatic conventions shaped discursive depictions and affective experiences of the terrorist attacks, which then influenced how the events were processed, interpreted, and experienced in U.S. politics. The power of news media, in Michael Schudson's words, lies not only in its ability to declare things to exist and be true "but in its power to provide the forms in which the declarations appear."[27] The news media thus harbors particular power for the constitution and circulation of political knowledge and national identity, especially during one of the most visually spectacular political crises in U.S. history, and helps to forge and sustain a sense of American nationhood through widespread mediated consumption of the event.[28] Watching the news was the way that most people participated in the event, and it was also a way that they participated in the national identity that developed in the wake of the attacks.

Laura Frost writes, "For most people 9/11 was so out of the range of typical experience that there was no clear framework in which it could be assimilated."[29] And yet one of the most remarkable parts of melodrama was the rapidity with which a moment of horror and chaos became legible through its genre conventions. Many different people and institutions, situated in and through the news media at various nodal points, drew from melodrama in an unsynchronized and uneven but widespread fashion. Varied sites, speakers, montages, editing processes, and images from across the political landscape and zones of coverage drew from melodrama within hours after the attack, sometimes even within minutes, to articulate a national identity out of the debris. In many of these different sites, that operate quasi-independently yet feed off of each other, Americans became a unified and virtuous people bound by their innocent love of freedom, connected by shared experiences of terror and suffering, and now morally called upon to pursue freedom by violently rescuing itself and the world from evil.

By the afternoon of September 11, melodramatic political discourse could be found in much of the news coverage, and for the rest of the chapter I analyze one hour of news coverage, Fox News's coverage from 5:00 to 6:00 p.m. EDT (2:00 to 3:00 p.m. PDT), to flesh out melodrama's operations. I examine the hour between five and six in the evening because it was close enough to the attacks for the shock to be new (the first plane hit the World Trade Center at 8:46 a.m.) yet far enough from the original events that the images were already depicted through an increasingly stabilized narrative.

Melodramatic conventions, at this time, were varyingly embedded within voice-overs, political speeches, and imaging and editing decisions. Edited montages of the day's past events regularly begin around this time. I examine Fox News because it became the most popular news channel in the United States precisely because of its coverage of the 9/11 events. Melodrama is not limited to Fox, however; as Brian Monahan notes, melodrama is visible in the news coverage of many stations, including CBS and CNN, and in many of the speeches and interviews that all channels covered.[30] I use Fox's coverage to scrutinize what enabled its success at this time—a success that reveals less about its conservative views, I would argue, and more about the compelling conventions in which it depicts the events.[31] Many various and unaligned sources from across the political spectrum drew from melodrama in this hour to help conceptualize the events: popular political figures from both parties, newscasters, the president, videographers, interviewees, and producers. Melodrama was thus more than a depiction imposed upon citizens from above by a tiny political elite from one party or cabal of media producers who stand outside of melodrama and control its employment and the political subjectivity it effects. I focus on Fox News's footage because, in focusing on the *what* rather than the *who* of post-9/11 depictions, Fox best illuminates what made melodrama so compelling to so many viewers that it catapulted the channel to the top of the ratings system.

5:04 P.M.

A newscaster begins an interview with the former secretary of state James Baker; both are unseen, but Baker's voice projects over a full-screen collage of images from the attacks on the World Trade Center earlier that day. Baker, an authoritative presence in the political arena, discusses the possibilities for attacking the perpetrators of terrorism. We do not see his face, but hear his words:

> It's a terribly tragic event in my view and it moves us into probably another era, one that we have feared for some time would get us here, as far as our vulnerability to terrorism is concerned. Some of the things that we are going to have to do is to beef up particularly our human intelligence capability so that we're able to penetrate these groups. We've let those slide ever since the mid-seventies. Somehow it has always been a little offensive to us to do the kind of things you have to do to be a clandestine spy and penetrate those groups. We're going to have to get

back into that messy business. We're going to have to beef up our security measures.[32]

Baker's comments fuse with a sequence of visual images that lasts for about a minute, and they are repeated eight times throughout the hour. The first shot of the sequence follows a man frantically running up the escalator of a bombed-out building, and the camera runs after him, as if just on his heels, into the smoky dust of the building where he then disappears. At this moment Baker argues in a voice-over that Americans are unwillingly placed in "another era" by this attack, one that "we have feared for some time" and that exacerbates "our vulnerability." Baker's speech facilitates the interpretation of the visual images, as the destroyed building illustrates the new era of lost innocence that has been feared, while the man runs away into darkness. Baker invokes a sense of lost American innocence in his comments about this "new era," which both defines the nation's position and begins the justificatory power of the venomous eye; retribution seems mandated by the visual images in his reading. The time before this "new era" is retroactively signified as better, more innocent. It is an era in which, like childhood, vulnerability felt unthreatening, and offensive action was unacceptable. This era is now past, and a new one has unexpectedly commenced, with more adult roles and darker imperatives for political action.

According to the audio-film theorist Michel Chion, when sounds and images are produced at the same time on-screen, they reflect each other and are fused into a new whole; sound-image fusion is "the spontaneous and irresistible weld produced by a particular auditory phenomenon and visual phenomenon when they occur at the same time. This join results independently of any rational logic."[33] In this manner, the importance of the voices and sounds overlapping the moving pictures provides new meaning to the image, especially as one of melodrama's primary designations is its emphasis on melos, on music and nonverbal communication. The fusion of voice and image is part of melodrama's discursive process, as meaning becomes encoded and reinforced in multiple sensorial registers throughout the viewing experience. Baker, by virtue of his political expertise and name recognition as an elder statesman of American politics, is ceded authority to place the events in a comprehensible narrative of victimization that necessitates increases in "the messy business" of surveillant and security forms of state power. As the drama in the pictures merges with Baker's seemingly understated words that call for retribution, the pictures highlighting this "terribly tragic event" and "our vulnerability" provide visual justification to "beef up" human intelligence, "beef up" security measures, "penetrate" groups, and "get back into that messy business." These are things, Baker tells the spectator, that we "*have* to do," that are *necessitated* by the violence of this new era, an era when Americans have lost the innocence of an earlier time in which we were free to refuse what was "messy" and "offensive." The "we" who are now face-to-face with our vulnerability makes "our" imperative for action obvious.

Voice-overs hold particular authority; they provide verbal narration that captions the images and renders them legible through a narrative form. During this hour, news spectators have little access to the actual audio that accompanies these images. The sound-image fusion erases all real sounds from the shots. Sounds are either voice-overs from interviews with officials or news anchors interpreting the day's events. The lack of real audio further imprints the images with melodramatic codification, as the narrative of morality and victimization serve in part to reify the visual landscape and become a primary framework for understanding the images on the screen. The voice-overs will repeatedly iterate agency through victimhood, villainy, and heroic retribution, and even at this early stage the voice-overs narrow how the events can be represented in other ways.

A following shot in this sequence is a skyline picture of New York City from which the Twin Towers are conspicuously absent, the sky blemished by yellowish smoke. This shot fades into the walking body of an ash-covered and disoriented businessman, and is followed by a close-up of a photograph half-buried beneath the debris of ground zero that depicts a young, white, smiling, seemingly heterosexual couple (figure 1.1). This shot quickly zooms outward to expose the destruction surrounding the photograph and causing its violent relocation. Structures, both the building and the normative social relations pictured in the photo, have been razed by these attacks. The empty skyline, the disoriented businessman, and the debris-covered photograph of a happy couple all become the image and proof of pre-9/11 innocence and virtue, a world that has been defiled and disrupted by the day's events. The photograph shot then rapidly zooms further outward to all of ground zero, exhibiting the widespread destruction that defines the lost era by its contrast. The zoom occurs as Baker explains for the second time how clandestine spy activity, though "offensive," is necessary. As Nietzsche's concept of "the venomous eye" highlights, visual images of pain and destruction make clear, in a moral way, why Baker's claims are necessary, and they project national identity through the zoom, in which the retrospective designation of the nation as a virtuous innocent is retemporalized into

FIG 1.1. Close-up of a photograph buried beneath debris. Fox
News footage from September 11, 2001.

a linear narrative. The photo is situated as proof of the pre-9/11 virtue destroyed by the attack; the photo is the image of what has been lost, what
must be redeemed, and what morally legitimates the "beefing up" of state
violence. The photograph, retemporalized as the old era of innocence,
merges with Baker's words in support of state violence to provide their
legitimating ground.

At the bottom of the screen, present throughout this sequence and
throughout the entire hour of coverage, is the tagline "Terrorism Hits
America": the word *terrorism* is in red, with uneven and disjointed letters,
while the word *America* is white, orderly, and bold. This caption frames every
moment of news coverage. From the outset, viewers are presented with a bipolarity that will literally caption the representation of the spectacle throughout the entire coverage: America as pure and innocent and unwillingly attached to a destabilizing and threatening force; the color red has indicated
terror and villainy in American political culture at least since the Red Scare.
With this tagline, the interpretation of these events becomes more uniform
and legible as America is continually framed as an innocent nation-state attacked by the fracturing, disorienting, and terror-inducing forces of evil.

5:07 P.M.

One particular shot in the visual sequence shown alongside Baker's words
stands out. It offers a medium close-up of the face of a black woman covered in white ash as she struggles for breath while lying on a stretcher

FIG 1.2. Medium close-up of an injured woman struggling to breathe. Fox News footage from September 11, 2001.

(figure 1.2). A wider shot of her body surrounded by paramedics quickly follows.

The images of the woman clearly situate her as a victim of tragic injury. She is struggling, covered with debris from the fallen towers, clearly overwhelmed and in pain. The medium close-up of her face asks viewers to feel pathos for her clearly observed trauma. The close-up exposes her face in a way only possible in unmediated life by the removal of personal space between the viewer and the viewed; as a visual tactic, the close-up asks viewers to step into the personal space of the viewed subject, to identify with her experience and her injury.[34] Showing her suffering in detail, viewers are invited by the shot to identify with her struggle and empathize with her injury. For Peter Brooks, "the melodramatic body is a body seized with meaning. . . . Bodies of victims and villains must unambiguously signify their status."[35] The struggling face of the injured woman worker is seized with just this sort of heightened meaning. As she struggles to breathe, she becomes a stand-in for the ash-covered nation that Baker is describing in his interview. The horror of national injury is made manifest on her body. Through the close-up, spectators are invited to identify with this woman's body as their own, to imagine her suffering as theirs, even while her body also becomes available as the national body in the context of a shared victimization that transcends difference to bind the nation together.[36]

In melodrama, national identification is opened across racial lines, because suffering affects all people who identify as Americans regardless of their racial or gender markers. Racialized differences are irrelevant to the suffering that unifies all people in sorrow, or perhaps it is more accurate to say that the irrelevance of racial differences is a necessary feature of nationhood, because this irrelevance proves the virtue of the nation in its capacity for inclusiveness. National identity is strongest, at this moment, when it centers on the moral virtue of national citizens, and this virtue comes about in part because of the way that melodramatic political discourses present the nation as able to transcend inequalities of race and gender. This discourse participates in what Melani McAlister has diagnosed as "a slow move away from the modern construction of a unified (white, masculine) national and racial identity toward the positing of national subjects as disjointed and diverse, gendered both masculine and feminine"; for McAlister, "when U.S. nationalism has succeeded, it did so because racial diversity and gendered logics were incorporated into the stories told about the moral geographies that underlie U.S. power."[37] The close-up of the injured black woman and the identification it solicits begin to congeal a post-9/11 national imaginary in image that will underlie the use of U.S. power in the months ahead. This visual image and the affective experience it solicits ground the national identity that emerges in political rhetoric and that legitimates the war on terror. This identity will define the injured nation as inclusive and tolerant in response to its opposing identity, which constitutes its boundary limit: terrorism. It will align with what Jodi Melamed has identified as the way that contemporary discourses of a racially inclusive U.S. national culture underpin justifications for U.S. empire.[38] Melodrama's depictions of the nation united in sorrow will capitalize on this claim of inclusiveness—and the moral virtue that attaches to injury—to eventually justify war against villains who are evil in part because they are deemed unable to include difference in their own constructions of political identity.[39]

5:13 P.M.

The Israeli prime minister Ariel Sharon holds a press conference in Israel. He shares a split screen with sequential images of the World Trade Center attack and collapse simultaneously shown with his speech. Sharon states, "Tomorrow will be a day of mourning in Israel, as we bow our heads and share in the sorrow of the American people." These words occur as the picture to his left on the split screen contains a shot of the plane flying into the South Tower of the World Trade Center. At 5:14 a former American ambassador states over a shot of a woman hugging a fireman tightly, "This is a day that will live in infamy." He later continues, "Whoever did this is going to regret this dearly."

Shown while Sharon speaks, the shot of the plane hitting the tower emphasizes the reason for mourning referenced in his speech. Sharon's sentence classifies all Americans together, as equally deserving of the Israeli people's sorrow. Through the perspective of a different national leader, Americans are categorized together: injured, unified, and bound by sorrow into a shared national territory. Sharon implies that each of us, as members of "the American people," has been victimized. This "spatial montage" conjoins the two disparate events—Sharon's speech and the montage of attack and collapse are shown alongside each other, so that both reflect upon and recontextualize the other in order to form a new experience for screen spectators.[40] Conjoining Sharon's words with the shot of the plane flying into the tower, the split screen helps to generate this community; together, all spectators become catalogued as Americans, the ones for whom sorrow is felt.

In the second section, the ambassador's words explain how Americans suffer together through a day of infamy. When the ambassador names the "infamy" of this day, he is speaking in hindsight about past events that now must be made meaningful. *Infamy* is a designation that can only be applied to an event retrospectively. Here it helps to establish the horror and world import of this day from the perspective of history. The language copies word for word Franklin D. Roosevelt's speech from the day after the Pearl Harbor attack, in which he names December 7, 1941, "a day that will live in infamy." While both events were surprise attacks on U.S. territory, the ambassador's use of the phrase connects the meaning of today's events to a past military attack by a state entity during an ongoing world war. The ambassador's language has two political effects. First, it names this a day like Pearl Harbor, in that its injury will herald a new exceptional power: the day will mark a pivotal nationwide shift that will significantly increase the use and capacity of U.S. state, military, and corporate power with the aim to establish a kind of global sovereignty. Second, by linking Pearl Harbor to today's events, the ambassador tells a story about them that helps to clarify their status; they are an announcement of war—attacks aimed at the nation that call for military retaliation. The use of Pearl Harbor as a reference contributes to the normalization of a military- and state-centered rejoinder to an event that occurred outside conventional understandings of war, attack, and violence.[41]

In the dynamic of melodrama's venomous eye, national victimization here begins the labor of birthing the legitimacy for heroism as it grants heroism moral authorization. Williams writes about the melodramatic form:

FIG 1.3. A fireman hugging a woman at the scene: united in grief. Fox News footage from September 11, 2001.

"To suffer innocently, to be the victim of abusive power, is to gain moral authority, to become a kind of hero."[42] Seen and heard alongside the ambassador's claim that the perpetrators will "regret this dearly," the image of the embracing woman and fireman emblematize the national victim and hero, especially when spectators are told of the infamy of this day. Presumably strangers, yet unified in grief and pain, they together encapsulate the rhetorical work of this melodramatic media coverage (figure 1.3). The victim and the hero, the crying woman and the fireman, merge together here into an inseparable whole.

The unification of victim and hero is produced out of the violence of this day. The moral status and pathos-laden affective charge of their hug sutures them together. The nation becomes the victim-hero, an entity that has both the moral power garnered by unjust victimization and the physical power to enact punishment for the attack. For Nietzsche, the venomous eye of ressentiment creates an identity invested in its own powerlessness, so that the claim that injury proves moral virtue can sometimes work as a substitute for action. Here, by contrast, the legitimating strategy of victimization is not a substitute for an action but a justification for it. The heroic capacity of the nation is predicated on the moral legitimation it gets from victimhood; the nation's injury underpins its subsequent (violent) heroic actions. Indeed, the injury prelegitimates them. Hugging each other, the woman and fireman become a microcosm of the nation. They model and signify the national identity of post-9 / 11 America and the strength it will draw on as a victim-hero for the subsequent war on terror.

It would seem obvious to map gender stereotypes onto the national identity being constructed here, to claim that national victimhood is feminized and state heroism is masculinized.[43] While positions of victim and hero are often gendered in melodrama, and in cultural life more broadly, they do not directly map onto this mode of national identity in the post-9/11 moment, as the situation seems more complex than this. This is not to say that gender stereotypes do not impact this coverage: almost all of the voices providing commentary over visual footage from the attack are male figures of political leadership; spectators are merely told of each man's credentials and thus are expected to assume that his words have legitimate power to authoritatively interpret the pictures. The first female authoritative face we see is Hillary Rodham Clinton's, at forty-five minutes into the coverage this hour. But as in the national identity that McAlister notes, the national identity that melodrama articulates in political discourse traverses gender binaries—anyone can be a part of the identity that melodrama constructs. The constitutive terms of nationhood are less about gender per se than about power, moral virtue, inclusiveness, suffering, and the inevitable associations of what evil arrays against it: terrorists. These are terms that are, at the level of discourse, available to all Americans who choose to accept them. This picture is a microcosm of the way that male and female figures are stitched together into the national whole through melodrama's construction of the national victim-hero. Spectators are encouraged to identify with them at once, together, in a way that again indicates how this national identity aims to transcend a nation organized by differential forms of power and possibility in gendered, racialized, and economic classifications. The national community that the image gestures to asks everyone to identify with both the woman and firefighter. Everyone is a victim, and everyone can be a hero.

In melodramatic political discourse, the nation is bound by its shared virtue, victimization, love of freedom, and desire for future heroism in the service of virtue. The image of these two people embracing assists in the development of national unification on this day of infamy, a shared experience of watching and suffering injury together with the promise of future retribution. For Nietzsche the experience of ressentiment is based on literal pain, a clear and observed wounding of the body. Post-9/11 incarnations of the venomous eye rest on the visual image of other Americans' bodily pain and trauma that merge the individual injured bodies on the screen to the more nebulous body politic to form the "us" who have been harmed. Melodrama on September 11 draws credence from the wound seared into the body of the nation. The media coverage even participates in carving the wound—it wounds its spectators in the act of watching, in how they are depicted as victims of the attacks they see on the screen, in how they are petitioned in sensorial and rhetorical registers to share in the suffering from terror as a constitutive part of their national identity.

5:18 P.M.

Another authoritative voice speaks over the same sequence of images shown at 5:04 p.m. This time, a former American ambassador to NATO explains why the American population should support intelligence agents' ability to assassinate a perpetrator of terrorism, a practice that is currently banned. The sequential images of pathos, first seen at 5:04, are repetitively looped to become a primary illustration for naming the national victim, for legitimating future increases in state power, and for expressing the nation's justice. The persistent repetition reiterates the wound that justifies the moral virtue of the injured, and this reinscription of the wound is necessary for the legitimating function of wounded attachments.[44] Nietzsche's reference to a venomous *eye* emphasizes the importance of visuality, and even spectacle, to a ressentiment-infused production of political subjectivity grounded in its own injured goodness.[45] The venomous eye is a strategy of identity production that works through both visual and discursive registers to interpret scenes of overwhelming force and to generate claims for power.[46] The live coverage of the events visually reveals the operative truth of an evil villain out to harm the nation in a way that spoken designations alone never could, and this coverage helps to bring the nation together in many interlocking registers—visual, aural, rhetorical, affectual—as a community of the unjustly victimized. Nietzsche's reading allows us to see how visuality is a key part of political subjectivities that claim power out of injury, a necessary factor that consolidates wounded attachments, and thus a key part of melodramatic political discourse.[47]

This sequential repetition of the images helps to consolidate national identity based on these images and also offers the visual confirmation of victimhood and villainy. As in melodrama more broadly, visuality is assumed to show an unmitigated truth: the visual spectacle of political events signals the apparent truth of victimhood and villainy, good and evil. Melodramas suggest that images tell their own story and provide unmitigated reality. "Sensation scenes," according to Frank Rahill, are a key aspect of the melodramatic form in which a dramatic visual spectacle of suffering encourages pathos in the spectator, and the "sensation" registers aspects of seeing, feeling, and hearing to reveal the moral goodness found in both the visual scene and in the spectator who empathizes with the victims on-screen.[48] The media coverage of the 9 / 11 attacks became a sensation scene, merging morality and feeling with the visual spectacle of the attacks. The reliance on visual spectacle to jump start the narrative is partly why melodrama operates so powerfully in times of crisis; it generally relies on the visual scene of violence to prove the act of villainy it endures. As Jacques Derrida says of the attacks, "This target (the United States, let's say) has it in its own *interest* (the same *interest* it shares with its enemies) to expose its vulnerability, to give the greatest possible coverage to the aggression against which it wishes to protect itself."[49] The visual repetition of the day's events offers the visual proof of evil that delineates the Other of America and justifies the legitimacy for assassination that the ambassador offers. The repetitive images are assumed to be self-evident; they prove their own truth, they tell their own story, and they will justify the violence of the war on terror.

Melodrama's heroism combines with the medium of news to promise mastery over the events; the television format itself provides a sense of control over events on the screen by reducing overwhelming events to lilliputian size. Television scales down images and challenges the images of destruction with the seeming capacity to control their representative medium. According to Robert Stam, television news "prosthetically extends human perception, giving an exhilarating sense of visual power to the virtually all-perceiving spectator[,] . . . turning us into audio-visual masters of the world."[50] Audio-visual mastery is one of the key reasons that people's reliance on news media substantially increases during times of crisis.[51] Watching the news coverage of 9 / 11 seems to counteract the felt disorientations and catastrophe of 9 / 11 even as the coverage serves to illuminate them— the clear narrative, authoritative interpreters, and medium that places the events inside a thirty-inch frame carry a sense of mastery over terror even as the images demonstrate the uncontrollability of national crises. The venomous promise to engage in "messy business" seems more possible when the destruction it responds to is bound within a small screen. The audio-visual form provides the visual counterbalance to the invasive identification of the close-up in the sequence. The repetitive close-up of a victim's face seen at 5:07 p.m. does not contradict the shrinkage from the medium; instead, these two tactics synergistically work to combine the moral virtue of identificatory suffering (close-up) with the promise of mastery over horror (a medium that diminutizes events). Together they support the melodramatic cultivation of the victim and the hero.

Senator Chuck Hagel is interviewed over a full-screen montage that presents, in sequential order, images of the towers' attack and collapse.

> People came together in a very precise project and effort [*full-screen fade-in to the moving image of the plane nearing the South Tower*] to do this terrible, terrible, terrorist act [*the impact of the plane into the tower is timed exactly on the word* act]. That is what we do know. . . . Now we will unfold this, and we will pull it apart and we will get those facts and there will be punishment [*continuous footage of the building exploding from the plane's impact*]. But right now what we must do, what we are doing in fact, is securing our country [*close-up of the fire on the tower*] and all our national security interests, helping those who need help [*fade-in to collapse of the South Tower*], pray for the families and the loved ones who have been lost, and then we've got a lot of work we need to do ahead of us.

This combination of speech and image generates melodramatic meaning in the spectacular montage of the World Trade Center's attack and subsequent collapse. The montage is a narrative unto itself, defining the event by a beginning (the plane flying into the World Trade Center) and an ending (the collapse of the Twin Towers). Starting the narrative with the plane flying into the tower means that everything that comes beforehand is not part of the story: neither U.S. foreign policy nor Middle East politics, nor even motivations for the attack besides evil and terror. The narrative thus visually circumscribes broader accountability for the actions besides the suicide attackers and their immediate supporters, as they are outside of and thus irrelevant to the narrative. It will take years for official political discourses to expand, reemplot, and retemporalize this narrative trajectory. In this montage, the cause of the events is external to America; the nation suffers as a virtuous innocent entity without responsibility for the actions of this day. If the narrative starts only when the plane attacks, then the examination of earlier actions and engagements is rendered moot to the problem at hand.

Hagel's authoritative voice simultaneously codes compassion, pain, ressentiment, and loss into the sequential images of collapse and destruction. Hagel's voice-over embeds the opposition of good and evil into its plotline, while the image of the plane crashing into the tower gains signification as the grounds for "punishment" that will be served as just deserts by the good side: those who lost "loved ones" from this "terrible" act. Of course I am not disputing Hagel's claim that the event is terrible, but instead I want to highlight how "terrible" gets mobilized through melodrama's venomous lens to morally justify the nebulous yet intense claim of "punishment." In melodrama's venomous eye, victimization is a pure and unsullied category—one cannot be both victim and aggressor. Hagel's speech highlights that when the nation is the victim of unjust violence after 9 / 11, the injury makes the United States uniquely virtuous and uniquely victimized in the realm of world politics. Terrorism becomes the trump card of suffering, one that makes the United States both exceptional in its injury and exceptional in its capacity to respond—a response that will, within melodrama, only be understood as justice, as virtue, as freedom, and never as itself a form of violence or injury.

As Nietzsche might note in the link between virtue and injury, while fighting evil, the American victim-hero is free of responsibility for harming others or for becoming a villain. This is part of what makes melodrama politically useful. In melodrama, the violence that America inflicts on others is part of heroism; it is morally mandated by the need to protect virtue, avenge unjust suffering, and save humanity from what threatens to destroy it. The national victim-hero is thus unaccountable, responsible only for eradicating evil, not for causing it; the victim-hero lives a righteous form of national identity in which all wrongdoing is deemed evil. Indeed, melodramatic national identity works not only to bind the nation but also to erase responsibility for the violent exercise of U.S. power.

When looking at material objects through the lens of melodrama, Brooks proposes that "things cease to be merely themselves. . . . They become the vehicles of metaphors whose tenor suggests another kind of reality."[52] In this vein, it seems that the image of the towers, perhaps previously symbolizing capitalist, masculinized, or imperialist power on a global scale, has been transformed during the news coverage into a material symbol of freedom, virtue, and "the American people." Indeed the towers' wound is perceived as a wound on the body of the nation. Combined with melodramatic modes of narrative voice-over, the sequential images of the towers' attack and collapse become a rallying symbol for unity, and for justice best served by avenging unwarranted injury. The World Trade Center seemingly transmogrifies into the body politic—as the destruction symbolizes the injury to the national body. Neil Leach argues that after they were destroyed, the towers were able to define a collective identity; melodramatic political discourse helps to account for the content of the national identity that they came to symbolize.[53] The media's continued replaying of their destruction becomes the continual citation of national injury. Each iteration firms up the national identity of a virtuous and injured freedom that they stand in for.

Yet the elephant in the room during this news coverage is the visual absence of the villain's body to be made available for punishment. Melodrama's recourse to visuality as a site of truth relies on visual verification of the act of victimization. Seeing the villain assists in proving moral legibility; Brooks argues that for melodrama to prove evil, "the body of the villain must be publicly branded—identified as evil by all, and punished clearly and publicly."[54] This is part of the incredibly destabilizing effect of the attacks: there is no villain to observe, as all agents have died. There is no visual perpetrator of evil, no person whose act of victimization can be held responsible. The images of the attacked towers show the *effects* of violent action but not the body of the villain. Because there is as yet no visual image of the villain committing villainy, and thus no villain to mark, the images of destruction repeating throughout this coverage begin to serve as a substitute for the villain's absent body. The inability to see the villain is circumvented as the events themselves are personified as villainy. This is a switch that can only happen when the nation is united by injury and the buildings stand in for all Americans. As the towers have come to retrospectively symbolize "the American people," the attack on the tower serves to symbolize the central injury in the melodramatic narrative that remains unseen: the body of the villain attacking the national body of the victim. But at 5:36 p.m., a villain is found. A responsible individual is made visible on-screen.

5:36 P.M.

A disembodied newscaster's voice relays an official's remark that "there is a strong indication [that Osama] bin Laden is involved." After this revelation, the newscaster further conveys bin Laden's military capabilities and recent illegal activity. While the newscaster speaks, the viewer is presented with a full-screen slow-motion shot of the North Tower collapsing. This image, which in real time takes approximately fifteen seconds to complete, is temporally stretched and slowed down to fifty-five seconds (figure 1.4). This image fades into a video of bin Laden shooting a gun in front of a group of spectators and is followed by a close-up shot of his face during the shooting (figure 1.5). The video of bin Laden then cuts back to a repeat image of the tower collapsing in slow motion.

This back-and-forth fading between two disparate images is an associative montage. By conjoining two distinct shots one can create a new product; the film theorist and filmmaker Sergei Eisenstein—who first named

FIG 1.4 AND 1.5. Associative montage showing Osama bin Laden shooting down the Twin Towers. Fox News footage from September 11, 2001.

this editing process—explains that in merging two visual objects one creates the metaphoric representation of something that is unable to be depicted visually.[55] In this case, what is visually unrenderable is an identifiable villainous body attacking the World Trade Center. The use of associative montage accomplishes this vision for spectators. Bin Laden's gunshots cut to the image of the collapsing towers, so that the towers become his direct target. The lack of visual confirmation of the villain committing the deed becomes sublimated into this associative montage and helps to provide a visual proof of villainous action.[56] Through the montage sequence, bin Laden's face and shooting action cause the towers' painfully slow collapse and fall. The slow-motion draws out the agony of the injury, expanding and lengthening the moment of death and destruction. The substituting of bin Laden for the vision of the villain committing his deed reflects what the film theorist Tom Gunning calls melodrama's "epistemania": its desire to represent all, to know all, and to reveal the real truth working within the obfuscating complexities of surface experience.[57] This two-minute montage reflects the insistence on ascribing a clear doer for the deed of national injury. Even before there is any confirmation of bin Laden's involvement in this terrorist act, melodrama's epistemania demands rapid solutions for this crisis; the villain has been named and consolidated—and his deed has been documented.

Melodrama's ability to depict moral clarity and causality out of experience is not only enabled but also intensified this hour by the practices of media production and the singularization of the event's causal factors. The origin of terror is now a singular person, a solitary mastermind, as melodramatic political discourse personalizes the large-scale political and social problems that have contributed to this crisis. With the identification of bin

Laden, the complexity of global conditions, the networks of violence that contributed to the attack, and the uncertain effects of U.S. foreign policy can be swept aside; the location upon which to place accountability and responsibility is isolated and contextualized as a singular person. An individual, motivated only by evil, is the sole cause, not larger geopolitical entanglements, public policies, historical events, or political structures that enabled or conditioned individual action. The crisis will not require social, political, or economic change, nor will it provoke a rethinking of major political actions and policies that have contributed to the cause of the events. Instead, all the nation needs to do is terminate its villains. All actions in the service of that goal, including war, are now a moral obligation, and will serve as the very proof of the nation's virtue.

5:39 P.M.

Fox News rescreens Bush's official public address (given a few hours earlier) to the nation regarding the day's terrorist attacks. Bush is framed by two American flags stationed behind him. The coverage of his speech shares a split screen that repeats the shots of attack and collapse looping throughout the day (figure 1.6).

Both the Bush administration and the news media draw from melodrama to articulate the 9/11 events, and at this moment they combine to intensify melodramatic genre conventions for understanding the day's events and for refashioning U.S. nationhood in their wake. The speech is a heightened moment. As Lisa Wedeen notes, national political spectacles, whether scripted or not, often work to solidify the bond between state and nation, citizens and institutions of governance, ruler and ruled.[58] The visual spectacle of the 9/11 events, with Bush's speech shown alongside them, generates a similar effect; together they are a key component of the glue forming the national identity out of wounded freedom. Bush's speech merges with its attendant media coverage to give his words the highest authority for shaping the national narrative and for linking the spectating nation with melodrama's depiction of a venomous national identity. Bush begins,

> Freedom itself was attacked this morning by a faceless coward, and freedom will be defended. I want to reassure the American people that the full resources of the federal government are working to assist local authorities to save lives and to help the victims of the attacks. Make no mistake: the U.S. will hunt down and punish those responsible for these cowardly acts. I've been in regular contact with the vice president, the

FIG 1.6. George W. Bush's speech shown alongside a plane crashing into the World Trade Center. Fox News footage from September 11, 2001.

secretary of defense, the national-security team, and my cabinet. We have all taken appropriate security precautions to protect the American people. Our military at home and around the world is on high-alert status and we have taken the necessary security precautions to continue the functions of your government.

Bush's first sentence is crucial for how it shapes the U.S. response to the events. The victim in Bush's speech is "freedom." It is an *ideal* that was attacked, and an ideal that must be defended. Through Americans' devotion to and identification with that ideal, Bush implies that all who value freedom, all who *are* free, are victims. Naming freedom as the victim broadens the notion of what has been attacked as it concurrently subsumes all Americans under that designation; it is an ideal so nebulous, and so loaded with different meanings, that it dramatically expands the scope of attack beyond its physical parameters. In his prime-time speech given two hours later, Bush will further conjoin *freedom* with *the American people* by using the terms interchangeably to reference what must be protected and defended by the state. Melodrama creates retrospective bodily wholeness of the nation, binding the nation around a jointly experienced wound caused by terror. Inscribing the images of attack and collapse with the suffering of the virtuous, Bush's speeches aim to accomplish many things: to clarify the events, to manage the nation's terror, to unify his viewers by expelling any differences among the American people save for the concept of freedom and its injury, and to encourage the viewer to fuse victimization to the American people. During the speech shown this hour, Bush utters "American people" at the exact moment the screen shows a plane flying into the World Trade Center. Whether unintentional or not, it is a powerful synchronizing point that indicates the conflation of both concepts circulating in visual and spoken communication. The American body is here defined by an ideal of freedom, by the moral goodness attached to that ideal as something that has been victimized, and by the action needed to protect it. Indeed, Bush's merging of the terms *the American people* with *freedom* and what *has been attacked*, and with the action verbs *to hunt down and punish*, illustrates how this version of American national identity aims to habilitate a nationalism containing both ideals that have been victimized and the militarized state action required to defend them.

As president, Bush symbolizes the ultimate authoritative voice in the space of U.S. politics, and in this speech he additionally references other authority figures to further ground his power. Especially in this time of crisis, the president is not only "the decider," as he will later name himself, but also "the definer." His position as president establishes his capacity to define the import of and the response to the events, and to acknowledge and redress the suffering of the victimized populace. Part of his presidential authority derives from his presumed capacity to define and manage catastrophic events for the nation. His words evoke the pain of loss, the inherent virtue of freedom, and the American people as situated squarely within these two poles—Americans, at this moment, are a people both injured and freedom loving. What binds and unifies them in the post-9/11 moment is a national identity formed around loose connections of suffering, injury, and love of freedom, with an opposing term of evil that produces an identity of goodness through its opposition. Melodramatic depictions of wounded bodies seem to produce the national consensus they claim to be preexisting, recapitulating the logic of the venomous eye. Identification with other injured Americans—and with others who identify with injured Americans—becomes a moral act. In Bush's speech the perpetrators of the attack are twice referenced as "cowards." Cowardice is a specific type of evil, as it immediately implies the weakness of the evildoer and the strength of the victim; thus, rearticulating the terrorist attack as an expression of weakness also suggests the success of the injured in their future response.

On one level, as Nietzsche might note, the opposing terms that constitute U.S. nationhood are simply moralized as evil and terror. National unity is staked on the shared ideals of freedom and procedural standards for public life that encode it, but also on the shared wound that all have had simultaneously inflicted by their very attachment to those ideals. These qualifications form a civic nationalism that binds Americans to the nation at a rhetorical level through shared attachments to general values and the shared experience of injury to those who hold these values. Civic nationalism is consequently different from more ethnic or religious nationalisms in which national identity is supposedly inherited, rather than chosen, in part because it allows for, and encourages, racial and ethnic difference as markers of civic virtue.[59] On another and more unspoken level, however, as the events progress, participation in the wound will be denied to many Americans—the use of evil will extend to people who, as Leti Volpp argues, "look like" Arabs or Muslims, even when that exclusion is explicitly denied under a language of inclusiveness and antiracism.[60] Volpp notes, "September 11 facilitated the consolidation of a new identity category that groups together persons who *appear* 'Middle Eastern, Arab or Muslim.' This consolidation reflects a racialization wherein members of this group are identified as terrorists, and disidentified as citizens."[61] Melodrama helps to explain one form in which this consolidation became the outside of U.S. national identity after 9/11.

The developing melodramatic national identity implicitly filters out people with Arab or Muslim backgrounds as more similar to terrorists than to Americans, and thus unable to choose membership in the common civic ideals that have been injured—unless they explicitly profess their intense love of the nation, demonstrate how they share in its woundedness, and repetitively engage in exaggerated performances of patriotism (and, more implicitly, monitor their own racial and religious communities in search of others who critique state power or refuse to demonstrate their love of nation and are, therefore, un-American).[62] The national identity constructed around the wound of post-9/11 victimization thus explicitly consolidates an inclusive and tolerant nation that loves freedom and experiences its injury after 9/11, but implicitly consolidates people who neither "look like" terrorists nor critique the use of state power deployed to redress that injury.

Many scholars have noted the way that discrimination against Arabs and Muslims was cultivated in official post-9/11 political discourse not through traditional ways—by directly calling out people in those groups as evil—but through the way that cultural language mapped an implicit racism marking Arabs and Muslims as unable to share in the virtue of freedom that defines nationhood.[63] McAlister notes that "through categories of culture that worked like race, a confused but powerful mapping fused Islam, the Middle East, and terrorism: it marked entire groups of people as immutably and intangibly inferior."[64] As Melamed writes of the broader work of racism in the contemporary moment, it relies less on overt discrimination than on deploying "economic, ideological, cultural, and religious distinctions to produce lesser personhoods," and the president's speeches in the coming days will begin to draw more heavily from a civilizational discourse that describes U.S. enemies as non-Western, as uncivilized, as intolerant, and thus as viable targets for U.S. violence and viable exclusions from U.S. nationhood.[65]

Suffering in melodramatic political discourse becomes part of national identity, yes, but it is only a very specific form of suffering; suffering is legible only if it is effected by the 9/11 attacks, only if one is wounded by one's role as a victim of terrorism, only if suffering can be redressed by "punishment" of the evildoers through the war on terror. As Judith Butler argues, this form of discourse effects violence through its exclusion; the problem is less that the discourse generates violence directly, but that it effects violence through what it omits from its categorization of victims and victimization.[66] This discourse enables the invisibility of suffering produced as a by-product of eradicating evil and leaves unmarked the products of systemic inequality and unaccountable power that often constitute more daily experiences of powerlessness. And this discourse certainly excludes in the wake of the attacks the effects of racism, hate violence, and racial profiling of people who look Arab, Muslim, or Middle Eastern.

5:44 P.M.

The New York Democratic senators Hillary Rodham Clinton and Charles Schumer stand together in a shot that takes up the full screen as Schumer begins addressing reporters: "We are here today to express our solidarity with the people in New York and America. First, we are completely appalled, shaken but resolute as a result of this awful action." At this moment, the shot is halved and the two senators share a split screen with the images of attack and collapse that are beginning again. Schumer continues,

> This is Pearl Harbor, twenty-first century, and it's an unknown enemy, although they will be known. First, to the families, those who may have losses, we feel your pain. So our first feeling is for the families and the suffering and pain in New York and throughout the country. Those who did this must be brought to justice. We now know that none of us, as

Americans, can avoid that terrorism unless we take strong action against it. . . . We will be united in this fight. America can never turn its back from this point. We are in a new era, where we realize the world is an interconnected, but sometimes very nasty, place.

Schumer doesn't just acknowledge the victims; he feels "their pain," he identifies with their injury and through the pathos of identification becomes a victim himself. Schumer models the proper national subject: one who experiences pathos—the sorrow of the American people, who identifies with the pain on the screen, who feels the suffering of strangers as his own suffering, and who is unified with other Americans through this shared national response. Through his speech, Schumer explicitly positions himself as a victim, as one of "us"—American—and as a future hero; by seeing Schumer, the viewer can more easily identify with him as a model American who demonstrates these traits. Melodrama is often personalized; *good* and *evil* refer to people who, in a clear and unambiguous way, characterize these qualities. The fact that Schumer is not faceless, and even occupies the full screen for much of the speech, allows the spectator to visibly distinguish him as a sufferer, a man of virtue. In a metonymic substitution, Schumer stands in for all victims, for the national victim, for the suffering body politic. His pathos works to unify citizens around him, who also feel a part of the national victimization, and his stated felt experience of wounding further conveys a sense of Schumer's own moral goodness. Melodrama's petitioning of all news viewers to identify as victims of 9/11 assumes that by watching the suffering on the screen, and identifying with it, each spectator's experience can, like Schumer's experience, stand in for all other Americans.

Schumer is the only person this hour to explicitly mention the fact that the perpetrators of this attack are "unknown." However, he can only mention this unknowingness in the context of a future knowing; he follows, in the same sentence, with a certainty that the enemy "will be known." Schumer points to the uncertainty and ambiguity underlying the day's events, but then he promises that this condition will be overcome. And overcoming the condition of unknowing only happens through and as state action; in Schumer's language, state action is a form of knowledge production that learns the nation's enemies in order to take action against them. Schumer's pronouncements to "take strong action," to "be united in this fight," and that "America can never turn its back" will combine with Baker's earlier claims to "get back into this messy business" and Bush's claims to "hunt down and punish those responsible." They are all necessary and categorically moral national actions in response to the suffering body politic. They are not seen as one possible choice in a range of many options, or as one made by specific political actors. Schumer, as an "American," and as an embodiment of suffering, calls for a "united" fight and for "strong action" against terrorism. Schumer's capacity to be appalled and shaken is grounded in part on the condition that these emotions will transmute into strength. In emphasizing urgent responses throughout his speech, Schumer infuses the images of attack and collapse with an insistence on active retaliation, especially as his reference to Pearl Harbor—the second one this hour—helps to justify militarization for the "new era" in which the world has become a "very nasty" place.

Melodrama creates a politics in which state action requires national suffering. Virtue and heroism are only legible through victimization, through the visual scar of injury; the legitimate exercise of state power requires the express pain of all Americans. If America is explicitly defined by goodness and freedom, and implicitly by the pathos of the nation's pain and the state power necessary to protect America, then state action seems an inescapable part of American identity. Melodramatic politics in its venomous expression is about heroism, about strength, about the capacity to respond and the promise to overcome. The designation *America* cannot be understood apart from heroic state action. In order for this to be the case, the notion of America as a national identity must be so blurred, abstract, and vulnerable to victimization that state action in the service of finding freedom and eradicating suffering becomes its primary mode of expression.[67]

6:00 P.M.

At exactly 6:00 p.m. dramatic music begins, packed with thundering beats and jarring mechanical jolts. As the loud music resonates, a screen-filling sequence of images materializes: a shot of the first plane flying into the North Tower, the tower collapsing in smoke, a shot of the South Tower collapsing, and an image of the collapsed wall of the Pentagon. This sequence is rapidly followed by an image growing out of the bottom of the frame into full-screen size (figure 1.7). It is the digitalized title seen throughout the news hour at the bottom of the screen. The word *terrorism* explodes in flames (figure 1.8), and when the flame disappears we see again the title of the coverage: "Terrorism Hits America." Though still red, the typeface of the word *terrorism* is even more broken and dramatic, with fissures disrupting the formation of the letters. The typeface of *America* by contrast is white, clean, and impeccably straight (figure 1.9).

FIGS 1.7, 1.8, AND 1.9. Videographic overload: "Terrorism Hits America." Fox News footage from September 11, 2001.

No melodramatic spectacle would be complete without fire and music, the astonishment and the melos of melodrama. The spectacular, rapid-fire images heighten the drama of the events, while the music fixes the intensified affect. This is high-action melos. The energetic music matches the affective intensity of the images; together they create a high emotional pitch and convey emotive meaning viscerally. They aurally conjure up a chase scene and a racing heart, simulating the adrenaline rush of excitement, while the discordant notes of the music and the shattered typeface gesture to nervousness, fear, and shock. Yet the music and images also evoke anticipation, the desire to see what is next, what will be resolved. They are familiar from Hollywood action films. The music signals the beginning of a fight sequence, of imminent heroic action. The music is heart pounding, energizing, and anticipates the hero's destructive violence that all spectators can rally around, because it is in the service of fighting villainy.

This musical pattern signals a heightening of the mood already rooted within the images. Embedding this music into the dramatic three-second narrative of the day's events increases the appeal to an urgent action-filled response to America's victimization. The moral legibility embedded in the title becomes even more insistent after it is blown to pieces while implanted within high-action rhythm; the title grows to take over the screen and override other forms of information. The intense pathos and frenzy of the present moment impels the nation to act violently to sanction the legitimacy of future heroic action in an explosive expression of righteous rage that promises to conquer all villainy. The national victim-hero makes retribution a required by-product of violated goodness, and so the nation is already rendered unaccountable for the effects of its response, responsible only for eradicating evil, not for contributing to it.[68] At this moment in the news coverage, melodramatic political discourse reaches its apotheosis; the fusion of word, image, and melos cement the events within a narrative, a truth, and a moral polarity that round out the dramatic construction of the national victim-hero.


Melodramatic political discourse is heightened and intensified in the early moments of the twenty-first century because of the way its genre conventions seem able to make sense of an unprecedented spectacle of mass murder, one that's terror will influence the tenor of national politics and foreign policy for years to come. It seems safe to presume that the orchestrators of the attacks intended them to be televised, so that much of their horrific murder and destruction would be captured live; they were "designed," in Marc Lynch's words, "for maximal media exposure."[69] As Derrida posed rhetorically, "What would 9/11 have been without television?"[70] And yet melodrama is not intrinsic to the attacks' violent spectacle, as this analysis shows, and in contrast to what Michael Schudson argues in response to this analysis.[71] Schudson contends that melodrama is an inherent quality of the attacks themselves, because Osama bin Laden viewed the world manicheistically and because he designed the attacks to be spectacular. Yet this seems to confuse intent and effect: to claim that the events are necessarily melodramatic because bin Laden wanted them to be suggests that viewers of the news can read back from their mediated experience of an overwhelming and unexpected event the true intent of one of its designers, which then determines the way that the event is processed in U.S. political discourse and U.S. political subjects.[72] This claim not only assumes that knowledge about bin Laden or his desires is accessible but that these desires are, in Schudson's words, "manicheistic" and about "hatred of freedom"—the very terms offered by melodramatic genre conventions.

Melodramatic depictions offer a social reality in which the violence that the United States will soon inflict on others is already morally mandated by the need to protect the virtue of the tolerant and inclusive, to avenge unjust injury, to fight against destruction of freedom, and to do so as a dramatic spectacle of heroism. These depictions, on Fox News and other media platforms, will help to stage the post-9/11 political landscape. They will hang like a backdrop behind public speeches and political decisions in the coming months and years, conditioning the legitimacy of expansive state power, reiterating the nation's injured status, and emplotting the nation's future freedom. These depictions will also open to the more theoretical material of this book, which investigates melodrama's broader work on the formations of political subjects and the circulations of state power. Before turning to those investigations, which form the heart of *Orgies of Feeling*, I first ask the question of genealogy: how did melodrama gain such prominence for narrating political crisis? I take up this question by examining the trajectory of melodramatic political discourse, starting from melodrama's origins in postrevolutionary French theater and tracking melodrama's transformations into U.S. politics during the cold war.

# TWO

# THE MELODRAMATIC STYLE OF AMERICAN POLITICS
*A Transnational History*

Woe to the Author Who Leaves the Spectator Unmoved!
—Guilbert de Pixérécourt, "Melodrama"

On the night of September 11, 2001, President George W. Bush wrote in his diary: "The Pearl Harbor of the 21st Century took place today."[1] As early as midafternoon on September 11, many people were comparing the day's attacks to Pearl Harbor and claiming that this was a new "day that will live in infamy." Despite the proliferations of this comparison, however, there were fundamental distinctions between the two attacks, and they were articulated though different genres of political discourse. The tenor of political discourse shifted throughout the intervening sixty years, and these shifts had implications for the representation of violent political events and for the expansion of violent state action that followed them.

President Franklin D. Roosevelt's speech the day after Pearl Harbor was grave. In his first nationwide radio speech, he calls December 7, 1941, "a day that will live in infamy." He proclaims the attack's "unprovoked" nature and catalogues Japan's deceptions leading up to it. His assessment is not depicted through a transhistorical narrative pitting goodness against evil. Instead, in an even-keeled voice he lists examples of Japanese hostilities to the United States and other nations, each example tied to a specific action and political grievance. The speech contains few descriptive adjectives of the Japanese or their attack on Pearl Harbor. The prose is relatively dry, lacking emotive expressions or a detailed description of the suffering on the ground.

Describing the effects of the attack, Roosevelt only states: "[The attack] caused severe damage to American naval and military forces. I regret to tell you that many American lives have been lost." Japanese actions are described as "treachery," but victimization is not used to characterize America or Pearl Harbor. The speech claims that the "American people in their righteous might will win through absolute victory," but Roosevelt does not classify the upcoming struggle through categories of victimhood or villainy. The speech assesses the situation in a terse way: "So far, the news has all been bad." The speech ends not with an exhortation of inevitable retribution and victory but with a call for hope and shared sacrifice. The speech employs what we could name a genre of objective rationality, popular in midcentury U.S. politics and media, that uses moderated affects, claims of rational judgment, and the even-toned pronouncement of factual evidence to claim objectivity and thus authority for depicting events.

Sixty years later, on the evening of September 11, 2001, Bush spoke to the nation to explain a new surprise attack on U.S. territory, but the intervening years had seen significant changes in political discourse. This president's speech was quite different. The speech was televised live and begins by explaining, "Our way of life, our very freedom came under attack." In the speech, the ideal of freedom is targeted for destruction. Bush describes the motivation for the 9/11 attack not through political strategy but through a moral worldview both outside and above concrete political strategy. "Today, the nation saw evil" and "thousands of lives were suddenly ended by evil, despicable acts of terror." Bush uses the word *evil* four times, and the speech shapes a moral economy for situating the attack and its agents. The speech individuates the people who died: they were "secretaries, businessmen and women, military and federal workers, moms and dads, friends and neighbors," people the audience can empathize and identify with, people just like them and others they know. The speech emphasizes the experience of suffering caused by the attacks and uses heightened language and descriptive adjectives to describe the pain that the nation is collectively experiencing: "The pictures . . . have filled us with disbelief, terrible sadness, and a quiet, unyielding anger." Bush goes on to explain that government agents are responding to the attack and will "find those responsible and bring them to justice." The speech highlights the nation's grief, constructs a moral economy of good and evil to describe actions and their perpetrators, individuates the victims of the attack, and promises the heroic triumph of the United States over evil. The focus and the structure, the affect and the tone, are far from Roosevelt's address.

Although many people likened 9/11 to Pearl Harbor, the events themselves are obviously different: Pearl Harbor was a military attack on a military base perpetrated by another nation, and it was part of an ongoing, larger war. The 9/11 attacks were perpetrated by nonstate actors on financial and federal military buildings using unconventional weapons and occurred in a vacuum of information about their agents and cause. The 9/11 attacks were intentionally spectacular, crafted to be broadcast live on television; the Pearl Harbor attacks were not viewed live but were transmitted retrospectively on radio and newsreel. And yet aside from the difference in events, there is a fundamental difference in the political discourses used to depict them. There is a change in the contouring of crisis, in the description of injury, in the framing of political agency, and in the individuation of the dead, differences too large to be reduced to the personalities of the speakers. Even if one wanted to attribute these different speeches solely to the temperament of their orators, the question remains not whether Roosevelt or Bush imposed his way of thought upon the nation, but whether Bush's language and mode of communication would have allowed him to be elected sixty years prior; what makes Bush's speech resonate in the twenty-first century when it may not have in 1941? If we shift critical scrutiny beyond elite figures in order to investigate the larger conditions of representation and accountability they draw upon to depict political life, we see something different. Melodrama marks the difference between these speeches.

Starting in the second half of the twentieth century, melodrama increasingly shapes political discourse in the United States, becoming one of its most prominent forms. Melodramatic cultural genres originated in postrevolutionary French theater and quickly migrated to American culture before becoming a prominent part of political discourse. Following the migration of melodramatic political discourse—from France to America, from stage drama to presidential oratory, from the nineteenth century to the twentieth—allows us to examine melodrama's historical development. How does a theater genre that originates after the French Revolution in order to represent bourgeois suffering at the hands of the aristocracy become serviceable for describing state power in post–World War II America? How do melodramatic stories about class injustice mutate to depict national imaginaries of freedom? How does melodrama generate political utility in U.S. politics?

This chapter first examines melodrama's instantiation in early nineteenth-century French theater and then traces its influence in the United States.

French melodramas were a new theatrical form that dramatized the suffering produced by class inequality. Melodrama was, from the outset, a mode of political expression, and its genre conventions reverberated with the liberal political theories prominent in its historical context. Melodrama's parallel origins with institutional liberalism in France made melodrama amenable to articulating political power. Both melodrama and liberalism insisted that individuals stand above and against overweening political power, and both dramatized the self-determining individual. Melodrama quickly moved to America in part because of these affinities, and melodrama's dramatization of injustice became widespread in American theater, novels, and eventually Hollywood film. In America, melodrama allied with American versions of a masculinized, liberal individualism to reformulate the melodramatic hero as a virtuous and self-reliant character free from complicity in the evil he fights against. Melodrama eventually became a popular genre of political discourse by the onset of the cold war, as its spectacle-driven story of the heroic triumph of innocent and virtuous people became part of the national narratives that legitimated the national-security state. At the end of the chapter I construct an archive of melodramatic political discourse by examining different instances of political rhetoric in the second half of the twentieth century. Reading political rhetoric as melodrama, I argue that melodrama's moralization of injury and heroic individualism become compatible with, and indeed foment, the expansion of postwar state power.

This chapter attends to melodrama's transnational migration. It follows the flow and travels of melodramatic genre forms across different media, continents, and historical moments. It emphasizes the way that melodramatic genre conventions mutate as they help to make sense of unsettling shifts in the relationships between citizens and structures of power.[2] This history and this archive are necessarily incomplete; they skip over many changes and movements in mass culture and political discourse in order to tell a particular story of melodrama's popularization in twentieth-century U.S. politics.[3] I pull from different strands of a larger, heterogeneous, and international archive of melodrama, highlighting certain products, moments, and forms while glossing over others in order to emphasize the particular themes that are most important for understanding how and why melodrama becomes a way of narrating nationhood, envisioning freedom, and legitimating dramatic expansions in postwar state power.

## French Melodrama: "The Morality of the Revolution" and the Spectacle of Liberalism

Melodrama originated in the context of the revolutionary changes in France at the end of the eighteenth century and the beginning of the nineteenth. Melodrama's birth story highlights not only how melodrama arose as a critique of unjust social power but also how its development was intimately connected to the institutionalization of liberal politics. Melodrama began as a theatrical form that attended to the dramatic economic and political changes of the revolutionary era.[4] Melodramatic plays typically performed a spectacle-laden unmasking of class privilege and absolutist power that had, until that point, structured social relations.[5] The plays postulated that individuals suffered because of the injustice of social hierarchy. They employed a gendered vocabulary of righteous female victims and dastardly male villains to clarify the complexities of revolution, modernity, and the redistribution of political, economic, and social power.

Jean-Jacques Rousseau invented the term *mélodrame* in 1774, drawing from the Greek term for music (*melos*) to describe a theatrical production that conveyed emotion and narrative clearly and accessibly through the intermixing of music and gesture.[6] While moral clarity, high emotionalism, and narrative accessibility would continue to be part of melodrama, the term quickly moved beyond Rousseau's definition to encompass a larger set of plays that depicted the heroic struggle of ordinary people who were victims of social injustice. Melodramas told stories about the sufferings of ordinary people, rather than kings and queens, who were similar to the audience in terms of class and social position.[7] The plays aligned with larger social forces working to denaturalize social hierarchies and shift the representation of political and social action away from the idea that history is shaped by great actors and toward two ideas: that ordinary people are central to the social fabric and that collectively experienced problems that cause individual suffering are not the product of nature or divine will but are the product of unjust social institutions and structural forces. Writing in 1843, the French theater critic Charles Nodier argued that melodrama "was the morality of the revolution."[8]

In illustrating how class inequities produce suffering, melodramatic theater also helped to articulate class inequity in the popular consciousness. The historian Lynn Hunt writes that melodramas "were creative efforts to reimagine the political world, to imagine a politics unhinged from patriarchal authority."[9] Often using the allegory of young bourgeois women seduced by evil aristocratic villains, melodramas clarified and moralized into story form the ambiguities of social inequality through gender stereotypes that represented victimhood in young women and heroism, sometimes, in ordinary male characters. In allegorizing rape in terms of the injustices of class hierarchy, melodramas identified structural causes responsible for affective experiences of powerlessness and suffering and condemned (while reinstantiating) sexual domination. A form of social whistle-blowing, melodrama exposed and denounced the unfairness sustaining aristocratic privilege, and in that way functioned as a continuous instigator of bourgeois revolutionary sentiment.

The 1800 play *Coelina, ou l'enfant du mystère* (*Coelina; or, The Child of Mystery*) is considered by many theater historians to be the first true melodrama, and it shaped the subsequent development of the genre.[10] The play was written by Guilbert de Pixérécourt, the first and most famous French melodramatist of the nineteenth century.[11] Pixérécourt called his melodramatic plays "spectacular prose dramas."[12] They contained thrilling action, ominous music, and heightened scenes of persecuted innocence, with the specific intent of instilling moral messages about proper behavior and social injustice in their bourgeois audiences. In *Coelina* the eponymous protagonist is an orphan living with her gentle uncle Dufour, who guards her modest inheritance. Coelina and Dufour's son are in love, but Coelina's other uncle, the rich Truguelin, wants to take Coelina's inheritance by betrothing her to his own son. Before the marriage with Truguelin's son is sanctioned, Truguelin is caught trying to kill a mute and scarred beggar, the victim of a violent crime years earlier who now lives with Dufour. Truguelin son's marriage is refused, and Coelina is slated to marry Dufour's son. Incensed, Truguelin reveals that Coelina is not who they all assume: her real father is the mute beggar, who was not even married to Coelina's mother: she is "the child of crime and adultery!"[13] In a pathos-laden scene of suffering and tears, Coelina and her mute father are cast away from Dufour's home. It is eventually revealed that rich Truguelin was the father's initial attacker years earlier, and that the father was in fact Coelina's mother's rightful husband. After a spectacular chase scene through the countryside, Truguelin is caught by the police, and Coelina is welcomed back to the Dufour home. She finally marries Dufour's son, her true love, with her father by her side. The drama ends with a lesson:

Always treat the beggar fair,
his misfortune is no disgrace;

A turn of fate, unless you share,
And you the poor man in his place; . . .
For happiness does not stay,
unless the heart is at the core. . . .
Good words, good deeds will advance
the delight of our little tune.[14]

*Coelina* oriented the beginnings of the melodramatic genre form to illustrate how the lives of the less powerful—often symbolized by innocent young women, beggars, or children—were cruelly injured by socially produced inequities. In addition to kings and aristocrats, ordinary people such as Coelina and her father had lives invested with meaning and value; they too suffered in ways that society was obligated to rectify. The play makes a narrative of class inequality in the story of the wealthy Truguelin's unjust attacks on Coelina and her father. Truguelin is an avatar for the dominations of the aristocratic class writ large. In the play, domestic suffering is a product of class inequities and is illustrated by the horrifying mistreatment of the mutilated beggar, the unjust banishment of the good Coelina, and Truguelin's initial escape from responsibility. Melodrama emphasizes scenes of injustice from the point of view of those who suffer from it; in the words of the historian David Grimsted, melodrama is "an echo of the historically voiceless."[15] In this play the voicelessness is literal, as Truguelin had cut out the beggar's tongue so that he was unable to indict Truguelin. *Coelina* sentimentalizes Coelina's and her father's experiences of victimization as they become objects of pathos, and spectators are encouraged to identify with their suffering. The play was wildly popular at the time of its creation, and part of its appeal was the way it encouraged identification with Coelina as a victim not of bad luck but of aristocratic malfeasance that demanded rectification by the authorities.

Melodramatists frequently aimed to impose moral lessons upon the bourgeois audience they aimed to educate. In the final speech of this early melodrama, responsibility for Coelina's and her father's injustice is placed on "fate," but this fate is the arbitrariness of aristocratic whim. It is only rectified by the revolution's shift in social structure that enables the police to hold accountable those with more wealth and social status. At the height of his career, Pixérécourt argued, "Through performances and reading melodrama, *the people learn to become better.* . . . Melodrama should thus have a useful influence on our manners and morals, because the eternal morality that one finds there consists of rewarding good actions and punishing bad."[16] *Coelina* is part of this moral mission: the play models proper behavior and shows the inevitable downfall of aristocratic injustice. The final speech makes what Pixérécourt calls "eternal morality" available in ordinary life and asks the audience to reshape their behavior toward the "good words and good deeds" of the final lines. *Coelina* imbued the ordinary travails of daily life with deep power and moral value.

Peter Brooks argues that melodramas were part of a larger epistemological shift that came out of the European destruction of the Catholic Church and monarchy, which decimated inherited modes of organizing society.[17] The French Revolution was generally understood to mark the end of a process in which hierarchical political and social representations lost their legitimacy. In locating revolutionary justice in domestic scenes of family drama, melodramas revealed the "hidden" structures of power that had previously allowed this system to function and yet also ameliorated the anxieties generated out of the nobility's and church's dissolution.[18] Brooks contends that melodrama helped to entrench two responses to the crumbling formations of revolutionary France: the liquidation of aristocratic and class privilege and the dissolution of the church and traditional concepts of morality. First, melodrama depicted the cruelties of aristocratic privilege by dramatizing its excesses and attaching moral condemnation to its inequities, as in *Coelina*. Individual injuries arising from this system were not seen as individual burdens but as socially, politically, and economically conditioned; the act of villainy illustrated with spectacular pathos and energy the unjust victimization of the weak.

Melodrama's second development—out of the dissolution of the Catholic Church—took a different form. The waning of church power portended the termination of traditional markers of meaning and morality; good and evil became untethered to specific moral imperatives. Yet melodrama countered this condition by insisting that an eternal moral law can and does exist. The location of that moral law, however, was in the world, not above it, often inside the home or within individual conscience. The inherent moral significance of daily life was resacralized in the "City of Man."[19] Thus, melodrama not only critiqued society but also provided reassurance, as in Pixérécourt's claim, that an eternal morality did operate to order the world. Melodrama insisted that ordinary social interactions and individual experiences had a deep, even cosmic moral meaning that exceeded the routine grind of daily life. As in *Coelina*, melodrama made daily life seem rife with extraordinary events. Melodrama arose, then, at an unpredictable era to restabilize certain key tenets that underwrote the social order. Hunt writes that melodrama's "stage managing of anxiety" worked to clarify and assuage the disorientations of a confusing social epoch with moral stability and with the promise that virtue can still be recognized even within a reconfigured social structure.[20]

Brooks's thesis does not note, however, the contradictory political message of *responsibility* that these two different origins create in the melodramatic genre. Melodramatic critiques of class power trace responsibility for suffering to social and economic structures that must be held to account for the injustices they perpetuate. Yet the amelioration of this anxiety reestablishes a traditional social and moral order by personifying the social problems it diagnoses in individual actions that can easily be overcome by individual heroes. In many melodramas, the larger changes that would be needed to redress expansive social problems are truncated by the end of the play, as they are ultimately solved in an isolated fashion by individuals. The cultural theorist John Cawelti explains the problem by arguing that melodrama relies on the conventional moral vision that particular political and cultural eras wished to see affirmed; melodrama "needs a proper order of things to fall back on," which reinforces prevalent social norms.[21] But it seems instead that the problem is less about the type of morality that is reinstated than about where responsibility is placed for suffering and evil. Villainy, initially established as the effect of large-scale social injustices, eventually becomes personified in the body of the singular evildoer. Once the villain is punished or redeemed, social injustice is eradicated.

This distinction becomes more pronounced in the American context. However, even in France the individualizing aspect of melodrama produces contradictory levels of responsibility for class inequity. We can see this in *Valentine, ou la séduction* (1821), another of Pixérécourt's most famous plays, and one that was translated into English as *Adeline, Victim of Seduction* within a year of its creation. Innocent Valentine, "a simple and inexperienced girl," is seduced by a wealthy count who cloaks his identity and pretends to marry her. When she finds out the ruse, she is devastated, and when she tries to escape she is locked inside a castle. Her seduction is first explained in the play through class inequalities and the unfreedom this produces for those without title; a butler who witnesses the seduction laments, "I'll go back to my native village— better the crust and cold water, earnt with the sweat of the brow amongst the honest, than fortunes without toil at their hands who delight in making the simple and innocent as wicked as themselves."[22] Her seduction signifies a larger structural problem in which class hierarchies dominate human freedom and noble rank is inversely proportional to moral virtue. Extending the play's condemnation of class privilege as moral iniquity, Valentine's father cries, "I claim a signal vengeance! A vengeance to strike terror into the titled, and the wealthy youth, who heedless of the example they ought to set their inferiors, seek among them for victims, laugh o'er the fall of humble innocence, and mock the desolation of the poor man's home."[23] But by the end of the play blame is solely placed on the shoulders of Baron Remberg, the seducer's evil friend who masterminded the seduction. The count is morally refigured as a good man, motivated only by love for Valentine, just a bit bumbling and manipulated by his friend. The count's father, the noble prince of the land and thus the sovereign ruler, calls himself "the father and friend of all who suffer," and reminds his servant that the prince "is always at home to the unfortunate."[24] On hearing of Remberg's actions, the prince—and by extension all class domination—is let off the hook for Remberg's violence; the prince grumbles, "How often is the ruler hated for the vices of the servant, whose real character he is often the last to know."[25] And the beneficence of his sovereignty and wealth are cemented at the play's climax, when he intones, "Believe me, 'tis the noblest exercise of wealth to share it with the unfortunate."[26]

The accountability for injury thus transforms from structural inequality to the personal cruelties of Remberg—"the most dissolute, the most depraved"—and the initial and damning judgments of class injustice are dissolved into a personal condemnation of the single evil malefactor.[27] Remberg's punishment is to be outed to the prince, who promises to personally tell the king about Remberg's deed. In *Valentine*, as in *Coelina*, the violences depicted in the initial scenes of injustice and domination do not require a wholesale restructuring of society by the end of the play, as the climax individuates the rectification of injustice and thus mollifies the anxiety created out of the vastness of the play's initial social critique. Thomas Elsaesser notes of early French melodrama, "Complex social processes were simplified either by blaming the evil disposition of individuals or by manipulating plots and engineering coincidences and *dei ex machina*."[28] With recognition of Valentine's injured virtue and the villain's evil deed, injustice is quickly righted and the status quo is restored.

Scholars of melodrama have built on Brooks's thesis to examine melodrama's other origins, including capitalism, urban modernity, and the bourgeois family structure.[29] Yet in melodrama scholarship, juridical changes in the late eighteenth century and the early nineteenth often receive short shrift, as if they were merely carried along with other tidal changes rather than themselves functioning as a generative force for melodrama's conventions.[30] The origin and development of melodrama cannot, however, be separated from the origin and institutionalization of liberalism. The rise of liberalism in the eighteenth and nineteenth centuries—as a normative theory of just politics, as an ontology of human nature, and eventually as an impetus for the shift in formal political structures from rights of the king to rights of the individual—was popularized by melodrama's dramatizing these themes within the lives of the ordinary people they would affect.

Melodramatic theater and the French institutionalization of liberal political ideas (drawing inspiration from Rousseau, Montesquieu, and John Locke but also moving beyond them) began at the same historical moment. During the revolution, melodrama entered the playhouse as liberal theory entered the statehouse; both initially harbored a critique of hierarchal domination. Undermining traditional models of authority, they illustrated the injustice of absolute power, sharing a dramatic reconceptualization of power that shifted its origin from the monarch to the people. While it would be impossible to do full justice here to the claim that melodrama is intimately connected with early liberalism, I want to highlight a few key similarities that I develop throughout the rest of the book in a more contemporary context. Both melodrama and liberalism argued that tyrannical power hampers human freedom. Locke's liberalism, for instance, inspired political thinking and French revolutionary action one hundred years later; his claim that "nobody can desire to have me in his absolute power unless it be to compel me by force to that which is against the right of my freedom, i.e. make me a slave. . . . Reason bids me to look on him as an enemy to my preservation who would take away my freedom which is the fence to it" is the written counterpart to the melodramatic play that visually illustrates the "slave" and his "fence" through the triumph of the ordinary individual over the "enemy to my preservation."[31]

In *Valentine*, for instance, the protagonist is literally fenced in by the boundaries of the count's courtyard for the first act of the play, and her escape is articulated through recourse to the desire for liberty and freedom. Political theorists' use of metaphors to describe an unjust society—for example, Rousseau's chains and Locke's fences—were illustrated most vividly in a melodramatic genre that performed them. Melodrama and liberalism nourished the belief that one could become one's own master, and as both argued that individuals are free to determine the shape of their own lives, they exemplified modes of being in which individuals triumphed over claims of transcendent authority. Like the early moments of liberal theory, melodrama was a form of protest, dissent, and mobilization against what it identified as the repressive and illegitimate conditions of prerevolutionary monarchical society.[32] In melodrama power took form as moral virtue and natural justice, and it was anointed on those who had traditionally been denied the capacity and capability to share in public authority.

Melodrama's protest narratives harbored the credo of "freedom *from* power"—a liberal conceptualization of freedom that contained a critique of domination, a fear of absolutist authority, and an insistence that political subjects can and should exist not as subject to others' power but as a subject without subjection, as the maker of one's own imperatives.[33] Instead of suggesting that individuals passively submit to the desires and predilections of the most powerful, melodrama, like liberalism, helped to denaturalize claims to transcendent mastery. Early French melodrama was probably more consciously styled on the works of Rousseau than Locke; Rousseau was "the patron saint of the revolution" as well as the creator of the term *melodrama*, and his writings encouraged desires for self-determination at both the individual and collective levels.[34] Rousseau's ideas guided not only the revolution and certain iterations of liberal theory but also the melodramatic form he first identified, which grew to perform in part his insistence that "no man has any natural authority over his fellows."[35] Both melodramatic theater and postrevolutionary French politics, including the *Declaration of the Rights of Man and of the Citizen*, insisted that ordinary people and the conditions of their existence were the locus of social power. Liberal theories contended, across their different iterations, that every individual, not just the monarch, is capable of becoming a self-determining subject; as Rousseau argued, "[Man] becomes his own master."[36] Both liberalism and melodrama grew out of a historic moment that engendered the development of the self-determining subject, one who is able to triumph over lived conditions and challenge its injustices. Both normalize an abstracted relationship to the world that conditions them, and, in the case of Locke more than Rousseau, find ways to deflect political responsibility onto individuals by using certain forms of socially produced injustice to erase the effects of others.

Melodrama was, in many ways, a cultural reconfiguration of the theoretical underpinnings of liberal democracy, though its message shifted depending on the context in which it was adapted and reworked. In postrevolutionary France, at least, part of self-mastery included willful submission to legal institutions. *Coelina*'s climax ends when the villain is captured by the police, the most familiar and daily symbol of the juridical order in postrevolutionary France. French stage melodrama emphasized respect for legal institutions as the new form of a just political order. While the police officers often had no speaking roles, they were frequently the figures who controlled the fate of the evildoer. Perhaps the police and juridical institutions were assumed to reflect the desire of each person as equal members of a Rousseauian general will. If the individual will subtends the political order, then obeying police authority is a way of obeying a law that the individual took part in authoring; it would therefore be experienced less as a form of submission than as the very example for how one can be subject to the law without being subjected by it. But the trope of just submission to legal authority, however, weakens when melodrama reaches American shores.

## Melodrama in American Culture I: The Rise of Liberal Individualism

American melodrama has been described as a "democratic" genre in film studies, literary theory, and theater history.[37] The theater scholar Daniel Gerould argues that American melodrama is part of "the democratic revolution in thought and feeling" not only because it was one of the first cultural forms designed for a mass audience but also because the genre trusted in the triumph of justice and illustrated a can-do self-determinism in which individuals were not hemmed in by authority.[38] Grimsted calls American melodrama democratic because it was produced by and for the middle class and takes ordinary people seriously, endowing them with the claim that the individual's gut-level wisdom is superior to the dictates of social conformity.[39] Yet democracy here seems to be conflated with something that looks a lot like liberal individualism: the valorization of self-reliance against overweening authority, the individualist challenge to social conformity, the trust in one's own gut instinct, and the hope that one can be free from domination through sheer force of individual willpower. In American melodrama, protagonists generally do not come together collectively to debate and author a course of action for addressing political problems, nor do they show governing powers or political authority dispersed and equalized across a large swath of the population. Instead, the solution to large-scale problems is typically individuated, so that individual problems are placed above community ones and the rectification of their grievances is a substitute for solving larger injustices. In many American melodramatic plays, the individual alone is often responsible for fighting injustice and is guided by the alluring promise of individual sovereign freedom.

Melodrama's travel to American culture was fast and furious. Grimsted's account likens it to a "tidal wave" of influx and influence that started at the beginning of the nineteenth century.[40] Gerould argues that melodrama had a prominent role in nineteenth-century sensibilities: "Melodrama determined to a large extent how Americans saw their world and imagined their place in it."[41] French melodrama's liberal sensibilities and story of emancipated bourgeois virtue primed it for American audiences, who found parallels in their own national narratives of independence. Faith in ordinary people, a critique of unjust power, and a heroization of the underdog allied with a newly formed America bound by a sense of emancipation from political tyranny. Its sense of political critique appealed to American audiences who found its use of dastardly villainy a productive way to illuminate social problems. The historian Lawrence Levine emphasizes melodrama's relationship to the national imaginary: "Melodrama transmitted ideas so pervasive and so apparent to Americans that we often find them hard to identify as ideas."[42] American culture both appropriated melodrama and rearticulated its tenets within American national fantasies, values, and modes of experience. American audiences took both their seating and their participation in the theater as expressions of a democratic ethos; spectators called audience participation "exercising their sovereignty," in which theater audiences had an "*undoubted right* to see and applaud who they please."[43] They described the melodramatic viewing experience as a Tocquevillian New England township in which individual power and civic participation structured the space and experience of the theater; though in the theater, as in politics, participation and access were varyingly curtailed, in particular for blacks and female prostitutes.[44] As Bruce McConachie writes of melodramatic theater, "Americans worked through their political anxieties not by listening to speeches on political philosophy, but by applauding heroes, scapegoating villains, and weeping for victims."[45]

The melodramatist Dion Boucicault's famous 1857 play *The Poor of New York*, a sentimental critique of capitalism and financial speculation, can help to flesh out how French melodrama shifts when it comes to America.[46] *The Poor of New York* begins in the financial crisis of 1837, when the hardworking and innocent Fairweather father deposits his life savings with the crooked bank owner Bloodgood. Bloodgood plans to steal the money, Fairweather finds out the plan, and when Bloodgood refuses to return his savings, Fairweather dies of apoplexy. Bloodgood keeps the money. The play then flashes forward twenty years to the financial crisis of 1857, which spectators were personally living through at that moment. The remaining Fairweather family now lives in abject poverty, while the wealthy Bloodgood squeezes them for rent money that they cannot pay. One character explains, making Bloodgood a placeholder for the cruelties of capitalism: "Wall Street is a perch, on which a row of human vultures sit, ready to fight over the carcass of a dying enterprise. Amongst those birds of prey, the most vulturous is perhaps Gid Bloodgood. . . . Last week by a speculation in flour he made fifty thousand dollars, this operation raised the price of bread four cents a loaf, and now there are a thousand people starving in the hovels of New York."[47] The Fairweathers are unjust victims of this speculation, but they are not resigned to their condition. They try any honest means to escape abjection and gain employment, even as they are stymied at every turn by the exigencies of the crisis.

Meanwhile, Bloodgood's old bank clerk threatens to reveal that Bloodgood stole the Fairweathers' money years earlier. Bloodgood attempts to burn down the clerk's house in order to incinerate evidence of his crime. In the spectacular climax of fire, danger, and rescue, the house and the evidence are saved in the nick of time by the Fairweather son and the bank clerk, with the help of other impoverished souls. The Fairweathers regain their savings and become wealthy, while Bloodgood is sent to jail. As the play ends, the Fairweathers will never have to worry about poverty again. *The Poor of New York*, like *Coelina*, finishes with its moral lesson directed clearly to the spectators: "Have the sufferings we depicted in this scene touched your hearts, caused a tear of sympathy to fill your eyes? . . . When you leave this place, as you return to your homes, should you see some poor creatures, extend your hands to them, and the blessings that will follow you on your way will be the most grateful tribute you can pay to The Poor of New York."[48]

*The Poor of New York* was adapted for American audiences from a French melodrama, *Les pauvre de Paris* (The poor of Paris), which also critiqued financial excess but spent much of its dramatic pathos on a suicide scene where each woman in the family tries to kill herself so that she will not burden the others.[49] This scene devolves to only a short moment in its American version, as the American family instead actively fights against its circumstances. The emphasis in *The Poor of New York* is on the can-do spirit of the protagonists. Their work ethic proves their virtue, whereas in *Les pauvre de Paris* virtue is proven by self-sacrifice. *Valentine* ends in a similar way to *Les pauvre de Paris*, with the recognition of the female protagonist's virtue yet also with her sacrifice: the brokenhearted protagonist secures financial support for her ailing father from the prince and then commits suicide. Her virtues are made manifest in these actions, and she dies right after she is publicly exonerated by the prince and her father. Gerould writes that in American melodramas, unlike French ones, "when confronted with extreme misfortune, American melodramatic heroes and heroines do not suffer passively or contemplate suicide—they fight back, get to work, start a new life."[50] In *Les pauvre de Paris* the impoverished family relies on public welfare to survive; in *Coelina* justice is served when victims seek help from juridical authorities. There is no such lesson in America, where virtue is not found in dependence on others, and public welfare is absent from the available resources offered to protagonists. Both the French and American plays end with the virtuous protagonists acquiring their righteous wealth, but in *The Poor of New York*, individual heroes are required to rescue themselves from the Wall Street–caused bank crisis. The final words of the play place responsibility for further poverty reduction solely on the voluntary contributions of individual theater patrons. Its final moral message disregards the bank speculation that situated the play's actions and produced the financial crisis in the first place.

American liberal individualism circulated within and reshaped melodramatic messages, rewarding the individual who fought hard for virtue against demeaning situations or conformist behavior.[51] Many of the changes that melodrama underwent when it arrived on the American stage center on changing formations of heroism and individual agency. Heroism becomes a much larger part of melodrama in the United States than it does in France; neither *Coelina* nor *Valentine* focuses on the heroism of a single courageous actor, even as both find courage in the virtuous and selfless acts of female victims.[52] American melodrama, however, emphasizes the hero's unlimited capacity to forge his or her own identity.[53] Neither God nor class, nor history, nor political institutions can predetermine the capacity of the liberal individual to pursue emancipation from authoritarian domination and to find happiness through self-assertion. Melodrama's liberal message of "freedom from power" resonated strongly in America, which had taken this message in a radically individualist direction, situating the fight for freedom as an individual burden and codifying it as an inalienable individual right in the Bill of Rights. These values were vivified in the body of the melodramatic male hero.

American melodrama's themes of overcoming social evil through self-determination and inner goodness developed out of earlier forms of both liberal theory and melodrama, which were extended and formalized in their American instantiations, perhaps aligning with Locke's greater influence in American politics. For Locke, the right of the individual to be autonomous is a right defined negatively: "Not to be the subject to the inconstant, uncertain, unknown or arbitrary will of another man."[54] Connecting to American individualism's imbrications with transcendentalism, American melodrama insisted on the certitude of basic ethical truths, but then located them in the interior wisdom of the individual, an individual who could shed the constraints of social orthodoxy and heed an inner call. This natural nobility of the hero expressed an affinity with the political theories that underwrote both liberal democracy and Emersonian self-reliance. Individuals had an inner divinity that, once freed from the dictates of domination (either by the state, economy, others' actions, or public opinion), would fully express that individual's virtue and grace. This individualism thus harbored a gut-level trust of self that eschewed interdependence in favor of a self-reliant subject constructed outside social dictates. As Grimsted states of American melodrama, "The heart is the sure compass that, if left untampered, would guide toward truth; emotional sensibility is the real criterion for virtue."[55] American melodrama thus reflected a liberal individualism that combined both a Lockean conception of liberty (which views the individual as an ontological category) and a transcendentalist conception of self-reliance (which views the individual as a moral category, a norm marking the ability of the individual to heed inner wisdom). By being true to one's natural self, anyone could possess heroic greatness if given the opportunity.

The melodramatic individual hero, typically a man, is often deindividuated, consisting of no specific qualities other than his ordinariness and superlative virtue, so that any spectator can identify with his deeds and identify himself with the hero's quest for emancipation. Heroes were average people, like the spectator, who happened to find themselves in dramatic situations and who develop self-reliance by learning to trust their inner strength.[56] All individuals harbor the capacity to determine their own form of existence; this is part of melodrama's ability to make ordinary life so extraordinary. In the melodramatist Augustin Daly's most popular play, *A Flash of Lightning* (1868), the working-class everyman Jack learns to listen to his inner virtue, which allows him to bravely and selflessly rescue a female victim from a burning steamship.[57] In *The Poor of New York*, Fairweather's son similarly highlights the virtue of individual heroism in the pursuit of justice. Responsible less to the community than to their own virtue, American heroes can single-handedly fashion their own fate via hard work, perseverance, and the repudiation (though not reformation) of institutions that smack of injustice. Perhaps borrowing from liberalism's general tendency to universalize the abstract individual as the individual par excellence, melodrama also argued that what was good for the hero was a universal good.

The melodramatic hero often *is* the universal liberal individual: a self-determining man with an innate sense of goodness, who can free himself (and his helpless yet grateful female and child dependents) from the chains of social domination.[58] Liberal individualism is deeply gendered; individualism is often understood to be a capacity generally available only to men, as women are deemed less able to achieve the promise of self-determination it offers.[59] Melodrama, in drawing from its tenets, also masculinizes its self-sufficient heroism: it is often the men who are self-emancipating and self-making; men are self-made upon women's suffering.[60] This is not always the case, however; historically, melodrama's gender conventions are themselves somewhat unstable. The archetypal scene of melodrama—the female victim waiting helplessly for the male hero to rescue her, epitomized in popular tied-to-the-railroad-tracks scenes—was in its first instantiation a man tied to the tracks who was rescued by a heroine.[61] The original scene in Daly's *Under the Gaslight* (1867) has young Laura bravely rescue an older man. Gender norms are further complicated by silent serial films in the 1910s; in serials such as *The Perils of Pauline* and *Exploits of Elaine*, as Ben Singer has shown, female action heroes find themselves imperiled but just as often rescue themselves and others.[62] Female action heroes, perhaps, wax and wane in loose alliance with the gains and losses of American feminism, but it is important to see that the gender norms of melodrama have never been neat and tidy. More commonly, however, American melodrama at this point reassures spectators that individuals, usually male, have an ontological capacity for self-making.

While American melodrama equates victimhood and heroism with individual moral virtue, it is a different worldview than that generated out of more explicitly religious genres of political discourse in America, and this shapes the way that melodrama cultivates responsibility for the evil it depicts. Take, for example, one of the most popular national genres, the American jeremiad. The jeremiad, according to Sacvan Bercovitch, is a genre form that bitterly laments the state of society and its morals and contains prophecy of its downfall unless the members of society return to their roots.[63] While certain conventions of the jeremiad and the melodrama overlap—both draw upon moral clarity to criticize society, provoke vengeance, argue for a return to a golden past, and seek to unify their spectators or participants to fight for justice—their moral worldviews are actually quite different. The jeremiad assumes that all members of society are accountable (though in different ways) for the problems it laments; the jeremiadic subject understands itself as part of the problem it seeks to overcome. In contrast, melodramatic subjects externalize all responsibility for society's problems to an evil Other, and once the villain is removed, society can go back to its smooth functioning. Social problems are not produced by the protagonist but by the villainous forces that try to shackle the protagonist. In the jeremiad, individuals must rid themselves of evil before they can serve the community. In melodrama, however, there is no positing of a split subject that is morally riven; the subject is completely good or completely evil. The self-work so crucial to the jeremiad is rendered obsolete in melodrama, where protagonists and spectators are always understood to be virtuous. As an innocent victim, the protagonist is free from personal responsibility for the problems that are diagnosed and cannot be held accountable for their effects. Unlike the jeremiad, in melodrama responsibility is not an act of soul-searching or a question of personal complicity in large social cruelties. Compared to the jeremiad, melodrama leaves its unriven protagonists and their social world blameless; both are free of accountability for the social problems that melodrama dramatizes.

The contrast between the melodrama and the jeremiad reveals what makes melodrama so appealing in its contradictory locations for placing blame for social problems. The blame placed by melodrama's diagnosis of victimization contradicts the blame produced by the articulation of heroism. Melodrama's diagnosis of victimization often identifies villainy as a social or political problem: aristocratic privilege, unfettered capitalism, gender domination. Positioning victimization as the unjust effect of a social problem figures the responsibility for that problem as structural, social, and broad in scale. The only way to heal the victim's injury is to change the larger social and political system from which injury emerges. Yet this message contradicts melodrama's other tenet, which depicts individuals not as delimited by societal status but as self-reliant actors. From the perspective of heroism, the only way to solve problems or eradicate villainy is by individual action.

The shift of responsibility is twofold: the source of injustice moves from social conditions to villains with bad morals, and the responsibility for eradicating injustice moves from large, collective efforts toward social transformation to the individual hero. *The Poor of New York*, for example, begins as a critique of speculative and unregulated capitalism but ends when an evil businessman is punished and the poor protagonists become wealthy. As responsibility devolves from broad social exploitation to a dastardly villain, Bloodgood is jailed, the Fairweathers become rich, and the problem of capitalism has been solved. The final words of the play recommend individual charity for beggars rather than large structural transformations of a political-economic system that produced two financial crises in twenty years (again, this is not a democratic genre but a liberal one). The hero, in the end, is responsible only for penalizing the villain, not ending exploitation. As Henry David Thoreau argued in his individualist treatise *Civil Disobedience*, social problems might be widespread, but they are best redressed through changes in individual behavior.[64]

## Melodrama in American Culture II:
## National Virtue and Racialized Power

While melodramas often portrayed political problems in this individuated fashion, they simultaneously transformed the political fields they depicted. We can see this transformation in two of the most powerful melodramas in U.S. history: *Uncle Tom's Cabin* (1852) and *The Birth of a Nation* (1915). Both of these melodramas trafficked in racialized power to transform the worlds of slavery and racism they depicted, but they did so to very different ends. *Uncle Tom's Cabin* is perhaps the most prominent and visible example of melodrama's power to inform and define broader social and political conflict even within an individualist ethos.[65] Whether or not President Abraham Lincoln was correct in supposedly calling Harriet Beecher Stowe the "little woman who wrote the book that started this great war," it is clear that she helped to reformulate public discourse on slavery leading up to the Civil War. Her book integrated a critique of the institution of slavery with a melodramatic worldview, and in so doing convinced millions of white Americans that slaves were victims of an unjust and immoral social practice. In dramatizing the terrible suffering of Uncle Tom and his fellow slaves at the hands of white slaveowners, Stowe's novel theatricalized and denaturalized the horrors of the slave system. Cawelti writes, "The extraordinary impact of *Uncle Tom's Cabin* was a testimony to Stowe's ability to express her sense of deeply felt social wrongs in terms of the melodramatic conventions her readers were predisposed to respond to."[66] Stowe, in other words, used a familiar melodramatic genre form to construct a new scenario that encouraged pity for black slaves.[67]

Yet James Baldwin's devastating reading of *Uncle Tom's Cabin* argues that the pure, impeccable virtuosity that describes Uncle Tom and enables his moral legibility is just as brutal to him as the slavery he cannot escape. It refuses him any human complexity and thus denies his humanity. The melodrama of slavery in *Uncle Tom's Cabin* requires slaves to be one-dimensional in their moral virtuousness in order for slavery to appear unjust. Baldwin calls the book "everybody's protest novel," though he is not condemning protest per se, but the way that the melodramatic narrative of *Uncle Tom's Cabin* defangs antislavery and antiracist protest through sentimentalizing characterizations of the black characters, which describe their actions, motivations, and desires only through moralized categories of unambiguous virtue. He writes of Uncle Tom: "In overlooking, denying, evading his complexity—which is nothing more than the disquieting complexity of ourselves—we are diminished and we perish; only within this web of ambiguity, paradox, this hunger, danger, darkness, can we at once find ourselves as the power that will free us from ourselves."[68] Baldwin further notes the comforting aspects of everybody's protest novel in the way it divulges to its readers their own virtue made manifest by their very willingness to read the book and empathize with Uncle Tom's plight.[69] Part of what dehumanizes Uncle Tom is the way he becomes an object for readers to use to mark their own virtue. Proving one's own goodness through one's empathy is a melodramatic tactic that, as Scott Loren and Jörg Metelmann note, "foregrounds a sensitive self in a mode of self-enjoyment."[70] If the readers can feel sorrow for Uncle Tom, they are aligned with Tom's utter goodness, and they gain a kind of pleasure through the self-acknowledgment of their virtue. Feeling sorrow for Uncle Tom and hatred at his owner, Simon Legree, somehow absolves readers of any of slavery's reverberations in the present, or of action in the present, to, as Baldwin writes, "free us from ourselves," as if all readers need to do is read the book and, in feeling virtuous about slavery's eradication, posit their own antiracism.

At the beginning of the twentieth century, the melodramatic genre's racialization of U.S. power quickly jumped into film; melodrama was, arguably, the most popular film genre in the United States among silent and then sound pictures, and melodrama's depictions of moral nationhood through race also become prominent in film.[71] The most explosive and controversial melodrama of early cinema, *The Birth of a Nation,* directed by D. W. Griffith, generated one of the first mass formations of American national identity through a racialized melodramatic narrative.[72] *The Birth of a Nation* reimagined a post–Civil War political order in which mischievous and undereducated black former slaves take control of the levers of national political power. These former slaves threaten the formal institutional practices of freedom and the virginal bodily purity of white America, as embodied in the actress Lillian Gish, the stand-in for both. In the film (and the novel that the film was based on), Southern and Northern whites come together to defend the nation from black villainy by joining the Ku Klux Klan. In the climax of the narrative, the Ku Klux Klan at once heroically prevents Gish from rape by a black man and restores the political order of the nation to its rightful white leaders. Pitting white American goodness against black aggressive villainy, the film united a post–Civil War nation by moralizing and sexualizing heroic vengeance against the racialized oppressor of American virtue. In Linda Williams's analysis, the film's emotional power generated "a national rebirth on the heels of the film's white hero."[73] While there is extensive scholarship on the racial connotations of U.S. nationhood that both stem from and exceed *Uncle Tom's Cabin* and *The Birth of a Nation*, what is most relevant for this chapter is *The Birth of a Nation*'s particular formation of national identity through potential domination and national victimization: the film performs national unity by turning black victims of white racism into oppressors of white goodness.

*The Birth of a Nation* thus draws upon melodrama's sexualization of structural inequalities from its French inheritance and *Uncle Tom's Cabin*'s moralization of racial inequalities to confer the moral power of victimhood upon white men, former slaveholders, and by extension the white nation it constructs in their shadow. In the film, the so-called real nation, the nation bound by whiteness, becomes both victim and hero, spurred to fight for its own self-preservation against the villains that aim to destroy its hard-fought freedom (i.e., rape its white women). Screened at the White House for an approving President Woodrow Wilson, *The Birth of a Nation* creates a representation of history that morally legitimates the use of aggressive heroism and violent state power against racial minorities. It makes war and expansive state power moral imperatives for experiencing freedom, and for protecting the nation from the very people violently injured for centuries by state support for slavery and by national imaginaries of black inferiority.

Whereas earlier forms of melodrama often gained popularity by anointing moral power upon the powerless, *The Birth of a Nation* names the powerful white majority the powerless innocent victim in order to garner the moral legitimation for heroic aggression against the black minority. *The Birth of a Nation* thus performs two feats that together stand the melodrama of *Uncle Tom's Cabin* on its head: the film sentimentalizes white Americans as victims of black Americans' desire for power, and then combines victimization and heroism into a virginal national identity that loses any need for a critique of its own practices and norms. The nation becomes that which has been unjustly injured by black violence, and the nation gains unity through its injustice, as well as the moral authority to aggressively fight the attacker that covets its freedom. Creating this identity at the expense of the very population that had been decimated by slavery, *The Birth of a Nation* presaged the work of melodramatic political discourse in post–World War II formations of U.S. nationhood that legitimate dramatic expansions of state power aiming not to support the flourishing and freedom of people's lives but to extend oppression over exploited populations in the name of freedom. Yet the racialized power so explicit in *The Birth of a Nation* is subsumed in melodrama when it becomes a political discourse, especially in presidential oratory; melodrama will unify the nation in part by making racial distinctions seem unimportant to the experience of being an American, of being part of a citizenry unified in victimization by un-American forces. Melodramatic political discourses will often depict the nation as racially inclusive, in part to legitimate violence against enemies presumed noninclusive.

The victim-hero national identity that melodrama eventually develops will be one all people can join if they accept the norms of freedom in the United States and the affective solicitations of melodramatic political discourse. As Karl Marx noted about the work of liberal politics more broadly, melodrama less erases racial, economic, and gender inequalities than accepts them on the condition that these differences are subsumed by a civic nationalism defined by the abstract promise of freedom granted to its citizenry.[74] In *The Birth of a Nation*, for example, the black people who side with the white people are included in the rebirth of the virtuous nation and gain access to its new national identity so long as they refuse to claim racial or economic parity, so long as they refuse to note that their racialized inequality undoes the claims of virtuous nationhood, and instead accept that American national identity makes their inequality irrelevant to the nation's virtue. The national identity constructed out of melodrama can thus elide the unequal realms of freedom as they are lived in the daily particulars of American lives marked by economic disempowerment, racialized exploitation, and unequal access to power, among other forms of inequality. Melodrama hails a particular type of citizen: as long as you believe in the goodness of the victimized nation and trust state institutions to enable individual freedom, then this form of melodrama accepts you as a virtuous citizen. But your inclusion, and virtue, is predicated on your acceptance that your particular and racialized experiences of inequality and unfreedom are irrelevant to the construction of American goodness.

Melodramatic Political Discourse: Victims and Heroes
on Both Sides of the Counter

After World War II, melodrama began to regularly shape national political discourse about American identity and its place in the world. The rest of this chapter examines different forms of melodramatic political discourse by reading key political addresses about U.S. state power in the second half of the twentieth century. As a political discourse, melodrama de-emphasized racialized descriptions of nationhood to focus on civic ideals of freedom and morality, which broadened its inclusiveness and scope of power. Melodrama's popularity in postwar U.S. politics drew from the widespread popularity of the melodramatic tradition in theater, novels, and film, and also from other national discourses, political conditions, and technological changes in American life that consolidated around a national identity grounded in the assurance of America's virtue and commitment to fighting villainy. This is not to say that melodrama had not been politically influential beforehand, as *Uncle Tom's Cabin* and *The Birth of a Nation* make clear, nor is it to say that there were not prior instances of melodrama in political discourse, as melodramatic elements might arguably be found in the rhetoric of westward expansion, in the newspaper coverage leading to the Spanish-American War in Cuba, and in discourses goading entry into World War I.[75] Yet only after World War II did melodrama shape political discourse on a regular basis, as the binarism of the cold war mapped onto and was nourished by a melodramatic moral worldview of good and evil, victims and villains.

Two changes occurred that encouraged melodrama's pervasiveness. The first is the rise of televisual communication. Melodrama's rise was enabled by significant changes in the medium of political discourse, which took new form with the invention of television. Political communication via the news media drew on melodramatic visual spectacle as it entered the living rooms of Americans, connecting domestic life with a nightly world-political spectacle of important events. By the end of the 1950s, 90 percent of Americans had televisions, the most rapid uptake of new communications technology in American history.[76] Melodrama also made the media shift from film to television, as its visual tableaux brought the spectacles and events of *public* life into the daily lives and *private* spaces of Americans, working to connect the ordinariness of daily domestic life to extraordinary global events.[77] The domestic environment became filled with visual spectacles previously associated only with the public sphere, and the televised evening news became, in the words of the media scholar Michael Schudson, "the symbolic center of the national agenda and the national consciousness."[78] Melodramatic genre conventions proliferated at the center of the national agenda as a way to conceptualize political events though a gestural and visceral language that could unify the nation and personify state power as the virtuous and sovereign hero of geopolitics.

Second, political changes after World War II, which included the dramatic rise in U.S. political, economic, and military strength, guaranteed or at least made credible a melodramatic narrative promise of heroic triumph. The shift in American influence that contributed to melodrama's political popularity was due to the rise in U.S. global power after World War II, as the nation became a world superpower, and had in addition proven its willingness to use nuclear bombs against other populations.[79] A popular national self-understanding arose to depict the United States as the hero who saved the world from domination, and after the war the nation found the need to save the world again: this time from the forces of communism and Stalin. The confusion of post–World War II politics was eventually mapped onto a global binary of the United States versus the USSR, and the cold war became legible in part through the heightened language of melodrama. Sheldon Wolin argues that postwar developments rendered state power restless and expansionist and that the onset of the cold war marked the moment when power was viewed not in terms of constitutional limits on different branches but as a potentially *unlimited* power that operated in the service of American needs and universal freedom, "creating forms and magnitudes of power hitherto unknown."[80] Postwar state power expanded through military engagement, national security, executive-branch growth, economic privatization, nuclear proliferation, corporate expansions, technological surveillance, and mass media. Bureaucratic power extended and consolidated the national-security state as did the regulatory intensifications that shaped how individuals qualified for services in the welfare state.[81] Melodramatic political discourse helped to justify these continued expansions of U.S. power, both at home and abroad, deemed necessary for ensuring the freedom enabled by global supremacy. I examine five iterations of melodramatic political discourse to flesh out these claims.

SENTIMENTALIZING THE DOMINO THEORY

One of the most significant early moments in the development of melodramatic political discourse was the Truman Doctrine speech given in 1947. President Harry Truman sought support from the American people for his aggressive postwar foreign policy toward communism, and he wanted to convince Americans that a massive accumulation in arms, military personnel, and economic power was necessary to ensure U.S. global strength. Truman used the speech to ask Congress and the American people to support the buildup of U.S. power while offering military and financial aid to Greece and Turkey. Relying on the concept that would later be known as the domino theory, which made the protection of other countries a necessity for American freedom, Truman assumed that if one communist nation spread its ideology to surrounding nations, all would "fall"; Greece and Turkey became the symbol of potentially falling dominoes. The domino theory linked the internal politics of other nations directly to the strength of the United States. While details about the suffering of foreigners had often been a motivating factor behind U.S. military action, in the logic of melodrama, the nation needed to be either a victim or imminent victim in order to legitimate foreign intervention. The domino theory thus became the crucial link that made Greek and Turkish suffering portend America's own, and that began to justify virtually unbound exercises of U.S. military and economic might.

On March 12, 1947, Truman laid out his doctrine in a speech that was seen and heard not only throughout the United States but also throughout the world. It was first broadcast live and then rebroadcast the next day, translated into twenty-five different languages by the U.S. Department of State.[82] After reading a first draft, Truman told his speechwriter to toughen the speech, simplify and clarify its dictates, and expand its scope—to make it more like melodrama. Truman explained, "I wanted no hedging in this speech. This would be America's answer to the surge of expansion of communist tyranny. It had to be clear, and free of hesitation and double-talk."[83] His message about freedom had to be morally unambiguous and expand beyond Greece to encompass the United States and the entire world order. The Truman Doctrine speech simplified the complexities of postwar politics into a melodramatic moral binary that sentimentalized European populations and authorized not only enormous expansion in state scope but also an entirely new position for U.S. foreign policy.

The speech begins urgently: "The gravity of the situation that confronts the world today necessitates my appearance." From the first moment the speech stages a "race to the rescue" that must be performed by U.S. power. Truman opens onto the initial scene of victimization and marks the compulsion for heroism brought about by dire worldwide conditions.[84] He details the suffering of the Greek people through melodramatic tactics that make vivid the unjust suffering of a virtuous people through humanizing details and broad-stroked images: "This industrious, peace-loving country has suffered invasion, four years of cruel enemy occupation, and bitter internal strife. . . . More than a thousand villages had burned. Eighty-five percent of the children were tubercular. Livestock, poultry, and draft animals had almost disappeared. Inflation had wiped out practically all savings. As a result of these tragic conditions, a militant minority, exploiting human want and misery, was able to create political chaos which, until now, has made economic recovery impossible." Greece is the Valentine of World War II: virtuous and hardworking yet cruelly mistreated, an innocent, childlike nation—it is no coincidence that the plight of sick children is mentioned here, as melodrama often links virtue to childhood—on the verge of seduction by the violent forces of Baron Remberg–like evil. Truman's speech stages the scene of injury to generate a critique of communism through its heightened and pathos-laden description of suffering. Truman creates for his listeners an emotional identification with victims, encouraging the audience through his heightened language and detailed examples to identify with the plight of the Greeks and to *feel* postwar Greek suffering as if it were the listeners' own.

Yet the speech presents a melodrama only midway through its story: the conclusion of heroic triumph has not yet been achieved, and it can only be achieved through the use of military and economic power. The hero, as state power, is conjured into being by the rhetoric of the speech. Truman warns that no other country but the United States has the capacity, the power, and the will to help Greece defend itself from totalitarianism. "The very existence of the Greek state" and "the future of Turkey" are at risk. Truman says, "We are the only country able to provide that help." The world is presented with a stark opposition, according to Truman, as "every nation must choose between alternative ways of life. . . . One way of life is based on the will of the majority, and is distinguished by free institutions, . . . freedom of speech and religion, and freedom from political oppression. The second way of life is based upon the will of a minority forcibly imposed upon the majority. It relies on terror and oppression . . . and the suppression of personal freedoms." Truman organizes the world into two all-encompassing conditions, one of freedom and individual liberty, and the other of "terror," "oppression," and "suppression." Truman uses the scene of injury and bifurcation of political agendas to legitimate his request for expansive power to fight against the encroaching unfreedom of communism: "I believe that it must be the policy of the United States to support free peoples who are resisting attempted subjugation by armed minorities or by outside pressures." The United States was the most powerful nation in the world and thus its special mission was to protect worldwide liberty; the ability of the United States to save other nations—proven, in this discourse, just two years before with the conclusion of World War II—implies both that the country had the capacity to end the suffering of others, and that if it doesn't act it condemns the world and itself to totalitarian subjection. Virtue is doubly accrued to the nation in Truman's melodrama, both in the act of rescue and in the nation's own potential for unjust suffering. The United States, in this speech, is both Coelina and the heroic forces of good that rescue her. Truman's language is dire as he warns that the legitimation of the heroic expansion of state power is an urgent request: if communism wins out, the consequences "would be disastrous not only for [Greece and Turkey] but for the world."

At this point in the speech, Truman puts forth the domino theory to highlight how the Greek and Turkish problems affect his listeners; the domino theory is the lynchpin that transforms Greek domination into a foreshadowing of America's own: "We must take immediate and resolute action. . . . The free peoples of the world look to us for support in maintaining their freedoms. If we falter in our leadership, we may endanger the peace of the world—and we shall surely endanger the welfare of our own nation." Greek and Turkish suffering from unfreedom foretells America's own suffering if it does not intervene. Truman used a pathos-laden description of Greece and Turkey to affectively connect Americans to the plight of these nations, subsuming postwar complexities into a moral imperative that mandated U.S. intervention to ensure the freedom of two virtuous nations and also the United States of America. Melodramatic political discourse thus departed from other generic formulations of melodrama as it began to generate legitimacy for state action. Primarily, the victim-hero was now permanently sutured into one character, a national character, so that the nation-state became both at once. The virtuous victim-hero signifies America: a single entity that garners the moral superiority of virtue and innocence as well as the physical power and righteous retribution of heroic rescue. This combination had occurred in past forms of cultural melodrama, as in *The Poor of New York* and *The Perils of Pauline*, but became the norm when melodrama described the nation in political discourse.

Truman's scene of overwhelmed suffering, moralized options, heightened emotionalism, and dire circumstances yoked together melodramatic cultural conventions to support a policy that broke squarely with America's past—a break that was immediately recognized as a world shift. The *New York Times* contended that America's foreign policy had undergone "radical change in the space of twenty-one minutes," and called America, not un-admiringly, the new "world police force."[85] This new national purpose, manifesting in the Truman Doctrine, transcended concrete national, eco-nomic, military, and social issues—a transcendence that highlighted melodrama's ability to generate cosmological significance at the expense of historical specificity. The affective power of the domino theory made the Truman Doctrine less about humanitarian intervention or doing what was good for others and more about doing what was necessary to protect one's own nation from villainy. The speech thus shaped a differ-ent form of national identity than what was found in humanitarian forms of political discourse, because in melodrama the nation is not just the hero called in to fight unfreedom; the nation is unfreedom's victim too.[86] The nation is not just a third-party heroic intervener but also the injured first party, and this position as a victim-hero compels its necessity for ac-tion. Melodrama deepens the moral justification for international inter-ventions, as the nation is motivated by its own survival in addition to its altruism.

The domino theory legitimated the Truman Doctrine's large expansions of state power, arguably the largest increase in the national-security state until after 9/11. The expansions it legitimated were not limited to foreign intervention in Greece and Turkey. Within the next year of the speech, the Truman Doctrine and Marshall Plan were enacted; the National Security Council (NSC), the CIA, and the Department of Defense were all created; and National Security Council Report 68 (NSC-68) was written, which called for America's "immediate and large scale build up in military and general strength"; NSC-68 required the United States to "assume unilaterally the defense of the non-communist world."[87] Truman's second inaugural ad-dress in 1949 draws even more from melodrama: an American way of life is defined through the victim-hero character that takes identity as the exact opposite of communism. The heroization of U.S. state power is now in full effect: "The peoples of the earth . . . look to the United States as never be-fore for good will, strength, and wise leadership."[88] The nation, which only wants "peace and freedom," finds itself "directly opposed by a regime with contrary aims and a totally different concept of life." In his speech, Truman lists communism's evils in overwrought language: "Communism is based on the belief that man is so weak and inadequate that he is unable to govern himself, and therefore requires the rule of strong masters." Truman then counters with America's liberal virtues: "Democracy maintains that govern-ment is established for the benefit of the individual, and is charged with the responsibility of protecting the rights of the individual and his freedom in the exercise of his abilities." He repeats this circular pattern multiple times: "Communism holds that the world is so deeply divided into opposing classes that war is inevitable. Democracy holds that free nations can settle differences justly and maintain lasting peace." By the end of the speech the opposites of communism and American democratic government become symbiotic upon each other, so that America's goodness is predicated upon communism's tyranny. The United States is responsible for the world's "justice, harmony, and peace" and therefore needs unlimited power for its task. The threat of communism mobilizes the nation's virtue and condones its production of military and national-security power. As in most melodramatic political discourses, a virtuous identity depends on injury to generate heroism. Yet within its narrative logic, melodrama could only justify power if that power operates in the service of righting American victimization and safeguarding global freedom; thus, with increasing frequency the victim-hero national character affectively links the suffering of U.S. citizens to the policies of other nations.

Truman's early form of melodramatic political discourse might at first seem to drop the individualism that played an increasingly important role in melodrama's theatrical instantiations, but I would argue that individualism is still present, just in a new form. For Truman and other policymakers of his era, world problems would now only exist if the United States couldn't muster the will it needed to solve them effectively. A new belief arose that as long as the United States married its world-historic self-reliance to its political and military might, it could control world events.[89] The tenets of individualism began to narrate political crisis by articulating various state actions and practices of freedom through the concept of the heroic, self-determining subject. Melodrama contributed to a trend that nationalized the dictates of American individualism and anthropomorphized disparate state actions into a form of individual and unilateral self-making. Through the conventions of melodramatic political discourse, liberal individualism began to describe state action. Nation-state individualism capitalized on a melodramatic heroism applied to the nation-state: that heroic will could conquer all evil if the nation-state tried hard enough and maintained perseverance. It was a liberal individualism, like that in American political subjectivity, that contained norms for proper action; this individualism assumed that international politics could be controlled and molded to America's needs, and failure demonstrated only a lack of unified desire, not lack of capacity.

This melodramatic form of individualism is therefore not antistatist, as liberal individualism is generally positioned, but is fully realized at the state level. Filtered through melodramatic political discourse, liberal individualism is not opposed to the state but maps onto, and directs, the very notion of state agency. Individualism here leads *to* the state, not to a distrust of state power but to its support. When read through melodramatic political discourse, state action seems not to be shaped by realpolitik; its aim is not limited or practical or amoral. State power demonstrates a form of agency that has the moral and physical strength to overcome the problems of the world and exist beyond its dictates, a world where freedom can become a static and settled achievement of U.S. power. What is so odd about this nation-state individualism is that it comes at a time when all of America's expansions of power are actually making it more interdependent and reliant on other nations. U.S. military power depends on its bases around the world; U.S. national security depends on the stability of other nations, especially with the inception of NATO and the policy of interventionism; and U.S. capital increasingly depends on foreign markets. America's expansions were making it more interdependent at the same time that the rhetoric of heroic individualism drove foreign policy. This foreshadows the way that melodrama will be employed after 9 / 11 to revivify the crumbling dictates of individualism once the illusion of individual and state sovereignty is shattered by the terrorist attacks.

GOING PUBLIC WITH GOOD AND EVIL

The early 1950s took melodramatic political discourse to a new level, visually and verbally, as the Eisenhower administration began to explicitly use the terms *good* and *evil* to define a bipolar political world. President Dwight Eisenhower also took advantage of television to speak directly to the American people, giving greater credence to his policies through the sheer spectacle, at the time, of watching the president speak, and of being able to do so in one's own personal space. The rise of mass visual communication became an important aspect of melodrama's rise in political discourse. Viewing the president speak live, in intimate close-up shots that made it seem as if the president were directly talking to each individual, was itself an astonishing attraction. Throughout its transnational and multimedia formations, melodrama's heavy use of visual spectacle to prove moral truths placed great purchase on action, violence, thrills, awesome sights, and spectacles of physical peril.[90] Many politicians began to capitalize on televisual media, bringing their policy demands and worldviews straight to American viewers through the visual spectacle of the televised public speech. Samuel Kernell's study *Going Public* investigates the executive branch's strategy, starting in the 1950s, of using television to communicate its desires directly to the American people.[91] Presidents began to promote their policies and rally public support for their agendas by televising speeches and adapting new methods of communication in order to shape the national agenda. Far from an equal exchange of information between representative and represented, it was a clearly unidirectional imparting of knowledge that allowed the president's views and statements of national need to bypass traditional filters of congressional representatives and journalists to enter right into the homes of the American people. The intimacy created by seeing the face of the president live and close-up heightened the affective power of the speeches. Through the use of visual props, including symbols of U.S. power or signifiers of presidential compassion, the president could mold the sphere of political communication by pushing national political discourse on the use of power directly, simultaneously, and visually to the nation. *Going Public* more deeply links state action to the mobilization of public opinion, helping the executive branch legitimate political power framed in affectively galvanizing ways.

In 1953 Eisenhower harnessed melodramatic conventions and the rise of television in his first inaugural speech. Employing the strategies later identified in *Going Public*, Eisenhower capitalized on television's personalization of power to generate an affective sense of legitimacy for the actions he proposed. For his first inaugural speech, Americans gathered together in living rooms across the country to watch the presidential inauguration live. While Truman's second inaugural address was also televised, only a few people owned televisions at the time. Eisenhower's speech was offered right when television began to saturate American homes, and the inauguration became an exciting national viewing event in and of itself. The speech was a spectacle of presidential intimacy, its very televised liveness a way of making Eisenhower's speech an extraordinary event that average citizens could participate in through the act of spectatorship.

Eisenhower's inaugural speech focuses on the specter of communism and America's political and moral mandate to inhibit its spread. The speech reads nationalist movements across the globe as communist threats to American existence, calling for the necessity to expand U.S. power to overturn foreign governments around the world. He outlines his interpretation of the global condition in a heightened drama at the beginning of the speech: "We sense with all our faculties that the forces of Good and Evil are massed and armed and opposed as rarely before in history. . . . This fact defines the meaning of this day."[92] The speech structures the world through a "fact" of melodramatic moral bipolarity that organizes world power into a violent standoff that simultaneously valorizes the nation. This political moment has transhistorical significance, as "the forces of Good and Evil are massed and armed and opposed as rarely before in history." Jodi Dean argues that Eisenhower was the first modern president to use evil as a way of defining America as its opposite; evil demonizes the nation's "enemy" and maps goodness onto the pursuit of freedom.[93] In the speech Eisenhower orates about the nation's villain in overheated language: "The enemies of [the spirit of the free] know no god but force, no devotion but its use. They tutor men in treason. They feed upon the anger of others. Whatever defies them, they torture, especially the truth. . . . No principle or treasure that we hold, from the spiritual knowledge of our free schools and churches to the creative magic of free labor and capital, nothing lies safely beyond the reach of this struggle. Freedom is pitted against slavery, lightness against the dark." This is villainy that would make Bloodgood blush, so horrific that anything done to defend against it is already legitimate. Detailing the scene of victimization in dramatic and spectacular imagery, everything that Americans hold as dear as freedom is now under attack, from the magic of capitalism to the spirituality of the classroom. The explanation of present dangers reveals that Americans are also part of something much bigger: the transhistorical fight for freedom and the generic fight against darkness.

After detailing the dramatic conditions of victimization, Eisenhower moves to another melodramatic trope: the valorization of the hero. Luckily, America is now at "a summit unmatched in human history." He draws, as Truman before him, on American exceptionalism to frame U.S. global power in melodramatically heroic terms. Americans "are called as a people to give testimony in the sight of the world to our faith that the future shall be free." Eisenhower uses the term *history* multiple times to paradoxically dehistoricize America's global position as a generic opposition of good and evil, one that will require a dramatic yet abstract expansion of U.S. power in the service of freedom. "How far," he asks rhetorically, "have we come in man's long pilgrimage from darkness toward light? Are we nearing the light—a day of peace and freedom for all mankind? Or are the shadows of another night closing in upon us? . . . [Our] domestic problems are dwarfed by, and often even created by, the questions that involve all humankind." This language is ripe with transcendent significance, now placed upon the role of the U.S. military. Humankind's generic problem of darkness trumps domestic squabbles, and U.S. power must be in the service of these historic fights in which the nation alone has the capacity to sort and win. Evil's power is so overwhelming that it requires heroism to be matched in its potency. Eisenhower states that America "can help defend freedom in our world" and that the nation is "a trust upon which rests the hope of free men everywhere." This assumes both America's *capacity* to defend worldwide freedom and a *compulsion* that America *must* do it: "Destiny has laid upon our country the responsibility of the free world's leadership." His claim for explosive heroism places agency for state action elsewhere, on destiny rather than on mere mortal political calculation. His claim is only possible in the postwar context, because it presupposes sufficient state power to carry out this moral vision and weighty imperative.

Similar to Truman's speech, which conflated military and economic expansion with heroism, this speech offers a melodrama midway through its familiar narrative trajectory of triumphant heroism in order to motivate the support for the policies Eisenhower deemed crucial to fighting communist villainy. It worked; the following year Eisenhower received a blank check from Congress to do, literally, whatever he thought needed to be done to protect freedom.[94] Congress's relinquishing of power was a monumental shifting of political power, one that primarily congealed in the executive (and military) branch, yet one that passed virtually without protest in Congress. In the following decade the national bureaucracy expanded exponentially, economic control of foreign markets grew significantly, multiple invasions of foreign lands were conducted, nuclear proliferation grew, and what Eisenhower criticized as "the military-industrial complex" also solidified its existence in small part through his speeches that heroized its power as a massive force for reshaping the global order. Eisenhower's administration dramatically expanded the scope and reach of state power while simultaneously protecting it from legislative oversight, in part because the melodramatic reasons justifying this expansion needed to no oversight—in a war of good and evil, all actions done in the service of combatting villainy are always already legitimate.[95]

The national victim-hero in postwar melodramatic political discourse recapitulates the same problems of responsibility for social problems seen earlier in American melodrama and that now recur at a national level. Like the powerful but good prince in *Valentine*, the nation-state is free of accountability for effecting conditions of unfreedom, or for instituting problems that cause the victimization of innocents. Instead, the nation has only a mandate to unseat the forces of evil. Problems are externally generated by others, and America is only responsible for diminishing villainy and restoring freedom to the world. The nation embodies the trait of unsullied innocence, as the United States only aims to do what is right while under constant threat from the Truguelin-like forces set on acquiring its economic and ideological capital and undermining its morals. It is a national body morally unriven, free and clear of blame. Eisenhower articulates it in this way in his inaugural address: "We feel this moral strength because we know that we are not helpless prisoners of history. We are free men. We shall remain free, never proven guilty of the one capital offence against freedom, a lack of staunch faith." It's the nation's moral requirement to buck predeterminism, indeed to emancipate itself from the very prison of history, while refusing any responsibility for the effects of the nation's efforts other than the triumph of freedom.

In linking national identity to the expression of state power, melodrama became a site of convergence for multiple ideas already circulating in American politics. Melodrama yoked together manifest destiny, exceptionalism, and individualism into a form of political demonization, doing so through its already enormously popular cultural thematics. Melodramatic political discourse wove together exceptionalism's claims that America serves as a model of just governance commanded by God with manifest destiny's notion of divinely inspired imperialism. With exceptionalism—at an all-time high after World War II—the nation's heroism is due to its unparalleled goodness and love of freedom. Exceptionalism assumes America to be a transhistorically inspired nation, one that is not only uniquely virtuous but also serves as a blueprint for just governance on earth. As seen in Truman's speech, melodrama relies on exceptionalism to figure the justness of foreign intervention and the mandatory quality of national retribution. Manifest destiny has also always contained a moral component; not just that America has a right to the land but that the country's destiny is compelled by a moral ideal that takes precedence over other concerns. America's mandate comes from a "higher law" that makes spreading democracy obligatory upon the state.[96] Melodrama draws from both of these ideals to articulate the expansion of state power as a melodramatic imperative.

Melodrama also takes part in what Michael Rogin has diagnosed as political demonization, a form of countersubversion that names as monstrous any form of opposition to mainstream politics and policy.[97] In melodramatic forms of demonization, political foes are not just monstrous but evil and cast outside what is properly inside "America." Melodrama's demonizing named the moral superiority in the nation; however, because this demonizing discourse operated through the terms of melodrama, the nation had to be seen as a victim in order to justify its superiority. When Rogin looks at this moment in U.S. politics through demonization, he reads national discourse as something closer to noir or horror. He observes a doubling in which U.S. national identity mirrors the very qualities it vilifies in communist monsters, acting out "forbidden desires for identification with the excluded object."[98] Communism, in Rogin's analysis, is viewed as a form of sexual seduction that penetrates the family sphere; in order to prevent this penetration the U.S. state must on its own penetrate family life by expanding domestic surveillance techniques and regulating familial behavior. Rogin's reading shows how cold-war discourse projected onto communism America's own violent qualities, yet his reading does not exhaust the different ways that political discourse pitted the nation against communist villainy, and it also does not account for how the moralizing qualities of political discourse could work as a form of state legitimacy. In melodrama the problem is not a weak and susceptible family structure but a form of villainy external to internal life in the United States. In Eisenhower's melodrama the nation is not a source of evil, unlike in Rogin's reading. Melodrama, unlike noir, uses moralization, detailed scenes of innocent suffering, and the personification of state actions to construct the state as the spectacular and heroic avatar of a freedom-loving and virtuous citizenry undivided by domestic problems.

## LOVABLE DOGS AND THE DOMESTICATION OF MELODRAMATIC POLITICAL DISCOURSE

During the postwar era, one of the most ingenious and visually spectacular engagements with melodramatic discourse came out of presidential campaigns—to articulate individual relationships with domestic politics. Richard Nixon's 1952 "Checkers" speech intended to save his faltering bid for the vice presidency amid accusations that he accepted large gifts from constituents. The speech situates Nixon himself as the victim-hero of American politics. Using televisual communication in an unprecedented way, Nixon gave an extended public service announcement on his candidacy by painting himself as the victim of a ruthless smear campaign. He informs his audience: "The best and only answer to a smear or an honest misunderstanding of the facts is to tell the truth. And that is why I am here tonight." His announcement attempts to demonstrate how he could single-handedly overcome unjust blights on his reputation by publicly performing his virtue. He states, "What I am going to do—and incidentally this is unprecedented in the history of American politics—I am going at this time to give to this television and radio audience, a complete financial history, everything I have earned, everything I have spent and everything I own, and I want you to know the facts." And he proceeds to describe his biography and provide intimate details about his financial situation.

Presenting himself in the same manner as the Fairweather family, Nixon tells the nation how grew up in a poor but hardworking home: "Our family was one of modest circumstances, and most of my early life was spent in a store out in East Whittier. It was a grocery store, one of those family enterprises. The only reason we were able to make it go was because my mother and dad had five boys, and we all worked in the store." Nixon sentimentalizes his suffering and turns himself into a virtuous victim whom his audience can identify with. He states, after describing his marriage: "We had a rather difficult time after we were married, like so many of the young couples who might be listening to us." He is a man just like his audience, but thrust into extraordinary circumstances that require his dire action in the form of a public service announcement. Revealing the details of his plain car and small home, Nixon succeeds in making himself ordinary, victimized, and heroic at once. At the end he states, "That's what we own. It isn't very much. . . . Pat doesn't have a mink coat. But she does have a respectable Republican cloth coat, and I always tell her she would look good in anything." He demonstrates his integrity (by appearing in front of the American people), his honesty (by reading out loud his modest financial picture), and his moral courage (by standing up to his bullies in an unprecedented and media-saturated way). To hammer the point home, he explains to the audience, "It isn't easy to bear one's life on television as I've done."[99] Even though he has been cruelly attacked by entrenched wealth and greed, he can stand up for himself by the sheer force of his moral rectitude and can-do spirit. Nixon is both similar to the people and able to achieve heroic feats of strength out of adverse and injurious circumstances.

Nixon's most effective astonishment of ordinariness is his reference to his lovable little dog, Checkers. Checkers was the only gift from a constituent that Nixon kept, because he became the gentle companion to his young daughters. Checkers was the only "truth" to the claim that Nixon took bribes, and his reference to Checkers turned a damning accusation of corruption into a childlike misunderstanding of his own big heart. Nixon states, "It was a little cocker spaniel dog, in a crate that he had sent all the way from Texas, black and white, spotted, and our little girl Tricia, the six year old, named it Checkers. And you know, the kids, like all kids, loved the dog, and I just want to say this, right now, that regardless of what they say about it, we are going to keep it." Checkers symbolizes Nixon's innocence, his relatable commitment to family. Nixon then asks his audience to contact their representatives directly about whether he should resign from the Republican vice-presidential ticket—which is a strategy laid out in *Going Public*—to motivate Americans to act upon the ill treatment of a virtuous family man. He controls the televisual spectacle by using a studious library setting, and interlaces the speech with reverse shots of his wife gazing up adoringly at him while he talks. The announcement choreographs a sequence where Nixon stands up to visually demonstrate his heroism and punches his fist upward to emphasize how he will clean up Washington if elected. Nixon embodies the melodramatic celebration of the underdog—"they want to smear me . . . but I'm not a quitter"—to usher in a new popularization of melodrama that spread beyond cold-war strategy and into the fabric of individual performances of domestic politics.

## REAGAN'S NEOLIBERAL HEROES

Throughout the cold war and up until the 1980s, melodramatic discourse was periodically deployed to justify foreign and domestic policy. Other genres of political discourse rivaled and overshadowed melodrama during this time, especially during the Vietnam and Watergate years, when the jeremiad rose in popularity to limit state power, tamp down America's language of manifest destiny, and mollify cold-war passions by requiring the nation to examine the effects of its violence both inside and outside the country.[100] The jeremiad's claim that evil is partly caused by one's own actions counteracted melodrama's refusal of responsibility for state violence, even as different jeremiads shifted the source of blame for the Vietnam War; jeremiads on the left found fault in government turpitude and military aggression, whereas jeremiads on the right located blame on a permissive and undisciplined youth culture that harbored no respect for authority.

Yet in the 1980s, melodrama resurged in political discourse, and with it the expansion of securitized and neoliberal state power under Ronald Reagan intensified. Perhaps the culminating exemplar of cold-war melodramatic discourse was Reagan's inaugural address in 1981, one just as rhetorically powerful as his famous "evil empire" speech but more visually spectacular, and given two years prior. So deeply attuned to the power of melodrama and the strategy of going public, Reagan's administration changed the location of the inaugural address for the first time in history to a more visually arresting spot on the Capitol grounds closer to the Washington Mall. News cameras could now cover him as they looked onto the vista of the Washington Monument and various presidential memorials, all of whom Reagan names as heroes and yet who serve as homages to the heroism of Reagan and the America he will explicitly embody in this speech. In the media coverage, more than ten different camera angles capture Reagan against different backdrops, with varying levels of closeness. Some are extreme close-ups so that Reagan can communicate intimately without any other visual distractions, while others show Reagan at the helm of hundreds of thousands of admirers present to hear him speak. The media coverage of the speech took advantage of new developments in cinematic technology, including one astonishing shot that starts from Reagan's face and zooms outward, capturing first the Capitol, then expanding to the hundreds of thousands of people watching him, broadening again to the national monuments, and finally encompassing the expanse of all of Washington. Through scripted camerawork, these iconic American images are seamlessly linked to Reagan as he performs his melodrama in the service of individual American heroes.[101]

Reagan begins his speech by inscribing his very presence on stage with miraculous significance. He states, "This every-four-year ceremony we accept as normal is nothing less than a miracle." As Brooks argues about melodrama more generally, Reagan succeeds in making the ordinary moment extraordinary by revealing the hidden majesty in what would otherwise appear to be the business as usual of liberal democratic politics. Setting the tone in this way, Reagan then immediately addresses the plight of the nation mired in an economic recession. He starts out at the origin point of all melodramatic plots—the scene of victimization—just as *The Poor of New York*, Truman, and Eisenhower do: "These United States are confronted with an affliction of great proportions. We suffer from the longest and one of the worst inflations in our national history. It distorts our economic decisions, penalizes thrift, and crushes the struggling young and the fixed-income elderly alike. It threatens to shatter the lives of millions of people. Idle industries have cast workers into unemployment, causing human misery and personal indignity." Reagan uses overwrought language to convey the suffering of American people embattled by an economic recession, using emotively powerful terms such as *affliction, threaten, shatter, distort, crush, penalize,* and *misery* to describe their plight. He sentimentalizes the economic recession in its production of national victimhood. His pathos-laden language would have been unheard of even during the darkest days of World War II to describe America.

In the speech America is the Fairweather family of the economic recession, and Reagan asks his audience to interpret their living conditions as a
political victimization caused by an unjust oppressor. Similar to Truman,
Reagan aims to create an emotional connection to the suffering he depicts,
but as opposed to Truman the victims are not filtered through a third-
party proxy. They are his direct audience: Americans. The villain is quite
different from the villain in Truman's and Eisenhower's speeches; not exclusively a communist enemy outside proper American life—the "evil empire" that Reagan will describe two years later—the enemy is internal, part
of the fabric of American nationhood that should, however, be cast out of
it. Melodramas often use victimization to point out oppression and injustice, and here—in a cruel but not unusual melodramatic twist—injustice is
caused by the very force that claims to protect individuals: the government.
The villainous cause of national suffering is government's unjust domination of American individuals, its bloated regulation of business and provision of social services the direct cause of national pain and individual unfreedom. America, according to Reagan, can push through its suffering if it
adopts his neoliberal plan of tax cuts and limited social services. Only then
will the nation regain its strength to "preserve this last and greatest bastion
of freedom." Government regulation is now the external enemy, banished
from its role as a constitutive factor in American goodness. Of course, this
plan for limited government service does not restrict state power but merely
diminishes its accountability, as the plan decreases financial support for needy
individuals while it increases the subsidization of corporate power, extends
regulatory expectations into areas of political life assumed to be private,
and relocates former state functions to private firms not beholden to any
electorate but still able to mobilize state power and collective resources.
Reagan's rhetoric of limited state power obfuscates the ways that varied
state powers will deepen and disperse into individuals and other nations
during his presidency, as neoliberal corporate-state mergers will unleash
cannibalistic corporate growth and increase disciplinary control over individual agency.

In this speech the solution to the economic recession is a personal one.
The only way to emancipate the nation from the recession, according to
Reagan, is not reliance on a paternalistic government; the key is the heroic
self-reliance of the individual American. As in *The Poor of New York*, economic and social unfreedoms can be righted by individual heroism and
voluntary, private action. Reagan transfers responsibility for ending the recession from government to the individual: he wants to "unleash the energy

and individual genius of man" so that we Americans "are ready to act worthy of ourselves." He describes his solution through a quote written by a man who died in World War I: "America must win this war. Therefore I will work; I will save; I will sacrifice; I will endure; I will fight cheerfully and do my utmost, as if the whole struggle depended on me alone." Reagan's speech asks its listeners to develop individual self-reliance by referring to their effort against economic hardship as a war. This a war to the death against the debilitating dictates of the welfare state, fought by individuals on their own, "as if the whole struggle depended on me alone." As in *Valentine*, when the accountability for classed injustice switches from the aristocracy to individual bad behavior, the larger economic problems of injustice, inequality, and fear that Reagan diagnoses through the language of victimization can be righted by individual behavioral shifts: by "individual genius" or the personal capacity to "work," "save," and "fight cheerfully." Reagan draws from melodrama's conventional trope of individualizing structural problems to find accountability for bureaucratic growth in personal action alone.

Heroism, in Reagan's melodrama, is found in performing the drudgery of work under neoliberal capitalism. Reagan tells his audience, "You can see heroes every day going in and out of factory gates; others produce enough food to feed all of us and the world beyond. You meet heroes across a counter—and they are on both sides of that counter." Reagan's examples of heroism are solely related to employment, devoid of political, civic, or communal action. None involves engaging, harnessing, or checking governmental power, even though governmental power is the villain in this speech. Instead, the speech brings heroism to the daily toils of the ordinary person and makes the daily toils of that life seem deeply meaningful. Reagan's melodramatic individualism valorizes ordinary heroes and the benefits of perseverance. In this speech heroism is distinctly not found in state action, especially when state action is tasked to provide benefits for poor and vulnerable people. Yet state action will be deemed heroic two years later in Reagan's speech about the "evil empire," when state power is directed to expand significantly in national security and defense.

The heroism that Reagan outlines in this speech is found by sanctifying the ordinary person who becomes extraordinary in situations of government-organized duress by eschewing government support and relying on an inner moral core. This version of heroism models the depoliticized citizenry that Reagan cultivates throughout his presidency. The neoliberal policies he outlines here, articulated and legitimated through the melodramatic discourse of heroic individualism, will decrease social safety for individuals and families at the same time that they demand individuals' personal responsibility for their own social and economic security. Yet perhaps most cruelly, the melodramatic formulation of neoliberalism makes the destruction of policies that aim to modestly support human flourishing, however flawed, seem *desirable* in the pursuit of individual freedom.

Just in case his viewers have not yet understood his message, Reagan cements viewer identification with the description of heroism he is painting in a clear and unambiguous way: "I have used the words *they* and *their* in speaking of these heroes. I could say *you* and *your* because I am addressing the heroes of whom I speak—you, the citizens of this blessed land. Your dreams, your hopes, your goals are going to be the dreams, hopes, and goals of this administration, so help me God." This gambit is a double move: First, it alchemizes his listeners into the celebrated ordinary heroes he has outlined. Reagan links the heroes he paints with me and my life; my personal daily toil is now explicitly transformed into heroism. I am a hero individually, and also collectively with all other Americans who work hard. Second, the end of the quote makes Reagan the ultimate heroic savior of all ordinary heroes. Not only am I a hero but Reagan will make my heroism his heroism—conflating my identity with the actions of his administration and refashioning the melodramatic trope of nation-state individualism into the body of the president. Reagan anoints all citizens with heroic virtue and then immediately harnesses their heroism for himself in one bold stroke, further depoliticizing citizenship in asking Americans to experience heroism by relying on his policies—a particularly stunning move in a speech about self-reliance as the cornerstone of freedom.

The speech ends by using melodrama to further couple the individual and the state, and yet also to keep citizens politically powerless in the face of corporate deregulation and militarized state expansion. America's "crisis requires . . . our willingness to believe in ourselves and to believe in our capacity to perform great deeds. . . . After all, why shouldn't we believe that? We are Americans." By not asking Americans to perform great deeds, but merely to *believe* that they can be performed, Reagan leaves his heroic citizens in their workplace and outside politics. He limits the people as a force in their own right by diminishing their power to oversee political and economic matters beyond going to work each day. Americans' role is to go to the factory or the farm or the counter, and to believe, but not to perform politically—that role can safely be left to Reagan in his capacity to enact our dreams for us. In fact, there is no political role available to this heroism other than belief. The mode of heroic political action, for citizens, is no action. Reagan uses the melodramatic framework he both inherits and rearticulates to outline a neoliberal citizenry that is victimized by the welfare state, heroic when it performs economic reproduction, and simply believing when it comes to the practice of citizenship. After all, "we are Americans."

## LAMENTING MELODRAMA AT THE END OF HISTORY

As Reagan's neoliberal melodrama extended into the 1980s, individuals were expected to take personal responsibility for the burdens of a life lived under the strictures of unaccountable state and corporate power, while simultaneously legitimating massive expansions in the national-security state deemed necessary to maintain their heroic individualism. Reagan's concept of an "evil empire" both expanded and depoliticized state and corporate power even further, not only by reinstantiating Eisenhower's bifurcated world order and reinscribing evil outward but also by moralizing and necessitating all state action done for the protection of good in the pursuit of global freedom. In the 1980s and beyond, domestic- and foreign-policy expansions not infrequently depended on evil for their moral tenor and for the obligatory positioning of the nation as a victim-hero to justify the expansion of foreign, neoliberal, and governmental power.[102] The end of the cold war, like the end of World War II, fortified America's heroic triumph and virtue in relation to the global order. The downfall of communist evil consolidated melodrama's power as both a clarifying political discourse and a triumphalist national identity.

The breakup of the Soviet Union seemed to prove the truth of melodrama's narrative promise that virtue and heroism win in the end, that freedom is achievable by expansions of U.S. state, military, and economic power. The fall of communism would seem the ultimate proof of American triumph, the end of a long-standing narrative that could finally climax with heroic victory. This climax signaled not merely the triumph of American power but also, in Francis Fukuyama's wildly popular and infamous phrase, the "end of history" itself.[103] Fukuyama's Hegelian claim in "The End of History"—that liberal democracy had dialectically overcome its communist Other and would usher in a new global order of peaceful coexistence underpinned by free enterprise—became the tagline of foreign policy in the 1990s, shorthand for explaining why the USSR's downfall was a global triumph. At an earlier moment in melodramatic political discourse, Eisenhower argued that Americans had liberated themselves from the prison of history; now, Fukuyama explained, the virtues of American-style governing liberated the entire world from history. The world was now free for sovereign and enterprising actors. The communist melodrama had ended with a resounding triumph for liberal capitalism: America overcame evil, and the world was unipolar. The post-1989 world was also a postmelodrama world.

Yet the end of the communist era temporarily left America's self-definition in ambiguity. America was again the dominant superpower, but it was also without a world order with which to map its virtues and showcase its strength. Without a constant threat of evil, the melodramatic promise of national virtue could not be invigorated—without villainy, virtue had no defining negativity. All America had left was an "end of history" mentality that, while proving the heroism of the U.S. nation-state, also left it bereft of a constitutive evil Other. Yet in a surprising twist that received scant attention when the essay first appeared, Fukuyama deeply mourns the loss of communist evil. He fears that strong nationhood will weaken without the vivifying effect that monstrous villainy has on U.S. power. He even refers to the end of history as "a very sad time." He continues: "The willingness to risk one's life for a purely abstract goal, the worldwide ideological struggle that called forth daring, courage, imagination, and idealism, will be replaced by economic calculation, the endless solving of technological problems, environmental concerns, and the satisfaction of sophisticated consumer demands. . . . I can feel in myself, and see in others around me, a powerful nostalgia for the time when history existed. . . . Perhaps this very prospect of centuries of boredom at the end of history will serve to get history started once again."[104] Fukuyama's argument ends, then, not with triumph but with the affective pull of lamentation. He mourns not merely the rise of economic rationality but the loss of a melodramatic way of viewing global politics, and thus the capacity for courageous melodramatic heroism. He bemoans the end of a national and individual ethos that requires intense struggle to prove its heroic courage and self-determination. He yearns to inhabit a melodramatic identity that gains both moral legibility and political legitimacy from standing against evil. Fukuyama points to a larger condition in which the nation-state gains strength and self-legitimacy primarily through a world order depicted by melodrama's moral economy, when the state and individual daringly fight on the side of the unconditional good for the very survival of human civilization.

What will we become, Fukuyama fears, without the affective force of a heroic state power fighting treacherous villainy, a power that exists beyond the individual citizen and yet to which each individual feels personally connected? For Fukuyama, melodramatic tactics for galvanizing national purpose will founder after America's triumphalism in 1989. This causes his despair about the end of history, a nontime in which U.S. power and identity cannot survive without pathos-laden struggles with evil. A victim-hero with no villain loses its capacity for moral power and remains mired in the drudgery of ordinary life—a life, he emphasizes, without extraordinary significance. A life without melodrama. But a decade later the 9 / 11 events will regalvanize America's extraordinary victim-hero identity when the nation-state battles a new villain intent on the destruction of the United States. The attacks of 9 / 11, then, as articulated in melodramatic political discourse, may serve to get history started once again.

# THREE

# FELT LEGITIMACY

*Victimization and Affect in the Expansion of State Power*

Melodramatic political discourses often construct legitimacy for antidemocratic forms of state power. Melodrama is part of a process whereby military action abroad and security, surveillance, and regulatory expansions at home garner vast popular legitimacy, even though they are not subject to typical institutional or deliberative channels for authorizing power. From the perspective of liberal-democratic theory, for example, state actions in the twenty-first century such as the War in Afghanistan and the creation of the Department of Homeland Security are not legitimate. Congress relinquished its constitutional duty to declare war through the Authorization for the Use of Military Force against Terrorists (AUMF), which conceded authority to deploy military force to the executive branch. The AUMF upended established juridical procedures for determining whether the nation goes to war by rerouting all authority to the president. In the months and years after the 9/11 attacks, more informal participatory and deliberative processes for authorizing power were also truncated. Political and corporate media sources tightly circumscribed public debate over large-scale domestic, foreign, and military policies, and even transfigured political contestation into an immoral and un-American activity. Many of the state actions enacted during this time were not approved by democratic deliberation or by juridical legal procedures. Nevertheless, they were sanctioned by a vast majority of the U.S. polity.[1]

A majority of the population legitimated the War in Afghanistan and other key policies in the war on terror outside the procedural or deliberative channels that compose established modes of liberal-democratic decision making. Legitimacy for these policies, I argue, was achieved in part by a melodramatic political discourse that depicted these actions as imperatives and as already anticipated. These depictions in turn shaped the affective terrain upon which legitimacy was granted. Melodrama offers particular ways of authorizing state actions, figuring them as necessities, as plot expectations, as uncontestable, and as categorically righteous. It generates *moral imperatives* for state action that combine with the genre's familiar *narrative expectations* for heroic triumph. Hannah Arendt insists that the making of imperatives is antithetical to a democratic politics, as the imperative silences the very possibility of contestation over collective decisions.[2] In this sense, melodrama's imperatives and expectations diminish contestation over authorizing power by depicting state action as always and already authorized. Melodrama depoliticizes the very process of legitimation. Yet this depoliticization also seems to instigate a felt sense in the larger population that state action in response to the 9/11 attacks is always legitimate. This felt sense of legitimacy obviated the need for other modes of legitimation; the actions under scrutiny are justifiable because they feel justified.

What I call *felt legitimacy* refers to an affective experience of authorizing state power. It names the way that the legitimation of state action is often generated out of subjectively experienced affect. Felt legitimacy is as powerful and meaningful as any formal consent, even when nothing procedural or deliberative has occurred to instantiate that feeling. People often participate in politics through felt legitimacy; they feel the legitimacy of the policies up for consideration, even as their judgment of legitimacy can occur outside the procedural or deliberative channels that compose conventional ways of authorizing power. Felt legitimacy exposes how processes of legitimation can work through the discursive forms and affective states that cultivate perceptions of legitimacy. The study of melodramatic political discourses reveals some of the complicated legitimation processes at work in contemporary politics and can help to investigate what it would mean to *feel* the legitimacy of state action. Melodramatic tactics in twenty-first-century political discourse depicted war and state surveillance as necessary for healing the nation's pain and for practicing freedom, which solicited the felt sense that these actions were necessarily legitimate. Felt legitimacy that is cultured by melodramatic modes of political discourse incorporates the sense that feeling the pain of national injury is equivalent to feeling the legitimacy of state power that will respond to it.

The study of felt legitimacy taps into an age-old question in political theory regarding who, or what, should be the primary determinate for whether political actions are ultimately justifiable in a polity. The question underpins many studies of the state and the people, from Thomas Hobbes onward: who consents to state power? And, consequently, how is this consent legitimated and secured? Many contemporary scholars, working in a liberal-democratic tradition, argue for participatory or representative processes of legitimacy for state action, processes that are also supported by the popular beliefs shaping American political norms. Bernard Manin states this argument in an exemplary way: "As political decisions are characteristically imposed upon all, it seems reasonable to ask, as a central condition for legitimacy, the deliberation of all or, more precisely, the right of all to participate in deliberation."[3] Manin offers a compelling normative claim for evaluating democratic legitimacy, one that many people might agree furnishes a vision of a just and democratic polity. Yet the study of felt legitimacy reveals how the authorization of state power can work differently from how it is presupposed, desired, and normatively sanctioned by liberal and democratic theorists.[4]

When political theorists study legitimacy, they often circumscribe their analysis to the creation and evaluation of legitimating norms. Yet this comes at the expense of other important—though less institutionally grounded or philosophically coherent—political dynamics that contribute to legitimation. Studying legitimation by judging the rightness of evaluative norms, or by measuring the illegitimacy of an action in accordance with proper procedures or deliberations, can miss how widespread perceptions of legitimacy are generated and sustained. Political actions can acquire legitimacy independent of an institutional or deliberative declaration of "rightness." The study of felt legitimacy, therefore, does not evaluate whether particular state actions are truly legitimate or illegitimate, nor does it offer a new normative schema to evaluate legitimacy. Instead, it questions how particular state actions *become* legitimate.

The study of felt legitimacy through melodrama aims to bring different authorizing dynamics into view by highlighting the importance of political discourse for cultivating an affective experience of legitimacy. While the concept of felt legitimacy runs counter to liberal and democratic traditions in political thought, I would suggest that its antecedents can be found in key political theories on power: Max Weber's and Michel Foucault's writings on the legitimation of power highlight the discursive and affective production of legitimacy. Weber argues that legitimacy is an effect of subjectivity—a subjectivity cultivated in part by "affectual states"—and Foucault suggests that discourses cultivate subjectivities that produce legitimacy as their effect.[5] Drawing upon their instigations, I argue that the judgment of legitimacy can be a subjectively experienced affect solicited by political discourses. Felt legitimacy can be mobilized for different political ends, and the affects of legitimacy attach to different political actions. The question I am interested in is how felt legitimacy operates in specific contexts and discourses, and I argue that melodramatic political discourse's moral imperative and narrative expectation for vast state actions cultivate the feeling that these actions are legitimate.

This is not to say that institutional or deliberative legitimating practices are not cultivated discursively or experienced affectively. Affect itself is not antithetical to deliberations on legitimacy, and, as Sharon Krause argues, formal decision-making processes operate through affective registers.[6] Juridical procedures surely cultivate their own discursive conventions and affective states, and felt experiences offer reasons for the judgments they offer. Felt legitimacy is not irrational, as it offers a rationale for its judgment; it offers that the state action under review feels right, and that this feeling offers the proof of democracy at work. The problem, then, is not that felt legitimacy is unreasonable. Nor is the problem that felt legitimacy doesn't follow established juridical procedures for sanctioning state power, especially because, as Marx and Foucault would note, juridical procedures themselves often serve to occlude more unaccountable forms of power.[7] The problem is a felt legitimacy untethered to democratic practice: by equating a felt sense of legitimacy with a moral imperative for state action, and with the very act of participation itself, felt legitimacy in melodramatic registers depoliticizes the capacity to partake in governing decisions. It further demobilizes a citizenry already left out of most if not all decisions for authorizing the vast military, economic, and regulatory powers exercised in their name, including war. If real democracy, beyond procedures and deliberations, is about the collective harnessing of power for creating a shared world, then felt legitimacy in post-9/11 melodrama deepens the antidemocratic practices of contemporary politics and further eviscerates the capacity of the people to directly engage in collective action.[8]

This chapter examines legitimation in five sections. It first engages Weber and Foucault to investigate discursive and affective forms of popular yet nondemocratic legitimacy. It then examines melodramatic political discourses to see the various ways legitimacy is cultivated through discursive means. The third section combines the observations from the first two sections to make the case for the production of felt legitimacy through melodramatic political discourse. The fourth section examines the fleeting nature of felt legitimacy by examining the ephemerality of the affective states and discursive claims that sustain it. And the chapter concludes by considering how alternative forms of felt legitimacy expose their own discursive cultivation as a crucial part of the legitimating process. This section examines the film *Three Kings*, a melodrama about decision making in war, to show one way that the inevitably affective components of legitimacy can be reconnected to participatory and agonistic registers for exercising power collectively.

Deborah Gould argues, "Power operates affectively: it is exercised through and reproduced in our feelings, and it is forceful and effective precisely because of that."[9] The work of power operates through feelings, but, in addition, these feelings are themselves a form of power. Felt legitimacy, in this sense, helps to produce the legitimacy it presupposes. The expansions of state power legitimated by melodramatic depictions of political life are actually the *effect* of felt legitimation. In melodrama, then, it is not that state power produces its own felt legitimation, as Weber and Foucault would contend. It is, rather, the opposite: felt legitimacy enables state power. Power becomes an effect of its prior affective legitimation. In other words, it is not that state power generates felt legitimacy, but that felt legitimacy generates state power as its effect.

## Legitimacy as Subjective, Cultivated by Discourse

In political theory, *legitimacy* is conventionally defined as the acceptance of power as authoritative, as the polity's consent to the rules that emanate from governing structures, and as the justified use of force or violence. Most political theorists working in a liberal-democratic tradition examine the normative dimensions of legitimacy and argue that legitimacy for state action is achieved either by mutually agreed upon procedural requirements for evaluating power or a democratic decision-making process. Jürgen Habermas argues, blending both procedural and deliberative models of legitimacy: "The binding character of legal norms stems not just from the insight into what is equally good for all but from the collectively binding decisions of authorities who make and apply the laws. . . . The law can satisfy this condition [of its legitimacy] only if it has come about in a legitimate way, namely according to the procedures of democratic opinion- and will-formation that justify the presumption that outcomes are rationally acceptable."[10] Habermas combines democratic participation with procedural standards to offer a normative schema for rationally evaluating the legitimacy of state action in democratic polities.

Yet the disciplines of political psychology and sociology examine legitimacy differently, less by establishing norms about what legitimacy should look like, and more by studying how perceptions of legitimacy develop. Some of these scholars locate the production of legitimacy in the belief of those participating political subjects tasked to legitimate state power.[11] Weber, who instantiates this line of thought, argues: "It is only the probability of orientation to the *subjective belief* in the validity of an order which constitutes the valid order itself."[12] In this tradition, initiated by Weber and extended by Seymour Martin Lipset into the American academy, the way for a state or any governing authority to guarantee legitimacy is to secure political subjects' belief in legitimacy. The establishment of legitimation is thus not necessarily or even normatively bound to laws or procedures but works through subjective processes of perception and knowledge acquisition that are often politically unaccountable and difficult to trace. Legitimate state action is that which is ultimately, in Weber's terms, "*considered to be legitimate.*"[13]

How does this belief arise, and under what conditions it is nurtured? What produces a belief in the rightness of state action? Weber argues that belief arises through techniques of political domination often organized by state apparatuses. In a legitimate political system the people living under that system believe its domination over them is valid, and they sanction the commands it issues. Belief in legitimacy is the way that individuals consent to obeying power. For Weber the order one consents to is either a total political system or "simply the order governing a single concrete situation," as both governing systems and specific instances of the exercise of power are legitimated through belief.[14] Belief is solicited by the power that aims for legitimation: "Every system attempts to establish and cultivate the belief in legitimacy."[15] Belief is thus the product of a political subjectivity cultivated by a dominating power that often originates in state dynamics. In bringing Weber's account of belief to American social science, Lipset severed Weber's analysis of domination and socially constructed knowledge acquisition from the theory of legitimation. For Lipset individuals first generate their own personal values outside consideration of broader social and political concerns, and then legitimate state action based on their belief that its operations generally match their privately held principles. In jettisoning Weber's insistence on state domination as a generative force, Lipset thus presents belief as a subjective claim made by autonomous liberal subjects, which they develop independently of societal norms and social power. Legitimacy, in Lipset's reading, is the very proof of liberal pluralism.[16] Lipset's approach, while enlarging the source of legitimacy beyond neutral norms to subjective perception, also set a path for the study of legitimacy that assumes that belief in legitimacy arises from sovereign subjects making their own autonomous judgments. Lipset's approach excluded the question of *how* legitimacy is cultivated, both in the individual subject and in the social body.

Foucault's work refocused the study of legitimacy back to that excluded question by arguing that subjects are nonsovereign, conditioned by discourses that encourage the legitimation of state action. Rather than a measurement of the objective quality of institutions or the normative evaluation of policies, belief in legitimacy, Foucault contended, is an effect of political discourses that cultivate legitimacy in political subjects. For Foucault subjectivity is partly an effect of discourse, of the ways that power operates through discursive constructs that enable and support certain forms of knowledge while inhibiting or diminishing others. The powers generative of political subjectivity do not operate only, or even primarily, through the law or a contractual constitution but are a series of relations that circulate between individuals and social bodies; they work through discourses, regulating techniques, and biopolitical practices that shape subjects and manage populations. For Foucault as for Weber, legitimacy is a form of rationalized obedience, but Foucault argues in addition that the very concept of legitimacy effaces the complicated dominations of political power by implying that it can be limited primarily by laws and authorized primarily by institutions or individual consent. He writes,

> [In the Western juridical system] if power were to retain its legitimacy, it had to be exercised within certain limits. From the Middle Ages onwards, the essential role of the theory of right has been to establish the legitimacy of power; the major or central problem around which the theory of right is organized is the problem of sovereignty. . . . The essential function of the technique and discourse of right is to dissolve the element of domination in power and to replace that domination, which has to be reduced or masked, with two things: the legitimate right of the sovereign, on one hand, and the legal obligation to obey it, on the other. . . . Right must, I think, be viewed not in terms of a legitimacy that has to be established, but in terms of the procedures of subjugation it implements.[17]

The concept of legitimacy is part of a theory of politics that, for Foucault, is tied to institutional models of power as sovereign and to the belief that consent limits power. The idea of legitimated power ignores the regulatory and subject-cultivating operations of power and functions as a smoke screen to obscure the specific modes of domination that operate through the belief that consent and institutions keep domination or unaccountable power in check. Foucault's intervention crucially disrupts the assumption that one can make judgments about state legitimacy that are neutral, objective, and free from power. Yet he uses the critique of legitimacy as justification to turn away from further inquiry into how state power becomes legitimated. For Foucault any further study of legitimation is unnecessary, as it merely colludes with legitimacy's obfuscation of subjugation.[18] But if legitimacy is a crucial nodal point for effacing the work of power (as Foucault himself points out), then I would argue that the subjective production of legitimation deserves a *central* place in political reflections on the authorization of power. By condemning the study of legitimacy as only a perpetuation of the effacement of power, Foucault too misses a range of complex mechanics involved in legitimation processes.

Weber, however, anticipates Foucault's provocations and provides the missing link between Foucault's critique of legitimacy and noninstitutional processes of legitimation. By redefining legitimacy as belief, Weber laid the foundation for studying legitimating practices that work in nonjuridical and subjective registers. Rather than abandoning the interrogation of legitimation after diagnosing its subjective and oppressive operations, as Foucault does, Weber offers a way to trace legitimation's mechanics in nonprocedural and nondeliberative registers. Crucially, he specifies the role of affect as a key aspect in legitimation's development. Weber argues that one way that belief is cultivated is through "the actor's specific affects and feeling states" that orient his or her social action.[19] These affects are not internally generated by autonomous subjects but by the powers that shape social action and behavior. Weber suggests that affects are in part an effect of power, and he thus forges the link between affective measures of legitimacy and the discursive production of legitimating norms. Foucault attends to the ways that discourses are a productive form of power that condition subjectivity, and his reading implicates a significantly larger array of political, social, and cultural modes of power than Weber's reading of domination, which maintains focus on institutional origins and on repressive, rather than productive, power. Rearticulating Weber's claim that belief in legitimacy can be created by affective states mobilized by social forces, through

Foucault's claim that power and discourse produce legitimacy, opens up a new claim that the affective states conditioning belief in legitimacy are shaped in part by political discourse. Legitimation processes involve discursive tactics that can cultivate and sustain affective states, and that condition belief in the rightness of state action.

Weber's use of the term *affects* to describe how legitimacy can be achieved aligns his claims with the work of contemporary cultural studies in the *affective turn*—which contends that affects are historically constituted and publicly and politically shared even when they are interpreted as personal experiences—in ways directly relevant to the development of legitimacy.[20] The discursive production of legitimacy has a necessarily affective dimension that circulates through citizen subjectivity and state discourse. Legitimacy connects to what Suanne Ngai calls our "sociopolitical" feelings, which describes how "feelings are as fundamentally social as the institutions and collective practices" of politics and infuse "models of subjectivity, collectivity, and agency."[21] Legitimacy is, in this sense, in part an affective experience, a sociopolitical emotional experience that circulates among political subjects as a common feeling of rightness.[22] The evaluation of legitimacy works in part through tactics in specific political discourses that solicit belief in legitimacy through the cultivation of particular affective states and public feelings. Evaluations of legitimacy extend into the discourses that delimit how we conceptualize power, that address different affective experiences of political life, and that emplot potentials for nationhood and political identity.

In claiming that legitimation processes work on subjectivity through discursive and affective means, I am not arguing that there is no difference between legitimate and illegitimate political action, that legitimacy is impossible, or even, following Foucault, that legitimacy only functions to obscure the expansion of power and the cultivation of subjects. Mutually agreed upon and broadly applicable measures for evaluating state action are necessary for a democratic polity to permit certain actions and inhibit others deemed wrong, illegitimate, cruel, or unjustifiable. The evaluation of legitimacy can be a crucial tool for demarcating the exercise of political power and for marking the public capacity to activate and challenge power. Yet the complex operations that enable subjects to impute legitimacy to state actions are only partially captured by deliberative and procedural frameworks of analysis that shape normative accounts. Examining legitimation in discursive and affective forms does not demand the abandonment of legitimating norms, but instead demands acknowledgment of the often-unaccountable investments of power, and the affective experiences of power, that structure any legitimating claim.

## From Politics to Evil: Legitimating Tactics of Post-9/11 Political Discourse

The post-9/11 legitimation of various expansive state powers, which took place partly within melodramatic genre conventions of political discourse, can specify the production of legitimacy for post-9/11 contemporary state actions. The feelings of legitimacy for the wars and state surveillance were solicited by deployments of melodrama's generic emplotments of retributive state action, deployments that began on September 11, 2001, but continue to influence U.S. politics. I first examine the discursive production of legitimacy in post-9/11 deployments of melodrama before moving to the work of affect. Key speeches legitimating war and state surveillance reveal how melodramatic forms of legitimacy take shape within official political discourse, especially presidential rhetoric. I primarily though not exclusively focus on the speeches of executive branch officials precisely because of their power to enact the policies they proclaimed as legitimate, and the national audiences they are able to command, especially in the wake of 9/11, when the president garnered extraordinary support and capacity to shape public discourse.[23] Yet my inquiry is not primarily concerned with why the Bush administration used melodrama, which is not to say that it did not purposely construct the legitimating tactics it deployed or is unaccountable for the violence it produced. Of course the administration intended to garner widespread approval for its policies, and it did so in part by the way it told the story of national politics. Administration officials certainly drew upon melodrama to legitimate their political program, but at the same time the administration was also submitting to the widespread accessibility and popularity of the melodramatic genre. Melodrama was present on September 11 in the news media and in public speeches, by political commentators and by newscasters, before Bush and other administrative figures spoke to the nation about the events.[24] While official rhetoric is key to producing legitimacy for state actions, melodramatic processes of legitimation, not the administration's machinations, are the focus of this story. I use these speeches to ask: when state action is legitimated as a narrative expectation and a moral mandate, what is discursively placed beyond the influence of power?

"Freedom at War with Fear," a speech given by Bush on September 20, 2001, is one of the most important speeches of the twenty-first century to date, and perhaps even the most influential. In the speech the president announces the key state actions that will compose the war on terror. The speech draws on melodrama to discursively legitimate both the War in Afghanistan, which will begin less than three weeks later, and the creation of the Office of Homeland Security, which will become the Department of Homeland Security in 2002, the largest reorganization and consolidation of federal governance and national security in fifty years. Thus, a single speech intends to legitimate the most extensive expansions in violent, antidemocratic, and securitized state power since the onset of the cold war, when (as I examine in chapter 2) Harry Truman similarly capitalized on melodramatic conventions to legitimate a new order of national security and foreign intervention. Bush states at the beginning of his speech, "We have seen the state of our Union in the endurance of rescuers, working past exhaustion. . . . We have seen the decency of a loving and giving people, who have made the grief of strangers their own. . . . Today we are awakened to danger and called to defend freedom. Our grief has turned to anger, and anger to resolution. Whether we bring our enemies to justice or justice to our enemies, justice will be done."[25] Bush's argument goes something like this: America is a unified group of loving and giving people unjustly injured by terrorism—a nation virtuous precisely because of its victimization on September 11. America is virtuous because of the way its citizens shared in the suffering of others and made "the grief of others their own"—because of the pathos it demonstrates. Retributive action is an extension of that virtue and becomes morally just. As Christine Gledhill writes of melodrama, "Its central protagonists become objects of pathos because they are constructed as victims of forces that lie beyond their control and understanding."[26] This speech claims that state power was morally mandated by the virtuousness that attends an overwhelming national injury, that state power is already legitimated by the forces arrayed against it, that it is legitimated by the very fact of its imperative.

Even as it is being announced for the first time, the war and the office are presented as already settled, already legitimate. In the speech the push for justice is a "resolution." As Bush explains it a few days earlier: "Americans are generous and kind, resourceful and brave. . . . Our unity is a kinship of grief and a steadfast resolve to prevail against our enemies."[27] Judith Butler argues, looking at this speech, that grief is something Americans were supposed to have moved through eight days after the terrorist attacks, and in such a way that grief becomes "a cry for war."[28] Melodrama helps to answer how the pain of grief laid the groundwork for both a shared national identity formed out of injury and a justification for violent retribution couched in the name of heroic defense of freedom that the nation has already resolved to enact. A unified and loyal nation is conjured out of suffering, which binds America's virtue into a kinship network and then grounds the "steadfast resolve" to fight the nation's enemies. This narrative directly translates suffering and virtue into support for intensifications of political power, so that "steadfast resolve to prevail" becomes an expression of national goodness.

Melodrama is particularly well suited for legitimating homeland security because it is often the genre of the home space, as its depictions allegorically transform domestic scenes into political scenes laden with heightened moral and social significance. *Homeland security* similarly gestures to the sacredness of the home. The very term *homeland security* was virtually unheard of in public discourse in the United States to describe the geographic territory of the nation-state until September 11. The speech's melodrama invokes the sacredness of the home space in justifying the massive bureaucracy of the Office of Homeland Security now needed to protect it. Under the new office, according to Bush, "life will return almost to normal" and "we'll go back to our lives and routines." It is necessary because the office was meant to protect sacred space and maintain ordinary life, and thus it was a matter that did not require public deliberation for its validity. In this speech, the nation is *awakened* to a new reality after 9 / 11: this verb implies a world, and a home space, changed without our noticing, without our input, a new home shaped by terrifying acts of violence that we are wholly unimplicated in cultivating.

Within the conventions of melodrama, the nation's injury and the sacredness of its home prevent the possibility that the United States could act villainously; that the nation could unjustly injure others; that others could suffer violence, unfreedom, and injustice as a result of its policies aiming to end evil; and that the United States could be accountable for any suffering its actions create. The speech states of its orders to the Taliban in Afghanistan: "These demands are not open to negotiation or discussion. . . . They will hand over the terrorists, or they will share in their fate." It states of the Office of Homeland Security: "These measures are essential. The only way to defeat terrorism as a threat to our way of life is to stop it, eliminate it, and destroy it where it grows." Moral claims for what we ought to do accede to moral imperatives for what we *must* do, what we *need* to do, what we have no other choice but to do. These actions are unquestioningly required even and especially when we do not understand the workings behind political action. The president explains three days after the war begins: "We cannot fully understand the designs and power of evil. It is enough to know that evil, like goodness, exists."[29] This explanation to justify war makes questioning the war or its justness not merely unneeded but misguided; when the stakes are defined through transhistorical dynamics of good and evil, the proper response to political confusion is state obedience.

Bush performs the virtue and moral strength of which he speaks through the giving of the speech "Freedom at War with Fear." His tone is one of vehemence, which fuels his righteousness, and his gestures of righteous anger are clear and readable. He enacts heightened affects as he references them—grief and anger—in order to show how they demand resolution, a resolution that will be the very end of fear. The hypervisible expression of righteous anger is its own legitimating tactic, performing the obviousness of the moral obligation to combat terror in this way. The intensity of Bush's tone testifies to the virtue inherent to this fight, what Lauren Berlant calls the "vernacular of the viscera, its effort to put forth politics as the practice of moral transparency rather than juridical validity," which works as shorthand to describe the discursive tactic of legitimation in the performance of this speech.[30] Gledhill writes that melodrama "stresses unpremeditated feeling as an index of moral status and social value"; in this sense, the vernacular of the viscera is also a moral vernacular, a performance of moral virtue.[31] It attaches to both Bush and to the state actions he describes as morally obligatory.

Melodramatic political discourse's reassuring and familiar narrative expectation that freedom triumphs over tyranny contributes to the post-9/11 discursive production of legitimacy. The speech on fear and freedom describes the 9/11 attackers as "enemies of freedom" and argues that "freedom is under attack," thus making the target of all of these policies "those who hate freedom." Freedom—as the subject and object of state action in this speech—offers a predigested legitimacy to an American nation that defines its policy agency and ontological existence through a vocabulary of freedom (a vocabulary I examine at greater length in the next two chapters). This language gestures to a teleology of freedom in which its spread is guaranteed, a guarantee that is a liberal inheritance, part of the progress narrative of liberal modernity.[32] Melodrama's moral imperatives and narrative expectations thus intersect at an expectation for freedom, as the title of the speech contends. Bush explains, "Great harm has been done to us. We have suffered great loss. And in our grief and anger we have found our mission and our moment. Freedom and fear are at war. The advance of human freedom—the great achievement of our time, and the great hope of every time—now depends on us." Using nationwide suffering to justify, and indeed animate, the desire for "our mission," both the war and the Office of Homeland Security become heroic, part of the nebulous yet energizing cry for transhistorical action in "the advance of human freedom" that conceals their disputable, arbitrary, and culturally specific formations. Of the terrorists Bush argues: "They are the heirs of all the murderous ideologies of the 20th century," implicitly lumping together for his American audience all of the recent foes that symbolize unfreedom: Nazism, fascism, totalitarianism, terrorism, and communism, a claim that is at one level incoherent, but at another level is a powerful legitimating tactic that suggests that the particular conditions of the post-9/11 moment are irrelevant to the legitimation of the actions detailed in this speech. It comes as no surprise that the military action for the War in Afghanistan is named Operation Enduring Freedom: the freedom the nation is required to protect, and thus the war itself, endures beyond this mission into "the great hope of every time," beyond mere human inquiry or self-examination.

This speech's moral imperative and transhistorical demand for the "defense of freedom" also constructs legitimacy through a civilizational discourse that legitimates state violence against enemies because they are uncivilized and less than human, a claim that grows out of racist imperial discourses. Bush argues, "This is the world's fight. This is civilization's fight. This is the fight of all who believe in progress and pluralism, tolerance and freedom," against those who "hide in countries around the world to plot evil and destruction."[33] The Office of Homeland Security and the War in Afghanistan are demanded by a civilizational fight with a mission to protect and sustain those who are tolerant, virtuous, and civilized in the "homeland" against those who are uncivilized and attack these values. The moral imperatives in this speech cull from a civilizing discourse used in past forms of legitimacy to justify imperialism through liberalism's goal to expand shared values of liberty (presumed to be held by all peoples) to those people, usually of color, who don't yet know they want it.[34] Drawing on an explicit language of tolerance and pluralism, the speech implicitly draws from a racist discourse older than J. S. Mill in which justifications for imperialism come about in order to spread civilization as liberal freedom to non-Western peoples of color.[35] The obligatory and fervent nature of the civilizational fight will prelegitimate future state actions in its service. The civilizing mission that Bush outlines is so obligatory that only two options are left for the world in melodrama's moral economy: "You are either with us. Or you are with the terrorists." In this discourse that separates the world into good and evil, us and terrorist, civilized and uncivilized, the gray zone of those who might be neither simply becomes evil precisely because they refuse to acknowledge the unquestionable moral rightness of U.S. state action taken in the service of this fight; the refusal to legitimate action as a moral imperative becomes, therefore, a sign of one's uncivilized nature. Those who are "with the terrorists" are uncivilized in part because they do not read the performance of U.S. state violence to be automatically virtuous.

Within the genre expectations of melodramatic political discourse, designations of injury promise something better—they portend the eradication of suffering, the heroic triumph of freedom over what has caused one to suffer. The speech ends on this point: "The path of this conflict is not known, yet its outcome is certain. Freedom and fear, justice and cruelty, have always been at war, and we know that God is not neutral between them." The Office of Homeland Security draws sanction from America's initial victimization in order to spearhead a fight for freedom larger than the nation, and in fact larger than this historical epoch; a war, the president explains, between good and evil has "always been." It is a war in which God is on the side of those who are virtuous. Bush's rhetoric insinuates that God has sanctioned the Office of Homeland Security. The creation of the office now gained overt theological justification, one that often lurks in melodrama's subterranean workings but here is outwardly employed; the insertion of God's nonneutrality toward the pursuit of freedom makes the national response permanently obligatory and eternally approved. If the office becomes part of a transhistorical battle approved by God, then its existence and methods cannot be subject to question, and yet neither is the administration responsible for its effects: responsibility lies with a higher power that promises freedom as its outcome while it also leaves the nation unaccountable for its own actions.

It would be imprecise to describe the melodramatic deployments of *good* and *evil* here as Manicheistic, even though that term is often used to describe both melodrama's operations and Bush's rhetoric.[36] In the original Manicheistic concepts of good and evil, good is understood to mean fully rational, pure, peaceful, and "of the mind."[37] Evil is rage unmodified, irrational, uncontrollable, and "of the passions." Evil is, specifically, an *invasion* of the good, a hostile force determinedly focused on good's violation. For the Manicheans, evil was timeless and indestructible, fated to eternally lock heads with its nemesis; evil could be restricted, but its complete eradication was impossible. Good was passive, defenseless, always threatened with im-

pingement by evil's ferocity, relying solely on the force of its purity for protection. These Manicheistic understandings of evil contribute to melodrama's present political use. What has transformed, however, is the ontological
status of evil and the submissive quality of the good. Now, in the use of
these terms in American politics, evil's ontology stands in contradiction to
itself: it becomes mortal as well as immortal. The annihilation of evil is possible, yet the fight against evil is an eternal one.[38] And goodness, in contemporary melodramatic political discourse, harbors the violent, passionate
power to accomplish the extermination of evil. Speculations for this complex historical shift are beyond the scope of this inquiry, but it is important
to note its transformational differences: good acquires aggression and violence without tarnishing its purity. And evil becomes both vanquishable
and unvanquishable, immortal as well as earthly.

Rather than condemning the incoherence of melodramatic evil's polysemy, however, it is vital to question what a mortal and immortal evil, pitted against a violent goodness, allows in the context of post-9 / 11 political
discourse. If the stated goal of the war and the Office of Homeland Security
is to spread freedom by fighting evil, then there is no conceivable limit to
the power they require. If evil is mortal, then the nation must mobilize all
of its resources to vanquish it; if evil is also immortal, then this fight is unending, and the legitimation for the resources it requires must also be unending. Within evil's polysemic deployment, there is no discernible end
point for these actions, and thus there are neither boundaries on the power
needed to accomplish the actions nor measurements to know when they
have been completed. As both mortal and immortal, evil allows for triumphalist assertions and unlimited increases in state action in the service of
fighting evil, as evil's eternal existence means we must always be engaged in
battle. And if the enemy is that which must—but can never be—eradicated,
this legitimation permits an unending need for heroism. Indeed, *evil* in
this context dramatically increases the scale of tolerable violence when it
is anchored within the political, because it mandates, as a moral injunc-
tion, the impossible destruction of a transcendent and immortal concept.
While analytically illogical, an evil that can both be destroyed and not be
destroyed tactically requires an endless legitimation of state action to
combat it.

The policies and powers that are endlessly legitimated in "Freedom at War
with Fear" are widespread and intense. The War in Afghanistan is the longest
in U.S. history. In the service of combating evil and protecting freedom, the
War in Afghanistan has killed tens of thousands of Afghans, imprisoned

thousands of others illegally and without due process, killed thousands of American soldiers, enabled a corporate- and state-organized neoimperialism that promoted vast levels of exploitation of Afghan land and people by multinational corporations and Afghan elites, and destroyed rural patterns of daily life that paradoxically strengthened the Taliban forces. The war put an entire country under U.S. control for a decade and counting. In the service of combating evil, the Office of Homeland Security (and then the Department of Homeland Security) dramatically increased the capacity and centralization of civilian regulation, behavioral surveillance, financial monitoring, and border patrols. Homeland security consolidated twenty-two different government agencies, making it the largest amalgamation of federal power since the National Security Act of 1947.[39] Homeland security institutionalized racism against Arabs, Muslims, and Mexicans; it dramatically expanded domestic police powers and attempted to create an impermeable border with Mexico. Many of these expansions involved thousands of private and multinational corporations subject to virtually no political accountability. Similar to the U.S. forces in Afghanistan, the homeland-security network spawned huge apparatuses of governmentality that rely on myriad surveillance strategies spanning state and private systems to order, manage, and monitor persons and things from micro- to macropolitics and to suspend "inalienable" rights and data mine citizens; most of these actions generally occurred outside of legal, democratic, and political liability. Yet these actions are legitimated in a discourse that proclaims their existence through world-transcending, morally requisite, and narratively obvious terms that solicit their creation as already legitimated.[40] In the weeks after this speech, 92 percent of people sanctioned Bush's handling of the war on terror and 90 percent of Americans sanctioned war in Afghanistan, while central governing institutions and leaders gained high levels of approval from the populace—from Congress to Attorney General John Ashcroft, who created the USA Patriot Act, to Homeland Security Secretary Tom Ridge.[41]

Operating as Foucault would suggest, legitimation here works around institutional and accountable practices of governance, because strategies and bids for political power—including contestation, active judging, contingent and collaborative decision making, political wrangling, uncomfortable compromises, cutthroat power struggles, and agonistic deliberation—seem irrelevant to the creation of the Office of Homeland Security and the decision to go to war. In his influential *New York Times* article supporting the Iraq War, titled "The Year of Living Dangerously: A Liberal Supporter of the

War Looks Back," Michael Ignatieff used melodramatic conventions to depoliticize the legitimacy these actions should garner by claiming their nonpolitical nature. Ignatieff explains why, even though Americans did not find weapons of mass destruction in Iraq, and even though the war caused thousands of casualties, citizens should still continue to support the Iraq War. Particular justifications for the war were fungible if America was motivated by its injury to perform goodness, which prelegitimated the action the nation would take in its moral mission.

Ignatieff explains that "the essential issue" for going to war was "the malignancy of [Saddam Hussein's] intentions," and that "Hussein ran an especially odious regime." Therefore, "the fundamental case for war" is captured in a quote by an Iraqi man who explains what America has the capability to provide: "This is the first and only chance in my lifetime for my people to create a decent society."[42] Ignatieff's "fundamental case" is the effect of the melodramatic discourse that claims its legitimacy by speaking on behalf of a morality that exists prior to and beyond itself. Ignatieff argues that when the U.S. military is fighting evil ("an odious regime") and establishing good ("a decent society"), its methods for achieving this virtuous goal become a priori legitimate. In other words, the state's political operations are divested of political significance and reinterpreted as a transparent expression of moral goodness that requires no further political evaluation, only the commitment to maintain belief in their legitimacy.

Yet this depoliticization is different from what Foucault may have expected, because the actions it sanctions are not hidden in secret recesses out of public view but are placed very much at the center of national attention. While for Foucault legitimation processes obfuscate the operations of power, here these operations are clear, recognizable, and overt. Ignatieff's melodrama directly petitions for the continued support of the Iraq War. The Office of Homeland Security and the War in Afghanistan were announced on primetime television to hundreds of millions of Americans, and by extension to the entire world, with dramatic flourish. Legitimation processes in "Freedom at War with Fear" depoliticize state power not by hiding the actions the speech intends to sanction but by repositioning them, so that they seem to be a clear sign of an apolitical moral mandate and an obvious outcome of generic expectations. In other words, this legitimation makes state actions invisible only as *political* actions available for deliberative legitimacy, even as it simultaneously and explicitly mandates their operations.[43] Melodramatic discourse thus legitimates state power in a counterintuitive way, depoliticizing the very power it subjects to authorization. Indeed it makes the power it overtly legitimates also seem unavailable for evaluation. Melodramatic discourse needs no further elaboration.

The depoliticization of state action is a prime tactic for defending against the erosion of legitimacy for actions that may seem unlawful, excessive, or outside the scope of conventional political acceptability. Habermas argues in *Legitimation Crisis* that the creeping and consistent encroachment of the state into areas of life previously unregulated by its management can potentially bring about a crisis in the legitimacy of state action.[44] For Habermas, the legitimacy of liberal states generally erodes with increased state intervention, in part because the ideologies and traditions used to justify state power under liberal capitalism—that define the state as a limited power over its citizens with impartial affiliations—are now not capable of justifying its new increases.[45] Without validation for its broadening movements, state action, and the legitimating beliefs it had relied upon, becomes exposed to contestation. By increasing its scope, then, the liberal state unintentionally repoliticizes the exercise of its power, an effect that leaves belief in its legitimacy open to public challenge. Habermas's analysis of legitimation crises points to the problem facing the contemporary U.S. state in the post-9/11 moment: the overt, dramatic, and wide-ranging intensifications in military power and securitization encompassed by the War in Afghanistan, the Iraq War, the Office of Homeland Security, and Patriot Act, among many other things, can potentially delegitimize America's authoritative power as a liberal state that limits intrusive powers through proper procedural governance. Because the actions that the Bush administration aims to legitimate are not hidden or obfuscated but are overt and highlighted, there is a problem for larger discourses of limited state power that validate U.S. politics. To avoid a politicizing or more democratic challenge, then, legitimacy is shored up by keeping state action outside the realm of political contestation—but not by altering or minimizing state action so that it recedes to earlier boundaries, nor by coercing obedience.

Melodramatic tactics thus aim to depoliticize not only state power but also the very act of legitimation. They encourage legitimacy in a register different from agonistic, formal, or contestatory political judgments about power. Bush makes contestation over political expansion unnecessary when he states in his speech at the Republican National Convention in 2004: "We have fought the terrorists across the earth, not for pride, *not for power*, but because the lives of our citizens are at stake. . . . We are working to advance liberty in the broader Middle East, because freedom will bring a future of hope, and the peace *we all want*."[46] Fighting terrorism is placed

beyond the scope of "power," that is, placed outside the realm of the political. Actions to fight terrorists and start a war are a priori legitimate because
they are separated from the oppressive and amoral power relations that
constitute the realm of politics. They are required for life itself, the very
demand of Ananke (the mythic force of necessity and constraint) that shuts
down questions of validity or choice. Melodramatic politics articulates a
world *beyond* politics, beyond the machinations and calculations of power,
beyond the daily squabbling and dissimulations of political life to the realm
of not only of basic survival but unmediated moral truth.

Advancing liberty is thus not about "power" or individual desires for
"pride"; it is about things "we all want," and consequently so natural and so
obvious that they are not even worth elaboration: life, hope, and peace. The
universalism of the "we" who "all want" these things marks action in their
service as universally desirable. The speech constructs this "we" in the moment its existence is articulated, inventing the consensus of all Americans
by naturalizing and unifying their political desires as universal and then
normalizing state action in the service of these desires. Action to "advance
liberty" is a priori legitimate because it is part of what is necessary for life;
further discussion is therefore not simply superfluous but a sign of bad
character, indeed a sign of one's unfitness for membership in the "we."

The success of contemporary legitimacy in the liberal state, especially in
post-9 / 11 America, depends in part on the ability to quell the repoliticization of expanding state power. In Habermas's view, as state powers intensify
their regulation, monitoring, and disciplinary efforts, their concurrent requirement is to maintain belief in state legitimacy by keeping these actions
outside political visibility or intense public debate. Bush's acceptance speech
for the Republican nomination for president in 2004 aims for this depoliticization when he explains: "Freedom is on the march." And moments later
he says, "Freedom is not America's gift to the world[;] it is the Almighty
God's gift to every man and woman in this world."[47] In the first quote, the
state loses any sense of political agency; it is freedom that marches, and an
abstract ideal becomes the agent of political action. In the quote that follows, God becomes the overarching generator of action—agency is now
two steps away from the state—as the movement of freedom is bequeathed
to the world as God's gift. Similarly, when the Office of Homeland Security
becomes civilization's defender, the audience is asked to forget the office's
political functionality and, more broadly, the contestability of state agency.
State agency is always and already legitimate because its agency functions
to complete on earth the work of God; thus its agency is removed from and

is above terrestrial concerns of power.[48] Freedom's march makes state agency inevitable as it eclipses and renders unnecessary a substantive role for procedural, legal, or deliberative legitimacy in determining what, exactly, the march consists of.

In fact, active participation by ordinary citizens in any of these decisions, or in attempting to understand the logic of these events and their responses, is an illegible political demand. In "Freedom at War with Fear," Bush supplies a long list of what citizens can do in response to the massive changes arising out the terrorist attacks, as well as the government-organized response to them, in a passage worth quoting at length:

> Americans are asking: What is expected of us? I ask you to live your lives, and hug your children. . . . I ask you to uphold the values of America. . . . I ask you to continue to support the victims of this tragedy. . . . The thousands of FBI agents who are now at work in this investigation may need your cooperation, and I ask you to give it. . . . I ask for your patience with the delays and inconveniences that may accompany tighter security. . . . I ask your continued participation and confidence in the American economy. . . . And finally, please continue praying for the victims of terror and their families, for those in uniform, and for our great country.

In this rhetorically repetitive intonation that lists proper American behavior, citizens are asked to do everything but act politically and collectively, or think critically and reflectively, about the 9/11 events and the best course of action to respond to mass murder. In other words, good political subjects are those who respond to 9/11 by hugging kids, praying, accepting surveillance, and shopping. Consumption demonstrates one's trust in American freedom; consumption even seems to mark one's virtue.[49] Go about your life, Bush suggests, and let the expert elite actors take care of the response, one that is already foreordained in any case; in fact the response is prelegitimated by the virtuous members of the national victimized public. The nation had already resolved its course of action even as the course of action was being laid out for the first time in this speech. "Our grief has turned to anger, and anger to resolution," Bush explains. In claiming that Americans have already moved beyond sadness to anger and resolution, the speech positions state action to merely fill in the blanks for what resolve will actually entail; the resolution itself, we are told, has already actualized. Deployments of melodrama explain that virtuous citizens passively sit by, retreat to their private families and shopping malls, and wait for the action they have already legitimated to commence while they go back to "almost normal."

This deployment of melodramatic discourse aims to generate nation-wide legitimacy for the "world's fight." This deployment works in many ways: by claiming that legitimacy is free from power; by encouraging visceral responses to national victimization that bespeak citizens' belonging to a new national identity with other virtuous Americans; by constructing politics through a moral economy that generates imperatives for action and marks those who do not agree with its imperatives as evil, uncivilized, or terrorist; by narrating political events in a familiar trajectory of pathos and action in which freedom is the expected teleological conclusion; by offering that the pain of victimization on September 11 compels the legitimation of state power; by suggesting that one's belief in legitimacy is a sign of one's virtue; and by arguing that the war on terror is part of a timeless moral fight untethered to the specifics of the moment and always demanded of all who love freedom. The deployment's techniques of moralization and dehistoricization circumvent the politicizing of state operations even as they aim to gain legitimacy in the national political sphere. They solicit belief in legitimacy by keeping state movements outside the realm of political debate, already sanctioned and normalized.

### Feeling Legitimacy

Post-9/11 deployments of melodrama create a justification for state power that simply makes political debate or participatory action extraneous; justification happens through a discourse in which citizens are solicited to *feel* the rightness of state action through its various tactics. Melodrama's moral imperatives, plot expectations, and link between virtue and injury solicit a *felt legitimation* of state action, an affective cycle whereby discursive productions of moral imperatives combine with feelings of national victimization, and with generic expectations for the recognition of virtue in heroic retaliation, to transmute into a feeling of the rightness of state power.

The deployment of melodrama seeks to produce a mass affect of legitimacy, in which state action feels legitimate.[50] Melodrama helps to circulate "state emotion" between individuals, national imaginaries, and state rhetoric, bringing into being an individual and a collective feeling of legitimacy for state action. *State emotion* is Lauren Berlant's term for describing how the political sphere is constituted by *emotional* modes of contestation; state emotion is a "public feeling" that describes the way that mass media and state rhetoric orchestrate "an emotional style linked to moral claims about truth and justice [that] increasingly come to dominate ordinary political speech."[51] Those who feel and enact this moral clarity on behalf of injured citizens, and the moral outrage it engenders, are themselves upstanding citizens, and the experience of state emotion seems to be, in and of itself, public participation. Extending Berlant's argument, I argue that the post-9/11 scene of state emotion orchestrates not only public belonging and moral clarity but also the felt legitimation of violent state power that grounds the very premise of contemporary citizenship. Felt legitimacy describes how deployments of melodrama cultivate a moral imperative that solicits the public feeling of felt legitimacy for dramatic state expansions, and that, as Berlant writes, "makes it possible for the government to motivate a situation of unending war and juridical crisis as though these practices constitute the just response of a representative state to the felt needs of its citizens."[52]

Different genres of political discourse solicit different sociopolitical affects and state emotions as part of their legitimating tactics. The legitimating strategies deployed in post-9/11 melodramatic political discourse aim to cultivate an expectation for the heroic triumph of the nation, to feel the injury that wounds all citizens while marking their—and the whole nation's—virtue, and to demand state action because it is already morally justified. The state emotion of national victimization in post-9/11 melodrama thus simultaneously equals the felt sense that one has already legitimated state action, as have others with whom one shares the feeling of suffering from the 9/11 attacks. This felt legitimacy is constructed through a nonlinear temporality in which the feeling of legitimacy produces the feeling that legitimation has already occurred, so that the feeling seems to ratify the already-existing condition that it brings into being.

Through melodrama state action is discursively legitimated in a multitude of ways that solicit its affective production: it is a moral obligation in response to injustice, a narrative expectation for the trajectory of world freedom spearheaded by U.S. power, and a catalyst for an affective experience of vehement righteousness that will banish felt terror. Felt legitimacy even works by making state actions unquestionable. Indeed, further attempts to scrutinize or debate them seem suspicious, immoral, and even unpatriotic, because they challenge melodrama's foundational premise that virtuous victimization demands heroic action.

Solicited by the melodramatic speeches and writings examined earlier, felt legitimacy can incorporate the feeling of suffering from terrorism and the felt desire to banish it, as well as the feeling of virtue that this suffering offers. Melodrama is defined, of course, by the affective pull it generates, by the pathos it engenders; in film this is what makes melodrama a "moving" image, and in political discourse this is what makes the solicitations of its legitimating tactics so affectively intense.[53] Felt legitimacy in melodramatic political discourse includes the feeling of one's own moral goodness, and the comfort and surety of this self-evaluation. Linda Williams writes, "What counts in melodrama is the feeling of righteousness."[54] Felt legitimacy generates the satisfaction that one has participated in political life by feeling it. As Berlant might suggest, melodrama solicits the sense that one is part of a group of like-minded and virtuous citizens who feel when to do the right thing.[55]

As the title of "Freedom at War with Fear" contends, felt legitimacy also includes the anticipation of nonfear: the nation is at war with the affect of fear, and felt legitimacy authorizes state actions that promise to banish the felt experience of fear. In its stead, felt legitimacy anticipates the felt experience of something different—something that feels like triumph, like control, like sovereignty, and like invulnerability, which all are expected to end the feeling of fear. Felt legitimacy has a forward-looking aim: it aims to banish the felt experience of terror and feel freedom, as Bush intends: if freedom is at war with fear, then the feeling of legitimacy is appealing because it seems to anticipate the end of the affective experience of terror that the attacks incited. "Freedom at War with Fear" is part of the war on terror, and even though terror and fear might seem qualitatively different in their intensity, they are conflated in this discourse to be the opposite of the felt experience of freedom that legitimation offers. Felt legitimacy expresses the feeling that state action is capable of binding fear and is ameliorative for the nation's injury. Felt legitimacy anticipates the feeling of freedom that will arrive with the end of fear.

A felt sense of legitimation aims to bring claims for the legitimacy of state power into being long before legitimacy might be conceived through cumbersome efforts in deliberative, procedural, or legislative channels. While post-9/11 state action is not considered legitimate by many of liberalism's legalistic standards of measurement, in felt legitimacy state action is considered legitimate from the standpoint of state emotion, encouraged by a melodramatic political discourse that cultivates the production of felt legitimacy through the obligations it demands from a virtuous and injured nation. As Raymond Williams would note, this does not mean that felt legitimacy's affective charge needs to be concretely understood, fully rationalized, or tightly categorized to exert pressures and delimit individuals' actions and experiences in relation to that situation.[56] Yet my reading of felt legitimacy also does not pit the affective experience of legitimacy in opposition to rational experience, or as antagonistic to deliberation. As Sharon Krause argues in *Civil Passions*, a book that challenges many of the conventional liberal norms underlying how deliberation and judgment work, affects support democratic judgments and even enhance their fairness when part of a practice of self-cultivation.[57] Yet Krause pits affect as a tempering effect on reason, on its cold and calculating objectivity, and thus sees affect as a "civilizing" force that enables democratic deliberation. Rather than seeing affect as a tempering force of reason, I would argue that different affects produce different reasons and rationalities for state power. Different affects organize different relationships between individuals and the state powers they are tasked to legitimate, some of which may be democratic, while others may not. Melodrama's complex affective charge, for instance, produces a logic and a reason for war and surveillance. Felt legitimacy offers reasons for judgments that are compelling even if they are not objective or even impartial. Legitimacy always has a partial and subjective register, even when its affective pull feels autonomously generated and impartial.

Legitimacy accrues in post-9/11 politics in part through the felt experience of melodrama's moral imperative that merges the feeling of national virtue with the spectacle of victimhood to prove the unobjectionable righteousness and imminence of a reactive heroism. Melodramatic tactics depict a political problem within a field in which humans have little understanding, but deep obligations, and in which legitimacy is not only or necessarily fought over in conventional political channels but also a properly felt experience of injury and righteousness. Felt legitimacy feels the virtue of a judgment through its suffering and anticipates that state power will redress national suffering and fear. When melodrama locates morality in the feeling of legitimacy for state retribution, then it also makes the very feeling of legitimation into an expression of moral virtue. This felt legitimation becomes the mark of a virtuous citizen, and in turn it marks as immoral, as evil, as not American, all those who do not agree with these state actions. The felt legitimation of retributive action seems, within the logic of melodramatic conventions, not only an ethical demand to the nationwide injury inflicted by the forces of evil but also the very proof of moral rectitude. State action is rendered invisible as a political choice at the moment it is authorized, and citizens who support state action seem to sanction this depoliticizing transformation to invisibility because the feeling of legitimacy marks their own goodness.

Brian Massumi might call the designation of felt legitimacy an "affective fact," one that differs from an "actual fact."[58] He explains the distinction between them by examining one legitimating process for the Iraq War: An actual fact is that Hussein had no weapons of mass destruction. An affective fact is that Americans felt threatened by Hussein's weapons of mass destruction, and Americans assumed that even if he didn't have these weapons at the time, if he could have had them, he would have deployed them. The affective fact is that the feeling of threat is real, and thus can legitimate preemptive war. In other words, there is a split between what occurs and how the felt experience of what occurs generates a political response. In the legitimation tactic operating in melodrama, these distinctions merge: the affective fact of legitimacy is the actual fact of legitimacy. The affective fact that war is felt to be a legitimate response to terror matches the actual fact that these state operations have become legitimate, because legitimacy operates through and as the circulation of affects. The war is legitimate because it is felt to be legitimate, and felt legitimacy is the fact of legitimacy in this situation.

Felt legitimacy is thus not a false or fake legitimacy but a real form of consent, even though it is a separate process from civic participation or juridical accountability. Feeling the rightness of state action incorporates the feeling that citizens impose their virtuous desire for responsive action upon the state. The dramatic expansion of state action is seen as a necessity, but a necessity that is determined first and foremost by the injured citizens for whom this action operates. This affective dynamic feeds off the broader democratic legitimation process of U.S. politics—a politics that is self-justifying because state legitimacy is premised on the democratic consent of the governed. Felt legitimacy, like the "fountain of power" of the Federalist Papers that travels from citizens to the government, marks a transfer of consent for state action based on an interpretation of it as always originating in the desires of its subjects.[59] In felt legitimacy citizens feel that state action is right at the same time that they feel that they impose their demand for expansive action upon the state. Felt legitimacy solicits the felt sense that the state is responding to the needs of its citizens who demand, as a moral imperative, state action to protect civilization from terror.

Yet the circulation of political affect is not only monodirectional—it does not only originate in the autonomous desires of subjects, as liberal theorists generally posit, nor is it merely imposed upon subjects from above by state mandates or political oratory, though this certainly is a determining factor. Felt legitimacy resides at the muddy midpoint of the affective work that

Michael Hardt calls "our power to *affect* the world around us and our power to be *affected* by it."[60] Felt legitimacy at once produces and is produced by the politics in which it circulates. Specifically, the dual aspect of the term *affect* allows us to see how the affective feeling of virtue arising out of felt legitimacy helps to produce the moral imperative that then cultivates further intensifications of felt legitimacy and material expansions of state power. The dramatic intensifications in post-9/11 state power are thus concretely enabled by a legitimation that is experienced affectively, and that circulates between and blurs the boundaries of individual citizens, national communities, and official political discourses.

By relying on a form of American citizenship that views the legitimation of state power as part of its national identity, melodrama legitimates state power not only because citizens demand it or because it offers the truth of the nation's own virtue. The feeling of legitimacy proves the virtue of each feeling citizen, and thus captures why melodramatic political discourse becomes so potent at multiple affective registers. Felt legitimacy creates a way for citizens who experience the feeling of victimization to index that this feeling proves their virtue. Felt legitimacy then doubles to demonstrate one's qualification for membership in a national identity defined by goodness. Virtue accrues twice to the citizen in this form of legitimation: through the felt experience of nationwide victimization that melodrama links to the proof of virtue, and through participation in the shared sense that state action is a morally obligatory response to victimhood. Feeling that the exercise of state action is virtuous becomes the proof of a citizen's integrity and proof of belonging in the national virtuous "we," a "we" that is conjoined in part because "we" collectively feel state action to be a moral imperative. The mass experience of felt legitimacy here is an aggregation of individual virtue into one righteous body.

This citizenship is defined by a shared virtuous capacity to feel the pain of others, as well as a virtuous capacity to feel the legitimacy of state violence. Feeling the legitimacy of expansive power is what it means to feel like a good citizen, to prove that one deserves to belong on the side of the nationally virtuous. The good citizen feels the legitimacy of war and the Office of Homeland Security. The experience of felt legitimacy enables membership and recognition in the moral nation. In melodrama's moral-affective nexus, the widespread feeling of state legitimacy among citizens becomes the highest proof of American virtue. In the public feeling of legitimacy, the nation's broad legitimation of these expansions stand as a testament to the goodness of the nation. They become the very sign of America's moral virtue. This is why the forms of state power that are legitimated must be easily identifiable: their exercise becomes visual and concrete proof of the nation's morality. Citizenship, through melodramatic modes of felt legitimacy, is not about participation, legality, or contestation; it is about belonging to a nation of virtuous victims who feel that the exercise of expansive and violent state action is an expression of individual, and collective, goodness.

### The Fragility of Melodrama

Melodramatic political discourse, however compelling, also has difficulty sustaining felt legitimation over long periods. Because of the intense codependence of suffering and heroism for generating felt legitimacy, each situation on its own is difficult to maintain over a long span of time. As a result, melodrama's thematic situations and affective intensities are often short-lived. Melodrama's legitimation of heroic retribution cannot be upheld without the repetition of injury by evil—which is why, in literary and filmic forms of melodrama, plotlines fervently employ continuous cycles of victimhood and revenge, pathos and action. Yet in politics this cycle is usually not self-generating, and it tends to unravel without fresh injury; melodrama's instability as a political discourse partly resides in its inability to function without this constant dialectic. The state emotion of legitimacy is only sustained if the nation's virtuous victimization is continuously reinvigorated.

Melodrama's weakness as a long-term political discourse thus belies its robust short-term capability to cultivate legitimation for expansive state power. The constant references to 9/11 by political campaigners for years after the attacks testify to the predicament that occurs when the discourse of melodrama is used as a legitimating tactic. References to the pain, devastation, and injury incited by the 9/11 attacks can revitalize a weakened melodramatic framework for legitimating state power and leaders' decisions, and for justifying the necessity of a sustained militarism. This is partially why a sense of felt legitimacy did not stay firmly with America over the contingencies of the two wars; the moral legitimacy of state power could not be sustained, especially after clear instances of the horrifying nature of "collateral damage," after the revelation of torture and abuse at Abu Ghraib and Guantanamo, and in the wake of the Bush administration's original claim that war was necessary to prevent Iraq's use of weapons of mass destruction, which never existed. The pictures of torture from Abu Ghraib in particular reversed the melodramatic terms of victimhood and villainy, and in some media discourses the images reemplotted the narrative of state power to provide visual validation of America's slippage from victim to villain in a way that weakened felt legitimacy for war more than any other singular event. After Abu Ghraib and other widely publicized violences from the Iraq and Afghanistan wars, including the detainee program at Guantanamo, the political, arbitrary, and disputable dimensions of state action seeped through melodrama's moral imperatives. The repoliticization of state action came about when the dialectic of victimhood and heroism broke down, and, as Habermas would predict, actions previously under the radar—such as the specifics of state regulation and strategies of wartime violence—were opened for a more public and agonistic reevaluation of legitimacy.

The narrative expectations of melodramatic political discourse can be incompatible with the unpredictability and complexities of political life, and as powerful a constitutive force that melodramatic political discourse is when it begins, it can eventually fade out of favor. Its narrative promises that the hero will always succeed in eradicating evil and fear; there may be near misses and close calls, but heroic retribution and the establishment of the nation's mastery over the global order is assumed to be inevitable. The triumphalist worldview cultivated by melodrama requires the nation's heroic success to rarely be in question because the nation's motivation is grounded in innocence and virtue. This is part of what makes felt legitimacy so compelling. In post-9/11 melodrama, America's justification for the war on terror was grounded in moral righteousness, and thus melodramatic expectations for heroic victory asserted that the war would go well, that Americans would be greeted as liberators, and that the postwar reconstruction would be self-generating. The same trope that classified state action as a necessity, as an unquestionable moral imperative, also revealed the fragility of a discourse that could not account for the contingencies of a politics in which the claim of the nation's impeccable virtue would come undone, in which a static moral economy could not maintain its structure, in which the promise of heroic triumph inevitably fails if its goal is to eradicate all experiences of fear. It could even be argued that the state's lack of planning for the possibility of failure was partly because these circumstances existed outside the framework of melodrama's political emplotment.[61] Once the war went badly, and the policies that had previously received widespread legitimacy were reopened for more intense scrutiny, felt legitimacy faded away. Yet felt legitimacy allows citizens to refuse responsibility for legitimacy for these policies. When the feeling of legitimacy fades, it is easy to claim that state actions were made without citizens' formal, express, or deliberative permission. Once the feeling of legitimacy is lost, there is no institutional trace.

Perhaps this was part of the appeal of Barack Obama's candidacy for president—that he was, as the slogan had it, "no-drama Obama."[62] For a nation exhausted by the intensity of melodramatic imperatives, and by their eventual delegitimization, Obama's intentionally modulated affect and rational demeanor seemed to allow people to support him as a way to diminish their accountability for the wars they had earlier supported. This initial turn away from melodrama did not necessarily stop people from turning back to it at many points, however. On the one hand, the right-wing anti-immigration movement drew from a melodramatic discourse to cultivate an overheated sense of victimization for jobless white workers, and found an evil enemy in the Mexican laborers who migrated en masse to the United States after their ability to prosper in Mexico was decimated by NAFTA and other free-trade agreements with the United States. On the other hand, even Obama was asked to capitalize on melodramatic conventions in order to gain legitimacy for his stymied policy proposals. During debates on the Affordable Care Act, for instance, Obama's presentation of numbers and statistics to justify the proposal was hemorrhaging popular support, so the Democratic Party implored him to personalize the problem of the uninsured: he was asked to speak about individual sufferers, people such as young mothers suffering from cancer who could not afford either insurance or treatment. The assumption was that melodramatizing the act would galvanize mass support for it by generating felt legitimacy for its provisions.

The loss of felt legitimacy for the war on terror was not detrimental to the long-term legitimation of state power, however. Melodrama's failed promise of future heroic triumph may also and ironically have functioned to further enable state expansion. Although the failure of America's melodramatic claim to win the war on terror is by now patent, the nation's failure also serves other ends. The larger changes of events in American life after 9/11 are testament to an enormous expansion of varied forms of state power, including provisions created under the Patriot Act, the policies of indefinite detention, warrantless wiretapping and widespread surveillance through social media, the weaponization of governmental functions (e.g., militarized responses to public protest), racial profiling, and the increasing securitization of both public and private space. The institutions affiliated under national security have continued to grow so extensive, dispersed, and corporatized that no one person has full knowledge of how their methods of surveillance operate, or how their information is garnered, categorized, and safeguarded.[63]

A growing worldwide terror network still keeps evil alive and ferocious by maintaining the affective sting of victimhood and may serve in part to sustain the felt legitimacy for the war on terror even as it enters a new phase, operating more through drones than face-to-face combat. The increase in anti-American violence and worldwide rebuke that erupted over the last decade produced myriad new enemies, and therefore helps to sustain America's legitimacy for continuing to extend national-security provisions. The national-security complex now comprises 3,984 federal, state, and local organizations working on domestic counterterrorism alone, including more than two thousand private contracting companies. As the Obama administration's secretary of defense, Robert Gates, himself admitted: "This is a terrible confession. . . . I can't get a number on how many contractors work for the Office of the Secretary of Defense."[64] Without oversight even by the very agencies that employ them, agencies and contractors monitor individual lives, purchases, communications, and activities, to an unprecedented and unaccountable extent. Another way of putting this would be to say that if there are no more terror attacks, then massive expansions of state power are justified. And if there are more terror attacks, then more expansions are required. Either way, power expands both globally and micropolitically.

Perhaps the ongoing war on terror will not, in the end, destroy America's enemies as much as draw sustenance from them for large-scale policies, expansions, and intensifications of power. Melodrama may work best to continually expand militaristic, disciplinary, and surveillant state power mainly by showing and feeling how evil does still exist. The policies that make up the war on terror proliferate the evil and the fear of evil that expansions in state power then aim to eliminate. The failure of the war further reinforces the expansion of state power by generating more evil that state power must then destroy. The more that America is unable to triumph over evil, and the more enemies, insurgents, villains, and terrorists appear, the more money is spent on military action; the more drone strikes operate around the globe; the more regulations are insinuated in domestic- and foreign-security plans; the more maintenance and regulation strategies are outsourced to private companies with no public accountability; the larger the Department of Homeland Security grows; the longer the United States stays in Afghanistan; the more surveillance techniques are in effect by government agencies such as the FBI, NSA, the Department of Defense, and the

CIA; and the more that private surveillance agencies penetrate daily life. This is why evil's polysemy, though conceptually incoherent, is vital to the expansion of power; the mortality of evil demands immediate extensions in state power for its destruction, and yet evil's immortality also demands continued increases to fight an unyielding adversary.

The fragility of melodramatic discourse, then, might do more than diminish felt legitimacy; this fragility might also and at the same time provide conditions for the further extension of state power. The failure to destroy evil, achieve freedom, or eradicate fear, failures that are of course inevitable, are actually the conditions by which governing power expands most rapidly—the failure demonstrates the need to increase state action in order to reverse the failure. Wider expansions and further operations are then required in order to sustain the fight. The fragility of melodrama assists in greater extensions and impingements of power. It is even conceivable that melodrama's principal service to state power is less in its initial felt legitimation than in its failure to wrest freedom from fear. Perhaps in the end the effect of melodrama is not exactly to legitimate expansive power; more precisely the effect of melodrama may be to make the spread of state, military, regulatory, and securitization power less troublesome and more efficient.

### Countermelodramatic Legitimacy: *Three Kings*

Would it be possible for a melodramatic discourse to repoliticize the legitimating process that traffics in uncontestable moral obligation? Can melodramatic conventions explicitly account for how investments in power structure affective experiences of legitimacy? When melodrama's requirement of revictimization to sustain felt legitimacy remains unmet, then space opens for a counterdiscourse that can solicit different affective responses to challenge the legitimation of state power. When felt legitimacy begins to ebb, could the exercise of state power be rearticulated and refelt as a political decision rather than a moral obligation or narrative demand, perhaps even be articulated as an effect of state emotion rather than an "autonomous" judgment? I would like to suggest that possibilities for these shifts can be found, and I turn to film melodrama to see one instance for how melodramatic political discourse, depicted on screen, is deployed to analyze the production of felt legitimacy through more participatory modes of legitimation. *Three Kings* (directed by David O. Russell, 1999) a melodrama about the 1991 Gulf War, works within melodramatic conventions to reveal legitimating processes for certain political actions, in part by delegitimating spectators' expected claims that the actions the film depicts are morally obligatory, and it thus disrupts their naturalized affective support. I focus on *Three Kings* precisely for what it reveals about the repoliticization of legitimation and for how it captures Foucault's claim that designations of legitimacy obscure power relations; but the film moves on in the attempt to make known (in part) what it obscures as part of its legitimating work. *Three Kings* depicts the moral and political complexity lurking in the interstices of any political action, in which the affectively reassuring signposts of moral certitude remain out of range. It does not rest there, however, but uses disorientation to unsettle the audience's generic expectations of felt legitimacy for the state military action the film depicts, even as it acknowledges how felt legitimacy structures any legitimating claim.

*Three Kings* is by no means an antimelodrama, as it still works within melodramatic parameters: the good guys win; the victims are rescued; visual spectacle is employed to reveal morality in unexpected places; a state of virtue is restored by the end of the film; spectators are encouraged to identify with the good guys—and eventually to feel the rightness of their actions. Yet the film consciously employs melodrama's affectively galvanizing rhetoric to instigate a disorienting criticism of the Gulf War, and in particular to condemn felt legitimacy for the political decisions made haphazardly in its aftermath. At the same time, as countermelodrama the film also asks spectators to see and, more important for this chapter, to feel the limitations of melodramatic depictions for legitimating political action. *Three Kings* is a problematic film in many ways: it asserts that individual heroic mastery can right the problems of the world and that state violence can be autocorrecting. It depicts popular stereotyped scenarios in which American heroes rescue grateful third-world victims, the same civilizing discourse that contributes legitimacy to the war on terror. But I offer a reading alongside those depictions that sits uneasily with them, and pulls out the film's challenge to those same melodramatic modes of legitimation. The film's countermelodramatic narrative orients spectators to the ambiguous quality of moral readings for political events, to the limitations of grand imperatives, and to the possibilities for legitimating political action that can arise from this orientation.

The opening shot of *Three Kings* visually begins with a black screen. A title flashes: "March 1991. The War Just Ended." Whereas titles are often meant to center a narrative's actions, this one marks a nebulous moment after action has passed. The title provokes a further decentering as the black space fades into a scene in which the spectator does not view a character or a clear setting; instead the camera takes on a first-person perspective as the spectator's eye becomes the eye of the camera, bouncing through a surreal white landscape. The scene is a physical vacuum, with no markers or signposts to guide viewers for interpreting the scene. The perspective suddenly shifts again to place into view an American soldier sprinting in a desert. This character brings the scene into better focus, yet the initial disarming of expectations, its blank canvas and rapid movement from third person to first person and back again, signals the viewer's entry into unstable terrain. A felt sense of imbalance lingers throughout the scene.

A man soon appears in the distance, but he is too far away to see clearly. The soldier asks an unseen person behind him to clarify the situation:

"Are we shooting?"
"What?"
"Are we shooting people or what?"
"Are we shooting?"
"That's what I am asking you."
"What's the answer?"
"I don't know the answer. That's what I'm trying to find out."

It seems there is no answer: the spatial disorientation is now combined with moral and political disorientations initiated by this unnerving dialogue, which refuses to locate a source of authority to legitimate the violent actions it discusses. Questions abound from the dialogue's resolute antiauthoritarianism: What is the status of this man? Is he the enemy now that the war is over? Is it morally or politically legitimate to shoot him? Who is the soldier talking to and does he have the license to make these decisions? Political markers have been erased, yet the man's identity and the legitimacy of the soldier's action are tethered to them. In wartime, without the political key, the moral map is nonsensical.

The soldier stops shouting and the camera pans a dizzying 180 degrees across the stark desert landscape, creating a further felt unmooring. The camera stops at a few military soldiers in the distance, but they are engaged in an absurd conversation about sand. The soldier is left unguided by moral imperative, felt clarity, or narrative expectation. His next move will be unscripted by the stock military, moral, or political discourses that reveal their limitations in their inability to elucidate a reading or guidepost for this encounter. The mise-en-scène contains the externalization of the soldier's internal discordance. He has become situated in a discomforting position of felt ambiguity.

The soldier looks at the man through his rifle's viewfinder. He sees an Iraqi waving a white flag in one hand yet holding a gun in his other hand, though he is not brandishing it. His intention is unknown, and his two antithetical possibilities make the soldier's options even more unclear. Spectators watch through the viewfinder as the Iraqi notices that the American soldier is pointing a rifle at him and begins to pick up his own gun. His movement restabilizes the soldier: the soldier sees a gun in the hands of a potential enemy and sees that it is about to be pointed toward him. His military expectations come back, his options have diminished, and perhaps he experiences a desire to escape this dizzying state. The soldier shoots and kills the man, recognizing only afterward how his own actions may have provoked the man to hold up his gun, how his choices may have instigated the shooting. Although he experienced the limitations of the discourses governing his understanding of the event, the soldier has no resources at this point to work outside them. The scene ends when he turns away in disgust and shame while his fellow soldiers cheer over the dead man's body.

In this scene, delegitimating tactics work at multiple levels on the spectator to re-process the military action it displays from new affective, visual, and narrative registers. By disrupting the diegetic expectation to center the narrative, the aesthetic register to provide a still and balanced mise-en-scène, and the narrative expectation of an imperative to kill a gun-slinging enemy, the soldier's choices become repoliticized in Habermas's sense of a legitimation crisis. The soldier's motives are the consequence of a series of calculations and decisions that were neither inevitable nor obligatory, nor were they sanctioned by a comforting source of authority (which would also serve to make him free of personal responsibility for the killing). The scene does not provide any final judgment of legitimacy for his action, but instead opens a space where his decision can be easily challenged. The initial ungrounding provides new ground for examining, and feeling, how expected discourses and the confusions they promote contributed to the soldier's action.

In a later scene, the artificiality and fragility of melodramatic legitimation processes are revealed at a site where they are often least questioned: the moment of face-to-face contact with villainy. The American soldier from the first scene, who we now know as Sergeant Barlow, has become a captive of the Iraqi Army. The situation at first seems quite clear: Barlow is tied to a chair with electric wires attached to his ears, and an Iraqi soldier towers over him. Barlow is about to be interrogated by an angry Arab, a familiar trope, and we are primed to feel Barlow's virtue through the unjust suffering he is about to undergo at the hands of a well-worn villain. Yet the interrogating Iraqi soldier begins by asking Barlow questions about Michael Jackson, an absurdity that disarms narrative expectations for the moral clarity of villainy and paves the way for the dialogue that follows. The Iraqi soldier asks Barlow if the Americans are coming back to help the children of Iraq survive after the devastation of war. Barlow responds that they are not, implying that they do not care about those they came to free. The dialogue upends the moral necessity of state action, as American spectators view the decision to go to war from a different angle, one generally not available through official state discourses or media representations that heralded the war as an unqualified achievement of U.S. power. After Barlow admits the callousness of military strategy regarding children, other soldiers begin to apply electric shock to Barlow, which they do while shielding their faces from watching—their disturbed reaction is yet another complication to the assignation of villainy. While there is no condoning of the Iraqi soldiers' actions, this discussion complicates conventional moral coding and felt justification for U.S. intervention.

The Iraqi soldier tells Barlow that the U.S. military bombed his neighborhood, killing his son and paralyzing his wife. The film cuts to split-second scene of the bombing, as a ceiling crashes down over his infant son's crib. The man who first appeared to be the embodiment of evil, the torturing Arab enemy soldier, becomes a spectacular victim who suffers in an overwhelming way from U.S. military action. Barlow, our expected American protagonist—he is the primary focus of the film's attention and is played by the star Mark Wahlberg—commences the film by killing a man and in another scene wants to abandon Iraqi civilians to their certain deaths. Barlow and the Iraqi soldier are part of a larger military apparatus that arbitrarily protects some and kills others. And each is a perpetrator as well as a victim of his government's rhetoric; we hear the Iraqi's empty justification for invading Kuwait, and the American's flimsy explanation for invading Iraq: "for stability," he claims, and "to stabilize the region," not knowing how to describe it any further. In some sense, the two men become interchangeable: who is good now, and who is evil? The answer is neither; both have become too complex for either clumsy designation. *Three Kings* disrupts melodrama's felt legitimation of war—political designations of good and evil become slippery and mutable, and the legitimacy of political action based on the externalization of evil now becomes impossible. The scene is not asking us to reverse the melodrama, to decry America as evil and Iraq as purely good, but instead to observe more perspectival readings that reveal the insufficiency of moral absolutes for legitimating anyone's actions in this scene. This scene does not suggest that legitimating judgments are therefore unachievable, but rather that moral imperatives and conventional narrative expectations are incapable of grasping the complexity of the soldiers' identities, of legitimating their actions, of understanding their motivations in perpetuating state violence.

The film concludes when the American soldiers decide to challenge military protocol and the inattentive commands of official authority to help Iraqis slated for death by Hussein escape to Iran. Throughout the film, the American soldiers debate their possible courses of action. These debates range widely over various engagements, all seen in different lights as legitimate or illegitimate, as rational or absurd, as saturated by different modalities of power, and as tangled within contradictory moral and affective commitments. Yet each possibility uses the specific conditions of their situation as groundwork for generating their justifications. In the end, the soldiers reach their own collective judgment that works within—by pushing out—the boundaries of the military as an institution: they arrange for the media to film their assistance of the Iraqis' escape on live television. This act is illegitimate from the position of military protocol and from the treaty produced at the end of the war between the countries, yet it is potentially legitimate in a felt way for liberal-humanitarian reasons, which the film makes explicit yet also insists are debatable, to the court of world viewers and thus to film spectators. Barlow's disorienting experiences have affectively, morally, and politically challenged his assumptions of what is legitimate action; spectators can presume by the end of the film that his initial experiences subsequently enabled more responsive options to present conditions. While the question of the true legitimacy of this final action remains open, the force of the conclusion resides in the soldiers' collective effort to work through their previously unquestioned expectations in order to arrive at an agonistic decision-making processes in which many possibilities are seriously interrogated.

Even as the soldiers spend much of the film debating their possibilities for enacting or challenging military power, their specific deliberative process for settling on their final action is never revealed. Spectators only learn their decision as it is happening, and there are two ways to read this: that their seemingly democratic decision has its own form of mystification that obscures its political process to makes the final action seem indisputably correct, or that their democratic process does not have one single decisive moment but is grounded in their experiences and arguments throughout the rest of the film, and that the final decision is not clear or easily translatable outside the particular context in which it occurs. All that spectators know is that the soldiers' judgment takes into account the earlier delegitimizing and repoliticizing experiences they worked through, and that this judgment incorporates perspectives throughout the rest of the film on different modes of felt legitimation that could be read into their actions from different social standpoints. The process for achieving their final action seems to incorporate a delegitimization of stock expectations for legitimacy and an acknowledgment of the investments of power that structure different possible legitimating claims. Their process suggests that the practice of agonistic deliberation can be tied to a reckoning with state power in both its repressive and productive capacities.

Of course, the soldiers do not become miraculously self-transparent in their ability to trace the normative and affective commitments underpinning the felt legitimacy they construct for their final action. Yet they remain open to various claims of legitimacy that will be differently placed upon their action by the media, the military, humanitarian interventionists, Iraqi refugees, their spouses, and the court of media viewers, diegetic and extradiegetic. And the soldiers accept the consequences of their action without knowing what the predominant determinant of legitimacy will be in order to do what they eventually decide is the right option, with the hope that their justification for its legitimacy will appeal to others as well. They choose to prioritize the plight of the refugees over military law and, perhaps, their own physical freedom. Their action is not depicted in typical heroic fashion as a selfless gesture; the men are trying to avoid jail time. It is an action shaped by the impetus of intersecting powers, conflicting options, and the desire to do good, combined with the desire to further their own individual gain and escape punishment.

Yet the legitimacy of the American soldiers' action isn't ultimately left completely open. The felt legitimacy for their action is solicited in spectators in many ways: by the swelling music that marks their final action, by the expressions of gratitude performed by the refugees, by the conventional narrative the action deploys that upholds the rescue of non-Western victims by American heroes, by melodramatic expectations that offer that identifying with subordinated Others brings about a better world (in this case, the soldier's identification with the refugees), by the broader norms of antiauthoritarianism in American individualism that the soldiers embody when they buck military strictures, and by the desperate plea that underlies the end of this movie—the belief that Americans can do good after all, a belief that works in part to cancel out the horrors of the Gulf War. All of these legitimating tactics are on display. The action to rescue the refugees feels legitimate to the soldiers, and the film aims to solicit the same felt experience in spectators, but it also seems to cultivate a feeling of legitimacy that recognizes competing rationalities for other actions, that disrupts expected affects, virtuous identities, and moral tales. The film keeps the characters' motivations complex rather than pure, murky rather than transparent, disorienting rather than restabilizing, specific to their situation rather than universally implementable.

The countermelodrama of *Three Kings* offers one example for establishing more-agonistic processes in generating the felt legitimacy of state power. It does not provide one final answer for how to mark the best and most equitable form of legitimacy, and suggests, as Weber does, that no consideration of legitimacy could ever be absolute or final. But it does acknowledge that the sanction of state power is not prediscursive, decided by autonomous actors, available for gut intuition, or outside the constraints of power, but a product and an exercise of power, discourse, and the affective circulations between state discourse and individual action, between those offering judgments and the events they judge. *Three Kings* demonstrates a form of legitimacy that can partly reveal the effects of its own obfuscation, and can work this revelation into the process for collectively authorizing action. At the end of the film, the soldiers' decisions are still comfortably within and limited by melodrama's genre expectations for moral goodness and heroic rescue. Yet by questioning the melodramatic imperatives that first condition their expectations, the soldiers eventually disentangle themselves from some of these expectations and think outside their initial possibilities for political action. In *Three Kings* felt legitimacy is repoliticized. Its complex sources are acknowledged and harnessed for, rather than against, agonistic decision making and collaborative action.

# FOUR

# ORGIES OF FEELING

*Terror, Agency, and the Failures of the (Neo)Liberal Individual*

Melodramatic political discourses often legitimate expansive forms of state power, yet this alone does not explain why so many people would accept this legitimacy or support these expansions. Melodramas work on and through political subjects in complex ways that differ from how public, official, or state political discourses and popular news-media practices might intend. In the last chapter, I argued that melodramatic discourses cultivate a felt legitimation of state power. In this chapter and the next I turn to the political subjects who might feel this legitimacy or take part in the strategies of melodramatic politics. Film scholars define melodrama as a genre that produces a deep investment in suffering, pathos, and victimization, a genre in which suffering is heightened and experienced viscerally; in this chapter I trace the translation of these investments into modalities of political subjectivity. If, as Janet Staiger argues, melodrama is a "genre of affect" that offers "a location for laying out the emotional landscapes of the public sphere," then what do melodramatic political discourses tell us about the emotional landscapes of contemporary political subjectivity?[1] I argue that people who are compelled by melodrama may accept its legitimation of state action, but they also harness melodrama's genre conventions and affective investments for their own fantasies and desires. Melodrama seems to offer something different to the subjects invested in its depictions: the promise of freedom. And this promise of freedom takes shape through an *orgy of feeling* that subsumes chronic experiences of suffering into a singular spectacle of nationwide victimization, and proclaims a coming freedom for those who suffer.

The term *orgies of feeling* describes a dynamic in which overwhelming affects displace more routinized experiences of suffering. The term is Friedrich Nietzsche's, who uses it to pinpoint how intensified emotions can relocate confusing feelings of pain and powerlessness onto a new and more forceful experience of victimization. Orgies of feeling cultivate spectacular, agonizing, and shocking affects upon the sufferer, paradoxically inhibiting the original suffering by imposing more violent emotions over it. Nietzsche writes, "An *orgy of feeling* . . . [is] employed as the most effective means of deadening dull, paralyzing, protracted pain."[2] Orgies of feeling "deaden" dull and protracted experiences of pain by inflicting new pain upon the suffering subject. They aim "to wrench the human soul from its moorings, to immerse it in terrors, ice, flames, and raptures to such an extent that it is liberated from all petty displeasure, gloom, and depression by a flash of lightning."[3] Orgies of feeling overpower the initial pain and relocate its cause onto a new scene of intensified victimization by "a flash of lightning." Enfolding pain within a new narrative, orgies of feeling explain where the pain previously experienced as "paralyzing" now comes from, and then they aim to "liberate" the sufferer from its binds. For Nietzsche, orgies of feeling attend to specific types of protracted pain, those that seem to have no clear origin or reason behind them, and therefore put the sufferer in a position of powerlessness in relation to them. The lack of a reason for suffering creates an agonizing sense of helplessness over one's own life conditions; according to Nietzsche, this type of helplessness is a form of unfreedom. Orgies of feeling aim to gain power over causes for suffering and thus experience freedom; orgies express a desire for "this rare freedom, this power over oneself and over fate."[4] Orgies of feeling manage the suffering that arises from diminished possibilities for freedom by both offering a new explanation for suffering and implying that pain will soon be overpowered by a "liberated" self.

Orgies of feeling can help to describe the dynamic and affective work of melodramatic political discourse. Melodrama's heightened affects might be appealing to political subjects precisely because those affects offer a way to explain and overcome the protracted pains and "dull" paralysis in daily lives saturated by myriad and unaccountable forms of power. In contemporary politics melodramas solicit powerful affects through heightened scenes of victimization, which may seem to offer political subjects the ability to overcome long-standing feelings of suffering and ineffectiveness. Recent global shifts in the past few decades that shape daily life in the United States—such as increasing inequality, decreasing possibilities for political participation, the virtualization and rapid expansion of capital markets, climate change, globalizing norms for individual behavior and personal demeanor, multinational consolidations of political and extralegal power that further demobilize the political and economic agency of nonelites, mass immigration, global terrorism, and resource scarcity—all generate increasing experiences of vulnerability, precariousness, and distress across populations. Melodrama enfolds the paralyzing pain produced by these shifts into genre expectations that presume virtue and freedom for people who suffer. This new narrative implies that the new and orgiastic victimization will signal the end of commonplace experiences of pain that seem to have no singular site of origin or easily identifiable source of blame. Through melodrama, heightened experiences of injury and suffering offer a way for political subjects to manage the daily impotence and precarity of contemporary life by promising that new and intense affects will eventually enable their rightful, and unburdened, agency.

In post-9/11 melodrama in particular, the story of terrorism becomes the site of that displacement. The terror attack becomes the singular act of injury that orgiastically overwhelms and displaces experiences of fear and unfreedom commonplace in a neoliberal era. Through melodrama's orgies of feeling, the painful feelings of victimization that Americans endured on September 11 could seem to be a mechanism for overcoming daily experiences of vulnerability and diminished agency. The end of terror would herald the instantiation of power and freedom. Orgies of feeling offer one way to read the circulation of suffering in post-9/11 melodrama, as they articulate how melodrama might be appealing precisely because its heightened affects seem to offer the overcoming of unfreedoms that extend beyond and behind 9/11 into the fabric of daily life. Melodrama's orgies of feeling suggested that once terrorism is punished, killed, or overcome, individuals' commonplace experiences of foundering agency will be eradicated and their rightful freedom restored. The historical moment of post-9/11 terror contributes to the formation of a melodramatic political subjectivity that is novel and yet rooted in decades of demobilization. Through melodrama, the war on terror carries the implicit promise to overcome the vulnerability and despondency of everyday life in a globalized, neoliberal-capitalist, and manifestly unequal social order.

But the story of debilitated agency is more complex than this. In addition, melodrama's orgies of feeling are also directly related to a crisis in freedom as articulated in liberal individualism. Popular conventions of liberal individualism, especially within American politics, have generally held to the creed that individuals can be free from power, that they are independent of one another and of society in the first and last instances, and that by right individuals should be self-determining masters of their own destiny. The 9/11 events, no less than daily experiences of felt powerlessness, undermine this creed. Yet within individualism, especially in its neoliberal variants, the uncertainty, isolation, and limitations endemic to contemporary life are experienced by the individual not as effects of myriad and intensifying forms of power but as a personal failure to achieve freedom. The political subject of neoliberal individualism continually suffers the apprehension, anxiety, and torment of the failure to live up to the norms of the sovereign and self-reliant subject. The model of freedom that this type of individualism projects generates a norm of masterful sovereignty that is outmoded at best for understanding contemporary power and freedom, given not only the new world order of post-9/11 politics but also the more long-standing conditions of demobilized, overworked, undersupported, exploited, and overextended citizenries, and the general sense of helplessness produced by the disemboweling of liberal democracy. Neoliberal individualism thus *contributes* to individuals' lack of agency by misdiagnosing or disavowing the organization of powers arrayed through and against people, rendering their attempts to experience agency ineffective and self-defeating. Melodrama's orgies of feeling thus aim to overcome not only experiences of unfreedom but also the affects of their disavowal in neoliberal individualism. By promising to overcome unfreedom through intensified affect, melodrama's orgies of feeling address experiences of unfreedom that originate from 9/11 and the material conditions of the larger moment, and also from the inability to address these experiences in any fundamental way within the terms of neoliberal individualism that often dominate American political discourse.

Yet as Nietzsche would note, melodrama's orgiastic mechanisms for overcoming unfreedom find false sites of accountability for the original experiences of paralysis and pain, blaming terrorism rather than the broader structures of power and norms too complex and enigmatic to be easily overcome. Orgies of feeling thus further debilitate American political subjects shaped by expectations of sovereign freedom as an entitlement, making them even less able to grapple with the dizzying constellation of contemporary powers contributing to their felt experiences of ineffectiveness, nonsovereignty, and constraint. Melodrama's orgies of feeling catalyze the promise of sovereign agency but entrench the impotence and unfreedom their affects are deployed to overcome.

## Orgies of Feeling

Nietzsche's analysis of orgies of feeling in *On the Genealogy of Morals* offers a starting point for scrutinizing how a melodramatic narrative of national victimization might arise out of a desire to overcome unfreedom.[5] The term *orgies of feeling* describes how intense affects can be deployed to overwhelm more mundane experiences of pain and ineffectiveness, and the story he tells begins with an analysis of victimization. Nietzsche examines affective experiences of victimization that are bred of vulnerability to power, of an inability to express one's own desire and control one's external world. He argues that the experience of vulnerability to power produces intense suffering, and that this experience is a form of unfreedom. For Nietzsche, a claim of victimization works to point out an injustice or unfreedom in confusing experiences of powerlessness, as it locates blame for unfreedom in an evil enemy. Nietzsche links suffering to unfreedom, pain to powerlessness, and these links shape his understanding of the affective experience of power. The claim of one's victimization turns a confusing experience of pain and vulnerability into a scene of unfreedom. In Nietzschean terms, a diagnosis of victimization conceives a *doer* for the *deed* that causes one's feeling of powerlessness. He writes, "For every sufferer instinctively seeks a cause for his suffering; more exactly, an agent; still more specifically, a *guilty* agent who is susceptible to suffering."[6] Locating a site of blame, a villain, for an experience of diminished power satisfies the deep need to find a specific cause for this experience, and thus to possibly fight back or gain power over it. Further, finding blame also implies that there is, in fact, a villainous deed that causes one to experience stymied agency as a form of injury. Through a diagnosis of victimization, a confusing sense of powerlessness becomes an intentional harm committed by a specific agent.

The claim of victimization, therefore, arises from the impulse of resistance to oppressive power.[7] The claim condemns subjugating experiences and finds agents accountable for them. To find a doer for the deed of suffering, according to Nietzsche, is a way to oppose forms of power that limit, wound, or condition the self. By identifying an agent responsible for one's feeling of subjugation, the claim of victimization aims to shift relations of power. It is a claim for power against power, a desire that originates from those who feel bound by unjust forces. The claim works in part because victimhood revalues an experience of powerlessness as something undergone by a morally just and virtuous subject: to be a victim is also to be morally superior to what has caused one's suffering. The claim of victimization is thus a revolt that censures forms of power and agency interpreted as controlling or constraining, as they are now revalued as evil, wrong, unjust, and injurious. Arising out of the fear, pain, and anxiety that develop from a feeling of boundedness, the claim of victimization condemns experiences of social suffering and critiques the established conditions that would perpetuate these experiences.

Sometimes, however, the cause of one's feeling of powerlessness is elusive; one feels constrained or oppressed, yet no clear agent of oppression can be found. This is where orgies of feeling come in. Sometimes one experiences the *feeling* of victimization without knowing where that experience originates or who can be held accountable. Certain forms of power do not have a single agentic cause or site of accountability (especially, I would add, those produced at the nexus of capitalism, liberalism, and state power, including governmentality, biopower, and networked modes of social control, as well as many others that shape the late modern era). Their complex and nebulous functions produce unfreedom, constraint, violence, injury, and unease, yet they seem to have no locatable origin or no identifiable oppressor. When there is no easily marked doer for the deed of suffering induced by powerlessness, Nietzsche tells us, then not knowing what causes one's suffering generates even greater pain than the initial experience of suffering. Nietzsche writes, "[Man's] problem was *not* suffering itself, but that there was no answer to the crying question, '*Why* do I suffer?'"[8] In other words, the suffering caused by diminished power is not unbearable per se, but it becomes unbearable when it seems to have no responsible agent, no locatable source.

Orgies of feeling arise in response to painful experiences that produce a felt powerlessness because they do not have a clear source. In an orgy of feeling, a new experience of victimization arises to generate a new source when none is readily apparent. This new victimization is more intense, and thus displaces the confusing sense of subjugation by overwhelming it. According to Nietzsche, orgies of feeling overwhelm a dull and commonplace experience of pain that has become paralyzing by inflicting greater pain on the subject. Nietzsche describes them as "a desire to *deaden pain by means of affects.* . . . It is to *deaden*, by means of a more violent emotion of any kind, a tormenting, secret pain that is becoming unendurable, and to drive it out of consciousness at least for the moment: for that one requires an affect, as savage an affect as possible."[9] Orgies of feeling attenuate a protracted pain that seems unnamable, unlocatable, and without attribution. The claim of a new victimization generates a new injury that deadens the earlier "secret" and "unendurable" experience. Operating not as a cure but as an anesthetic, an opiate rather than penicillin, orgies of feeling deaden an initial hurt by unleashing strong affects on and within the subject, as an overpowering, surprise attack. "As savage an affect as possible" drives the initial pain out of consciousness. Orgies of feeling are, Nietzsche writes, an "affect medication."[10]

Orgies of feeling do not just name the doer for the deed of unfreedom; they also *generate a specific deed in order to find a doer*. Orgies of feeling attach to new experience of victimization in order to actively create a cause for confusing experiences of vitiated agency when none is readily apparent and thus find something accountable for the suffering one endures. This new experience of suffering and pain has an easily identifiable cause. Orgies of feeling displace the original experience of "secret pain" because they have a clear agent responsible for their affective frenzy. Orgies of feeling thus have a dual function: to displace the original pain by overwhelming it and to provide an agent, a source, responsible for them. They produce a new wound, and this new wound has a doer who causes a clear injurious deed. Offering a narrative of the pain caused by powerlessness, orgies of feeling describe what causes one's new feeling of suffering, explains why it happened, and thus offers a location for one to focus one's energies for overcoming pain. In this sense, the feeling of powerlessness loses its confusion because it now has an identifiable agent. This identifiable source both alleviates the confusion of why suffering exists and identifies a source that can be fought against and overcome. Seemingly so awful, orgies of feeling make suffering manageable by offering a narrative about its origins.

Nietzsche may at first seem to devalue, sexualize, and feminize heightened emotional displays with the term *orgy*, perhaps implicitly contrasting it to a desexualized rationality or masculinized stoicism. But Nietzsche's celebration of Dionysian characters in *The Birth of Tragedy* and other texts makes *orgies* a more complex term: it explicitly equates to an overwhelming celebration of life, an intense appeal to power that belies what might first appear to be the term's condemnation of orgiastic affects as vulgar.[11] In *Twilight of the Idols*, Nietzsche writes of "the psychology of the orgy as an overflowing feeling of life and energy within which even pain acts as a stimulus."[12] An orgy is both a destructive and yet creative and life-affirming force, which accords with Nietzsche's similarly complex view of *ressentiment* as creative and "yes saying" even in its mobilization of venom and bitterness.

Yet because orgies of feeling only offer false sources of accountability for their underlying suffering rather than rooting out its source, their overflowing feeling of life though the stimulus of pain only temporarily displaces the underlying affective experience of suffering. They cannot eradicate the initial feelings they displace because orgies of feeling do not address the real cause of these feelings; they only postpone or push the feelings away for brief periods of time. Eventually, the quest for attenuation becomes a continuous desire to experience orgies of feeling, in hopes that their overwhelming affect can repeatedly displace the nagging original pain. For Nietzsche, "one no longer protested against pain, one *thirsted* for pain; 'more pain! *more pain!*'"[13] The ability to identify a cause for suffering and thus contribute to its temporary alleviation makes the pain of orgiastic victimization desirable. It is an expression of an overflowing feeling of life, even as this mechanism for attenuating powerlessness never fully achieves its aims.

Nietzsche initially seems to suggest that orgies of feeling are motivated by humanity's existential fear of meaninglessness, rather than powerlessness, as if the reason that the underlying pain is so unendurable is only because it seems to have no reason behind it. He writes, "The meaninglessness of suffering, *not* suffering itself, was the curse that lay over mankind so far."[14] However, I would suggest that Nietzsche is not making a claim about humanity's innate or existential need for meaning; he is instead pointing toward a specific form of power that expresses itself through epistemology. The search for a meaning for suffering is a search for *power* expressed as a desire to understand and control one's life conditions. It is part of the desire to be powerful, to experience self-determination, to resist external domination, to fight situations of dependence.[15] Nietzsche explains the origins of orgies of feeling as such: "Man, suffering from himself in some way or another but in any case physiologically like an animal shut up in a cage, uncertain why or wherefore, thirsting for reasons—reasons relieve."[16] The lack of a reason for suffering creates an agonizing sense of powerlessness over one's own life conditions, a powerlessness over setting the terms and limits of one's formations, and a failure to interpret the intent of suffering and consequently to find ways to challenge it. Caging that has no specific, locatable reason means that one cannot figure out how to escape it, and thus has no control over it—and for Nietzsche a sufferer cannot relieve that suffering without first knowing its source.

This becomes more clear when reading the passage on the caged and uncertain subject alongside one in *Will to Power*, in which Nietzsche explains what inspires the desire to find meaning: "Interpretation is itself a means of becoming master in something."[17] The search to find meaning, to interpret phenomena, to find reasons for one's constraint, are all aspects of the desire for "becoming master," to resist unendurable experiences of powerlessness in part by controlling the epistemological field in which they are made legible. The metaphor of a cage, one that physiologically constrains and binds a confused and unknowing subject, highlights how a desire for power undergirds the desperate search for reasons to explain one's painfully felt sense of lost agency. Interpreting the feeling of cage-like constraint as an intentional victimization is a way to make sense of one's felt experience of oppression, to identify its cause and source of responsibility: this is an act of resistance to constraint, an expression of a desire for freedom, with the eventual goal of mastery over one's life conditions. The desire for orgies of feeling stems, Nietzsche writes, from a subject "which tries by all means to sustain itself and to fight for its existence. . . . Precisely he is among the greatest *conserving* and yes-creating forces of life."[18] Orgies of feeling have a specific goal: to fight for and control the conditions governing one's existence.

## 9/11 as an Orgy of Feeling

I read the nationwide affective response to 9/11 as an orgy of feeling, one encouraged and developed through melodramatic political discourse. The 9/11 attacks induced a series of painful and intense affects across the population, which circulated between individual and national sentiment. On one level the intense affects were a direct response to the mass violence of the terrorist attacks. These affects included a sense of helpless vulnerability to monstrous evil, empathic identifications with the wounded, angered cries for retributive violence, shock at the scope of the terrorists' violence, powerlessness at the inability to control it, and panicked terror of impending personal and civilizational destruction. A *New York Times* letter writer expressed this general sentiment the day after the attacks: "Shock. Anger. Terror. Confusion. Unspeakable sadness. Grief. Fear. These are just some of the emotions Americans are feeling today in the wake of the monstrous terrorist attacks on the United States."[19] But on another level, these affects also derived from widespread depictions of the attacks though melodramatic genre conventions. Melodramatic political discourse made legible the experience of helplessness against overwhelming forces through its narrative and affective form, which dramatized impotence and linked the expression of heightened suffering to virtue.[20] Melodramatic political discourse depicted the attacks and Americans' felt experience of them in a viscerally intense language that also solicited the suffering it described.[21]

The intensity of post-9/11 affective states was not only an instinctive response to a horrifying event but also, in part, an effect of political discourses that depicted the 9/11 events through melodrama's heightened emotional conventions of pathos, shock, distress, and virtue.[22] Consider the media coverage of the attacks examined in chapter 1, or the political speeches examined in chapter 3. Or consider the very first lines of the front-page article in the *New York Times* from September 12, 2001:

> It kept getting worse. The horror arrived in episodic bursts of chilling disbelief, signified first by trembling floors, sharp eruptions, cracked windows. There was the actual unfathomable realization of a gaping, flaming hole in first one of the tall towers, and then the same thing all over again in its twin. There was the merciless sight of bodies helplessly tumbling out, some of them in flames. Finally, the mighty towers themselves were reduced to nothing. Dense plumes of smoke raced through the downtown avenues, coursing between the buildings, shaped like tornadoes on their sides.

Opening with a forceful and terrifying description of 9/11, this article depicts the events through a written melodramatic tableau that evokes overwhelming power, astonishment, and extreme pathos, and that describes terrible injury and unfathomable horror through visceral imagery and a narrative of heightened suspense. The emotional tone of this reporting doesn't merely represent but *contributes* to the intensity of post-9/11 affective states. This is not to claim that the events were not distressing, or that terrorism would otherwise be experienced in a more emotionally flattened fashion if not for melodrama, but to inquire about the political work of melodrama's affective intensities. By reading them as an orgy of feeling, I argue that they seemed to displace more long-standing experiences of unfreedom and vulnerability onto the 9/11 attacks, which were imagined as the new site of origin for felt experiences of impotence. Situating terrorism as the primary source of contemporary powerlessness revealed a more frantic and orgiastic search to invent a singular cause for the forms of unfreedom that condition political life, of which terrorism is only one part. Melodrama's affective intensity worked as a promise to restore a vitalized agency to individuals and the state beyond the singular experience of terror.

While vulnerability, fear, and helplessness were effects of the 9/11 events, as well as effects of their mediated representation, they are also common and even daily political experiences that extend far beyond the singular effects of 9/11 or terrorism. Through melodrama, common and less potent but still tormenting experiences of ineffective agency—that are systemic in political worlds organized by unfathomable corporate power, state penetration, and the priority of profit over human flourishing, and which can seem to have no clear agent—were displaced onto a clear and familiar narrative of victimization and heroism that also offered a blameworthy villain. Melodramatic depictions of nationwide victimization made the terror of 9/11 manageable by naming the event's injustice and locating a source of blame, and they were also appealing to political subjects because their affective intensity overwhelmed more daily experiences of felt pain: what Nietzsche calls orgies of feeling's capacity to liberate "all petty displeasure, gloom, and depression by a flash of lightning." Feelings of paralysis, terror, impotence, and horror came to a head on September 11, but their affective resonances were decades in the making.

The "cause" of 9/11—terrorism—stood in for a much wider array of forces that produce the feelings of powerlessness shaping political subjectivity. As power has become increasingly globalized while ordinary individuals' ability to shape and participate in it has been continually truncated, experiences of what I call *unfreedom* have intensified and broadened across populations. Individuals are precariously positioned within global networks of power, impinged upon by multiple forces and relations that delimit subjectivity and agency in ways more systemic and unrecognizable than earlier political moments.[23] Unfreedom defines a set of conditions in which distant problems are selectively exposed but rarely imagined to have real solutions; in which power is often nonagentic and deinstitutionalized yet still experienced as a concrete and painful form of domination; in which global economic networks generate widespread reliance upon people, corporations, and structures of provision neither known nor understood; in which access to political decision making has become increasingly consolidated and ever more remote and inaccessible to ordinary citizens; in which corporations are persons and persons are commodities compelled to maximize their own value; in which overexposure to unyielding digitized quantities of news, tidbits, and facts breeds a kind of hyperstimulation fatigue that is at once addictive and exhausting; in which rigid behavioral norms have intensified, impinging more deeply into people and binding them ever more tightly to a limited set of expressive options; and in which governmental institutions merge with private companies to breed labyrinthine yet contingent structures of bureaucratic life support that simultaneously extinguish more sustainable sources of care.

Teresa Brennan diagnoses the contemporary era as "the destruction of life conditions for human beings." This destruction is wrought out of industrial and nuclear accidents, mounting debts, corporate nonaccountability, cuts in welfare and education, and industrial and postindustrial capital's often destructive effects on climate, livelihood, and labor markets.[24] These conditions generate a series of terrors that overlays the cheapening of human life, and Brennan names the experiences of these conditions the "terrors of globalization." These terrors are experienced in differentiated ways across the globe, depending on states' and people's positions of power and privilege in the transnational economy. In the United States, where the terrors of globalization come up against a culture also shaped by expectations of sovereignty as a national entitlement, this plays out through what Timothy Melley characterizes as "agency panic," a "sense of diminished human agency [that reveals an] intense anxiety about an apparent loss of autonomy or self-control." Agency panic is the product of a contemporary moment in which subjects who understand themselves to be sovereign find themselves defenseless against subjugating forces and at the same time unable to figure out the agent behind those forces; they are unable "to map networks of power too vast to be adequately represented."[25]

Experiences of unfreedom, agency panic, and the terrors of globalization are not only frightening but also confusing, as their causes can be difficult to discern.[26] They are often produced out of nonagentic forms of power, in which power seems invisible even as it impinges into subjects and even as it circulates as micropolitical affective dispositions as well as macropolitical networks of global force. Michel Foucault argues that the twentieth century witnessed myriad political struggles, from women's rights to patients' rights, which when combined point to a general struggle against new forms of unaccountable power—forms that, far from cultivating autonomy, aim to forge individuals into regularized, manageable, "normal" subjects. He writes that these struggles are resisting powers significantly more complex than "authority." Instead, "this form of power applies itself to immediate everyday life which categorizes the individual, marks him by his own individuality, attaches him to his own identity, imposes a law of truth on him which he must recognize and which others have to recognize in him. It is a form of power which makes individuals subjects."[27] In Foucault's diagnosis of twentieth-century subjectivity, subjects are increasingly formed by regulation and governance of the body; this type of power is often nonagentic and yet it still exercises a wide variety of techniques that gradually penetrate into ever more minute forms of daily life, not only normalizing but producing individual behavior. Jeffrey Nealon brings Foucault's diagnosis of subjectification into the twenty-first century, arguing that regulatory and normalizing forms of power are becoming even more minute, less obvious, more efficient, and more intense in their circumscription of action within a narrowing range of political agency.[28] Affecting people to significantly varying degrees depending on economic class, geographic location, gender, race, immigration status, ethnicity, disability, and religion, these shifts produce uneven yet widespread experiences of atomization, constraint, dependence, and exclusion. They are caused by global forces, and also, for the relatively more privileged, especially in America, by a sense of slipping freedom, by a potent nostalgia that wants the future to be a return to a mythic golden age in which privilege seemed secure and individual freedom seemed guaranteed.

Melodrama's orgies of feeling arising out of 9/11 overwhelmed these more routinized, different, and daily experiences of unfreedom and unaccountable injury. Capitalizing on the fraught experience of terrorism and the horrors it produced, melodrama displaced the confusions of more commonplace forms of diminished agency onto a singular terrorist action that created a dramatic spectacle of nationwide suffering, a suffering caused by a clearly defined external enemy attacking America. Melodrama is particularly well suited for this work. Christine Gledhill writes, "[Melodrama] attests to forces, desires, fears which . . . appear to operate in human life independently of any rational experience"; and then melodrama reemplots them onto its dramatic narrative story that clearly identifies victimization and redemption.[29] Melodrama's ability to clarify social complexity, as Gledhill notes, is one of its most important attributes: it "organizes the disparate sensory phenomena, experiences, and contradictions of [society] . . . in visceral, affective, and morally explanatory form."[30] Post-9/11 melodrama worked in this vein to flatten, generalize, and displace more complex and differentially allocated forms of vulnerability and unfreedom directly onto the 9/11 events. It named a cause for these experiences: the evil enemy of terror. This enemy could be easily verified, which also meant that it could be eliminated through national heroic force. The orgiastic displacement of lived unfreedom was possible because 9/11 dramatized and intensified experiences of unfreedom and fear in a spectacular and unavoidable way: the death and destruction of 9/11 forced many Americans to confront the experience of radical vulnerability, nonsovereignty, and defenselessness to contingent events, and this worked partly because confronting a namable, identifiable evil (even one as conceptually hazy as terrorism, a tactic more than an agent) seemed more achievable than confronting a chaotic and confusing range of structures, networks, and relations of power that affects individuals in different ways.

This affective work did not assume that the terror arising from 9/11 was equivalent to the daily injuries of neoliberal and bureaucratic capitalism—as Nietzsche notes, the frenzied pain of "terrors, ice, flames, and raptures" is not of the same order of magnitude as the "petty displeasure, gloom, and depression" it displaces. And the hyperstimulation fatigue that comes from endless sifting through the Internet in search of ways to make sense of (or escape from) the world is of a different order than the exhaustion and fear that come from trying to support a family with two low-wage jobs, which is different from the despair of a college graduate with insurmountable debt who is unable to find paid work. Yet orgies of feeling can show how those encountering each of these very different experiences might find it appealing to attach to the melodrama of national discourse in order to capitalize on its displacement of devitalized agency and promise of future freedom.

As Gledhill writes, "Melodrama [can] bring together the grandiose and the banal."[31] Here varying "banal" experiences of daily vulnerability and ineffectiveness are brought together under a grandiose narrative of terrorist villainy and heroic overcoming. We can see the discrepancy between the grandiose and the banal play out in the very terms of melodramatic political discourse: between the grandiose negative affect used to organize state action at this time (the war on terror) and the goal of these actions in Bush's speech "Freedom at War with Fear" (to banish the commonplace experience of fear). In this discourse that substitutes fear for terror, the massive mobilizations categorized as the war on terror intended to banish general experiences of fear. The promise of overcoming unfreedom means overcoming fear itself, overcoming familiar affects that attend to experiences of vulnerability and impotence. In fact, the discrepancy between terror and fear is part of the necessary strategy of orgies of feeling, in the way it intensifies, elaborates, and magnifies "terror, ice, flames, and raptures" in order to displace commonplace experiences. The confusing causality of those common experiences is precisely what enables orgies of feeling able to work in this way.

Through depictions of evil and terror, melodrama offered a clear and agentic source of responsibility for daily feelings of vitiated agency. Nietzsche writes of orgies of feeling that the sufferer "seeks a cause for his suffering; for exactly an agent; still more specifically, a guilty agent who is susceptible to suffering—in short, some living thing upon which he can, on some pretext or another, vent his affects."[32] By making terrorism the agent responsible for the condensed experiences of contemporary subjectivity, post-9/11 melodrama made terrorism a "doer" ("evil-doer") for the "deed" of daily unfreedom.[33] How did this work? Melodrama's orgies of feeling ameliorated the suffering that attaches to daily unfreedoms in three ways: first, by overpowering the older and less intense pain with more intense affects; second, by naming a responsible agent, a villain, who could be the source of the new pain; and third, by promising to end feelings of lost agency with grandiose claims of heroic mastery over terror. As one of the most infamous lines of post-9/11 presidential rhetoric framed the matter: "Grief has turned to anger, and anger to resolution."[34] This narrative of the war on terror tracks the orgiastic melodramatic trajectory: painful vulnerability and grief gives way to the empowerment of anger, and anger lays the groundwork for a new form of agency, resolution to go to war and win the war on terror—indeed, to triumph over all socially produced affective experiences of fear.

Melodrama's orgies of feeling aim to fight acute domination in a specific way; they draw on the melodramatic character of the victim who becomes the hero to describe the national political subject. The orgiastic feeling of victimization is thus not the final end point of the melodrama; the feeling leads up to the promise that the victim will become the hero and gain mastery over the agent that caused the injury. Then, in promising heroic emancipation from evil villainy, melodrama implies that this will solve all experiences of political powerlessness (a dynamic I explore further in the following chapter). And within melodrama the more the victim suffers, the stronger and more justified heroic action will become. The victim-hero is a self-rescuing sufferer who moves from wounding to triumph, impotence to power, and vulnerability to self-mastery. In welding heroism to victimhood, the injured victim can draw on its own strength to overcome the source of its obstructed power. The claim of victimization diagnoses experiences of suffering from unfreedom, and the claim of heroism promises a conclusive triumph over one's unfreedom through a singular, strong, willful, autonomous, and overpowering act.

Part of what makes orgies of feeling so compelling, indeed so ameliorative, is their presumed ability to *limit* affects that attach to the underlying paralysis. Melodramatic constructions of the 9/11 events insist that the American public's experience of overwhelming affects was contingent, limited to the injury of terrorism. The shock, anger, terror, and confusion explicated in the letter to the *New York Times*—the felt experiences of victimization by unknown forces—could now be overcome because their cause was located: terrorism. Orgies of feeling thus reconfigure what it means to suffer from the effects of political action. Melodramatic boundaries of legible victimization exclude social suffering not explicitly caused by terrorism. Suffering from poverty and structural economic inequality, global violence, the routinized effects of racism and sexism, blocked access to governing power, Islamophobia, the degradation of community fabric and wholesale destruction of the environment, anti-immigration violence, the experience of cage-like constraint at the hands of bureaucratic and corporate institutions, agency panic, and the terrors of globalization are all generally unmarked in the story cultivated by orgies of feeling, in which terrorist villains harm a formerly sovereign national subject. Contributing to these distinctions are post-9/11 melodrama's discursive conceptualizations of what causes suffering—terrorism, not war; hijacking, not daily impingements of power; al-Qaeda, not ordinary experiences of living on the edge; Osama bin Laden, not daily experiences of embedded racism and sexism. Melodrama's orgies of feeling circumscribe the boundaries of suffering's legibility by insisting on immutable distinctions between victimhood and villainy and between good and evil. If it is not victimization by a clearly identifiable evil villain, then politically inflicted suffering is irrelevant to the suffering addressed through post-9/11 melodramatic political discourse.

In an effort to alleviate a suffering bred by weakness and vulnerability, orgies of feeling thus misdirected responses and limited potential solutions to the problems of unfreedom they were employed to eradicate. The bitter irony after 9/11 was that the very site of blame itself—terror—could not be located, existing as a tactic and an affect more than a person. Even the eventual capture of bin Laden, the official end of the Iraq War, and the weakening of al-Qaeda's power did not substantially alleviate or counteract the long-standing suffering produced from experiences of widespread inequality, globalized accumulations of power, decreased possibilities for ordinary individuals to participate in the powers that govern them, the outsourcing and robotizing of care and human sustenance, the weakening of welfare provisions, and other causes that contribute to the daily sense of debilitated agency that orgies of feeling aim to eradicate. Experiences of precarity have only increased in the intervening years, in part because the global economic crisis—which partially originated in U.S. policies that funded the war on terror to the exclusion of other priorities, such as social welfare—diverted and defunded resources, finances, and policy priorities even further from the support of the most needy and vulnerable.

Orgies of feeling, as Nietzsche describes them, do not exactly match up with melodramatic political discourse, however, and their differences reveal the work of melodrama. Nietzsche primarily examines orgies of feeling in regards to a self-inflicted form of suffering. For Nietzsche, orgies of feeling are particularly nefarious because the agent of evil that they posit is one's own self. Part of the intense pain they produce is guilt that one's own immorality is the cause of one's suffering. For Nietzsche, orgies of feeling are first identified in Christian ascetic practices; while they eventually spread to Enlightenment discourses about science and truth, they begin in religiously inflicted forms of self-punishment that exact orgiastic terrors on the self in order to gain control over one's ineffective agency. Within melodrama, by contrast, the self is innocent. The evil cause of suffering is embodied in a villain outside the self, which is why melodrama's orgies of feeling are less predictable; they only come about through a crisis event that is unexpected and uncontrollable, rather than a self-inflicted wound. Post-9/11 orgies of feeling entail a mode of subjectivity that capitalizes on an unexpected event to enact its own orgiastic terrors; melodramatic orgies of feeling are thus more conditional and less systematic than the dynamic diagnosed by Nietzsche. These orgies of feeling are also, however, significantly easier to bear. They disavow their own accountability for their suffering and place blame on others, on villains outside the virtuous and victimized subject they construct. In melodrama, the self undergoing orgies of feeling is innocent of causing any of its injuries. Melodramatic political subjects, contra the ascetic subject of Nietzsche's reading, can place blame solely on an evil villain. In the short term, melodrama's orgies of feeling thus satisfy deeper desires for freedom and nonresponsibility in a way that Nietzsche's orgies of feeling do not.

Yet the melodramatic political subject still shores up certain aspects of agency present in Nietzsche's reading, as it undertakes an overwhelming experience of suffering in order to identify a specific cause for what it endures. Agency within Nietzsche's orgies of feeling is found *through* the sudden experience of "terror, ice, flames, and raptures." He writes, "Fundamentally, every great affect has this power [to produce an orgy of feeling], provided it explodes suddenly: anger, fear, voluptuousness, revenge, hope, triumph, despair, cruelty."[35] The agency in this sentence is with the affect that explodes, rather than the self alone. In this sense, orgies of feeling can be generated by unpredictable events in the world if subjects take on their heightened affects through orgiastic mechanisms. I am not claiming that 9/11 was a self-inflicted form of suffering, but rather that the act of interpreting the events through melodrama, and the sudden explosion of affective force that melodrama further intensified, allows the response to them to be understood as an orgy of feeling.[36] The purpose of this claim is certainly not to adjudicate who is or is not a proper victim of the events, or to mark who is conceivably allowed to suffer from their effects—an effort that would be futile at best, brutal at worst—but rather to examine why melodrama was so powerful not only within public political discourses but also for political subjects. The purpose is to examine the affective effects underpinning the interpretation that all Americans were victims of the events, and to speculate on the desires behind the claim that the attacks were caused by a singular form of villainy upon all Americans.

The 9/11 events were not self-imposed, but the turn to melodrama's affective interpretation of the events at once made the pain intensified and rendered less potent, in part because it was plotted and made sensible. As Marc Redfield carefully reminds us, the violence on September 11 did not occur on a nationwide scale, as for instance the violence of genocide, famine, or warfare, yet it was generally understood to be a nationwide victimization. A focus on melodrama's orgies of feeling can help to understand how this understanding developed and why it was widespread.[37] The depiction of each American, indeed the whole nation, as victimized by the events (rather than, for instance, interpreting the event as an attack on world capital via the World Trade Center, or on the U.S. military via the Pentagon, or on only those individuals directly or indirectly implicated, or even clumsily on "globalization" writ large, as a similar attack was planned for a Philippines skyscraper just a few years prior) aligns the victimized experience of melodramatic political subjectivity with a self-inflicted suffering. And the violent national response to 9/11 generated the feeling of control over powerlessness—the key feeling that makes orgies of feeling hold out the promise of mastering one's life conditions.

Orgies of feeling produce what Nietzsche calls "the error of imaginary causes."[38] In Nietzsche's diagnosis, the imaginary cause of one's suffering is the immoral self, while post-9/11 melodrama posits evil terrorists as the imaginary cause of nebulous suffering. In both cases, the search to find an identifiable agent for one's conditions narrows, narrativizes, and moralizes the cause of their experiences. This is not to say that contemporary experiences of powerlessness have no causes, or that pursuits of accountability are always futile. But it is to say that the accountability for widespread experiences of unfreedom, and the diagnoses of the structural, discursive, and governmental causes for them, cannot be captured by or fought against through a war on terror. The orgiastic positing that a singular cause of felt constraint exists, and is clearly locatable, reinscribes powerlessness by alleging that it has a lucid, singular cause that can be heroically overcome through the war on terror. Nietzsche writes, "The venting of his affects represents the greatest attempt on the part of the sufferer to win relief. . . . He combats only the suffering itself, the discomfiture of the sufferer, *not* its cause, *not* the real sickness."[39] Nietzsche notes that there are real causes for these initial discomfitures, but that they are impossible to diagnose through orgiastic mechanisms. Orgies of feeling place blame on that which does not, or does not only, cause individuals' experiences of helplessness, or only generate conditions of constraint and exclusion. The turn to orgies of feeling, then, aims to challenge unendurable experiences of unfreedom, but at the same time their misdiagnosis inhibits the very capacity to overcome them.

For Nietzsche, orgies of feeling—in positing the self as the guilty agent who causes the original and nebulous suffering—reveal what he calls "this instinct for freedom forcibly made latent[;] . . . this instinct for freedom pushed back and repressed, incarcerated within and finally able to discharge and vent itself only on itself."[40] Impotent rage is turned back on the self rather than toward the outward fight for freedom it seems to desire. But as post-9/11 melodrama shifts the "cause" of orgies of feeling—from Nietzsche's claim that the self is the guilty agent to melodrama's claim that external intruders, that is, terrorists, are the guilty agent—it also shifts the direction of that "instinct" for freedom. Post-9/11 melodrama thus reveals how a desire for freedom is not forcibly made latent after 9/11, but is still there, struggling, responding to underlying and unnamable experiences of unfreedom through vengeful violence against misplaced causes. The turn to orgies of feeling is, emphatically, not a turning away from politics as a site of agency in the face of demobilization and ineffectiveness. It is an attempt to recapture that agency, and to experience it as freedom. Yet melodrama's orgiastic pursuit of freedom entrenches the experiences of unfreedom it aims to challenge ever more deeply.

If orgies of feeling arise from the desire to alleviate experiences of "secret pain" caused by confusing yet common forms of powerlessness, why do the underlying forms of contemporary power seem unknowable? The most obvious answer is that contemporary political powers are, in their very structure, overwhelming, disabling, and obfuscating. Neoliberal, biopolitical, and late-modern forms of power are unquestionably complex, their operations so multifaceted and circuitous that it would be virtually impossible to fully map or diagnose them.[41] Yet this is not the only answer I want to supply for why subjects are so unrelieved by their confusing experiences of powerlessness. The operations of various dominating powers are not necessarily in and of themselves always inexplicable or unaccountable—the problem I am concerned with is why they often *seem* to be this way. Why do these commonplace feelings of unfreedom seem so confusing? Why are we often so unable to articulate their origins, to find their sources of accountability, to halt or redirect their oppressive operations? Confusion is not only caused by the fact that contemporary forms of power frequently appear nonagentic or unaccountable. Confusion is also deepened by the ways in which the American public often understands power and freedom. The answer, to my mind, is not only the nature of the powers under scrutiny but also the limitations of the discourses and norms usually used to understand them.

The problem, then, is not only the complexities of power but also their unintelligibility within the dominant terms for understanding power and agency in America—primarily, though not exclusively, through the terms of *sovereignty* and *individualism*, combined in an American form of liberal political individualism. Giving the problem a distinctly American twist that Nietzsche could not have anticipated, the freedom that melodramatic orgies of feeling promise is based on the tenets of American liberal individualism and their reuptake in discourses of neoliberalism—in which freedom is only freedom from explicit coercion, from domination by other individuals or concrete institutions. *Freedom*, in this normative definition, means sovereign agency and freedom from other forms of power. The main form of power that fits into freedom is singular, identifiable, and causally agentic. Yet given the range of powers arrayed against and through individuals in the current moment, and given the ways that power and agency are very differently experienced for different raced, classed, and gendered people, this understanding of freedom is inadequate to the task of either understanding the circulations of various powers or addressing particular experiences of unfreedom. Forms of power that elide sovereignty, and desires for freedom that exclude mastery, are rendered unintelligible, and individuals conditioned by their terms consequently lack the resources to address various unfreedoms or even make them legible.

The dilemma arising from this is twofold. First, the language of individualism often exhausts American understandings of power, freedom, and agency, and thus dedifferentiates all other ways that power functions to shape individuals. This language thus leaves unaccountable many of the various powers that condition individual and state agency. Indeed, it narrows possibilities for challenging unfreedom by *making illegible* nonsovereign and nonjuridical operations of power that shape and affect its possibility. Second, this exhaustion makes individuals feel *more* powerless than they are. By leaving out more detailed understandings of power and unfreedom, this type of individualism also prevents more productive ways of challenging them. The language of liberal individualism constitutes violence to social and interdependent ways of being. It devalues norms that posit humans as fundamentally social beings, and it views social interdependence as a threat rather than a resource for the practice of freedom. It does not enable the tools to produce and articulate notions of freedom and power that could be more effective in challenging current global conditions, or that could contribute to remaking society in a significantly more free and equitable way that would actively contribute to both individual flourishing and collective freedom.

Liberal individualism takes various forms throughout American history, so I will briefly trace the one I have under scrutiny, one that saturates political discourse in the United States and has often overshadowed other ways of thinking about the relationship among individuals, power, and freedom in recent years, perhaps because of the weight it gives to the value of mastery. The form is dominated by an emphasis on the capacities of individual agents, and, in particular, on individual mastery over the self and over the external environment.[42] The underlying norm bolstering this version of individualism is that it is the purpose, and unique capacity, of the individual to control the self and nature. This form values the mastery of power, of ruling over one's life conditions, conquering the unexpected, controlling the irregular, dominating the whims of Fortuna. It is within the individual's ability to tame contingency, to direct the state, and to use the external world as an instrument for one's own ends. This form of individualism is similar to what William Connolly calls "ontological narcissism"—a conviction that the individual is inherently sovereign, unconstrained by power save one's own will, and able to domesticate the world with hard work.[43] Ontological narcissism presumes a specific model of a normal and rational individual: unencumbered, masculine, almost omnipotent, this individual instinctually knows what he needs, has the capacity to get what he desires, is unbound by power save his own self-generating law, is autonomous and prior to the social system within which he operates, and is one to whom all individuals are compared in measuring whether they fit within bounds of these norms.

The version of liberal individualism I have in mind is historically traced in this way: after centuries of philosophy positing that subjects obey the law because of a willed obedience, and that subjects perform their own subjection to the legal order, the political revolutions of the eighteenth century posited a new type of political subject. Étienne Balibar explains, "He is no longer the man *called before the Law*, or to whom an inner voice dictates the Law, or tells him that he should recognize and obey the Law; he is rather the man who, at least virtually, 'makes the Law,' i.e. constitutes it, or *declares* it to be valid."[44] With this dramatic shift, the political subject becomes one who obeys his own law, not being subject to it or self-imposing the dictates of another. The subject becomes the legislator, executor, and citizen all at once, responsible for and accountable to the laws that he has made. This subject who makes the law that he obeys, one initially traced by John Locke, elaborated by Jean-Jacques Rousseau, paradigmatically formulated by Immanuel Kant, and concretely delineated in America's Declaration of Independence, held out the promise of a new definition of freedom: one that severs *subjection* from *subject* and conceives the practice of self-constitution as the cornerstone of modern freedom.

In American political discourse this larger project of subjectivity takes shape through the norms of liberal individualism that draw most prominently from Locke and John Stuart Mill, which understand the individual through conceptions of independence, self-responsibility, and a model of individual freedom defined as *freedom from*: from unwarranted state action, from other individuals, from power. Freedom is conceptualized as personal freedom and individual agency, and it is on this ground that the political order rests. The discourse of American individualism posits the individual as the source of one's own governance and will, separate from the choices and dictates of others. The American subject qua individual is typically constructed as a man, with women often serving as the counterbalancing force of dependence or the site of circumscribed agency. Women often signify subjection more than subject. The male individual, by contrast, is distinctly and personally responsible for his life experiences. From personal character to specific actions, from economic success to social value, the subject without subjection shoulders full accountability for his life trajectory. Complementary beliefs in personal freedom and equal opportunity place responsibility for all actions, and their consequences, squarely on his shoulders. The individual is the source of decidability, held directly accountable for what he does and what he is, and assumed to be unencumbered by external constraints in choices and decision making. This is the iconic narrative: that it is the individual's responsibility to pull himself up by his own bootstraps. It presumes everyone can, and everyone should.[45]

What makes this American individualism distinct from a broader liberal subjectivity, or even a broader form of individualism, is the uniquely American value of self-reliance, the oversimplification of an Emersonian inheritance that combines with a frontier mentality of mastery over self and nature. Ralph Waldo Emerson's influential ideas on heroism and self-reliance amalgamated into narratives of heroic individuals taming the wilderness, and these ideas transformed the concept of sovereignty from something an individual is born with into something that must be worked for.[46] Reliance on others is thus equated with social conformity, a chosen condition that signals a weak and ineffectual character. This self-reliant individualism inspires challenges to burdensome social conventions, encroachments of state power, and restrictive norms; it is a source of many projects and practices for greater freedom in American life. Yet this self-reliant individual also carries the premise that problems of subordination or dependence or incapacity result from a deficit in the strength and moral character of the individual, and the individual alone. Individualism as a moral norm does not supplant individualism as an ontology, but rather they coexist, so that any failure to live up to the standards of self-reliance becomes a personal failure. This version of American liberal individualism, as I've described it, is thus a site of the convergence of multiple discourses: eighteenth-century revolutionary promise (specifically its formal and juridical manifestations), a Lockean and Millian form of liberal individualism, an Emersonian self-reliance, and a neoliberal rationality that emphasizes personal responsibility and risky entrepreneurialism as the hallmarks of moral agency. Together they consolidate into a distinctive definition of political subjectivity that functions as both a norm and an ontology of individual agency.

In American neoliberal individualism, political subjects' inability to experience unconstrained agency signals the failure of one's very constitution *as* a political subject. As Dana Nelson argues, living up to the ideal of self-reliant, even aggressive, competitive individualism is impossible for anyone, an ideal no one can seemingly inhabit.[47] Yet within this discourse, larger social, economic, or political conditions cannot carry responsibility for limiting capacity, regulating possibility, or forming character. Even as this version of American individualism inhabits and shapes different discourses, norms, and political practices in different historical moments and social bodies, its tenets continue to be quite faithful to their nineteenth-century forms. The tenets remain a guiding force in contemporary politics, especially in neoliberal demonization of welfare-state power for disabling self-reliance, as well as in the heroization of individuals who are self-making and self-maximizing entrepreneurs.[48] While many people insist that the norms of individualism do not apply to them, that they are immune to their normative pull (and even imply that if they exist at all, it is only as an ideal inhabiting a foregone middle America that includes no one they know), it is important to recognize that individualism is a figure, an ideal, that significantly shapes national understandings of power and possibility. Many people may disidentify with individualism, assume that its dictates do not apply to them, that they do not buy into it, even as it marks a horizon for their personal, social, and economic expectations and norms.

The individualizing norms that organize this version of freedom are unable to account for how individuals are shaped in part by various fields of historical and social power. They abstract subjects from their lived experiences and material circumstances, even as they diminish the possibility of articulating those powers forming the subject. They exclude the conditions of daily existence that enmesh subjects within corporate, administrative, and governmentalizing structures, a well as the global political and economic networks that generate a material web of interdependency. These governing norms disavow the possibility that, as Karl Marx would insist, formally free individuals are often materially constrained by multiple and interweaving modes of social power, and that, as Foucault would insist, formally free individuals are also given particular form by the discourses that articulate the terms of their freedom. These discourses, practices, and norms entrench and expand normalizing forms of racial and sexualized power by leaving them unaccountable at the same time that they devalue the sort of public, collective participation in governing life that could work to diminish experiences of exploitation and regulation. The experience of contemporary power feels similar to the failure of the individual to live up to his or her capacity, the failure to be self-reliant, the failure to succeed economically, the failure to resist subordination, the failure to pull oneself up by one's bootstraps, the failure to control the vagaries of economic and state actions. Experiences of powerlessness and vulnerability are not seen to be a product of human relations or political conditions or gender norms or economic power or social atomization but instead arise only from one's own ineffectiveness as an autonomous agent. This disavowal casts the liberal individual into pain, from, as Wendy Brown argues in another context, "the failure to make itself in the context of a discourse in which self-making is assumed."[49]

The imaginary of freedom in American neoliberal individualism also disavows the constitution of subjective capacities through these multiple forms of power.[50] These exclusions are particularly disabling in contemporary politics and citizenship, as they severely delimit understandings of individuals' relationships to political life. If individuals are produced as subjects through regulatory and disciplinary forms of power, if individuals are materially circumscribed, or if global forces penetrate into micropolitical actions, then any insistence on personal sovereignty, or on an individual solely responsible for his or her actions and capacities, swiftly unravels. American individualist subjects, situated at the site of this challenge, bear an agonizing burden. Conditioned by corporate markets and regulatory norms, by confusing circulations of global as well as micropolitical powers, and by interdependent sustenance networks—yet primarily valuing themselves only when they feel autonomous and free from power—subjects experience failure, anxiety, and suffering from the very moment of their inception as political subjects.

Furthermore, individuals' dependence on others is not always or necessarily disabling; it can be a constitutive and enabling aspect of lived experience. In many cases dependence is not a painful experience and is even the very condition of political agency. As psychoanalytic thinkers from Jean Laplanche to Judith Butler argue, radical interdependence is the very fabric that constitutes subjectivity and lays the groundwork for the collective exercise of power.[51] Democratic theorists drawing from Hannah Arendt, including Patchen Markell and Linda Zerilli, argue that the practice of freedom has never been about sovereign power but is a nonsovereign and relational experience of world making that only exists between people acting in concert.[52] In more historically inflected claims, Saskia Sassen and Zygmunt Bauman, among many others, argue that interdependence arises out of changes wrought by globalization, capitalism, and the experiences of urban modernity, in which material developments reorganize human relations toward a more connected and interdependent mode.[53] Under globalization, peoples and societies become more interconnected and dependent on each other, which can be in many cases a cause not for fear but for vitalized agency and collective responsibility. For all of these scholars, whether interdependence is a constitutive condition of the human, the grounds of the political, or a structural by-product of modernity, it inescapably organizes the field of human relations and forms the ground for individual agency. Yet in American individualism all experiences of dependence become relatively undifferentiated. Any form of interdependence seems threatening or painful for subjects shaped by expectations of self-reliance and personal sovereignty.

Nietzsche emphasizes that the problem that kick-starts orgies of feeling is less the experience of powerlessness per se than the inability to figure out *why* one feels powerless. Figuring how to challenge a particular type of power involves knowing what, specifically, one is challenging. As Foucault insists, every form of power can be challenged and transformed—no forms of power are totalizing or all-encompassing. All offer possibilities for challenge, reworking, mobilization, and flight. Yet by preventing broader understandings of power, American liberal individualism inhibits this diagnosis and thwarts its premise of freedom. The desire for challenging overweening power motivates the turn to melodrama: a desire to end powerlessness, to make legible one's felt experience of precarity, to fight against unfreedom. Yet individualism's discursive disavowal of felt dependency produces as its effect even deeper distress than the feeling of situatedness within power; this condition fuels a gnawing anxiety, continually fed by increasing regulation as well as anxiety's inexpressibility.[54]

Even as individualism, like melodrama, animates a desire to challenge experiences of oppression and names that desire a desire for freedom, it organizes a subjectivity that no longer has a sense of what powers it aims to challenge, or what kinds of agency may be effective in this endeavor. Individualism's conceptions of power and freedom can thus contribute to the experiences of powerlessness that orgies of feeling aim to ameliorate by inhibiting a broader understanding of their causes and thus delimiting possible ways to address them. In other words, neoliberal individualism prevents a more critical understanding of agency and is also responsible for new experiences of anxiety and fear. In this way, it produces a deeper helplessness. It diminishes openings to form a critical knowledge that could help develop tools and tactics to challenge newer forms of power, forms more complex, nonagentic, noninstitutional, and specific to certain bodies than it addresses. This is not to say that other conceptions for understanding power and agency would magically make all forms of power transparent, or to say they would give subjects the singular key to challenge the problems composing the contemporary condition. But it is to emphasize how orgies of feeling aim to address felt problems of unfreedom that are often denied or rendered unintelligible in American public discourse, that are affectively experienced but formally disavowed.

American neoliberal individualism constrains individuals partly by producing individuals who understand themselves to be unconstrained. Orgies of feeling become so desirable in part because they seem able to fight against the vitiated agency commonplace in neoliberalism. Within discourses of freedom in the United States, to recognize oneself as constrained by expansive forms of regulation, as conditioned in part by globally produced forms of vulnerability, as living within conditions of governmentalizing power as well as producing them, undermines the very self-grounding presuppositions of the autonomous subject. These disavowals of dependence function most painfully within the subject itself, whose attempt at self-formation is constantly cast as ineffective and impotent, whose primary value as an individual is the capability for mastery over self, state, and world, for existing as a subject without subjection, yet whose ability to master in this way is always already impossible.

## 9/11 and the "Orgiastic" Revival of Individualism

Orgies of feeling, in promising to restore the normative vision of sovereign freedom to U.S. subjects, attends to the disavowed debilitations arising out of individualism. Through melodrama's orgies of feeling, 9/11 provided a stage upon which an experience of vulnerability could be autonomously overcome by grandiose acts of militaristic power that would re-instate or prove autonomy. The widespread devastation of the 9/11 events highlighted the limitations of the ontological narcissism of individualism. Its large-scale and indiscriminate violence challenged the ontological status of self-reliant individualism and self-making subjectivity. It revealed the chimerical possibility that one can control contingency and live bound only by one's own will. Yet through melodrama 9/11 was also, and simultaneously, coded to argue for just the opposite. In giving pain a clear meaning and a clear cause, melodrama's orgies of feeling displaced both the unknowing and the paralysis of unknowing that attends the original pain.

Yet liberal individualism also circulates widely in melodramatic political discourse, figuring its model of sovereign heroism, its promise of individual mastery, its personification of state power as an individual actor, and its diagnosis of villainy in a single nefarious agent; all are shaped by individualism's available parameters for power and agency.[55] Melodrama's ability to name and identify a unified agent of oppression for social suffering, and to promise heroic mastery over experiences of constraint, is the very stuff of individualism. Melodramatic political discourse insists on the possibility of a subject's capacity for autonomous self-making; the expectation of heroic self-mastery promises that one can resist power's injunctions and domesticate contingency. Melodrama implies that self-reliance is both possible and the norm of proper subjecthood, that social suffering has a single and easily identifiable cause that can be recognized and redressed by the individual (and by states that act in a unified way), and that all individuals can overcome heteronomy through their own agentic capacity.

Right at the moment when the 9 / 11 attacks revealed the impossibility of the claim for mastery and impermeability, melodramatic political discourse cultivated a subject that tried to reclaim the promise of heroic invulnerability. At the very moment that sovereignty is revealed as chimerical, melodrama looks back to sovereignty for its inspiration, challenging individual vulnerability by reconstituting the possibility for autonomous mastery. Melodramatic discourses thus reinscribe individualist mastery as an ideal, cast varied and disparate forms of contemporary power into a singular villainy, and legitimate dramatic expressions of violent and unaccountable state power as expressions of sovereign freedom. By positing the possibility of finding one particular doer, and even of finding one specific deed for the terrors of politics, orgies of feeling diminish the ability to bring into popular discourse an understanding of the complex operations of power and subjectivity that produce and regulate contemporary individuals. Within the terms of melodramatic victimization, autonomous individualism is conceived as the original subject position, but one currently thwarted by an external force (here, terrorism). *Yet the condition of thwarted agency is in part an effect of neoliberal individualist discourse.* The experience of political helplessness is partly an effect of individualism's impossibility; subjects of individualism are produced through an always already thwarted agency.[56] Melodramatic condemnations of unfreedom manifest through the available terms of American individualism and become: if only this one obstacle is removed, then unobstructed agency can be restored. The potential for a larger examination of unjust and unequal power, the effects of which animate the melodramatic form—the question of how to best challenge felt experiences of injustice and exclusion—becomes orgiastically displaced onto a false target.

The underlying supposition of orgies of feeling, that all experiences of dependence and vulnerability necessarily produce suffering, harkens back to Nietzsche, who implies that suffering from dependence is ontological, even biological. Nietzsche argues that all humans innately want "to become master not over something in life but over life itself, over its most profound, powerful, and basic conditions."[57] Nietzsche posits that a desire for mastery subtends all human activity, a claim that itself draws partly from the terms of American liberal individualism. Nietzsche explicitly relies in other parts of his work on Emerson's norm of self-reliance for similar claims.[58] Although Nietzsche suggests that the desire for mastery congealed in the will to power is ontological, it seems instead to be a variant of the same ontological narcissism that structures American individualism. By positing that suffering arises from the thwarted expression of an existential will to power, orgies of feeling ontologize a specific form of late modern experience: suffering cultivated both by the constant feeling of constraint and by discourses that produce subjects as failed masters. This pain derives in part because subjects have learned to desire the impossible experience of maximal power and individual mastery. Examined from this angle, Nietzsche's theorizing on victimization may be less a genealogy of morality than a prescient example of a late-modern experience that will come to shape lives structured by norms of neoliberal individualism. The claim of victimization arising out of the desire for mastery, and expressed as an orgy of feeling, operates within the same assumptions that support American individualism, by assuming that ontological narcissism, as the will to power, is possible.

Orgies of feeling developed from melodramatic political discourse can thus be viewed as a diagnosis and as a product of particular social conditions in which ontological narcissism becomes the governing ideal of power. In this governing ideal, pain caused by nonagentic or complex forms of contemporary power might appear to have no cause. Orgies of feeling can therefore help to understand responses to the felt experience of contemporary power; suffering feels so profoundly disorienting and anxiety laden not only because contemporary forms of power are increasingly restrictive but also because an understanding of these powers is discursively disavowed by the conventional terms of political discourse. The permutations of contemporary unfreedom that cause suffering, the circulations of power that work outside and through individual or state-institutional agency, that generate global instability, that penetrate and produce the self, and that inhibit the capacity to participate in decisions over one's lived conditions, are felt but remain unarticulated. The suffering produced out of contemporary forms of power thus seems to be a failure of the subject, and also to have unknowable origins. The movements of contemporary power cannot be productively gauged, and to the subjects conditioned by this discourse, pain feels unexplainable. Further, any sense of interdependence, even interdependence that may be constitutive, desirable, or a precondition for the practice of freedom, is experienced as painful to those for whom self-reliance is supposed to be both ontological and desirable.

In melodrama's victimized subjectivity, mastery and power seem most accessible through the condition of orgiastic victimization and produce the perverse desire to look for and cultivate orgies of feeling. The claim of victimization requires pain in order to challenge impingements of power. The effects of this phenomenon encourage subjects to find ways to insist on the nation's victimhood in order to bring about the promise of future sovereignty it heralds for both individuals and states. We can read the endless and orgiastic citations of 9/11 in political discourse in the years following the attacks as a repetition of the victimization that offers claims of moral goodness and the promise of a future in which one resists, fights, and shifts experiences of powerlessness and terror. In melodrama this form of fighting is tightly bound by the normative conceptions of individualism and is thus aimed backward: not as a prelude to more capacious understandings of power or radical political transformation, but to ideas of mastery and self-reliance, the very ideas that contribute to the subject's original pain. Nietzsche could be the prototype of this predicament: one who sees the productive capacity of power and its cultivation of specific and limited forms of subjectivity, yet one who also wants to overcome these conditions by, in part, relying on concepts of individual heroism and mastery.

In homogenizing all experiences of unfreedom into terror, melodramatic political discourse legitimates the war on terror in an effort to catalyze power and undo vulnerability. Melodramatic political discourse's orgies of feeling mislocate multiple causes of helplessness onto a singular type of evil and misdirect possible solutions. Melodrama deepens the problem its displacements intend to ameliorate, expanding violent incursions of state power upon individuals while bolstering the normative framework of individualism. The war on terror is thus charged with the herculean task of establishing conditions for sovereignty on the basis of a frenzied call to respond to a spectacular instance of helplessness. Melodrama legitimates dramatic expansions in state power over and within the very individuals who employ orgies of feeling to lessen their own experiences of vulnerability. The concern in this case, ultimately, is that an impulse to interpret, resist, and overcome contemporary experiences of dependence and constraint takes shape as an orgy of feeling that only increases the shock, anger, terror, confusion, unspeakable sadness, grief, and fear it is deployed to overcome. By way of desiring opposition to the pain bred by late-modern and neoliberal forms of contemporary power, melodramatic political subjects end up legitimating constraining power relations, repudiating a deeper interrogation into their lived conditions of precarity and unfreedom, and eventually sanctioning violence, surveillance, and war.

# FIVE

# HEROIC IDENTIFICATIONS; OR, YOU CAN LOVE ME TOO—I AM SO LIKE THE STATE

In the name of freedom, many Americans have recently supported war, occupation, empire, domestic surveillance, racial profiling, the willing curtailment of civil liberties, the criminalization of dissent, the militarization of policing, and other violent and invasive forms of power that have generally worked at the expense of the political agency of the people who supported them. While there were many Americans who did not support these actions, or fought against them, a majority did.[1] What political desires prop up these majorities? What investments sustain the support of state powers among Americans on whom they impose tight regulation, political exclusion, and disenfranchisement? Does this support demonstrate Friedrich Nietzsche's assertion that people so often seem to desire their own unfreedom? The consensus view in political theory, no less than public discourse, argues that Americans have willingly traded freedom for national security.[2] In this view Americans, seemingly cowed by the responsibilities that real freedom entails, are by and large willing to sacrifice their civil liberties and political agency for the promise of a stronger security state.[3] Yet I argue instead that their support for these actions reflects a more paradoxical situation than this account allows: it reflects misdirected attempts to *challenge* conditions of unfreedom. Many Americans have sought to enact a kind of freedom increasingly denied to them in contemporary political conditions of unfreedom, and they do so through their active support of state power. Their legitimation of state violence and regulation may have aimed to rehabilitate their *individual* freedom in a neoliberal era that challenges freedom at every turn.

What does it look like to read contemporary politics with individual freedom as a motivating desire and promised teleology? What is imagined when citizens legitimate invasion, surveillance, and the abrogation of their rights to secure the triumph of their personal freedom? If the goal of the war on terror is not only security but also freedom, surely this complicates readings of national security as a zero-sum game with individual freedom. Can individual freedom be entwined so tightly with national security that desires for individual sovereignty manifest as support for massive extensions in securitized power? The war on terror is, after all, not a war for safety and security per se but a war for freedom; its stated goal is "securing freedom's triumph."[4] The war on terror is tasked to abolish the terror that deprioritizes freedom. We can read the rhetoric of freedom as a cynical ploy to make violent executive expansion and military dictates appealing to a country that bases its national identity on its support of freedom, and this is surely a factor in the use of this language. But it is also necessary to take the desire for freedom seriously as a reason for the intensification of the national-security state and the militarization of foreign policy in order to understand why *freedom* is a lynchpin term legitimating them.

The promise of freedom crucial to the legitimation of state power, I argue, takes form through *individual identifications* with dramatic and violent forms of state power. For a melodramatic political subject—a subject who chooses membership in a virtuous and wounded national identity in part by supporting dramatic and violent state power—the expression of state action may seem to be an extension of one's very own action. Melodramatic political subjects envision a heroic mastery over the world performed by state action and yet also experienced by the individual. Their legitimation of state power is thus a consequence of identification with it, in which the power symbolized by the state becomes an internalized ideal of sovereign agency. Unilateral and dramatic performances of state power demonstrate a type of sovereign freedom that political subjects do not have but desire to possess. Individuals who support expansive state action may do so as an attempt to experience state power as their own individual sovereignty, and to imagine this experience as freedom.

State unilateralism, within the conventions of melodrama, serves as a proxy for the freedom and sovereignty denied to individuals by daily experiences of vulnerability, fear, and the sense of a lost capacity to be self-reliant. For U.S. political subjects—who often valorize (neo)liberal individualism's norms of heroism, rugged self-reliance, and individual freedom yet experience dependence, exploitation, constraint, and fear on a regular basis—the strength demonstrated by bold state actions seemed a viable model of sovereign agency. Individuals' investments in state power are driven by the desire to compensate for the loss of the horizon of freedom promised as a birthright of U.S. citizens.

My reading of state identification through melodrama disputes conventional interpretations of recent political-economic shifts grouped together under the term *neoliberalism*. These interpretations assume that recent political and economic changes have retrenched state power in favor of deregulated private enterprise, and also that this retrenchment is buttressed by individual disidentifications with the state as a site of sustenance and national identity. As the state decreases its mechanisms of support for citizens, it is presumed that citizens become less invested in the state as a source of support, identity, or assistance. Yet this chapter challenges both of those assumptions. I argue that the neoliberal norms inhabiting the U.S. polity enable state expansions (especially regarding national security and individual regulation) and incite individuals to reinvest in state power. In other words, neoliberal tenets of individual mastery, entrepreneurship, and self-reliance *encourage* identifications with state action. One surprising effect of the policies that eviscerate state welfare in order to uphold individual freedom is to spur individuals to reinvest in certain types of state power in order to buttress against the vulnerability these policies create.[5] Norms of individualism thus contribute to the increased identification with state power; unilateral state actions are imagined to revivify the individual sovereignty that is idealized and yet destroyed by neoliberal norms and policies.

The previous chapter and this one are two halves of a story about the political subjectivity of unfreedom in contemporary politics. Together they investigate how a melodramatic political subjectivity cultivates U.S. citizens as the victims-heroes of geopolitics in an attempt to mediate the effects of contemporary conditions of nonsovereignty and unfreedom. Melodrama cultivates a political subjectivity that aims to end more ordinary experiences of powerlessness through the orgiastic promise that an affectively overwhelmed subject will soon experience freedom from terror. While orgies of feeling displace daily experiences of vulnerability onto a heightened story of victimized freedom, melodrama's flip side to victimization is the promise of heroism, and identification is the mechanism by which melodramatic victims aim to heroically acquire their sovereign freedom. *Heroic identifications* is a strategy to overcome powerlessness, and in the process restore the individual sovereignty that seems to be the rightful inheritance of U.S. subjects.[6] Orgies of feeling and heroic identifications are the resources that melodrama offers for challenging experiences of unfreedom. The legitimation of intensified state power they produce does not necessarily reflect a political subject that desires security over freedom, or even desires its own subjection, however. Orgies of feeling and heroic identifications reflect a subject that obstructs its own freedom by the very methods it employs in its pursuit.

### "Look, You Can Love Me Too—I Am So Like the State"

The psychic process of identification may seem a peculiar place to begin examining how individuals could legitimate powers that diminish their own capacities as political agents, but identification is, at least for Sigmund Freud, the very point where the individual intersects with the political. Identification mediates the relationship between the self and others. Freud's seminal account of identification argues that it is the process by which the political and social world shapes individuals at the same time that it is a way for individuals to attempt to exert control over that world. Identification turns individuals into subjects through their engagement with what is outside of them. Identification does not produce one stable subject or singular identification but a series of subjectivating identifications throughout one's life that continually adapt to changes in the social world. It is no coincidence that Freud's most extended writings on identification come in *Group Psychology and Analysis of the Ego*, his examination of group formation and behavior. In Diana Fuss's reading, there can be no politics without identification; she argues, "Identification is not only how we accede to power, but it is how we learn submission."[7] Identification would seem to be the very point from which to begin taking the measure of the work of political legitimation, the process by which individuals sustain, acquiesce to, and influence political power.

For Freud, the process of identification begins out of an experience of losing something or someone that one has loved. This lost object can be a person, an abstract concept such as an ideal, or one's country. Identification is a way of managing this loss, and it requires relinquishing one's earlier desire to have what was loved and is now gone. In identification, individuals abandon a prior aim to possess their love object and adjust to more limited aims: *to be similar to* the loved one that is gone.[8] Identification is the "endeavor to mold a person's own ego after the fashion of the one taken as a model."[9] Part of the ego takes the form of the object of desire in order to satisfy other desiring parts of the self. Identification begins when individuals realize that they cannot have their loved ones but still feel attached to what they love, so they modify their desires: they become similar to the ones they had loved, and thus the individuals preserve their attachments internally. Freud explains, "If one has lost a love object, the most obvious reaction is to identify with it, to replace it from within, as it were, by identification."[10]

In identification, an unattainable external love object becomes an *internal ideal* upon which to pattern the self. Freud argues, "When the ego assumes the features of the object, it is forcing itself, so to speak, upon the id as a love-object and is trying to make good the id's loss by saying 'Look, you can love me too—I am so like the object.'"[11] In identification, one substitutes oneself, part of one's ego, for the lost object. Part of the ego transforms into the lost object in order to compensate other parts of the psyche for the lost original tie with something desired. Identification is the nexus of the self and the social, and marks a process whereby the individual internalizes something in the world (indeed it is shaped by its relations with the external world) at the very moment it turns away from the world in an attempt to satisfy its own needs. Identification constitutes subjectivity by its attempt to manage loss, an attempt to satisfy one's own desires when they are not satisfied by others.[12] Identification thus involves a reckoning with loss, but also with difference. As one becomes aware of loss, one becomes aware of the difference between who one is and who or what one wants to have. Identification marks a process in which the subject individuates himself or herself from something else. Identification is how the self grapples with personal identity through relationships to others, and it works by idealizing and modeling part of the self on someone or something that is now gone.

Freud's theory of the mechanisms of identification contributes to my reading of the development of a melodramatic subjectivity that authorizes violent state power. As in all identifications, the melodramatic identification with state power arises out of an awareness of loss—a knowledge of the impossibility of having something one had loved—and functions as a mechanism in order to be similar to that which one cannot have. For this type of political subject, the impossible loved one is, I offer, an ideal of power as sovereign, an ideal of freedom as the absence of impediments for individual self-making. These ideals have been "lost" by power's increasingly pervasive operations in late modern life, no less than by the spectacular demonstration of nonsovereignty on September 11. While this loss might always exist for subjects shaped by expectations of heroic sovereignty, it is also historically and materially configured, and it was brought to the forefront of national consciousness on September 11.

State identification happened in post-9/11 politics after the terrorist events revealed, in a spectacular way, the fiction of state power as autonomous and sovereign. The terrorist attacks punctured the fantasy of invulnerable state and individual boundaries that had, for much of the late twentieth century, shaped both U.S. foreign policy and the norms of liberal individualism. As Jodi Dean argues, it was a moment that entailed "the specific horror of the disintegration of the social link, the symbolic pact promising security and holding society together."[13] The events of 9/11 forced an acknowledgment of the nation's vulnerability to others, of the impossibility of state invincibility or sovereignty, of the triteness of an "end of history" narrative that dominated the post-cold-war 1990s and proclaimed the historic rule of an American-led neoliberal state militarism over all other political norms, desires, and institutions.[14] As *Time* magazine noted three days after 9/11, "If you want to humble an empire it makes sense to maim its cathedrals. They are symbols of its faith, and when they crumple and burn, it tells us we are not so powerful and we can't be safe. . . . It was strange that a day of war was a day we stood still. We couldn't move—that must have been the whole idea—so we had no choice but to watch."[15] The ability of a tiny group of individuals to maim the cathedrals of the U.S. empire in a way that "tells us we are not so powerful and we can't be safe" was a break in standard narratives of U.S. power. The perpetrators of mass violence worked outside, underneath, and through state forms; they were undetectable, elusive, and unaccountable. And yet the break they produced was so intense that "we stood still." Their actions left the nation powerless, impotent, and inert. The *Washington Post* wrote tellingly of a first responder's face after trying to help rescue others: "It was not the horror that she had seen. It was the impotence."[16] The 9/11 attacks gruesomely underlined helplessness, heteronomy, and vulnerability to unseen and violent powers. In an unavoidable and terrorizing way, 9/11 highlighted the impotence of individuals and states and the inability of singular heroic efforts to right the injustice of mass brutality. If sovereign freedom is defined, in its most stripped down and popular version, as a situation in which no one has a higher power over the self, then the unsuspected killing of thousands of people going about their usual routines by a few men without mass weapons deeply challenged the premises of sovereign power for both the individual and the state.

The loss of sovereign freedom as a national birthright was what melodramatic identification with state power aimed to recuperate. The state-organized response to 9/11 extended and performed dramatic military, state, and securitized action in unilateral exercises of global power. These various forms of power seemed to harbor the unbound drive and unlimited capacity to defeat terrorism, and identification with them aimed to eliminate the barrier between the subject and the freedom it covets. Identification with the state aimed, on the one hand, to shore up the weakened or failed belief in the U.S. state as global master. Identification with the state aimed, on the other hand, to reanimate the lost promise of individual sovereignty. Identification with state power, therefore, aims to revive not only the promise that the state can heroically overcome heteronomy but also the liberal promise that the individual has the ability to do this too. This is why a rugged and self-reliant individualism can be so enamored of violent state action and support a militant patriotism. These seemingly contradictory ideas share an intertwined fantasy of mastery over external events. In the post-9/11 moment, when the unexpected mass violence against thousands of people laid bare the impossible promise of individual sovereignty, unilateral state power seemed to be the one place where a robust sovereignty could still be displayed, and identification linked that display to one's own personal experience.

Analyzing the post-9/11 moment of intense state support and patriotic loyalty, Wendy Brown has similarly posited that citizens identified with the nation-state.[17] Brown argues that individuals idealized the desired object of the nation-state and identified with each other based on the collectively shared experience of idealization. The patriotic fervor in post-9/11 politics was a product of citizens who were together in love with the nation that none of them could singularly possess. She writes that in group idealization, "we are bound to one another through our collective experience of being in love with the same object." This joins the nation together partly through the strength that the nation expresses: "The attachment achieved through idealization is likely to glory in the power of the nation, a power expressed in state action."[18] After 9/11 idealization produced a patriotism that both stifled dissent and uncritically celebrated state power. The question that remains from this analysis is why the nation became idealized at the moment of a terrorist attack. What is satisfied, exactly, when the nation-state (and its power) becomes a love object in the wake of spectacular mass violence? What was it about 9/11 that created the desire to posses the nation-state, and what made the nation-state an unattainable object at this precise moment? My answer is not about the pleasures and aggressions satisfied by group bonds, which may seem the most obvious one, but about the specific forms of power that idealization satisfied: the *individualized* desire for omnipotence. The state was the weighted site of identification after 9/11 because it seemed to possess the sovereign power that individuals desired to possess for themselves, especially after a shocking event in which their intense vulnerability was highlighted and the possibility for individual sovereignty seemed threatened or impossible.

Identification with the state was, therefore, an individualized experience that aimed to cast off 9 / 11's spectacular unveiling of heteronomy by identifying with that which most prominently holds the promise of mastery: a subjugator, an enforcer, the sovereign hero. The counterpart to the virtuous victim in melodrama is the hero who vanquishes the cause of the victims' pain and eliminates the barrier between the subject and the freedom he or she covets. When combined into a singular character of the victim-hero—a character who is both injured and can self-emancipate from injury—this character, morally validated by prior victimization, has the imperative to eradicate villainy, overcome domination, and reverse powerlessness through a triumphant act of vengeful power that exercises the trappings of sovereign strength. As I argue in chapter 2, the melodramatic hero is the universal liberal individual who emancipates himself and his dependents from injustice and domination. In 9 / 11 discourse, various modes of state action were read as the performance of this singular, masculinized, self-emancipating heroism. Differentiated state actions were congealed into a great single actor that could reassert mastery. Unilateral state action seemed to express ontological narcissism: the belief that a single entity has an innate capacity to master contingency and domesticate the world, and is inherently sovereign, beholden to no power but one's own.[19] To put it bluntly, identification with state expansion thus posits that the subject can be similar to what he or she now idealizes: "Look, you can love me too—I am so like the state."

To subjects who want yet are unable to live up to a model of sovereign agency, bold and unilateral state actions can seem to be one place where a strong autonomy is still possible.[20] By dramatic and bold expressions of state action, I mean actions that are both visually spectacular and widely expansive. In foreign policy, this encompasses unilateral military and political actions such as war, declamations of empire, dramatic withdrawals from multilateral governing policies and transnational treaties, the dictating of international security policies for other countries, and prominent rhetorical demonstrations of state sovereignty.[21] In domestic policy, this includes large and often overt expansions in state penetration and surveillance; the explicit retraction of institutional civil liberties, such as indefinite detention, the retraction of habeas corpus, and the use of military tribunals; and dramatic and widely publicized restructurings and intensifications of governmental regulatory and monitoring capabilities. In my reading, widespread support for these actions was motivated by an individual desire for sovereignty. State action can seem to harbor the possibility of unrestrained power over the contingencies of the world, where the ability to control others and the world still gains credence.

One of the most freighted moments of intended sovereign power in the post-9/11 moment was the "Mission Accomplished" performance in spring 2003, a heightened site for the individual identification with state action. The body of President George W. Bush, situated beneath the banner reading "mission accomplished" after the rhetorical end of combat operations in Iraq, was an exemplar for the way that individual sovereignty merges with the expression of state power. Bush's melodramatic performance—landing a fighter jet on an aircraft carrier to announce the end of combat operations in Iraq less than two months after the start of the war—was full of potent gestures and intentional swagger that aimed to revive the fantasy that an individual can be as sovereign as a war-winning state. Bush personified in individualized, bodily form the belief, and omnipotence, of American mastery.[22] Clad in a military uniform, Bush merged the individual and the state into the presidential body, which, as Michael Rogin would remind us, is often figured to be both ordinary and heroic, at once mortal and institutional.[23] Bush performed the unilateralism of the Iraq War. The performance was a melodramatic attempt to prove that U.S. sovereignty is still possible, and to do so through the actions of the president at the nation's helm.

Aside from the many ways we could read "mission accomplished" as the culmination of Bush's own personal fantasies of military prowess, it is crucial to see how Bush was positioned for the U.S. populace as a deindividuated American hero whose actions were available to all Americans. He embodied in spectacular form the individual capacity to enact the full trappings of sovereign freedom. As Thomas Elsaesser and Peter Brooks note, melodramatic characters are often positioned less as unique individuals than as ideological positions: The "mission accomplished" performance, while starring Bush as its key player, was ultimately less about Bush than about the U.S. norms of heroism and individual sovereignty he stood in for.[24] Indeed, action figures in flight suits bearing Bush's likeness were subsequently marketed to children, so that children could literally imagine themselves as him. Bush, commanding a fighter jet and announcing the triumph of freedom, was the personification of the individualized norms of freedom and agency he embodied at that moment. The melodramatic identification with state action configured moments like this to personify and unify the fragmented conditions of state power into a heroic savior, condense the myriad possible responses to the events of 9/11 into an idealization of militaristic state action, and legitimate warfare as a morally requisite action for gaining freedom.

## State Identification and Individual Unfreedom

Yet the reasons behind individuals' identifications with unilateral expressions of state power did not originate on September 11; they began in two other more long-standing conditions that I detail in the previous chapter: the devitalized agency produced through commonplace forms of political disempowerment and inequality shaping daily life in the United States, and a general desire for sovereignty that figures prominently in U.S. politics as a norm and birthright. Understanding heroic identifications thus entails stepping back from the immediacy of 9/11 to examine the historical shifts and political discourses that embed it.

The post-9/11 desire for mastery that motivates the identification with state power derives from the juxtaposition between a desire for freedom and generalized conditions of political powerlessness in contemporary life. This juxtaposition stems from the ways in which formally free individuals are not only materially constrained by multiple and interweaving modes of social power but are also shaped by contemporary global crises such as empire, occupation, and imperialism across broad international populations— from the broadening control of the state and economy over aspects of social life previously ascribed to the "private" realm, such as education, child rearing, and welfare, and from capital, terrorism, ethnic wars, racism, sexism, entrenched and broadening levels of poverty, environmental destruction, security privatization, and resource scarcity. Under these conditions, citizens are excluded from national politics and made into consumers rather than active players in the operations of collective decision making; multinational corporate powers promote vast levels of exploitation while evading accountability and visibility in taking responsibility for the destructiveness of their actions; and individuals often seem unable to exercise freedom or effect change in the world. They are conditioned by the impinging effects of global capital and global interdependence, by the downward mobility and eroded security they create throughout most of the population, and by the sense that no individual or single agent has the ability to master or control the powers that shape ordinary and lived experiences of powerlessness. Lauren Berlant describes these experiences not as crisis but as "crisis ordinariness," in which survival is at stake even in the mundane experiences of daily life—in which the sense of crisis is not acute but has become an ordinary, lived condition.[25] Identification with the state addresses the very ordinariness of these experiences through a melodramatic narrative that insists upon their uniqueness, their nonordinariness, and then asserts both the state's and citizens' capacity for sovereign mastery over all experiences of crisis and fear.

Identification internalizes state violence as a way of undoing familiar experiences of unfreedom. Defeating terrorism is weighted with reversing long-standing experiences of powerlessness through a powerful act of sovereign triumph. The vital importance of the Shock and Awe military campaign in Iraq, for instance, was that its shock and awe were aimed as much at American viewers as the Iraqi military. The media coverage of the bombing of Baghdad was crucial to the maintenance of state identification; the visual proof of overwhelming power cemented and sustained it. Live video feed of bombing campaigns and detailed descriptions of military firepower did not merely reflect a national obsession with military hardware but an intense desire to see the moment of power's impact, to verify the massive forcefulness of state action. I'll address the misrepresentation that these military targets caused American powerlessness later in the chapter. For now, I am arguing that by delimiting 9 / 11 as a singular and clear moment of thwarted freedom, melodramatic political discourse held out the promise of a bound field to fight against unfreedom, to resist 9 / 11's exposure of more extensive, ordinary, and long-standing forms of powerlessness.

Working synergistically with melodramatic interpretations of victimhood, identification with the so-called heroism of state action became a second form of reclaiming power, one that aimed to overcome the devitalized agency in contemporary subjectivity by reasserting sovereign power. This reading of melodramatic identifications puts post-9 / 11 unilateralism in a new light: it was an attempt to prove that American sovereignty was still possible. Raymond Geuss argues of post-9 / 11 politics: "The problem is not that the United States represents a *hyperpuissance* with which it is no longer possible to deal on terms of rough equality, but rather that the United States is in fact now far too weak to play the role that it attributes to itself."[26] The legitimation and attempted performance of unilateral action contains a plea to prevent the twilight of the trust in state (and individual) sovereignty that had already occurred, and that was demonstrated by the 9 / 11 events.

The identification with the state as an expectation of sovereignty, however, is not conditioned solely by the unfreedoms of contemporary politics but also conditioned by the very discourses of freedom that shape norma-tive desires for sovereignty. The lost object that initiates identification with state power is more than the loss of freedom from terrorist attacks and the bewildering, indifferent, and violent forms of governmentalizing power circulating in contemporary life. The lost object also derives from a set of promises that originated in the seventeenth century yet still help to orga-nize the expectations for contemporary American political subjects about the possibility and ontology of self-reliance, mastery, and control over the self and world. Identification with state action is thus also, in part, an effect of a specific type of liberal individualism that saturates melodramatic politi-cal genre conventions and valorizes expectations of mastery over and au-tonomy from the social world. American political subjects are often shaped by liberal individualism's expectations of individual sovereignty and self-determinism, as well as neoliberalism's more extreme insistence on entre-preneurship and personal responsibility for risk as the normative ideals of political subjectivity.[27] Political subjects struggle intensely with the disjunc-ture between these norms and their lived experiences of dependence, in-effectiveness, and vulnerability. Inevitable dependencies seem to demon-strate subjects' failure to live up to individualism's ideal image: to be self-reliant, to master power, to pull oneself up by one's bootstraps, to actively and unilat-erally determine the course of one's existence while shunning all forms of dependence and support. Freedom is presumed to be a type of self-determinism that implies the capacity to control historical and political uncertainty. It is understood to be both the lived experience of mastery and the absence of power over the self. Interdependence of any sort is con-sidered unfreedom, so that freedom is sustained through an aggressive stance toward other individuals, nations, and even nature.[28] The desire for freedom here translates into a desire for mastery over the external envi-ronment, as only full control over the external world can guarantee the absence of constraint.

The juxtaposition between the norms of sovereign individual freedom and the political conditions of dependence and fear that subjects live within create the desire for sovereign agency, which intensifies in the post-9/11 moment into the identification with state power. Identification interprets state violence as a way of undoing unfreedom, specifically for melodramatic subjects shaped by individualism's expectations of self-reliance and mas-tery. Figurations of individualism actually set the conditions for the expan-sion of state power through the fantasy that this power is an extension of each individual's own. It is thus different from other patriotisms based only on identification with other citizens and on group bonds. Identification here is not primarily with other citizens, but with the very act of state power, and with the way it is imagined to be sovereign freedom.

The exercise of state power thus doubly functions as the lost object of identification, in both literal and figurative forms. Literally, the identifying subject realizes he or she has lost what is desired: mastery of, or domination over, the exercise of key institutions of political power that govern the subject. Figuratively, the state stands in for a certain type of power that the subject has lost but intensely desires: a sovereign power that is self-determining and unbound, a power that seems to be the expression of freedom and that is embodied in visible and spectacular articulations of state agency. Identification with sovereign state action aims to (re)claim lost power by overcoming the sense of powerlessness saturating melodramatic subjectivity, performing a spectacular experience of overwhelming power.

Identification with state power is enabled because the categories that define individual agency also often shape American interpretations of state agency. State institutions and processes are often rhetorically figured into a unified agent, a singular, self-reliant individual, so that varied and unaligned actions congeal into the expression of a sovereign subject. Disparate governmental agencies and actions are discursively consolidated into a unilateral, personified force that conquers its external enemies and manages the domestic population. Gelled together, these various state functions seem to signify the type of power recognized and understood within the possessive individualism of mainstream liberal discourses: an autonomous power that is self-governing and ontologically capable of self-emancipation in situations of duress or heteronomy.[29] In the late twentieth century, the discourse of individualism increasingly described and personified U.S. state power, especially with the onset of neoliberalism's ascription of personhood and accountability to corporations as well as to the state (as I argue in chapter 2).[30] The norms of American individualism shaped the possibilities for various modes of state power, especially their modalities in state-corporate mergers, and melodramatic heroism mapped onto the agency of the nation-state. This heroism articulated a personified notion of state action and state capacity through the concept of the heroic, self-reliant individual. Individualism narrated state action by categorizing various state powers qua individual.

Identification with state action relies not only on the mimetic constitution of self and state but also on America's particularly democratic promise that individuals author the state, as electoral accountability and the "people as the origin of political power" claim enable the fantasy that state action could be an extension of one's own. Identification with the state relies on the formal structure of America's representative democracy, which promises that state power originates in its citizens and is always accountable to them. State power is thus, uneasily, an extension of the civic self and a source of potential domination. It is both a potential site of democratic participation and a potential site of overweening power. State power is seen to be created by laws formally authorized by all, electorally accountable to the people, steered toward their vision of the good life, and an expression of the might of the nation. But it is also a likely tyrant that citizens are wary of and that threatens their freedom at every moment, and thus something that they must tame and steer through electoral accountability. This produces what Murray Edelman diagnoses as the continuous slippage in referents to the state as both "us" and "them."[31] Foreign policy provides the arena for demonstrating autonomous state power vis-à-vis other entities, and the democratic, state-as-civic-self model of governance yokes the individual to state power's operations.

Deployments of melodrama suggest a constitutive equivalence between the state and the individual, which works because the state continues to be the primary source of accountable public power. Even in a deterritorialized era of late-modern globalization—as multinational regulatory bodies and corporate powers might seem to make state capacities increasingly irrelevant to the flow of people, goods, capital, and power—the state remains the discursive locus of power, the conferrer of rights and political recognition in public life. Paul Passavant refers to this as the "strong neoliberal state" in order to highlight how neoliberal governmentality contributes to and consolidates, rather than weakens, state expansion and visibility.[32] Brown similarly argues that the state continues to be the primary power visible, and responsible, as political power.[33] This is certainly not to say that state functions are the only source of political power, but they are the primary ones that are formally accountable and publicly verifiable in political life, especially as corporate power is so often invisible in its governmental functions. State functions are aggregated as a key nodal point for political identity, knowledge, power, and influence. They seem to embody and employ instruments of protection and strength—military power, juridical authority, legal legitimacy—that wield power visibly and on a large scale. Within political life, the state is the most obvious symbol of sovereign power, and its symbolism leads to melodrama's figuration of state power as the singular hero of geopolitics.

In neoliberal policies state power is often considered a barrier or impo-
sition to individual freedom, but post-9/11 melodrama revealed neoliberalism's conviviality with expansive state power. Subjects turned to melodrama,
and its heroization of state action, in part to fight against their inability to
live up to the neoliberal norms of individual freedom. This inability to live
up to the norms of individual freedom is deepened by policies that rhetorically promote individual freedom but mainly work to undermine it at the
expense of corporate capital. Melodramatic identifications with state
power reveal how neoliberal individualism has not been necessarily opposed to the state but has also mapped onto, and directed, the very notion
of state agency. Neoliberal norms of individualism and personal responsibility, especially in melodrama, lead *to* the state, not only to a distrust of
state power but also to its uncritical support. These norms paved the way
for how the national identifications arising out of 9/11 melodrama involved identifying not only with other fellow Americans or with a larger
sense of patriotic nationhood but also with the very governing mechanisms of the federal state.

Yet identification only occurs with an object that is lost or dead, that
does not or cannot exist in practice. Identification with state action aims to
sustain the moribund promise of individualism by imagining its revivifica-
tion at the state level, so that the power of the unilateral sovereign state
could be imagined as an extension of each American citizen's sovereignty.
Yet heroism as state action only creates a vicarious way of experiencing
sovereignty. The individual identification with state power is, of course, experienced only as a fantasy of individual power. In relation to post-9/11
politics, the immediate source of blame for unfreedom was already dead
(the hijackers), or hidden (Osama bin Laden), or a complicated configuration of foreign affairs too convoluted to be singularly defined or bound as a
national entity. Yet blame was categorized in tidy and monological terms—
through singular causes (terrorists), national boundaries (Afghanistan,
then Iraq), and moral binaries (America versus the axis of evil). Identification drew from the impulse to overcome what had caused individuals to
"lose" their freedom—a loss that is perhaps constitutive of this contemporary political subject. Because the target for the hero's display of mastery—
terrorism—was not the only cause of powerlessness, nor were efforts to
personify terrorism's tactical nature successful, the feeling of unfreedom
remained unchallenged and even intensified.

Surely this is why the killing of bin Laden a decade after the terrorist attacks he orchestrated did not provide any real sense of national relief to a

population continually beset by glaring examples of their own political un-freedom and economic powerlessness, commonplace experiences that have nothing to do with terrorism—from the housing crisis and endless political corruption scandals to massive levels of unemployment, demobilizations of a dissenting electorate, and the *Citizens United* decision. Throughout the last decade, the expectation was that the killing of bin Laden would finally satisfy the long-delayed gratification of the "mission accomplished" trium-phalism over terror. Yet aside from the few students whose drunken late-night cheers at the White House on the night of bin Laden's death dominated the media coverage and stood in for American sentiment writ large, there has been no substantial nationwide, long-term sense of satisfaction or sense of settled freedom out of that moment.[34] Lived experiences of political and economic helplessness overcame any sense of the heroism or mastery seem-ingly generated out of his death.

And these experiences were intensified through the policies intended to recuperate sovereignty. The recuperation of individual mastery entailed the legitimation of policies that abrogated dissent and protest, that engendered individual surveillance, eviscerated civil liberties, increased regulation of individual action, and sanctioned brutal violence. The alleged solution for recapturing freedom became the state- and corporate-organized policies that composed the war on terror. Melodrama restored the fantasy of un-bound freedom to both the individual and the state, yet its identifications legitimated policies and powers that explicitly targeted the American citi-zens employing these policies and powers to challenge their sense of unfree-dom, the very citizens who turned to them to fulfill their individual capacity for heroic mastery over the dominations that shape their world. Identifica-tion with state expansion engrained the experiences of powerlessness it was employed to relieve, inflicting greater unfreedom upon the subject as well as greater violence throughout the global order.

### Omnipotence through Interdependence

Although the post-9/11 identification with state power was primarily based on a desire for individual freedom rather than group loyalty, it was part of the intense patriotism that arose in the wake of the 9/11 events. Steven Johnston describes this patriotism as a form of narcissism.[35] Patriotic nar-cissism posits the national subject at the center of the world order while demanding continuous national self-congratulation for its violent actions toward those both inside and outside national boundaries. Johnston names this a "self-excusing narcissism" in which professions of goodness translate into a vigilant enmity whereby "the world remains at America's disposal."[36] The identification with state power drew from the same narcissistic desire Johnston diagnoses while radically individualizing it. According to Freud, identification brokers a loss over the specific object one has desired and also a more primal loss originating in narcissism. In Freud's work "On Narcissism," the primal loss that initiates all identifications is the experience of omnipotence felt by infants in their earliest development. Freud understands infants to experience a state of primary narcissism, in which they assume mastery over a world undifferentiated from themselves, in which their needs are gratified instantly, their bodies auto-satisfying. This experience erodes rapidly once the infant gains a sense of his or her own dependence and vulnerability, but the desire for primary narcissism remains. For Freud, the work of identification in general is an attempt to re-create a psychic state of narcissistic omnipotence, a mastery over the external world through the capacity for self-satisfaction. Setting up the lost object as an ideal within the self is a way to recapture mastery out of the feeling of loss: "That which he projects ahead of him as his ideal is merely his substitute for the lost narcissism of his childhood—the time when he was his own ideal."[37] As Johnston notes, this process involves fantasizing away one's condition of dependence on others. It is repeated throughout the individual's life in all forms of identification. In melodramatic identifications with state power, when the very ideal of sovereignty is the lost object, identification occurs not only with a particular ideal of individual mastery but with the crux of idealization itself: the desire for omnipotence. When sovereignty is the aim of primary narcissism as well as the aim of the identification with state power, the longing for it can only be compounded. Identification with the state becomes that much more intense and intransigent.

While Freud reads primary narcissism as a universal formation of human development, I would interpret his diagnosis as a historically situated and culturally specific reading of human behavior, one conditioned by the Euro-American late-modern era that he contributes to and also prefigures. Freud sees the desire for omnipotence as a transhistorical, even biological, quality of human development. Yet he seems to make observations and assumptions that are either tied to their particular moment or read into it, fed by a specific historicity in which mastery is naturalized as the thwarted aim of human behavior. Perhaps Freud's very analysis of primary omnipotence is an effect of the desire for mastery grounded in a late-modern liberalism. While I do not want to claim that Freud is squarely situated within the terms of liberal individualism (he is not), I instead want to suggest that primary narcissism is akin to a historical configuration of ontological narcissism that posits mastery as the ground and aim of individual desire. The perpetual sense of lost power, one that can be regained through acts of self-emancipation, structures the operations of both primary narcissism and liberal individualism.

Melodramatic political subjectivity, shaped through an identification with state power, aims to generate experiences of power out of conditions of dependence. This subjectivity hopes to soothe the "loss" of autonomy by identifying with what it cannot be, and by justifying vengeance against the "cause" of its loss. Identification with state power challenges constraint by actively fighting what it deems its cause—terrorism—and reasserting the individual capacity for mastery. What is so confounding about this situation is that the process of identification is itself a profoundly relational and interdependent process. It involves the formation of the self through one's encounters with others and the social world. Identification is the formation of the ego through its relations with others; it reveals how subjects are constituted by internalizing their relationships with others. It is the very basis of sociality, as Mikkel Borch-Jacobsen, Judith Butler, Kaja Silverman, Jacques Lacan, and other scholars working in a psychoanalytic tradition contend.[38] Identifying with a figure of sovereignty is therefore a form of identification that works by denying the very process of self-formation. Identification with the state as a sovereign power is a profound act of disavowal, disavowing not only the relational constitution of subject but the very workings of identification itself.

Perhaps, then, the central crux of state identification is the act of disavowal. For Freud all forms of identification express a desire for independence from and mastery over the world, yet the process of identification also describes the constitution of the subject through its relations with others.[39] The subject is formed as the ego takes on the characteristics of its external love objects. Identification is the satisfaction of mastery through interrelationality. It is the desire for unconstrained action expressed within conditions of interdependence. In this way, identification with state power dramatizes desires for sovereignty particular to contemporary politics and a more long-standing and deeply problematic disavowal of human interdependence in the late-modern era, one that is perhaps, in part, the effect of a widespread liberal individualist definition of human agency that equates mastery and limitlessness with what it means to be free.

## Conclusion: Desires for Freedom?

I have argued that identification with the state as a melodramatic hero posits that individuals legitimate state power because violent unilateralism models an autonomy denied to them and the state after the 9/11 attacks disrupted the premises of sovereignty, premises that had already been eroding in daily life and in global politics for decades. The loss of sovereignty that subjects experienced came from three sources: (1) the spectacle of nonsovereignty on September 11; (2) the historical changes referred to by the umbrella terms *neoliberalism* and *globalization* that often isolate and render individuals vulnerable to dominating powers they neither know nor understand; and (3) a widespread norm of freedom as mastery and sovereignty that makes its pursuit always unattainable. In an attempt to recapture these losses, many Americans authorized violent and expansive state power as a way to experience sovereign freedom, not to buttress their desire for security.

Melodramatic forms of state identification thus demonstrate something more than false consciousness—an individual subject blind to his or her subjection by oppressive power—and more than a subject who actively desires subjection. Because if anything, the process of state identification presupposes an acknowledgment of unfreedom, as well as an acknowledgment of the limits of individualism, of the losses and failures that individualism demands from subjects who gain value solely though their mastery over power. Through identification with state power, the subject must first sense the "loss" of autonomous mastery—the subject's failure to self-make, to control contingency, to experience unrestrained action, and to author the politics that governs his or her existence. To identify with what he or she wants to be similar to, the subject must first differentiate the state ideal from the self. The subject must posit that while the self wants to be *like* state unilateralism, the self exists as separate from it and does not have the power it signifies.

Freud's varied theories of identification all insist that the loss of the love object *must be acknowledged*, in some unconscious way and by some part of the self, for identification to commence. The process of identification can only happen after a subject recognizes a difference between the subject and the subject's ideal, as identification arises to help mitigate the pain of this recognition. Identification presupposes an acknowledgment, however nascent or unconscious, of what the subject is not and does not possess. In this case, the subject must acknowledge the loss of sovereignty (if it ever existed). This includes reckoning with the effects of contemporary intensifications of power, which include, though are certainly not limited to, those exercised by state functions. It also includes reckoning with the failure or unattainability of achieving the norms of neoliberal individualism. Some part of the self must acknowledge that the model of individual freedom as unconstrained agency no longer serves the self in a meaningful way. For Freud and the psychoanalytic tradition that came after him, the nature of this acknowledgment and the specific part of the psyche that acknowledges this loss remains murky; it is ultimately left undertheorized.[40] What remains clear, however, is that in identification the loss is registered and expressed, even if it is subsequently denied, displaced, or repressed: the loss is experienced by the "bodily ego" even if it is not consciously articulated.[41]

Moreover, the desire for identification is derived from the desire to *challenge* conditions that cause experiences of constraint. Identification is a way for a subject to resist the loss of sovereign freedom in an ingenious way: reinstituting a facsimile of sovereignty inside the self.[42] The initial awareness of one's inability to be a sovereign subject illuminates how identification is animated by the subject's sense of his or her own situated and interdependent experiences, and by a desire to challenge them. Identification highlights the subject's awareness of the difference between what one is and what one wanted to be, between heteronomy and sovereignty. Identification highlights the subject's desire to resist power and experience a type of freedom—one primarily defined as unbound and masterful action.

The identification with state action is then, at its outset, an attempt to recapture a lost sense of sovereign power, to challenge experiences of regulation and exclusion, to recapture a capacity for freedom. Animated by the loss of what the subject desires but cannot have, state identification idealizes what the subject "should have been"—sovereign, self-making—and what the subject now desires to be "like."[43] Once state power is differentiated from the self, it is then set up internally as an ideal. Through the subject who salves her loss by imagining herself like state power, identification operates to fortify the very terms of American liberal individualism that contribute to loss—insisting that subjects can master contingency and can exercise heroic overcoming of their dependence. Perhaps because of its very unattainability, the ideal of individual sovereignty always produces loss as its effect. It creates a bind in which the type of freedom that individualism recognizes as desirable is always already unattainable.

The subject's initial awareness of a discrepancy between oneself and one's ideal thus does not lead to broader recognition of *why* this discrepancy exists, or perhaps to a reevaluation of the object the subject desires, but leads instead to a reidealization in new form. Heroic identification with the state illustrates subjects' incipient awareness that sovereign control is not possible, that heroic mastery over the self and the world is fictive. However, identification reinstates the lost object as an internal ideal. Identification subsequently represses this incipient recognition while embedding the operations of impinging and regulatory power ever deeper into subjects. It refigures awareness of power's expansions back into the terms of individual heroism and deflates the possibility for a more productive critical engagement. Post-9/11 identification with the state hinders the fight against forms of power that sustain unfreedom. By way of desiring opposition to forms of contemporary power, melodramatic political subjects identify with and legitimate oppressive forms of power, repudiating a deeper interrogation into their lived conditions of unfreedom, and eventually sanctioning violence, surveillance, and war.

Following 9/11 a decathexis with the state did eventually happen, but only after the slow realization that the "mission accomplished" of the war on terror did not actually accomplish its mission, and especially after the Abu Ghraib images were uncovered. The Abu Ghraib images had a profound effect on the disidentification with state power. This was due, of course, to the horror they engendered by revealing detailed pictures of torture and cruelty perpetrated by U.S. citizens on detained individuals. Yet part of the images' horror was their revelation of the squalidness of military power: the images uncovered a form of state violence normally shielded from public view. They did not depict smart bombs targeting a hidden enemy outpost or a cutting-edge U.S. Air Force jet shooting dehumanized evildoers from above, images that dominate media coverage of the war on terror. Instead, the images revealed the small, individualized, even routinized aspects of violence, suffering, and death in war. The Abu Ghraib photos countered the antiseptic heroism of "shock and awe" with the literal and metaphoric blood of bodily torture and human cruelty; they revealed the misery that the pursuit of unbound mastery can inflict on other humans, the distinct lack of strength that is required to overpower and brutalize another person in situations of structural domination. The pictures directly countered the melodramatic claims of U.S. military justice as clear, or U.S. strength as based on superior moral and technological capacity. In deglorifying the pursuit of mastery, the images showed the ordinary brutal tactics of calculated terror behind the glittery green curtain of smart-bomb videos. The gradual failure of "mission accomplished," combined with the harsh immediacy of the Abu Ghraib revelations, weakened the idealization of U.S. state mastery and reexposed the larger experiences of global interdependence and individual constraint that animate a sense of lost sovereignty, a loss intensified for national subjects who assume that sovereignty is their inheritance and birthright.

The weakening of state identification, however, could have taken different forms, and the desire for freedom could have been expressed in many alternative ways. What would it look like to sustain the acknowledgment that loss engenders: that the object of desire is gone, that one's ideal is no longer tenable and perhaps was never viable? For Freud this involves a mourning process that concludes by rerouting desire to a new, more tenable, more live object. This process is not clearly delineable or fully predictable. The desire to contain contingency and garner complete knowledge of the future is itself a derivation of the desire for sovereign freedom—its satisfaction clearly impossible. The rerouting of desire can thus never be predicted in advance, and this is part of its danger. Yet static and predetermined ideas of freedom are also insufficient to predict the rerouting of desire in the wake of mourning lost sovereignty. Freedom entails more than a stable and binary condition, in which one is or is not free, or in which the settled terms of freedom's experience are laid out in advance of its pursuit. Part of the practice of freedom is a keen responsiveness to the specific experiences of domination and exploitation that one wishes to change or overcome. This responsiveness is the first step in the very hard and necessarily collaborative work of finding new languages and new practices to respond to present unfreedoms.

The animating impulses of both individualism and melodrama derive in part from a desire for freedom—a desire to expose and resist dominating power—yet refiguring their post-9/11 legitimating functions could include sustaining recognition that freedom does not entail sovereignty even as freedom demands accountability for the actions that shape political life.[44] This recognition might open the space for new modes of political agency that are necessarily collective and interdependent, that account for the actions they enable and support, and that work to challenge material and structural experiences of unfreedom. Peter Fitzpatrick argues that post-9/11 politics requires reconceiving freedom to entail responsibility for others as a necessary precondition.[45] A desire for freedom as nonsovereign responsibility can enable tools for pushing more resourcefully against encumbrances of power, instead of rehabilitating the lost, dead object of individual mastery. As Butler, Jill Bennett, and many other feminist thinkers have suggested, by acknowledging lived conditions of interdependence in the contemporary era, challenges to structural unfreedom might draw more deeply upon the resources of collective life for establishing conditions of social justice, freedom, and human equality, using interdependence as a source of strength that works with collective resources rather than against them.[46] This might also assist the crucial work of distinguishing foundational social interdependence from the increasing binds of governmental and neoliberal power. While melodramatic political subjects who legitimated war and increases in the national-security state were partly motivated by a desire to resist the rapidly intensifying regulations of power, it remains to be seen whether those desires could be transformed into a more productive challenge to the specific conditions they aim to change, and whether they can nourish different conceptions of agency and freedom from those that sustain the unfreedoms of current politics.

# SIX

# LEFT MELODRAMA

Melodramatic conventions catalyze desires for freedom across the political spectrum. Given melodrama's popularity in the conservative and neoliberal policies of current politics, it would be easy to diagnose melodramatic political discourse as a right-wing phenomenon, or as a genre that primarily infuses lowbrow and uncritical political discourse. It might even be easy to assume that melodramatic conventions do not take hold of radical or theoretical addresses, as if theoretical critique and radical politics confer immunity from either melodrama's affective charge or its promise of freedom for virtuous sufferers. Yet the melodramas I address in this chapter circulate in both radical and theoretical forms, and they draw inspiration from a more emancipatory politics of freedom than the melodramas examined in earlier chapters. These melodramas are deployed through leftist political theory to critique war, imperialism, and oppression. What I call *left melodrama* merges the narrative structure and thematic elements of the melodramatic genre found in literary and cinematic texts with leftist political commitments, fusing them into a form of critique that dramatically interrogates conditions of unfreedom, exploitation, and inequality in contemporary politics.

Melodrama takes an alternate shape in leftist politics and high political-theoretical contexts, and this chapter examines its distinct history, operations, and effects. Left melodrama unfolds within a heightened moral drama of good and evil in which U.S. empire, oppressive state power, and the forces of administered capitalism are arrayed as villainy. The proletariat and other marginalized and vulnerable people across the globe subject to the violent whims of imperialistic and corporate power are melodramatic victims. Exemplary practitioners of this analysis include Michael Hardt, Antonio Negri, and Giorgio Agamben, theorists whose important works have captured the interest of a generation of scholars, as well as the interest of a reading public broader than that enjoyed by most academics. Left melodrama's appeal derives from the moral clarity it confers on the complex powers organizing politics and subjectivity, from its ability to identify the victims of these powers (i.e., what Hardt and Negri term "the multitude" and what Agamben terms *homo sacer*, or people living under conditions of bare life), from the virtuous power it bestows upon conditions of subjugation, and in the case of Hardt and Negri from the assurance it offers that heroic emancipation can conquer the villainous source of oppression.

Left melodrama is, in many ways, a countermelodrama to melodramatic political discourse's legitimation of imperialism and securitization. Left melodrama draws from melodramatic genre conventions with the aim to counter affective investments in empire, war, surveillance, detention, antidemocratic power, and nationalism. The image of freedom that animates left melodrama challenges deployments of melodrama in the service of expansive anti-democratic state power and violence, offering instead visions of emancipation that aim to cultivate real equality and collective freedom across national boundaries. Yet while left melodrama intends to galvanize its audience for radical social change, its conventions and attachments limit its capacity to depict the distinct challenges and specific conditions of political life.

The differences between melodramatic political discourse and left melodramatic political theory are, on one level, surface differences: different identities for who is included as a righteous victim and what qualifies as a scenario of overwhelming power, different depictions of the actions that are nested under heroism, and different visions that animate the promise of future freedom. As Christine Gledhill argues of melodrama, "Anybody can occupy positions of victim and oppressor, serving any ideological configuration."[1] Yet left melodrama originates in a different historical tradition than American melodramatic political discourse: in the pervasive use of melodrama in revolutionary contexts, as opposed to its use in U.S. nationalsecurity strategy. Left melodrama also draws from a different theoretical tradition: from Karl Marx rather than John Locke and John Stuart Mill. Left melodrama therefore takes sustenance from a different imaginary of freedom: one more communist and collective than liberal and individualist. And, crucially, left melodrama is a different form of melodramatic politics because it is an effect of left melancholy. It demonstrates a melancholic holding on to the Left's former power in a late-modern and neoliberal era in which leftist politics are often sidelined, marginalized, and ineffective.

Left melodrama is a recent form of political theory, but it recapitulates an older dynamic that Walter Benjamin diagnosed as "left melancholy."[2] Left melancholy, according to Benjamin, is a type of leftist critique in which scrutiny of the present is disabled by its attachments to past promises; it deadens what it examines because it employs analyses that are both insufficiently radical and outdated in relation to current inequalities and exploitations. Left melodrama stems from left melancholy in part because its attachments to older forms of critical scrutiny undercut and subvert a grasp of the contemporary objects it interrogates. Melancholy is defined by Freud as a refusal to acknowledge one's desire to repossess something that has been loved and lost. Contemporary left political theory is melancholic when it disavows its attachments to the failed but still-loved promise of left critique: that its methods will accurately gauge and help overcome the brutality of capitalism, and that left critique will provide a direct means to freedom and moral virtue. In other words, left melodrama is underpinned by a refusal to acknowledge the loss of left political theory's guarantee to provide a means to revolutionary freedom, as well as the loss of intrinsic moral virtue implicitly granted to its practitioners.

More subtly, left melodrama is melancholic because it incorporates the particular melodramatic narrative, style, and promise of *The Communist Manifesto*. *The Communist Manifesto* is a melodrama. It offers a heightened story about the suffering of virtuous people overwhelmed by nefarious forces, and uses dramatic language, polarizing binaries for diagnosing oppression, race-to-the-rescue chases, and the promise of heroic emancipation from villainy. It is a paradigmatic text for contemporary left melancholy, as it comes to represent what the Left has desired and lost: the guarantee of immanent freedom, the clear virtue of leftist political positions, and the promise of the Left's destiny as the harbinger of revolutionary emancipation. Left melodrama recapitulates the manifesto's melodramatic style in a melancholic effort to hold on to its promises and stave off these losses.

The current appropriation of *The Communist Manifesto*'s melodramatic form intends to be an important counter to the violence of empire and neoliberal capital, but it also inhibits the creation of new critical methods appropriate for analyzing these phenomena and occludes Marx and Engels's own counsel that the possibility of radical transformation is diminished when longing for the past colors the blueprint for the future. For Marx and

Engels, only when visions of the future are open-ended can they remain unburdened by the structural and imaginative limitations of the present. Contemporary left melodrama entrenches the deadening effects of left melancholy, and thus its countermelodrama impedes its political-theoretical efforts to challenge the specific forms of inequality, injustice, and unfreedom that shape our present moment.

## Left Melancholy and Political Critique

Benjamin once penned a brief scathing critique of left intellectuals whose writings seemed only to reinforce the exploitation they placed under interrogation. He derided the way their condemnations of society derived from habitual modes of criticism rather than a real desire for change and became reflex responses imposed upon difficult problems. Erich Kastner, the particular Weimar-era writer who served as an exemplar of this broader condition, was "as incapable of striking the dispossessed with his rebellious accents as he [was] of touching the industrialists with his irony."[3] Kastner's routinized forms of scrutiny betrayed a longing for the comfort of past sureties that precluded insight into present configurations of power and inequality, and thus stifled possibilities for more radical political critique.

Benjamin titled his critique "Left-Wing Melancholy," but he did not provide an explicit definition of the term in the text. The term is provocatively compared, however, to a "clenched fist in papier-mâché": a figure that outwardly gestures to revolutionary desire yet is reified, inanimate, frozen in place at the same time that it has no inside material.[4] Its core contains only "empty spaces," "hollow forms," an inner void where melancholy holds on to dead objects instead of engaging the world of animate life—even and especially when that world is increasingly oppressive, commodified, fascist, and in desperate need of radical social transformation to real equality and freedom.[5]

Benjamin's term *left melancholy* seems to imply not only the act of holding on to dead objects—the more conventional way of interpreting melancholy after Sigmund Freud—but also the frightening act of deadening live subjects in its grasp. In *The Origin of German Tragic Drama*, where Benjamin more directly engages in the concept of melancholy, he describes it in one iteration as "the deadening of the emotions . . . [that] can increase the distance between the self and the surrounding world to the point of alienation from the body."[6] Melancholy's deadening work creates distance between the self and the world it places under investigation, an act that can potentially provoke *distanciation*, Bertolt Brecht's term for the ability to distance individuals from the normative conventions that shape their lives, and which offers a standpoint from which to critique these conventions.[7] But it also harbors the dangerous threat of devitalizing that very world. In melancholy "the utensils of active life are lying around unused on the floor, as objects of contemplation."[8] Melancholy, in this regard, is a form of contemplation that makes alien the things in the world; in the particulars of left melancholy, this making alien turns active material into unused, inert objects.[9] In "Left-Wing Melancholy" Benjamin similarly describes Kastner's intellectual movement as accomplishing "the transposition of revolutionary reflexes . . . into objects of distraction, of amusement, which can be supplied for consumption."[10] Left melancholy is akin to a process of reification, as habituated forms of leftist scrutiny drain the vitality and energetics of both the melancholic and the objects he or she holds on to, vitality necessary for sustaining the critical push for freedom in a dark and dangerous time. By diminishing revolutionary potential, left melancholy reflects the outward trappings that signify work for social change while its animating core is inert, empty, and lifeless.

At the end of the twentieth century, Wendy Brown revisited "Left-Wing Melancholy" to ask how Benjamin's analysis could supply a diagnosis for the contemporary moment. In "Resisting Left Melancholy," Brown argues that loss now saturates leftist intellectual inquiry, as leftist academics must contend with the loss of legitimacy for Marxism and socialism, the loss of a unified movement and method, and the loss of viable alternatives to counter the nexus of liberalism and capitalism. These losses originate in part in leftist critical analysis, which has had difficulty accounting for recent formations of power and thus has become ineffective in challenging them. For Brown the difficulty in analyzing contemporary power is traceable to new iterations of left melancholy. She addresses the unanswered questions from Benjamin's piece by examining the content of the losses that left melancholy clings to, and by asking how left melancholy accomplishes its deadening work. Addressing the latter question first, she suggests that deadening arises from the conventional methodologies of left critical theory: economic determinism, totalizing social analysis, and a teleology of human emancipation have proven inadequate or unsustainable for grappling with the current conditions of contemporary politics. Significant historical shifts have changed how politics and the economy have operated and interconnected with individuals since the mid-nineteenth century, but leftist modes of critique have often been unable to keep pace with them. Drawing from Stuart Hall, Brown argues that attachments to older forms of critique narrow and devitalize the current dynamics they scrutinize, and thus impede discovery of the unexpected and particular. A more effective analysis would require a break with certain methods and assumptions that had conventionally defined what it meant to be part of the academic Left.

Yet attachments to outdated forms of critique are only one part of the problem, and they have already been confronted by key interventions from feminist theory, queer studies, and postcolonial studies, among other modes of inquiry. More influential, Brown suggests, is the loss that underpins the attachments: "In the hollow core of all these losses, perhaps in the place of our political unconscious, is there also an unavowed loss—the promise that left analysis and left commitment would supply its adherents a clear and certain path toward the good, the right, and the true?"[11] Melancholy, in Freud's "Mourning and Melancholia," is defined as the loss of what cannot be loved, the disavowed desire for something that has left or abandoned the subject. It is the refusal to acknowledge that a "love object" has been lost, or that one had desired this lost object in the first place. Incorporating Freud's analysis, Brown argues that left melancholy is formed by the refusal to acknowledge the desire for what the left has lost: the faith that leftist theoretical analysis and political commitment can provide a direct means to truth, moral virtue, and human freedom. This "hollow core" of loss, perhaps the core of Benjamin's papier-mâché fist, underpins left critical theory. Because it is unacknowledged it continues to inhibit the academic Left's reckoning with the present; the hollow core weakens and marginalizes leftist inquiry. The refusal to relinquish these desires, let alone acknowledge them, marks the refusal to grapple with the failed promise of inevitable emancipation, or as Hall puts it, the refusal to abandon the guarantee that left critique can "rescue us from the vicissitudes of the present."[12] Both Brown and Hall insist that the unsettling and difficult practice of self-critique can begin to undo some of these attachments and counter the disavowals of left melancholy. Sustaining leftist commitments paradoxically requires acknowledging the Left's losses and failures.

In the decade since Brown made her analysis, the topics, range, and methods of left analysis have further expanded and reoriented crucial aspects of critical thought. Widespread criticisms of America's post-9/11 politics reinvigorated leftist critical and political theory and remobilized its sustained commitment to social transformation. Influential authors in American academic circles, such as Agamben, have written trenchant political critiques of contemporary domination that do not privilege only class or capital in diagnosing experiences of unfreedom. Others, such as Hardt and Negri, have used multidisciplinary analyses to delineate complex formations of power and energize revolutionary sentiment. Do these changes demonstrate that melancholy has loosened its hold on leftist intellectual scrutiny? The answer to this question, I offer, is no. The attachments animating left melancholy are still present in particular modes of left theoretical work, though they have been reinscribed in a new form.

Left melancholy continues to shape a type of left political-theoretical inquiry, but the loss it holds onto is more specific than the earlier types that Benjamin and Brown diagnosed and it manifests in a different form, even as the inquiry draws from the dynamics Benjamin and Brown identified. Current left melancholy marks the loss of a particular love object. Freud's analysis of melancholy can help to interpret the nature of this object. Freud makes clear that the lost *object*—his psychoanalytic term for describing what or who is desired—can be a person, a group identity, an abstraction, a country, or an ideal.[13] The melancholic not only refuses to acknowledge that the self has lost or been abandoned by the object of love. He or she also takes on the characteristics of the lost love object. The melancholic subject incorporates the disavowed lost object into the self in order to hold on to what has been lost.[14] Melancholy, therefore, includes both a disavowal of loss and a part of the self that turns into that very object, so that the self begins to mimic the desired lost object. Through incorporation, the melancholic refuses to let the object go.

The lost object, in current left melancholy, is a paradigmatic text that has been weighted with representing the set of losses I have articulated. It is a text that provoked the promise and the dream of radical social transformation, that augured revolution, indeed that founded left praxis, all of which can now seem lost, failed, and out of reach. Most important, this text galvanized millions of people, and its widespread appeal, explosive moral power, and emancipatory guarantee engendered a century or more of transnational solidarity toward the project of human freedom.

### The Lost Object: *The Communist Manifesto*

In certain strands of contemporary critical theory, *The Communist Manifesto* has become the "hollow core," the lost and deadened object. Its style and terms of analysis are reabsorbed into contemporary political inquiry as a way of fending off the losses it represents. *The Communist Manifesto* is lost to the degree that it stands in for the failed twinned promises of leftist critical theory: inevitable emancipation and unwavering moral rightness. In this new form of critical theory, the manifesto represents a former era when leftist political critique seemed unquestionably vital and promising, when the moral virtue of left critique seemed valid, when the freedom it envisioned seemed imminent. Indeed the manifesto, when situated in this way, becomes the instantiation of those guarantees. The logic of the manifesto as the lost love object conjures up a past era when the Left's moral certitude seemed self-evident and aims to recover the possibility that a single text can energize populations for the collective pursuit of human freedom.[15] The Communist Manifesto also represents these failed promises because the collective movements it engendered often only entrenched the oppression they intended to overcome.

While this new form of left melancholy still interprets politics through older leftist frameworks, including monocausality, teleology, and moral certainty, it displaces the earlier analytic targets of capital, revolution, immanent dialectic, and the working class onto different targets. And more strikingly, left melancholy now adopts the galvanizing narrative form that *The Communist Manifesto* uses to tell its story. Left inquiry draws on the text's particularly *melodramatic* narrative form. Melodrama, I offer, shapes the foundational text that provides a key framework for left political analysis. What I call *left melodrama* is a new form of left melancholy that holds on to the manifesto's promises by incorporating its melodramatic narrative and style into its very constitution. *The Communist Manifesto*'s melodrama is melancholically absorbed into some of the most popular critical theory in left academe, particularly the work of Agamben, Hardt, and Negri.

Melodramatic cultural forms, particularly theater, have aligned with left politics for more than two centuries. Early melodramatic plays dramatized and moralized unequal socioeconomic relations, connecting poverty with virtue and wealth with venality.[16] They historically favored the cause of the dispossessed rather than those who held power, and their heroes were often those harmed by a bourgeois economy.[17] The imbrication of melodrama and revolution is well documented by theater historians and literature scholars, as many Euro-American leftists have at key points turned to melodrama "as the most effective means of conveying revolutionary sentiments to mass audiences."[18] And of course, Jean-Jacques Rousseau both invented the term *mélodrame* and posthumously inspired melodramatic critiques of unjust authority in revolutionary France. In the 1830s French and English melodrama contributed to shaping the organizing narratives of the working class and the consciousness of social injustice.[19] One French melodramatist even claimed that his plays organized the 1848 revolution.[20] After the Bolshevik Revolution, Soviet leftists created and subsidized a particularly expressionist form of melodramatic theater and film and proclaimed melodrama to be the most effective cultural form to explain revolutionary ideology.[21] In mid-twentieth-century America, a differently organized and more pessimistic form of melodramatic theatricality infused left sensibilities in the films of Douglas Sirk. For later film scholars, Sirk's Marxist critiques of capitalism and gender norms played out in the tawdriness and excess of his films' mise-en-scène; his films unmasked various forms of oppression using disheartening story lines permeated by alienation and depression.

In addition to melodrama's better-known leftist theatrical and film affiliations, I contend that melodrama also contributes to the political inquiry that structures *The Communist Manifesto*. Karl Marx and Friedrich Engels can be considered melodramatists for penning their challenge for collective emancipation. Reading the manifesto as melodrama shows how the text illuminates class oppression by molding historical relations into stark binaries, detailing the unjust suffering of the proletariat, promising the triumph of heroism, highlighting the righteousness of the oppressed, and employing all of these tropes with the aim to affectively motivate its reader into revolutionary action.

## Manifesto Melodrama

*The Communist Manifesto* takes shape through a melodramatic narrative that connects revolutionary heroism with the social victimization of the proletariat in order to both illuminate the violence of industrial capital and reveal its immanent overcoming. The presumable intentions of the text—to point to the economic forces that drive political and historical development and to motivate radical action to establish an equal, sustainable, and meaningful species-wide human existence—also turn the complex dynamism of history into a melodramatic unfolding. The manifesto promises the radical overcoming of economic domination, and like most melodramas, insists that rightness will eventually prevail. Even for all of Marx's and Engels's claims to the contrary, they still reassure their readers that the world is just: oppression will be eradicated and the oppressed will triumph.

Marx and Engels begin the first section of *The Communist Manifesto* by arguing, "The history of all hitherto existing society is the history of class struggles. Freedman and slave, patrician and plebian, lord and serf, guild master and journeyman—in a word, oppressor and oppressed—stood in constant opposition to one another, carried on an uninterrupted, now hidden, now open fight, a fight that each time ended either in a revolutionary reconstitution of society at large, or in the common ruin of the contending classes."[22] From the outset of the text, Marx and Engels reconfigure the history of social relations into various binary oppositions, which all become an opposition of "oppressor and oppressed." This opposition is not particularly civilizational, nor does it seem to partake in long-standing Greek-barbarian distinctions based on superiority. And neither does it seem to be a product of an ontological friend-enemy antagonism, even though Carl Schmitt melodramatically describes it as such: "This antithesis concentrates all antagonisms of world history into one single final battle against the last enemy of humanity."[23] Rather, this is a distinction that is specifically based on power. It is what Marx and Engels explicitly describe as having become a "simplified" polarity, juxtaposing two options: powerful and powerless, in which power is determined by economic production. For the authors, the modern industrial era has tidied the premodern clutter of human relationships into "two great hostile camps, into two great classes directly facing each other: Bourgeoisie and Proletariat."[24] They create their contemporary moment as a sharpening of hostility down to solitary and stark distinctions. These two classes do not merely face each other; they do so, as the authors state, "directly." This language heightens the back-and-forth drama of this clash of power—what Linda Williams calls melodrama's "dialectic of pathos and action"—part of melodrama's affective engagement with its readers.[25] For Marx and Engels, "political power, properly so called, is merely the organized power of one class for oppressing another."[26] This beginning to *The Communist Manifesto* inaugurates history as a dramatic narrative story about power antagonisms—a building up and compressing of myriad human relationships into one model with two possible positions.

The analysis of this power antagonism does not rest there, however; if read through the generic conventions of melodrama, it is moralized. The binary that Marx and Engels identify is "oppressor and oppressed."[27] Another way to explain this might be to say that it is a distinction based on villainy and victimization; in melodrama the experience of oppression by oppressor is depicted by categories of victim and victimizer, with victimization intensified by the unjustness of the injury. Oppression marks the inverse link between power and moral virtue, so that more of one entails less of the other. If we understand moralization as the overt making of absolute moral claims, then the authors do not explicitly moralize their distinction, nor is their critique reproachful or self-satisfied.[28] However, they do interpret history by drawing on distinctions that have deep-seated moralistic connotations. They do not make direct claims of goodness for the proletariat, but they do describe the proletariat's condition in heightened language that gestures to an organizing structure of good and evil, and they frame events in a cyclical narrative of victimization and overcoming.[29] In these ways, *The Communist Manifesto* signals the melodramatic claim that powerlessness marks virtue. Writing in the 1940s, the literary critic Wylie Sypher argued that Marx uses melodramatic tropes throughout *Capital*.[30] Sypher suggested that Marx's particular uptake of the Hegelian dialectic draws partly from melodrama's Manichean moral binary. For Sypher the social conventions of the nineteenth century were saturated with melodramatic ways of viewing the world; Marx was a product of his time period, and though he was not intentionally employing melodramatic conventions, he would have been hard-pressed to fully extricate himself from melodrama's pervasiveness as a worldview. Though Sypher's claims for melodrama's saturation may be overdrawn, his analysis supports how *The Communist Manifesto* can be read to employ melodrama's moralistic tropes in its depiction of revolution. The manifesto's initial paragraphs draw on the moral horrors of capital to presage the communist revolution and shape how readers interpret the rest of the powerful first section.

In arguing that the bourgeoisie acquires power by conquering all other classes, Marx and Engels diagnose one primary mover of modern history, one that subtends and subsumes other forces: capital. They isolate capital in order to draw attention to its pervasive force, and they place it above and in control of other social forces, which become its derivatives. Capital, and the bourgeoisie as the capitalist class, produces the political, social, and familial dilemmas that *The Communist Manifesto* diagnoses. Even the state is wholly in the service of modern industry. The bourgeoisie puts an end to all other human relations besides those based on exchange and labor; dramatically, the bourgeoisie has "pitilessly torn asunder" feudal ties, leaving only "naked self-interest" and "callous cash-payment." The bourgeoisie's actions are quite violent toward all other human relations. These actions have "drowned," "destroyed," "stripped of [their] halo," and "torn away" their organizing power using "naked, shameless, direct, brutal exploitation."[31] In undoing feudal structures, the bourgeoisie produces a system that resolves human worth into exchange value and generates power for the few at the expense of the working masses. Capital is everywhere, destroying everything, harming everyone. Melodrama's "metaphors of unfreedom," in Thomas Elasesser's words, are well suited for revealing and depicting capital's breathtaking violence.[32] Marx and Engels inform the reader that this power has created more massive and colossal productive forces than in all preceding generations combined. It has subjected nature, burst its own fetters, and cannibalized all other forms of human relationship.

The bourgeoisie absorbs responsibility for the horrors the authors depict; as the generative force of these injustices, it compels, batters down, and creates the world in its own image. *The Communist Manifesto*'s description of villainy makes it easy to champion its overcoming; the bourgeois villain becomes an identifiable target to mobilize against, the singular and clear agent of evil. Marx and Engels may be simplifying power intentionally in the manifesto in order to shed light on the then-underexamined role of capital in social suffering and to emphasize the disregarded conditions of the proletariat. In other texts Marx and Engels portray power and capital in significantly more complex ways. Yet presented in this way and in this text, the isolation of capital comes at the price of diminishing other important generative forces of history and social life, and quite possibly of limiting the possibilities for thinking about how to overcome the plight of the working class. This isolation antecedes the Left's current problem of narrowing the varied phenomena of power and may contribute to—though is not solely responsible for—the determinism that haunts contemporary analysis. With one singular source of accountability, analytic focus is directed at only one aspect of society.

Marx and Engels render in melodramatic detail the suffering of capital's victims. Marx and Engels emphasize the dehumanization of members of the proletariat by describing how they are "rendered worthless" by their burdensome and monotonous toils; they are, in body and soul, "enslaved by the machine."[33] Horrifyingly abject, they are not only without property but also without supportive family relations, without nation, without law, morality, and religion. Stripped of all organizing forces save capital, "the proletariat is [modern industry's] special and essential product."[34] *The Communist Manifesto* both denaturalizes economically produced suffering and makes the weak harbingers of emancipation. Because the proletariat is so stripped, the members' needs are selfless, aligned with all of humanity. The heroic possibility of human emancipation thus lies with them. They become what Karl Löwith calls the "universal human function of the proletariat," as their self-emancipation will necessarily emancipate all humanity.[35] Their abjection is exactly what makes them capable of a world-historic heroism.

After describing the power of villainy and the victimization that it inflicts, *The Communist Manifesto* moves along the melodramatic narrative trajectory and turns to the victim's heroic overcoming. At the end of the first section, Marx and Engels write of the "decisive hour," the classic heightening of suspense, the race-to-the-rescue last-minute tension that makes melodrama such an affectively engaging mode.[36] In their analysis, heroic overcoming will occur by the cruel and violent logic of the very victims of capital. Victims become the heroes and perform their own rescue. As Sheldon Wolin writes, "Not only is revolution to destroy the rule of capital, but the experience is to transform the worker into a heroic actor of epic stature."[37] As the proletariat's numbers grow and its strength concentrates, the future collision between the two classes fulfills the narrative promise, a teleology of revolution providing freedom in (and) equality. The melodramatic cycle whereby the injustice of victimization legitimates the violence of heroism is here made manifest in the authorization of revolution.

Combined with the detailing of villainy, this explanation of victimization and heroism intends to engender, viscerally, a new affective charge. It aims to motivate the desire, and the difficult work, for revolutionary change. The horrors endured by the proletariat inform *The Communist Manifesto*'s readers that this suffering is unjust, cruel, and yet eradicable. The film theorist Jane Gaines emphasizes melodrama's ability to motivate revolutionary sentiment: "Theatrical melodrama has historically been the preferred form of revolutionary periods for precisely its capacity to dichotomize swiftly, to identify targets, to encapsulate conflict, and to instill the kind of pride that can swell the ranks of malcontents. Revolutionary melodrama can be depended upon to narrate intolerable historical conditions in such a way that *audiences wish to see wrongs 'righted,' are even moved to act upon their reaffirmed convictions, to act against tyranny and for the people.*"[38] Gaines, drawing from Sypher, argues that readers of Marx, "like the melodrama audience, see patterns of injustice laid out before us, and we are appalled."[39] Melodrama's affective power, what the literary theorist Peter Brooks calls melodrama's "excess" and Williams calls its "pathos," is what makes melodrama so politically powerful for mobilizing large-scale transformations and can help explain the widespread transnational and transhistorical effects of the manifesto.[40] The manifesto ends with a galvanizing call to action: "The proletarians have nothing to lose but their chains. They have a world to win. WORKING MEN OF ALL COUNTRIES, UNITE!"[41] Having been shown the cruelties and exploitations of industrial capitalism, and asked to reinterpret their own experience through its injustices, *The Communist Manifesto*'s readers are energetically summoned to fight for revolution.

Left melodrama is a contemporary mode of political critique that aims to incorporate the affective force, explanatory power, and moral rightness of *The Communist Manifesto* by drawing on its generic form. Left melodrama details scenes of unjust victimization, employs cycles of pathos and action, divides social formations into moral binaries of protagonists and antagonists, and promises a heroic overcoming of injustice and inequality caused by the very policies supported in post-9/11 melodramatic political discourse in the service of the U.S. fight for freedom. Unlike the manifesto, however, left melodrama is oriented backward to the loss of the past ideals: it intends to regalvanize the twenty-first-century political imagination in the way that the manifesto did in the nineteenth and early twentieth centuries. The contemporary use of melodrama is thus different from the melodrama of the manifesto, as it is motivated by disavowed loss; left melodrama aims to recapture the specific losses represented by the manifesto and positions it to stand as proof of the Left's moral virtue, heroic promise, and capacity to instigate substantive freedom. When melodrama organizes contemporary critical inquiry in this way, disavowed loss sustains left melancholy in melodramatic form.

Incorporating yet irreducible to melodrama's moral economy, left melodrama is a complex phenomenon. It sustains older leftist critical modes such as monocausality when positing a singular and clear accountable subject for oppression (usually in the character of a villain); its villainization and victimization of assorted economic and political positions maintain simplified antagonisms for interpreting social change; and its teleology of heroic overcoming of oppression revives the guarantee that leftist theory inevitably guides toward freedom. Left melodrama even insists that leftist theory is itself an expression of virtue. While left melodrama is a powerful and dramatic way to expose domination and counter the violences enabled by standard versions of melodramatic political discourse, its melancholic grounding limits the comprehension of and response to the domination it seems to unmask. Even as it is an inspiring form of argumentation, left melodrama undermines the salience and critical capacity of left critique.

Left melodrama can be found in some of the most important and influential critical theory circulating in left academia at the outset of the twenty-first century, including Agamben's *Homo Sacer* and *States of Exception* and Hardt and Negri's collaborative works *Empire* and *Multitude*.[42] Left melodrama is partly a response to the violences stemming from the role of U.S.

politics in the global order, especially in the wake of 9/11. *States of Exception* and *Multitude* were written after 9/11 and incorporate scenes of domination and killing in the United States, in the wars in Iraq and Afghanistan, and in policies of indefinite detention and the Patriot Act. Whereas these policies and wars are part of the moral imperative for freedom in post-9/11 melodramatic political discourse, in the countermelodrama of left melodrama, they are the very scenes of victimization, injury, and powerlessness.

Agamben's work interrogates individuals' relationships to the state through the concept of homo sacer: human bodies that become bereft of social value, bodies that can be killed with impunity because their deaths lack social or political recognition. The sovereign power of the state is the ultimate arbiter for conferring bare life, as it can except itself from the law and designate bare life (homo sacer) at will. Homo sacer is a provocative and valuable concept for analyzing certain contemporary problems, particularly in *States of Exception*, where it responds to post-9/11 politics and interrogates policies of indefinite detention legitimated by melodramatic political discourse. Homo sacer critically scrutinizes the ways in which humans have been subject to state violence while stripped of legal protection and political recognition. For Agamben, critical analysis of bare life is the primary tool to interpret contemporary power. This analysis "has thus offered the key by which not only the sacred texts of sovereignty but also the very codes of political power will unveil their mysteries."[43] By offering methodological heroism, the very study of homo sacer promises to reveal the analytic truth of our historical moment and the horrors that will occur if it remains unheeded. And homo sacer may soon be an omnipotent villain; Agamben ominously warns that if left unchecked, state power as the permanent state of exception "will soon extend itself over the entire planet."[44]

Yet is the state really the only arbiter of power in contemporary life, as Agamben seems to claim?[45] In Agamben's left melodrama, the state is both monolithic and sovereign. Agamben's accountability, similarly to Marx and Engels's melodrama, points one sensationalistic finger of blame for social suffering. Most contemporary forms of abjection become the effects of the state. The texts draw clear lines of accountability for the suffering of bare life onto a villain whose motives are transparent: control, dehumanization, and domination. Agamben's form of left melodrama marks binaries between homo sacer and the sovereign state, victims and villains, oppressor and oppressed; even as his work aims to dispel antagonistic models with nuanced readings of indistinction, his descriptions instate new binaries in this effort. In a sense, the sovereign state has become capital, the great force of domination that leftist scholars can safely and rightly align themselves, without reservation, against. Perhaps part of Agamben's popularity is that he has given us a new enemy against which to mobilize in opposition.

The Nazi death camp functions in this argument as the archetype and epitome of the relationship of sovereignty and bare life, and it models modern individuals' relationships to the state. Agamben's treatment of the camp, which he calls "the hidden paradigm" of all modern biopower, weakens his analysis of present politics by diminishing the heterogeneity of power, the dynamism of juridicality, the multifaceted and nonlinear directionality of accountability for contemporary unfreedom, and the existing forms of nonsovereign politics.[46] If political life is captured only by the state of exception, and power is an all-encompassing form of dehumanizing sovereignty—one that seems to apply as much to Nazi death camps as to the suburbs—then all modern individuals become lumped together, categorized without differentiation as pure victims of a villainous entity that has full control over human life. Yet the melancholy that shapes Agamben's left melodrama is not simply found in the use of melodrama from *The Communist Manifesto* but in the longings that propel its use, especially the desire for unproblematic moral righteousness. Agamben takes pains to assure his readers that homo sacer "is the protagonist" of his book.[47] And later he says, "If today there is no longer any one clear figure of the sacred man, it is perhaps because we are all virtually *homines sacri.*"[48]

It is at the juxtaposition of these two claims that the "hollow core" of this argument shines through. Everyone is a victim of sovereignty; "we" are all homo sacer, "the protagonist" of Agamben's book. Each person who aligns politically and morally against the sovereign state, against indefinite detention, is a besieged and virtuous protagonist. Agamben's critique moves solely outward, against a force so sovereign and omnipotent that all can disclaim responsibility for the political horrors his texts depict. This juxtaposition nourishes leftist disavowed desires: we are right, we are beyond reproach, we are against camps, against bare life. As *homines sacri* living in a state of exception, we are innocent victims, free of complicity with oppression, harm, and violence effected in our world. Morality is clear, and the discomforting work of self-evaluation is unnecessary, even obsolete. The perhaps unintended effect of this move is that individuals are left somewhat bereft of the capacity to shape society, and in this respect Agamben's melodrama resembles those of Sirk. Agamben's Sirkian narrative offers up victims but denies a readily available hero, and thus undoes the guarantee that freedom will be imminent. Aside from his hopes that humans might create a nonsovereign politics, Agamben's individuals are left to passively wallow in the state of exception, the flip side perhaps to the passive protagonism of homines sacri.

This is where *Empire*, the book hailed as a "*Communist Manifesto* for the twenty-first century," steps in.[49] Using a different form of left melodrama, Hardt and Negri sew politics, culture, and the economy into a complex yet unified tapestry of global society dominated by the machinations of empire. Empire is "the political subject that effectively regulates these global exchanges, the sovereign power that governs the world."[50] It operates as an agent that governs, but supersedes, myriad variations of power and economy in order to permeate varied registers of society and regulate all of them. As the prime mover of contemporary political forces, empire is "the idea of a single power that overdetermines them all, structures them in a unitary way, and treats them under one common notion of right that is decidedly postcolonial and postimperialist."[51] The primary antagonism in *Empire* and *Multitude* is between empire and the multitude, the villain and the victim of this melodramatic story. Empire reflects and exceeds U.S. power, though America's violent response to 9/11 is one of the conditions of the present that the multitude is arrayed against. The multitude is, as in *The Communist Manifesto*'s proletariat, a "radical counterpower" composed of marginalized and suffering groups across the globe whose very existence signifies revolutionary promise.[52] Hardt and Negri see signs of revolution at the unraveling margins of society, in various resistances to surveillance, war, corporate domination, and government hegemony, among other forces. Hardt and Negri examine local resistance efforts in different and unaligned sectors of the multitude and argue that these efforts combined become a harbinger of a more total social transformation. With empire as the "parasitical" "single power" of oppression, all forms of challenge presage human emancipation.[53]

The antagonism between empire and multitude carries explanatory power for contemporary geopolitics by giving hope and meaning to many different conditions of domination. This antagonism highlights the moral rightness of the dominated and promises that they will overcome their conditions of unfreedom. This optimistic analysis and melodramatic rhetoric have captured the public imagination, reaching across academic audiences to a broader readership thirsting for social change in the wake of neoliberal globalization, including multinational corporate and U.S. state power. Yet Hardt and Negri's narrative of victimization and heroism, description of a "single power" as the agent of oppression, and prophetic overcoming of social suffering function similarly to Agamben's analysis to deaden the dynamics of the geopolitical landscape. Hardt and Negri's claims tidy the messiness, confusions, and contingencies of various forms of political life; narrow what formations of power and politics can be understood within its terms; and revivify the promise that emancipation from all felt experiences of domination is imminent. The aim of *Multitude* is in part to mobilize the multitude as a collective historical force that counters contemporary empire, but the authors' argument becomes, as Timothy Brennan states, "everything for newness provided newness is polite enough to appear in familiar forms."[54]

Hardt and Negri's left melodrama is thus an expression of melancholy because of how its structure is organized by loss. *Empire* demonstrates a form of political analysis too rooted in the disavowed loss of past promises of revolutionary emancipation to fully grasp the newness of the present. The melodramatic form often harbors a backward focus, in that its critiques of injustice stem from a desire to recapture an idyllic lost past, rather than to postulate a new and unknowable future. The injury that jump-starts melodramatic narratives often marks the loss of a past state of virtue that will be recaptured by righting the victim's injury and reestablishing a prior state of moral rightness. In Brooks's analysis, melodramas aim to reestablish a virtuous world that was seemingly destroyed by villainy, in which goodness, rightness, and truth are easily identifiable and ever present; this is the lost promise that left melodrama aims to recover. Referring to melodrama's backward gaze, Gledhill contends: "Melodrama's challenge lies not in confronting how things are, but rather in asserting how things ought to be. But since it operates within the frameworks of the present social order, melodrama conceives 'the promise of human life' not as a revolutionary future, but as a return to a 'golden past': less how things ought to be then how they should have been."[55] For Gledhill melodramas often dramatize the forces of revolution but from within the boundary of the dominant social, economic, or political order in which they are deployed. In this sense, melodramatic idealizations of the past eventually recoil social critique and reassert the status quo. Brennan captures this dynamic in the quote about newness, regarding how *Empire*'s premise of radical transformation in the future looks suspiciously like *The Communist Manifesto*'s nineteenth-century revolutionary promise.

The left melodrama of *Empire* and *Multitude* incorporates *The Communist Manifesto*'s emancipatory guarantee while refusing to evaluate the methods, promises, and style the text uses to secure that guarantee. Indeed,

*Empire* and *Multitude* may even deaden *The Communist Manifesto* by turning its forceful analysis into the empty papier-mâché fist that Benjamin so feared. Though they take into account the historic particularities of contemporary globalization, current political events, and recent identity politics, *Empire* and *Multitude* still search for a past ideal to ground their vision of the future. Using the manifesto as that ideal, they put forth immanent revolution, the moral virtue of their protagonists (readers), clear lines of social accountability, and, as John Brenkman puts it, a "root thesis": left theory's continual attempt (a melodramatic one, I would submit) to find one root cause that carries the explanatory power for all social ills.[56] The lost ideal, therefore, is less the possibility of freedom or the *The Communist Manifesto* per se than the guarantee that freedom is immanent and that moral virtue is necessarily conferred upon those who desire it.

By lumping together very different groups into the multitude—including its readers, including us—and then positing that undifferentiated and unstratified whole as the hero of humanity, *Empire* perpetuates the most problematic aspect of left melodrama. Like Agamben's analysis, in which the reader is likened to homo sacer, Hardt and Negri's analysis implicitly encourages its readers to identify as a member of the multitude.[57] The left melodrama of both analyses places the readers as victims of the horrifying forces the works depict. The melodramatic trope that links victimization to virtue works so that readers can disclaim responsibility for the injustices depicted in these texts. It renders unnecessary the work of reassessing one's own investments in and responses to inequality and oppression, including those to which one may be contributing, even unintentionally. The moral certainty of left melodrama and the inseparability of marginalization, victimhood, and virtue are, in part, a refusal of self-critique, a refusal that Hall insists has contributed to the debilitating weakness of left politics.

### Reworking Left Melodrama?

It is important to note that *The Communist Manifesto*'s melodrama operates differently from contemporary left melodrama in two ways. First, the sufferers in the manifesto's melodramatic story are not free of responsibility for creating or overcoming injustice. The agency of heroic emancipation is in a complex relationship to teleology: revolution is forthcoming but requires the action of the workers and the Communist Party. The overcoming of capital is both inevitable and yet must be nourished by collective political action. Both the weapons that will destroy capitalism and the people who wield them are called into being by capitalist forces. While the final source of emancipation is not fully worked out in *The Communist Manifesto*, or perhaps it is more accurate to say that the process of emancipation is *purposely* ambiguous and multifaceted, it still relies in part on the agency of the dispossessed and the Communist Party. After all, the bourgeoisie does not provide its own grave; it instead provides its own grave*diggers*.

Second, the analysis in *The Communist Manifesto*, unlike left melodrama, is not motivated by loss. Marx and Engels uproot melodrama's conventional backward-looking inspiration and forcibly turn its focus forward, to an unknown and unknowable future. The frustration and excitement of the text, indeed its necessity, is that it intentionally does not flesh out what a nonbourgeois, communist, postrevolutionary future will look like. For Marx and Engels, any description of the future would inevitably be colored by the framework of the present, and thus would diminish the possibility of motivating truly radical change. In not charting the future, therefore, they choose not to limit its transformative possibilities. This is not to say that Marx and Engels understand the future to have limitless possibility, but that they make a strategic effort not to offer a systematic vision of the postrevolutionary future. Gledhill suggests that most melodramas are motivated by a normative vision of the past that often serves to structure and limit future visions. Marx and Engels, by contrast, refuse to posit an ideal past that can be recaptured. They interpret history through cycles of violence that stanch nostalgia for any past epoch. Instead, *The Communist Manifesto* only gestures to the eventual dissolution of economic inequality and allows the vision of the future to be open-ended, unconstrained by the limited imaginaries of the present.

Reading melodrama in *The Communist Manifesto* draws out why melodrama may appeal to certain segments of contemporary political theory as a mode of analysis. Of course, reading the manifesto through melodrama does not, could not, exhaust the varied cultural modes and rhetorical devices that structure its logic and shape its worldwide effects; to claim *The Communist Manifesto* as fully explainable in this way would be its own form of melodrama. Much of the text does not conform to melodramatic conventions, and even disrupts its melodramatic elements: its forward-looking vision, its refusal to ground critique in the loss of a past ideal, its ambiguity in detailing the agency of heroic emancipation, and the proletariat's complex relation to the overcoming of the villainy of capital—as both its conqueror and inheritor—all disrupt conventional melodramatic tropes. *The Communist Manifesto* is not a melancholic text, and it refuses to generate a lost past ideal as a model for the future. Yet the current reuptake of its melodrama works in this way. While this certainly does not mean that contemporary thinkers should refuse the inspiration of the manifesto, melancholic incorporation of the manifesto's melodramatic tenets should limit the critical salience of contemporary leftist theory in pushing to resist the violence of empire, of unaccountable state and corporate power, of the intensifying administration of human life. Left melodrama appropriates *The Communist Manifesto*'s style in order to hold on to the failed guarantee of immanent freedom, and to reassure the present Left of its unwavering moral rightness in the face of its weakness and defeats.

I would like to be clear about my claims: I think it is imperative to diagnose and rectify conditions of social, political, and economic violence; injustice; and inequality and name their sources of accountability. And any strong push for real social transformation must be motivated and galvanized by moral visions of what is good and right. I am certainly not arguing that extraordinary political, economic, and socially produced suffering does not exist in contemporary life, that moral goodness is impossible, or that clarity must be forsaken in political inquiry. Each of these claims would be a melodramatic counter to what I hope to diagnose as a particular problem: the intellectual and political dilemmas that arise when *The Communist Manifesto*'s melodramatic tropes shape contemporary political-theoretical explanations of geopolitical inequities, when its tenets become normalized in current intellectual inquiry, when its narrative promises become future visions of heroic emancipation. My generation of political theorists, those of us in the United States who intellectually came of age closer to the millennium, have grown up with this type of loss. Loss constitutes part of what it means to be "left," which makes its working through more terrifying; the loss of loss could dissolve part of a political identity. In this vein, I am wary that this chapter could itself be interpreted as a product of left melancholy, read as a critique of left melodrama from a position of melancholic self-flagellation against the internalized lost object of moral promise. My hope is that, by attempting to identify the operations of some of these losses, this chapter derives from a different place, in which the very working through of loss marks an effort to transform it, in which the refusal to grant moral purity to cherished canonical texts, key modes of critique, and firm political identifications keeps them open to inquiry.

There are certainly examples of contemporary political theory that align with the self-critical working through of left melancholy. They include political critique that avows the loss of self-righteousness and sees it as mark of strength that can engender innovative and vital political diagnoses; work that emphasizes the tragic dimension of politics, highlighting the inescapable losses, and losers, inherent to all forms of political inquiry and collective self-governance; scholarship in which leftist individuals, collectives, and political groups are partly accountable for inequality and injustice yet also have the potential to change them; and scholars who accept a multiplicity of coexisting visions for radical political, economic, and social change in part by acknowledging the partial quality of their own assertions.[58] These modes of political theory address the precise problem of melancholy because they explicitly avow responsibility, reckon with loss, or refuse self-purity as starting conditions for critical interrogation. While no single approach could be a panacea for the leftist theory's current dilemmas and each of these options is limited in its own right, one thing is clear: recourse to left melodrama deepens the deadening work of left melancholy and intensifies the pressing violences and inequalities that leftist political theory aims to counter.

# MELODRAMAS OF FAILED SOVEREIGNTY

*The War on Terror as a Women's Weepie*

> If men wish to be free, it is precisely sovereignty they must renounce.
> —Hannah Arendt, "What Is Freedom?"

> It matters how the story is told and retold.
> —Bonnie Honig, *Emergency Politics*

## Melodrama and the Pursuit of Freedom

*Orgies of Feeling* has examined how melodrama, as a political discourse, enables public support for antidemocratic and violent forms of state power, including military occupation, securitization, and disenfranchisement. The book moves beyond conventional readings of this public support, which assume that people trade freedom for security, to argue that a *desire for freedom*, cultivated by melodramatic political discourse, paradoxically undergirds it. Melodramatic genre conventions—including a moral economy of good and evil, intensified pathos, the righteousness of overpowered subjects, and plotlines that travel from injury to freedom—circulate as political discourses that promise Americans that their legitimation of violent state power both marks their virtue and restores their imperiled freedom. Melodrama has become so prominent in the twenty-first century because its conventions promise that heightened affects and dramatic acts of power can revive individual and state sovereignty, in an era when both seem debilitated by global powers beyond their control.

In U.S. political discourse, melodrama's teleology of heroic triumph is often shaped by an aggressive liberal imaginary of sovereign power, in which the desire to be free from coercion manifests as a need to control the external world, to violently tame contingency, to shore up as invulnerable the borders of state territory and individual bodies. Yet melodrama cannot deliver its narrative promise of sovereign freedom for virtuous victim-heroes. Its unfulfilled guarantee has multiple sources. First, the powers heroized in the melodramatic pursuit of sovereignty, including war and widespread surveillance, do not assist either the people's collective welfare or individual flourishing, and they entrench ineffective and frustrated practices of political agency. The actions that melodramas often legitimate in the pursuit of sovereignty not only fail to achieve "freedom" even in anemic institutional forms but also further disable collective, participatory politics while they intensify individuals' felt sense of vulnerability to overpowering forces. Melodrama contributes to the devitalization of political agency, ironically, through the ideal of unconstrained agency that it deploys for imagining the practice of freedom.

Second, melodrama's failure to make good on the promise of sovereign freedom is compounded because sovereignty itself is deteriorating as a viable ideal. Sovereignty is not achievable in its state forms in a globalized era of transnational economies and nonstate governance, nor is it achievable in individualized forms, if it ever was, as the operations of geo-economic and micropolitical powers make clear that individual actors are neither masters of their own domain nor free from the powers, needs, and actions of others.[1] Deployments of melodrama work as strategies to refuse sovereignty's twilight as an organizing concept. They aim to revivify the possibility of sovereign freedom and revitalize a heroic form of political agency for both the citizen and the state. The popularity of melodrama thus indicates a struggle against a more long-standing decline of sovereignty as an operative norm in contemporary politics. As with Hegel's owl of Minerva, the melodramatic discourse of sovereign freedom in the post-9/11 era takes flight just as sovereignty is effectively eclipsed.[2] Melodrama's popularity as a political discourse indicates the dusk of an insufficient and outdated norm for understanding power and agency in the twenty-first century.

Though the norms of freedom proffered by melodramatic discourse are chimerical, violent, and self-defeating, the challenge to unfreedom that motivates melodramatic political discourse is politically indispensable. Melodramatic conventions name both enigmatic political conditions and felt senses of domination as concrete forms of unfreedom that should be challenged.

Melodrama's critique of unfreedom posits the *capacity* to fight against un-freedom and energizes the desires and capacities its critique presumes. Melodrama's power, and its promise, lies in its ability to catalyze desires to challenge unfreedom. The problem, then, is partly the analysis of unfree-dom and powerlessness that melodrama offers—individual villains or ab-stract concepts personified in particular actors (e.g., terrorism or com-munism) rather than systematic experiences of inequality and domination. And the problem is also in the solutions melodrama offers to the ills of felt powerlessness: melodrama offers "freedom" as liberal license and sov-ereign authority, and melodrama posits both as solutions to the problems it diagnoses even when they do not correlate to the problems under scru-tiny, and even when their pursuit leads only to more violence and greater unfreedom.

Yet the conceptual value of freedom is still salvageable from the wreck of its present uses. Freedom is not limited to norms of license or choice, or to sovereign power, or to a practice inescapably bound up with domination and mastery. *Freedom* is the best word for the norms, desires, practices, and ideals that prioritize how individuals and collectives can harness power to shape the decisions that govern their lives and to take part in the making of their worlds. It encapsulates the many ways that people can challenge the structures and forces of unfreedom that prevent them from participating in the powers that govern them.[3] What other possibilities for practicing free-dom in the present could grow from melodrama's indictment of powerless-ness and unfreedom? What other responses to contemporary conditions could be pursued through melodrama, beyond license, militarism, and sov-ereignty? Through what other lenses might melodrama refract a desire for freedom?

### Melodramas of Failed Freedom

While melodramatic political discourses often impede the pursuit of free-dom that they seem to support, melodrama has—in minor moments— nourished more-promising practices of freedom. Though it might seem more apt to conclude this book by recommending the eradication of melo-drama as a genre of politics because its capacity to energize desires for free-dom reflects an attachment to sovereign power and is not worth the vio-lence it validates, this recommendation does not attend, in the first instance, to melodrama's imbrication in American political imaginaries and national sentiments. A claim to eradicate melodramatic political discourse ignores its vast popularity and is itself a melodramatic gesture that aims to perform the heroic conquering of villainy while disavowing how melodrama's deep cultural investments will not magically disappear from American politics. Nor, in the second instance, does it acknowledge that melodrama's galvanizing capacity to motivate pursuits of freedom can operate in different ways than it does in typical forms of melodramatic political discourse. The same genre can refract altered imaginaries of freedom and different genre conventions that shift its narrative and affective experiences; as many genre scholars argue, and as Hayden White succinctly states, "the worldview inherent in a genre does not possess a *fixed* form. . . . Genres can be read in contradictory ways."[4] While genres are not infinitely malleable, their conventions certainly shift in different moments, and different iterations or viewing experiences can solicit different affective experiences. Genres can always be interpreted in different ways, redeployed in new contexts, and renarrativized at a different tempo.

Jacques Rancière emphasizes the political work of renarrativization. He argues, "An emancipated community is a community of narrators and translators."[5] Rancière reads collective narrativization as a tactic of power that involves remaking and participating in the key ideas, stories, strategies, and vocabularies that organize political life. The claim underlying his argument is that the stories people tell and retell—about political power, about the affects that circulate in a political environment, and about the subjects who participate, or do not, in political activity—are necessary to the formation of a politics organized around collective pursuits of freedom. This retelling does not guarantee the success of these pursuits, but it is a necessary factor undergirding this process. In making this claim, Rancière serves as an important reminder that every political event involves an act of depiction and translation and—to extend the claim in ways that Rancière might not have anticipated—that genre forms often shape how we interpret and thus come to live within political events.[6] With White and Rancière in mind, I argue that different deployments of melodramatic narratives and affective expectations take a contradictory or surprising tack to problems of unfreedom.

Remaining within a melodramatic imaginary, this chapter examines a subgenre of melodrama that differently articulates melodramatic conventions to refract their standard image of sovereign freedom. I call this subgenre *the melodrama of failure*, because these melodramas depict the very failure of melodramatic desires for the heroic overcoming of unfreedom. These melodramas reveal the failure of the freedom that their conventions otherwise seem to promise and interrogate sovereign practices of freedom conventionally idealized as the solution to socially produced experiences of impotence and vulnerability. Melodramas of failure are formed out of the same confluence of historical forces that shape more conventional forms of American melodramatic political discourse, including postrevolutionary French stage melodrama, nineteenth-century American individualism, mid-twentieth-century spectacularizations of mass culture, and the genre's general impetus to uncover oppression and injustice through the heightened revelation of virtue. But melodramas of failure refract familiar melodramatic conventions and historical antecedents to show how the very promise of freedom as license and sovereignty *contributes* to the unfreedom and subordination it critiques. These melodramas disclose the ways in which normative American practices of freedom undermine their own aims, and even suggest that the failure of these practices can reroute the pursuit of freedom to a more structurally emancipatory politics.

Melodramas of failure offer one way of delinking sovereignty and freedom, because they illustrate in spectacular fashion the terror of their conflation. Hannah Arendt famously argues, "If men wish to be free, it is precisely sovereignty they must renounce."[7] Sovereignty's promise of mastery enables a form of domination that views other people not as necessary interlocutors for the collective and thus political achievement of world making, but as obstacles to individual free will and thus as impediments to be overcome. Melodramas of failure disentangle freedom from sovereignty by telling a story about sovereignty as both a practice of violent appropriation and a nonviable model for both state and individual agency. I use the term *refract* to describe melodramas of failure in order to draw on the metaphor of rebreaking the direction of light to open it up and change its direction. Refraction separates out the constituent elements of a beam of light and shifts their trajectory to show something new—a multiple spectrum of possibility that did not seem to be available initially but was actually part of the original beam all along.[8] This multiple spectrum shifts the direction of light into various paths. Once refracted, the beam that was first viewed as something closed, linear, and unified becomes open, multiple, and prismatic. Melodramas of failure refract the conventional elements and narrative trajectory of melodramatic political discourse, rebreaking the conflation of freedom and sovereignty and redirecting the expected trajectory toward possibilities other than the familiar promise of heroic triumph. In the process, this refraction shows how melodrama can open different paths for envisioning new practices of freedom that are nonsovereign, collective, and radically participatory and that attend to the specific conditions of the late-modern and neoliberal unfreedoms they aim to overcome.

Melodramas of failure suggest that it is not the desire for freedom that must fail but the desire for freedom imagined as sovereignty. They do not suggest celebrating failure for its own sake but, I think, that there might be much to learn by affirming the experience of failed pursuits of sovereignty. Nor do melodramas of failure necessarily suggest that the desire for freedom must fail permanently.[9] As theorized by Karl Marx and Judith Halberstam, failure lays the groundwork for new languages and practices of freedom conceived out of the failure of earlier practices and imaginaries. The failure of freedom is what offers the possibility to open a space for asking, in Halberstam's words, "whether freedom can be imagined separately from the terms upon which it is offered."[10] Failure is not the opposite of freedom, then, but may instead be a factor that reenables freedom's possibility.[11]

The rest of this chapter first turns to a prime example of melodramas of failure—the women's weepie—before exploring its conventions in the contemporary context. I turn to the women's weepie to attend to America's historical investments and affective attachments to melodrama as a favored genre convention, to remain within its concerns over the problem of socially produced suffering and unfreedom, while using the women's weepie to refract melodramatic political discourse beyond its seeming attachments to sovereignty. The melodramatic story of 9 / 11, I argue, can be refracted as a women's weepie of failed freedom. Women's weepie melodramas help to retell the story of post-9 / 11 melodrama to show how incipient critiques of normative ideals of freedom are already available *within* the most violent iterations of melodramatic political discourse.

*All That Heaven Allows:* Women's Weepies
and the Failure of Freedom

Domestic melodramas, often referred to as the "women's weepies," present some of the best examples of the melodrama of failure, despite the fact that they may seem at first blush unlikely sources for political critique. The term *women's weepies* refers to midcentury films ostensibly concerned with the problems of women in their homes, including conflicts around family, love, relationships, and gendered codes of morality. Most scholars have assumed that domestic melodramas, in their sentimentalization of structural problems, mainly work to uphold norms and structures of social unfreedom, especially for women and the economically disadvantaged.[12] This claim was a key part of feminist film studies debates in the 1980s, which criticized the weepies for their ideological valuation of women's suffering and sacrifice, and has gained new relevance through Lauren Berlant's devastating critique of domestic melodramas as normalizing adaptation to, rather than revolt against, structural injustices. For Berlant, melodramas suggest that politically produced inequalities are best redressed by finding consolation in intimacy and by identifying with others' suffering to create community around feelings of injury, rather than by directly engaging in politics to transform the systems that produce inequality and suffering in the first place.[13] While many weepies reflect Berlant's depiction, I argue that others produce incisive critiques of unfreedom that undo the attachments to conventionality that they otherwise might seem to uphold; and these critiques present a basis for recognizing moments of refracted melodrama within post-9/11 political discourse.

Although still a popular film form, women's weepies achieved particular prominence in the mid-twentieth century, just as the United States was settling into its role as a global superpower. As melodrama began to shape political discourse and televisual political communication for legitimating national security provisions, films in the women's weepie genre—stretching from early weepies such as *Stella Dallas* (1937) and *Dark Victory* (1939) to later films such as *Mildred Pierce* (1945), *Letter from an Unknown Woman* (1948), and *All That Heaven Allows* (1955)—offered a different melodramatic reading of contemporary life.[14] They shifted focus away from the domain of state power and international politics to illustrate individual powerlessness and obstructed agency outside the ostensible political sphere. Similar to all melodramatic forms, the women's weepie of domestic melodrama takes the point of view of the subordinated and moves through cycles of suffering and action to identify virtue and diagnose causes of disappointed agency. The story lines of women's weepies center on the sacrifices demanded of the less privileged—primarily but not exclusively women and people inhabiting the lower economic strata—by the strictures of American society. Yet rather than offering the solution typically found in more action-oriented melodramas, including melodramatic political discourse—the promise of heroically overcoming one's limitations—women's weepies emphasize characters' lack of social agency and highlight in bold and pathos-laden gestures the sacrifices demanded of ordinary people to remain included in the normative social fold. These melodramas of failure unravel the very norms of unencumbered agency and conventional behavior desired by their characters.

Melodrama, as an object of scholarly attention, came into being through analysis of Douglas Sirk's weepies; as Christine Gledhill has argued in her historiography of melodrama, "through discovery of Sirk, a genre came into view."[15] As their presence on *Variety*'s polls of the top 20 movie money-makers indicates, Sirk's weepies were a significant part of the American filmic and social imaginary.[16] They would thus seem an apt place to begin the examination of the weepies. Sirk's films interrogate the crushing effects of capital, consumerism, and normative gender roles on individual lives, yet they also never offer easy solutions or heroic redemption from the bleak scenarios they detail. The films, including *Magnificent Obsession* (1954), *All That Heaven Allows* (1955), *Written on the Wind* (1956), and *Imitation of Life* (1959), are ostensibly about unfulfilled love; they are also about the limited possibilities for freedom within an entire cultural milieu, even in the most minute and intimate relations. They highlight how society demands that all its members (in very different ways depending on gender, class, and racial markers) limit and normalize their actions, gestures, and desires for freedom.[17] According to Thomas Elsaesser's formative essay on the subject, Sirkian melodrama "more often records the *failure* of the protagonist to act in a way that could shape the events and influence the emotional environment, let alone change the stifling social milieu."[18]

I focus on one of Sirk's most influential melodramas, *All That Heaven Allows*, which foregrounds unsuccessful attempts to overcome unfreedom. The film tracks the futile efforts of an upper-class widow and working-class gardener many years her junior to find love and happiness in a stratified society that rejects the possibility of their romance. Cary (Jane Wyman) lives in an artificial, consumer-saturated world made manifest in the garishly Technicolor mise-en-scène of the film. She is primarily confined to her upper-class home space, and when she ventures outside, she is usually reconfined both by the strictures of her gossipy country club and more insidiously by the class and gender norms that bear down upon her. Even at home, her bodily gestures and careful smiles seem tightly hemmed. Cary's only socially acceptable possibilities for intimacy are the town's elderly bachelor, who promises not love but mild companionship, and a television set, which one character refers to approvingly as "the last refuge for lonely women." Cary's daughter describes her lack of social agency allegorically: "The woman, after the husband has died, is walled up alive with him." In a moment of isolation, Cary strikes up a conversation with her gardener, Ron (Rock Hudson), and they tentatively begin a romance. Ron embodies the American ideal of the unencumbered liberal individual. He grows trees,

FIG C.1. The sovereign individual of melodrama: Rock Hudson in
*All That Heaven Allows* (Douglas Sirk, 1955).

lives in a wooded greenhouse cabin, and shrugs off the dictates of Cary's
society to live according to his own personal values (see figure C.1). As one
character tellingly describes him, referring to a copy of Henry David Thoreau's *Walden* that gets its own close-up: "Ron hasn't read it—he just lives it."

Cary and Ron's unlikely romance develops in fits and starts, with the
showy disingenuousness and policed cruelty of town society grating against
Ron's natural lifestyle. Cary's eventual acceptance of Ron's marriage proposal makes her a town mockery. It turns her spoiled children against her
in paroxysms of rage and tears. Cary's obligations, they explain, are to remain bound by the social norms that give them privilege and comfort: to
honor her dead husband and the wealthy lifestyle he provided and to prevent the children's panicked fear of "what people would say" if she acted in
unacceptable ways. The filmmaker Rainer Werner Fassbinder, who drew
inspiration for many of his own films from Sirk, describes the milieu of these
scenes succinctly: "The world around is evil."[19] Norms of class and gender
are so confining that in order to remain within the social field they monitor,
Cary must sacrifice her desires for love and social connection. She submits
to their regulatory demands, diminishes her capacity to act with others on
her own terms, and relinquishes even her modest possibilities for participation in creating or transforming societal norms in order to maintain the
safety of being socially acceptable. Cary breaks up with Ron, is soon cruelly
forgotten by her self-absorbed children, and remains isolated from the
town crowd that mercilessly ridiculed her. The television set makes it into
her glittery home (see figure C.2).

The end of the film at first seems to herald a familiar and tidy Hollywood
ending, in which the normalizing demands and disturbing actions of society

FIG C.2. Melodrama's "metaphors of unfreedom": the consumerist confines of Cary's home in *All That Heaven Allows*.

and family will be erased when Ron and Cary reunite. On a sunny day with swelling music, Cary goes to visit Ron's property, presumably to make amends. Once she gets there, however, she seems to have second thoughts and drives away. Ron spots her from afar, and in his rush to catch her he falls off a cliff. The film ends not with the hard-fought happiness of the reunited couple ready to brave the condemnation of town or escape it altogether in the woods, but with Ron barely conscious, in an uncertain recovery, Cary by his side.

All That Heaven Allows illustrates particular forms of unfreedom that actively limit the agency and expressive capacities of the characters. The film highlights the oppressions that ensue when socially produced economic and gender hierarchies are naturalized as moral hierarchies. It emphasizes how empty consumerism is intended to satisfy diminished possibilities for human flourishing and active public participation. As Elsaesser observes, "The social pressures are such, the frame of respectability so sharply defined, that the range of 'strong' actions is limited."[20] The film depicts a world in which social power and class inequality not only limit characters' freedom but also limit the strong action, the robust agency, of all individuals to live in the world and right the vast unfreedoms they experience. All That Heaven Allows thus personalizes the effects of impersonal domination in the bodies of Cary and Ron without reducing that power to individual autonomy or strong action. The film works hard to reveal the effects of gender inequality and the psychic violence of capital without identifying individual villains as their cause. All That Heaven Allows refuses the guarantee that these problems can be easily overcome by thwarting individual villainy, while also refusing to give up on its social critique with a tidy ending of personal success that would erase the critique offered in the rest of the film. It does not posit that characters can escape their unfreedoms by individual acts of redemption or success. The problems that beset the characters are too much for them to bear individually, and a single heroic individual cannot fix them.

Unlike most American narratives of individual agency—which promise that if you try hard enough, you can get anything you want (and conversely, that failure to get what you want reveals personal weakness rather than structural barriers)—*All That Heaven Allows* emphasizes the violence effected by those very individualizing and depoliticizing norms. It delegitimates the tenets of freedom conceived as individualism and self-reliance by revealing in intimate portrait the different limitations demanded not only of Cary but also of Ron, who functions as the stand-in for individualistic freedom—the explicit embodiment of Thoreau's rugged and socially nonconforming individual. Whereas Ron initially indexes the belief that resistance is possible if one individual is positioned against and outside social power, his debilitated condition at the end of the film brutally disabuses that belief. Indeed, the film shockingly forecloses the liberal fantasy of the unencumbered subject embodied in Ron: by the end of the film, his life outside the social fold is no more livable than Cary's life within. The film thus does not suggest that all social norms can be eradicated by living outside society, as Thoreau aimed to do in *Walden*. If it did, Ron would emerge as the triumphant hero over a degraded society, but he does not. And this is where *All That Heaven Allows* becomes more interesting.

Film scholars often focus on the film's critique of modern capital, contrasting Cary's artificial social world to Ron's naturalism and self-sufficient individualist ethos.[21] On this reading, the film seems to suggest the primacy of the individual able to live in a natural environment outside an artificial and tarnished society; it celebrates the personal freedom and rugged self-reliance still possible there but impossible to sustain within consumer capitalism's overbearing obstacles and indifferent cruelties. This reading is usually made by focusing only on Cary's experience in the film.[22] But my point is that the film also critiques Ron's world, or at least an American fantasy that Ron's rugged individualism can serve as a consumer society's critical counterpoint. Ron's environment is shown to be just as chimerical as Cary's, his wild outdoors scenes painted with the same garish Technicolor as Cary's sculpted interiors. Ron temporarily vivifies the liberal individualist fantasy of the sovereign subject—the same fantasy that structures post-9/11 melodramatic political discourse—but Ron is left powerless, supine, and crushed

FIG C.3. The failure of individual freedom displayed in Ron's broken body in *All That Heaven Allows*.

at the film's end (see figure C.3). While other film critics have read Cary, and her world, as the embodiment of failure, Ron seems to offer failure's most drastic performance. Ron's defeated body embodies the failure of freedom, when freedom is depicted as personal sovereignty and self-reliant individualism. His physical incapacity, acquired in his attempt to reconcile with Cary in the woods, allegorizes the impossibility of heroic individual mastery to right the problems that the film depicts, no matter how much American discourses of freedom proclaim heroic self-reliance to be the panacea for entrenched inequalities.

If the film ended by relegitimating the power of individual freedom to right social injustice, then Ron would triumph over social conformity and the town's regulatory demands. A different final scene would emerge, with Ron's attempt to reconnect with Cary being successful, and he would rescue her from the town's capitalist depredations, becoming her backbone and heroic savior. Cary would gratefully rely on Ron's strength to cast off her wealth and social access, and the two would create a new Eden in their wooded palace. Conversely, if the film relegitimated the structural hierarchies of capital that harm the characters at the beginning of the film, it would show Ron accepting the validity of social hierarchies by modifying his own behavior and attitude. Ron would embrace Cary's upper-class world: they would happily marry at the town's fancy social club, and Cary's wealth would underwrite Ron's successful landscaping business. They would become the most sought-after couple in town, and Ron would graciously receive the love of Cary's now-adoring children. Instead, the film ends when Cary expresses her decision to stay with a debilitated Ron. Ron remains dependent on Cary, physically crushed, and barely sentient. The way to fight unfreedom, according to *All That Heaven Allows*, cannot be to embody Ron's seemingly unencumbered existence outside of societal norms. Nor can it be, in Cary's more limited options as a female character, to escape social binds by riding atop the shoulders of the self-sufficient male hero. The film is steadfast in its refusal to accept the degraded and unfree terms of the society it depicts, but the film is just as steadfast in its refusal to create easy promises of individual mastery over or escape from the systemic problems it diagnoses.

*All That Heaven Allows* thus illustrates individual experiences of unfreedom while insisting that society in its current state cannot offer the freedom individuals seek—and neither can intimate relationships offer safe harbor from unfreedom. Berlant's critique of women's weepies, as a depoliticizing genre that drains its critical potential to galvanize larger social transformation, is pertinent here. For Berlant women's weepies locate the desire to challenge unfreedom within the desire to escape social suffering: to the extent that their sentimentalized diagnoses of structural unfreedoms identify solutions for unfreedom, they are found not within political participation, resistance, or structural transformation but in the solace of intimate relationships in which love and emotional fulfillment can offer shelter from unfreedom and palliate the emotional effects of injustice.[23] Berlant argues that women's weepies locate social agency in the "juxtapolitical": a place separate from but alongside politics where political and social grievances can be aired without requiring widespread social change to rectify them. In the juxtapolitical realm, consumers of melodramatic cultural products are encouraged to imagine others' injuries as their own and confine their disappointments about injustice to the juxtapolitical realm; both of these strategies deface the specificity of the injury born by subordinated populations into a general feeling of pain untethered to particular social, economic, racial, and gendered experiences and assume that empathy with subordinated Others offers the best way to resolve subordination and injustice.[24]

While many women's weepies, such as *Stella Dallas* or *Now, Voyager* (1942), "solve" specific problems of lived unfreedom by relocating their sites of injury and redress to the juxtapolitical realm, films such as *All That Heaven Allows* counter the depoliticizing tendencies that Berlant diagnoses and reject conventional intimate relations as a substitute for large-scale social change. The critical potential of key women's weepies such as *All That Heaven Allows*, and what will make them relevant to post-9/11 politics, is their ability to deindividuate political solutions to structural unfreedoms and to suggest that the unfreedoms they depict are not redressed, or even ameliorated, within the juxtapolitical realm or conventional social arrangements. It is the *failure* of intimate and personal solutions to unfreedom, combined with the refusal to rehabilitate the promise of heroic individualism as the model of emancipation, that allows women's weepies such as *All That Heaven Allows* to delegitimate the normalized social hierarchies that contribute to unfreedom. It is also what will allow the films' refracted conventions to contribute a critical counterpoint to the conventions of post-9/11 melodrama.

It is certainly possible to read *All That Heaven Allows* through the concern that melodrama offers relief from the world it depicts by constructing fantasies of transcending politically produced hierarchies through intimate relations isolated from larger social problems. The feminist film critic Laura Mulvey makes this sort of argument. For Mulvey the suffering couple eventually reunites at the end of *All That Heaven Allows*; even though they have lost their innocence and are wise to the cruelties of the world, they have found a different kind of happiness together, joined in Ron's recovery.[25] It is expected that Cary will find satisfaction in performing the normative female work of caregiving and in making her new home in nature. *All That Heaven Allows*, in this reading, would seem to reinforce privatized solutions to the problems of diminished social agency. According to Mulvey, the film locates a kind of closure in the juxtapolitical realm, where Cary's and Ron's socially produced suffering can be alleviated if they gain a measure of satisfaction within their newly configured relationship. Yet the ending is so deeply unsatisfying, even from the perspective of individual problem solving for Ron and Cary; Ron barely knows that Cary is there, and Cary's tight smile seems more a gesture of resignation than satisfaction. *All That Heaven Allows* produces and then crushes expectations of intimate closure by embedding and then denying the promise of a satisfactory ending. The story sets up the expectation that Ron will succeed in winning Cary back through his strength. Hudson's familiarity as an iconic and heroic persona, as one of the most popular heroic male protagonists of the 1950s, combined with the Hollywood conventions of the character's rugged individualism encourage the expectation that his victory is on the horizon. They make the ending all the more surprising and disorienting. Conventional expectations to secure individual contentment, either through individual triumph over injustice or intimate relationships, are harshly denied when Cary chooses to walk away from Ron's house without reconciling with him, and more dramatically when Ron falls. *All That Heaven Allows* evacuates the juxtapolitical as a space of redress. The film coaxes then denies the possibility of either intimacy or heroic individualism to loosen the character's binds, salve their wounds, or push for greater agency.[26] This melodrama produces its own nonfulfillment, critiquing the desire for a heroic or satisfying conclusion by inscribing both its promise and defeat within the actual story line. By tracing a narrative in which their experiences of unfreedom are not overcome or displaced but intensified, *All That Heaven Allows* refracts and breaks open the familiar melodramatic closure of radical social critique.

*All That Heaven Allows* illustrates the failure of freedom when freedom is envisioned as individual sovereignty and personal noncompliance with the politically produced inequalities and exclusions of an oppressive society. Overwhelming feats of heroic mastery or the smaller satisfactions of intimate happiness cannot displace the critical political concerns unleashed in the narrative. The concluding images of Cary and Ron's romance suggest that when individuals deny that their lived experiences of suffering and unfreedom are inextricable from the social world, when they try to evade or disavow their interdependence on collective social forms, this generates its own form of violence and effects even greater passivity and helplessness. Like other melodramas, *All That Heaven Allows* offers a powerfully affective experience of pathos with its injured protagonists, but here it is not orgiastically displaced into the promise of either strong agency or intimate satisfaction. Rather, it transforms into the failure to achieve anything redemptive.

In melodramas of failure, however, failed pursuits of freedom can serve as a platform for launching new modes of social critique and new imaginaries of freedom. For Marx, for instance, failed expectations for experiencing freedom can be a precondition for radical social transformation. Marx, one of Sirk's explicit influences, argues that the recognition of failed emancipatory efforts is the necessary condition for a critique in which aspirations for freedom are refracted through the specific problems of the present.[27] From the *18th Brumaire of Louis Bonaparte* to *The Communist Manifesto*, Marx grapples with failed attempts to overcome domination, and he argues that failure demands a critique of one's current ideas about how one understands the practice of freedom and its possibility within current social conditions. Failure can lay the groundwork for future efforts toward radical social transformation in which freedom—as the ability to participate and share in authorizing the decisions that govern one's life, as the collective emancipation from societal-wide oppression—can become a daily and lived practice. Failure means "that he himself and his party have to give up the old standpoint"; failure does not only demand a renewed critique of contemporary life but also a critique of one's standpoint in its situatedness to current social conditions, a revaluation of norms underlying one's goals to be free from domination and the methods one assumes will achieve this freedom.[28] When prior forms of freedom seeking have failed and lost their validity, a critical examination of failed emancipatory efforts enables a more exacting critique of unfreedoms and the search for more-precise and viable mechanisms to challenge them.

And yet drawing on Marx in this context is problematic: Marx's valuation of failure as the groundwork for a more emancipatory practice of freedom depends in part on his dialectical reading of history. Failure is the necessary antagonistic counterpoint that propels history forward; new historical epochs are born of the failures of old epochs, performing their overcoming into new historical configurations that generate their own failures and then move society forward again. Without a trust in a dialectical overcoming of the present—without the confidence that failure is situated in a teleological history that inevitably leads to radical equality and freedom—then failure may not have any critical purchase on the future. Without the promise of future success, failure can be devastating: it undoes one's desires and dreams, and it offers proof that what one has hoped for will not come to be. The experience of failure is thus significantly more precarious and devastating without a guarantee of overcoming it. Failed pursuits of freedom can lead to reactionary violence, to lashing out in vengeance and fear. This lashing out partly describes the push for war after the 9 / 11 attacks spectacularized failed sovereignty. The experience of failure can be enervating, despairing, and laden with ressentiment. But not only, and not necessarily.

Freeing failure from a dialectical history can also allow the critique it engenders to be more pressing and agentic; Halberstam's argument, for instance, that failure is potentially a site of freedom, is instructive here. For Halberstam the experience of failure from normative images of subjectivity can work to repudiate oppressive social relations and gives those who "fail" relief from the pressure to measure up to constraining and patriarchal norms of achievement, which are themselves a form of unfreedom. This experience discloses a different logic of being in the world than that of an idealized sovereign subject.[29] She writes, "Failure is a way of refusing to acquiesce to dominant logics of power and discipline, and is a form of critique"; failure "presents an opportunity rather than a dead end."[30]

Challenging the conventional grammar of freedom, failure reveals its breakdowns, aporias, and violences. It emphasizes what happens when governing norms cannot achieve their stated strategies and illustrates the lived effects of failed sovereignty on individual and collective bodies.[31] The experience of failure can thus be marshaled in the service of critique and human flourishing in the face of the unfreedoms produced not only out of contemporary forms of subordination but also out of the norms that contribute to subordination by offering a privileged model of a non-subordinated subject. Similar to Marx, Halberstam argues that failure does more than offer a critique of what has failed; failure opens up the world to reimagine alternatives to the present order, and one's roles in it. She goes further to argue that failure can offer its own space for practicing freedom precisely because it is not embedded in a teleology of progress; failure can free those who experience it to imagine lives, politics, and norms outside of available expectations of sovereign triumph, without guarantee of success, but with tools and techniques already available in the present. For Halberstam, "failure recognizes that alternatives are embedded already in the dominant logics and that power is never total or consistent."[32] Failure thus addresses how normative visions of subjectivity, even those as pervasive as sovereignty, are never totalizing, and thus offers a refracted reading of the present in which failure marks a challenge to sovereignty's claims of totalization, and therefore suggests that alternatives are always possible.

Halberstam's reading of failure addresses the dark experiences that failure confers, yet it is often optimistic, even playful, in part because it sometimes implicitly relies on a strong model of agency in which failure can become a chosen condition, and in which the losses it demands from subjects can be individually reworked into a more intentional subjectivity. But failure in *All That Heaven Allows* is devitalizing in many respects; failure signals so many losses for Cary and Ron that it undoes any modicum of safety in either of their worlds and threatens both of their integrity as subjects. Yet Halberstam's insistence that failure provides an opening for different norms to organize the present, an opening that can be pried apart by unrelieved subjects looking desperately for something more, makes for a powerful and energizing form of critique. In revealing the failure of individual freedom within current social norms, *All That Heaven Allows*, like Halberstam's argument, invites us to imagine new forms of social organization beyond what the characters experience, even though the film does not define them for us. Its refractions break open the possibility of articulating a more just future for Ron and Cary, and for the spectators who identify with their travails, outside of their present social organization and normative imaginaries of freedom. Opening a space, however, is different from delineating the content of that alternative vision; melodrama opens this space without detailing the content this vision must take.

*All That Heaven Allows* can thus be read to suggest, along the lines of Halberstam and Marx, that there must be other ways to challenge the unfreedoms the characters face—ways that emphasize collective organization rather than individual acts of heroism, that work through rather than outside society to transform possibilities for human flourishing, that deny the possibility that self-ostracism in the woods or in a commodity-saturated home space can be a successful strategy for renegotiating oppressive norms. The film suggests that a more free and livable society for all inhabitants can only be achieved by large-scale societal transformations that would significantly flatten the hierarchies and balance the forms of power that stratify populations and produce breathtaking levels of inequality. This possibility for transformation is found in a failure severed from dialectics; it is without guarantees, as Stuart Hall would assert.[33] The wager in melodramas of failure, and it is a big one, is that a devastating tableau of unfreedom that undoes all conventional grounds for reestablishing agency might become a galvanizing source for imagining, and working toward, a significantly more just and less oppressive society.

## Mission Accomplished: The War on Terror as a Women's Weepie

The refracted melodrama of failed freedom, as exemplified in *All That Heaven Allows*, offers a starting point to construct a different depiction of post-9/11 politics, which can sustain the critique of unfreedom animated but displaced by standard melodramatic political discourses. It is not a seamless move to read post-9/11 melodrama as a women's weepie: the latter is more often situated in a world just beginning to be organized by postindustrial capital (the 1930s to 1950s), while the former deals with a twenty-first-century radically reconfigured global political-economic order. Women's weepies circulate in a cinematic medium and often condemn villainies internal to the daily life of nation, while post-9/11 melodrama circulates in political discourse and often relegates villainy to outside the national body that melodrama constructs; women's weepies usually emphasize gendered experiences of unfreedom, whereas post-9/11 melodrama attends to feelings of constraint experienced by a nationally configured and more generalized population. Yet the conventions of women's weepies, and particularly the reworking of Sirkian melodramas, have remained a fixture of popular culture, infusing American cultural imaginaries as their conventions shift in response to the cultural and political moments in which they are produced.[34] And their differences do not preclude the way that the conventions of the women's weepie, and its critique of contemporary unfreedom, are available within post-9/11 melodrama, when viewed through a refracted lens.

The narrative trajectory and affective experience of post-9/11 melodrama breaks open when they are refracted as a Sirkian women's weepie; they tell a melodramatic story that does not culminate in the virtuous triumph of American heroism but in the *failure* of the American pursuit of freedom as envisioned in the war on terror. The narrative trajectory of post-9/11 melodramas of failure illuminate the collapse of melodrama's narrative promise for the nation's impending sovereign freedom. They demonstrate instead the inability of state and individual action to overcome diminished political agency, unexpected violence, and the terrors of globalization that shape the contemporary era beyond singular events of terrorism. As in *All That Heaven Allows*, the failures of freedom in post-9/11 melodrama also challenge the assumption that freedom can be found in sovereign and unilateral Rock Hudson–like heroic action. Jackie Byars describes *All That Heaven Allows* in this way: "Central to [this film] is a structuring absence, most frequently the result of a traumatic loss. . . . [It] confronted the inequities within American institutions and examined their influence on the lives of ordinary Americans."[35] The Sirkian politics of the post-9/11 events can also be described in this way: as the result of loss, a loss of the promise of sovereign freedom, a loss that has been extant for decades but that moved violently into political consciousness on September 11, 2001.

I initially argued in chapter 3 that the narrative structure and affective intensity of post-9/11 melodrama slowly faded out when its promise of sovereign freedom and triumph over evil endlessly receded into the future. The affective power of its legitimating conventions weakened as its cycles of pathos and action broke down, as the United States was unable to sustain the claim that the nation is only ever a virtuous and innocent victim; the felt legitimacy the United States cultivated for state action thus gradually dissipated from the affective experience of post-9/11 politics. Yet this chapter offers a different reading of the conclusion to post-9/11 melodrama to argue that it offers up the failure of sovereignty directly within its genre conventions. The least likely example of this melodrama of failure might seem to be George W. Bush's infamous "mission accomplished" performance. This performance, I argued in chapter 5, intended to provide the triumphant victory of sovereignty crucial to the narrative of 9/11 melodrama. Six weeks after U.S. military forces were deployed, Iraq was already under U.S. military occupation; the Iraq War was a cornerstone of the war on terror and had the stated intent to bring freedom to Iraqis and to ensure U.S. freedom by preventing Saddam Hussein from deploying weapons of mass destruction. At this six-week mark, Bush made a speech on an aircraft carrier announcing the end of combat operations in Iraq. Bush's speech was preceded by a televised spectacle of him landing a fighter jet onto the aircraft carrier. It was one of the most heightened melodramatic moments of the war on terror, the climax of the nation's triumph of virtue and freedom. It was the moment expected by the audience of *All That Heaven Allows*: the conclusion that demonstrates the triumph of the sovereign hero who pushes for freedom against the larger forces that constrain his agency. Yet as in *All That Heaven Allows*, "mission accomplished" overtly denied this triumphant conclusion.

The mise-en-scène of "mission accomplished" has as its backdrop the same action-oriented melodrama as the post-9/11 political discourse examined earlier in this book. In it America suddenly became a virtuous victim of evil forces on September 11. The nation had undergone a dramatic and intensely affective experience of powerlessness and horror in the wake of the terrorist attacks. America's response was the war on terror, which intended to overcome citizens' felt experience of unfreedom through the nation-state's morally righteous capacity to defeat evil and "secure freedom's triumph." In this melodrama the United States, initially overwhelmed by its injury, would secure the triumph of freedom by hunting down enemies of freedom through military, economic, and securitizing political strategies, always justified by the moral imperative to virtuously bring freedom to the nation and the world. For individual citizen-subjects, melodrama offered a related and implicit promise: to help regain a sense of individual power in an age of powerlessness and devitalized agency. Citizens' desire to live an unencumbered life, melodrama suggested, would be satisfied once the U.S. state eliminated evil from the global order.

At the time of its delivery the "mission accomplished" speech was supposed to be the culmination of post-9/11 melodrama. As chapter 5 argued, the speech intended to demonstrate both the triumph of righteous U.S. global power and the resurgence of individual freedom as embodied in the fighter jet maneuvers of Bush. The performance situated Bush, the first president to fly a fighter jet onto an aircraft carrier in the middle of the ocean, as the signifier of unbound individual and state agency. In this intended final scene, Bush piloted a high-tech jet, which had his name stenciled under his window, onto a carrier while news media from around the world covered his exploit. After a dramatic landing, he exited the plane to the wild cheers of service members, changed into a suit, and, under a huge banner reading "mission accomplished," made the speech announcing the end of the major combat operations in Iraq. Urban legend has it that upon landing the jet, Bush appropriated U.S. Navy lingo to announce to the carrier's flight control, "I have the balls." This story circulated widely in social media as proof of Bush's masculinized and aggressive individualism. Bush was the individual hero of U.S. power, the living stand-in for the successful pursuit of sovereign freedom at both the individual and the state levels. He performed a more violent, state-organized, and neoconservative version of liberal individualism than Rock Hudson's Thoreauvian-inspired self-sufficiency, though both performances drew from the same masculine norms of individual sovereignty. As I also argued in chapter 5, these characteristics of heroic individualism, through slippery identification of Bush with the body politic, were then bestowed upon the American population as a shared experience of unbound agency. As the media commentator Chris Matthews tellingly revealed: "I think we like having a hero as our president."[36]

The "mission accomplished" speech, given on the aircraft carrier, intended to mark the fulfillment of the promise of American freedom made in the wake of 9 / 11. The speech drew from melodramatic tropes to announce that the war was over and employed a telos of freedom aligned with virtue. Bush stated, "Everywhere that freedom arrives, humanity rejoices. And everywhere that freedom stirs, let tyrants fear."[37] Heated in its dramatization of damaged virtue by the unrelated 9 / 11 terrorist attacks, the speech claimed the moral high ground for Operation Iraqi Freedom. The United States "fought for the cause of liberty, and for the peace of the world." Bush explained that the U.S. military's cutting-edge technology made fighting wars fast and precise: the "shock and awe" of violence was carried out in a way that "the world has not seen before. . . . We have witnessed the arrival of a new era." New precision technology not only avoided civilian casualties, Bush explained, but was also a weapon for those who are morally virtuous enough to employ it: "It is a great advance when the guilty have far more to fear from war than the innocent." In this melodrama, "shock and awe" marked the very innocence of those who enacted it. The performance also

FIG C.4. George W. Bush performing the desire for sovereignty. The "mission accomplished" speech given on an aircraft carrier on May 1, 2003.

spectacularly demonstrated the global supremacy of U.S. might. Its technological, military, economic, and political power congealed in a dramatic spectacle of sovereignty that also proved the goodness of the nation that powered the spectacle. "Mission accomplished" announced the intent to create a new era of freedom for the world with the United States at its helm (see figure C.4).

*All That Heaven Allows* embeds a false promise of an airtight and familiar happy ending, which gives way to a recognition of weakness in an ambiguous climax that invalidates both the social world of the characters and their ways of struggling against it; so too does "mission accomplished." From the first moment of its delivery, "mission accomplished" was derided as fake, staged, and hyperbolic. Nothing was accomplished at that time, as many popular media and political commentators noted: it was not the end of the war on terror but only the end of the beginning; the Iraq War would continue for another eight years, with the U.S. occupation in Iraq continuing even beyond the official end in 2011, and the war on terror ongoing in Afghanistan, Pakistan, Yemen, Sudan, and the United States, as well as other shadow sites. As in *All That Heaven Allows*, 9 / 11 melodrama ends not with a scene of heroic triumph, as expected, but with obstructed pursuits of freedom. The grandiose and garish performance of sovereign triumph in "mission accomplished" emphasizes the impossibility of global mastery, territorial invulnerability, and individual self-sufficiency, and thus reveals the collapse of the promises of freedom as they take shape in popular discourse. "Mission accomplished" was never able to be the heroic-action melodrama its orchestrators planned, but instead became the women's weepie scene of unfulfilled desire.

From the very moment when "mission accomplished" ended, mainstream news and political figures noted the fractures within the executive branch's intended narrative of virtuous power, masculine heroism, and triumphal freedom. The staged and canned nature of the performance, in which Bush—who hadn't flown a plane since his days as an absentee national guardsman thirty years prior—swaggered off the plane with the pilot who "assisted" him, was noticed immediately and became part of the story about the performance. It was scorned as "tailor-made for television" and "choreographed" by no less than NBC and CNN, even as their coverage also glorified Bush's heroism.[38] Major news outlets highlighted the artificiality of the scene; the *New York Times* reported, "He hopped off the plane . . . with a swagger that seemed to suggest he had seen *Top Gun*. . . . Even in a White House that prides itself on its mastery of political staging, Mr. Bush's arrival on board the Lincoln was a first of many kinds."[39] Media outlets both praised Bush's commanding performance and noted the brash excess of it: Bush claimed that the fighter jet was necessary for landing on the carrier that visually appeared to be in the middle of the ocean, but PBS reported that it was just off the shore of San Diego. Bush was even called out as a caricature of masculinized individualism. One pundit noted, though not unappreciatively, how Bush's pilot costume intentionally accentuated his crotch. "It makes the most of his manly characteristics," G. Gordon Liddy reported (figure C.5).[40] These comments were not in rarefied or marginalized realms but in mainstream media coverage and national political discourse: the artifice of the event, the patent falsity of Bush's piloted landing, and the desperate attempt to cull masculine brawn from the scene, were all part of the ordinary reception of the performance. The very fact that Bush's likeness was turned into a children's action figure became part of the narrative of disingenuousness. "Mission accomplished" was just as lurid and spectacular as any Sirkian film. Its garishness was the new Technicolor, the excess of its mise-en-scène clearly revealing to its audience the artificiality of its attempted resolution.

Refracting the "mission accomplished" melodrama through a women's weepie, we can see that the melodramatic narrative of virtuous heroism that legitimated the Iraq War was also subtended by a critique of this narrative. The reading of "mission accomplished" as a women's weepie was right

FIG C.5. "Manly characteristics": the failure of sovereign freedom revealed in the excess of its performance. The "mission accomplished" speech given on an aircraft carrier on May 1, 2003.

in the center of the political discourses that framed the events for the public. The weepie refraction of "mission accomplished" is now part of the war's established chronology, one that signifies the general failure of the war and occupation to grant freedom to either Iraqi or American citizens. As many commentators argued at the time, and has now become a commonplace observation in almost all mainstream political discourses, the Iraq War was a miasma of moral terror and horrifying violence. The urgent necessity of finding weapons of mass destruction—the ostensible yet patently false motiving force behind Operation Iraqi Freedom—never came to fruition. The violence, surveillance, and regulation that attended the war on terror caused even greater bloodshed throughout the world over the following decade. As Operation Iraqi Freedom caused the deaths of tens of thousands of people and officially ended in the rubble of a violent, broken, and terrified country, and as the war failed to eradicate evil or bestow genuine freedom, even a freedom as anemically construed as fair elections, America's failed efforts become part of a standard story we now tell about "mission accomplished." The term *mission accomplished* now works as an ironic epithet for any failed endeavor.

The "mission accomplished" performance demonstrates failed pursuits of freedom at two levels that melodrama often conflates: the levels of state sovereignty and individual sovereignty. The endless occupation and losses of the war reveal the chimera that the U.S. state can unilaterally ensure stability of the globalized order, let alone secure it own porous border, in an era of intense technological, political, and economic transformations. The story suggests that the melodramatic promise to triumph over evil, especially through feats of heroism, cannot adequately address the systemic problems of unfreedom that the term *evil* indexes, of which 9/11 is only a small part. As the story of "mission accomplished" is now conveyed, its hyperbolic and gestural declarations of sovereign freedom reveal the vulnerability underpinning the declarations, the realization that sovereignty is a fiction only maintained through attempts to spectacularize it in actions such as shock and awe. The promise of post-9/11 melodramatic political discourse (to escape or overpower contemporary unfreedoms through the virtuous use of unilateral state power) takes the form of a Technicolor fantasy that promises the righteous capacity of state functions to eliminate easily identifiable sources of unfreedom.

The fantasy of "mission accomplished" as a performance of state sovereignty is undone within its very diegesis. Just as *All That Heaven Allows* unravels the story of freedom within its telling, "mission accomplished" promises, and then crushes, the possibility of heroic triumph. As in the end of *All That Heaven Allows*, the violence that attends "mission accomplished" refutes current ways of struggling against felt disempowerment. "Mission accomplished" spins out to show how freedom imagined through the Iraq War takes the form of mass sectarian murder, chaotic violence, the privatization of national industries that only benefit an elite few, and sham elections that can barely claim to serve a free and democratic nation. It not only highlights how the attempt to gain freedom by conquering terror is always already a failed endeavor but also exposes the injustice, inequality, and oppression that are the disavowed but very real remainders of this pursuit of freedom. Yet unlike the post-9/11 story told earlier in the book, the refracted post-9/11 melodrama of failure does not devolve into a continual investment in the imaginary promise of heroic overcoming of evil. Instead, it emphasizes the inability of disparate and expansive state powers to congeal into the image of the heroic individual.

On another level, "mission accomplished" emphasizes the failure of unbridled freedom as individual agency. It suggests that hyperbolic gestures of individual sovereignty are the very signs of the refusal to face and grapple with individuals' interdependence, vitiated subjectivity, and inescapable social enmeshment. As in *All That Heaven Allows*, when Ron literalizes failed self-reliance with his broken body and physical dependence on Cary, "mission accomplished" depicts how grandiose gestures of individual sovereignty do not actually bestow this type of agency to individuals. Both Ron and Bush are in fact overwhelmed by outside forces, and their respective quests for sovereignty issue in false and impotent gestures. They share a lack of social agency and pursue futile attempts to establish self-sufficiency and liberal freedom in the societies in which they are inextricably intertwined.

While Bush's performance of heroism was intended to embody individual and state sovereignty, as both were conflated in his persona as president, his outsized gestures and artificial staging clearly reveal their fantasmatic nature. Just as in Sirkian melodrama, where "violence, the strong action, the dynamic movement, the full articulation and the fleshed-out emotions . . . become the very signs of the characters' alienation, and thus serve to formulate a devastating critique of the ideology that supports it," the excess bravado of Bush's performance betrays the impotence in which it is grounded and illuminates the very experiences of vulnerability and passivity it is intended to ward off.[41] The truth behind the urban legend of Bush's "balls" comment shows this most strongly. Although Bush actually said to the carrier's air control, in a correct use of military terminology, "Navy One, Viking ball, seven point oh," no one on the flight deck heard his comment because he pressed the wrong button on his cockpit radio, and thus failed to transmit his message.[42] His action, intended to convey his fighting prowess in alignment with individual heroism, misfired instead as a gesture of impotence, ignorance, and dependence. It bares the bluster and helplessness behind the bravado, the weakness underlying the staged scene of masculinized toughness intended to stand in for sovereign power.

These refracted elements of failed sovereignty continue throughout the war on terror. To cite a more recent example, the shooting of Osama bin Laden in 2011 by an elite wing of the U.S. military was, from the perspective of melodramatic political discourse, situated as the new long-delayed climax in the pursuit of sovereign freedom, one that could substitute for the failure of "mission accomplished" with a successful finale to the war on terror. Yet even for all its heightened rhetoric and dramatic unfolding, the killing of bin Laden could not offer the heroic victory of freedom for a public that, a decade after 9/11, continued to experience a lack of political, social, and economic agency perhaps even more profound than ten years earlier, as the global economic crisis intensified experiences of economic vulnerability and political disempowerment while making access to political power, economic stability, and experiences of sovereign freedom recede even further from nonelite Americans. Lived experiences of obstructed agency could not be resolved by the death of bin Laden. Indeed, national polls reveal that in 2012 Americans felt just as anxious and insecure as they had in the year following 9/11.[43] Bin Laden's capture and death neither ended the war on terror nor "secured freedom's triumph." His death primarily provided a temporary feeling of relief that in its brevity reiterated the breakdown of the fantasy that sovereign freedom was imminent. It was akin to the final reconciliation of Ron and Cary, which in its fundamentally dissatisfying finale did not mark the success of virtue or of heroism, but rather bared the breakdown of the fantasy of sovereign agency.

President Barack Obama admitted as much in his announcement of bin Laden's death when he stated that "the cause of securing our country is not complete," though he only offered that candor by immediately following it with his assertion that "we are once again reminded that America can do whatever we set our mind to." His quick admission of national vulnerability was already dismissed by the end of the sentence, displaced by the more politically winning ideal of unbridled license that aimed to reinvigorate American heroic self-sufficiency in a new decade when it is experienced as even more remote. In the larger context of post-9/11 melodrama, Obama's claim—while different from Bush's overheated performance of sovereign agency not only in its more modulated affect but in the material proof of its claim that the action it described was indeed accomplished—still shared the desires both revealed and destroyed in "mission accomplished" and *All That Heaven Allows*: that one can overcome the vulnerabilities and interdependencies of late-modern life by spectacular acts of heroism that both power sovereign mastery and shelter individuals from structural violence.

Even the film *Zero Dark Thirty* (directed by Kathryn Bigelow, 2012), a dramatized account of the hunt for bin Laden by the U.S. military and CIA, illustrates the failure of his death to substitute for the achievement of sovereignty. The film's end confounded many commentators: after bin Laden is confirmed dead, the CIA's most dogged pursuer of him sits in a cargo plane by herself, wordless and forlorn, tears streaming down her face as she leaves Afghanistan without having a new destination in place. Many commenters made sense of this ending by interpreting it as a character portrait of a driven and ruthless woman whose life-engrossing pursuit left her with nothing after bin Laden's death—she has no friends, no partner, no other interests that would fulfill her life—and so she cries at the vast emptiness now in front of her. Yet another way to read this scene is not through individual character pathology but as the very revelation of the fundamental inability of the killing of bin Laden to provide the heroic closure it was expected to deliver. The death of bin Laden could not restore U.S. sovereignty, nor could it enable personal liberty, nor could it provide any substantial finale to the war on terror. His death was not the culmination of freedom for the virtuous. In the last line of the film, the pilot of the cargo plane asks the protagonist, "Where do you want to go?" She has no answer. The killing of bin Laden is unable to point to any redemptive future. The unhappiness of the main character and the disappointment of the final scene more generally mirror the very dissatisfaction of the killing of bin Laden, which was weighted to provide so much more but could never live up to those expectations. *Zero Dark Thirty* reveals the truth that the killing of bin Laden did not provide a satisfying conclusion to anything.

Melodramatic political discourse, I have argued throughout this book, proposes that protagonists who are victims of injustice and inequality are absolved of their own complicity in the injustices and inequalities of others; they are rendered innocent and even virtuous through their own suffering. But reading "mission accomplished" as a refracted melodrama shows something different: it is perhaps possible for a melodramatic narrative to detangle virtue from injury. The women's weepie rendition of "mission accomplished" is unable to moralize America's position of injury after 9/11 as justification for the Iraq War. *All That Heaven Allows* illuminates a mode of this detangling: Cary is positioned as a victim of social and consumerist expectations, of her children's privileged self-absorption, and of strict gender norms, but she is by no means virtuous. Her social injuries are marked as unjust and undeserved, but she also acts in morally complicated ways that do not fit into a binary of good or evil. She not only blithely luxuriates in the class privilege that harms her and Ron but also refuses to marry Ron in order to stay within its warm fold. The film thus refuses to valorize her condition, even rendering her partly accountable for Ron's violent accident; even though she is not precisely its cause, she stands accountable for its painful consequences.[44] The film denies Cary's wounds an immediate moral righteousness that would erase her complicity in upholding and sustaining the cruelty of the social injustices that also injure her.

Similarly, melodramatic political discourses after 9/11 depicted the horror, cruelty, and violence of 9/11, but they can also be read to have refused to identify those who suffered as unquestionably virtuous. Melodramatic accounts of "mission accomplished," especially in addressing events *after* the mission was supposedly accomplished, account for the continuation of the occupation, the ongoing practices of indefinite detention at Guantanamo, the falsity of going to war in Iraq in pursuit of terrorists and weapons of mass destruction, the thousands of people killed as "collateral damage" in the war, and the U.S. torture of prisoners in Abu Ghraib—events that delegitimize claims of U.S. moral innocence within U.S. political discourse.[45] By suggesting that one can be both terrorized by the 9/11 events and also accountable for legitimating the violent deaths of thousands of others, the women's weepie conventions of 9/11 melodrama sever the link between U.S. injury and U.S. virtue. Delinking virtue and injury thus inhibits the a priori moral legitimacy for any action taken in the name of defeating villainy, assuaging injury, or restoring a victim's capacity for sovereign freedom. This delinking doubles back on post-9/11 melodrama's earlier moral legitimation of state expansion, weakening the felt legitimacy that it had earlier encouraged, locating complicity, discomfort, and moral complexity where the comforts of righteous certitude may have earlier reigned. The delinking creates a space for those who suffer from the effects of unfree conditions to account for the ways they also contribute to these conditions.[46] Melodramatic political discourse offers outsized and grandiose gestures of power, ressentiment, and mastery as the proper response to experiences of unfreedom, while showing in refracted moments how these gestures are unsuccessful. Rather than performing the disavowal of U.S. violence, the melodrama of "mission accomplished" performed in a spectacular way both the state's failure of sovereign power and the country's responsibility for global violence.

## Twenty-First-Century Politics of Sovereign Failure

Melodramatic political discourse does not offer a new vision of freedom's practice or a more promising genre form for interpreting political life. Gledhill argues, "Melodrama does not hav[e] a programmatic analysis for the future; its possibilities lie in this double acknowledgement of how things are in a given historical conjuncture, and of the primary desires and resistances contained within it."[47] What melodrama offers is a ground to scrutinize the forms of unfreedom that inhabit contemporary life and the failure of existing attempts to overcome them. Bonnie Honig has recently argued that melodrama can be a key genre of social critique, as its depictions of the impotence and paralysis that saturate late modern life *interrupt* political resignation rather than reinforce it.[48] Melodrama's staging of paralysis in the face of overwhelming power, for Honig, does more than resign individuals to powerlessness; this staging interrupts more common ways of depicting political subjects as permanently helpless against contemporary power. The women's weepie version of "mission accomplished" also works in this vein, albeit in a different way than Honig envisions. Refracted weepies of post-9/11 melodrama stage an agentic scene of aggression and acting out that is expected to undo powerlessness but instead illuminates the failure of that effort. Melodramas of failure thus offer a different type of agency than a passive staging of interrupted paralysis. "Mission accomplished," for instance, offers a melodrama in which massive and violent state-organized actions, intended to fight back conditions of powerlessness, achieve the very opposite of what they intend. And yet the failure of sovereign power that melodrama depicts does not necessarily demand resignation, but it can incite the pursuit of new options for challenging the unfreedom and powerlessness that animate its use.

The failure of "mission accomplished" undoes attachments to sovereignty as the final position of freedom, but this failure does not offer new options or attachments in its stead.[49] Rather, it asks political subjects to actively grapple with the impossibility of mastery, the lived conditions of demobilized agency, and the complex operations of various and interconnected powers that penetrate and condition contemporary life. This grappling begins the hard work of collectively engaging with the political violence, felt powerlessness, waning sovereignty, and structural unfreedoms of the contemporary moment. These experiences include the 9/11 events but are certainly not limited to them, and they include reckoning with the ways that individuals are themselves imbricated or complicit in the exploitation and demobilization of others. Failure, in this context, shows how individual acts of heroism or state practices of unilateralism are no match for the larger and abstracted yet individually experienced powers that must be challenged to practice freedom in a substantive and transformative way. Only large-scale, collective, and solidaristic change, failure implies, can achieve the world-making and self-governing capabilities that individuals and collectivities seem to desire in their pursuits of sovereign power.

Yet melodramas of failure are a difficult and limited place to pin the possibilities for reimagining freedom. In women's weepies, for instance, the characters are based in conventional stereotypes and are ultimately self-defeating in their ability to get what they desire. Spectators of these films rarely if ever see characters acting in ways that promote human flourishing, social transformation, or acts of world participation. However, as Linda Williams argued decades ago in a debate about the weepies that energized feminist film theory, the participants in melodramatic stories—characters, spectators, all—experience not only the resignation of obstructed agency but also the anger, sorrow, and, yes, furious critique of a society that demands so much from its members and offers so very little in return.[50] Failure enables one to reattend to the discrepancy between desires for freedom and the specific unfreedoms shaping lived experience, without yet having a new genre of interpretation to suture back up what discrepancy opens.

Melodrama's scenes of failed freedom thus take failed efforts to achieve freedom as a space for opening, not for frantic cauterization. It opens a space to imagine alternatives to sovereign triumph, besides humiliation, powerlessness, or oppression. To ask this of "mission accomplished" might seem to be a tall request, but "mission accomplished" and the war on terror more broadly make our present; they are what continue to be worked through and subjected to this kind of demand. Neither *All That Heaven Allows* nor "mission accomplished" provides the key that turns scenes of failed sovereign desire into energetics for structural transformation. But both do more than hold up the fantasies we might expect. The heightened dramatizations of failure in *All That Heaven Allows* and "mission accomplished" can undo the feeling of resignation from failure by refracting and thus, as Arendt would suggest, breaking apart freedom from sovereign agency or heroic individualism.

Where that opening to failure may lead is not predictable. Perhaps most likely, it leads into a panic that reinvests the social world with those aspirations for sovereignty yet again—as the depictions in melodramatic political discourse often did in the wake of 9 / 11. Or the opening leads to a reactionary vengeance against one's own society, a society that now seems unable to live up to the dreams of sovereignty that power so many of the norms stabilizing individual identity. This path holds onto individual sovereignty while blaming society for individuals' failures to achieve it—the Tea Party takes the path from this opening. But melodramas of failed sovereignty can also offer a different path: a path in which resistance to experiences of powerlessness and terror does not demand heroism but a deep and collective engagement with, through, and on power—whether this engagement takes form as active antiwar protests; solidarity movements with people under occupation by the United States; mobilization of antiracist and antisexist counterpowers against racial profiling and structural inequality more broadly; local movements for equality and freedom still in incipient formation or under the radar; or, in more risky and imaginative ways, in radical emancipatory and transnational world-making projects for true democracy and equality across borders, bodies, and regimes.

Reworking Halberstam's provocations for a post-9/11 political context, I would argue that the women's weepies' insistence on failure challenges what traffics as political freedom and also offers a felt space for confronting unfreedom in ways unimaginable through the norms one has "failed" to live up to. As Halberstam would note, an acceptance of failure, and a facing up to the losses that failure entails, already serves to challenge debilitating norms of sovereignty. They undermine the assumption that the failure of sovereignty means the failure of freedom itself. The acceptance of failure can also free freedom from the opposite assumption: that freedom is an inescapably violent or dangerous desire that should be altogether jettisoned or relinquished as a conservative norm or tool of imperialism. Instead, acceptance tarries with failure as a source for reconceiving what freedom can and should demand. Failure thus presents a way to sustain the impulse that animates melodrama—the desire to identify and undo experiences of unfreedom. But in addition failure makes it possible to imagine and practice freedom within situations that would seem to offer unfreedom only from the perspective of governing norms of sovereignty: heteronomy, vulnerability, distributed agency, and dependence on others.

Failure can offer fecund ground for cultivating different forms of freedom beyond the norms of sovereignty, militarism, and individualism, none of which correlates to the powers, networks, and social unfreedoms that each is assumed to challenge. The melodrama of failure in contemporary politics encourages reckoning with the specific forms of unfreedom shaping the present, ranging from vast levels of economic inequality to the manufacture of military occupation. This melodrama also encourages reckoning with loss: the loss of sovereignty as a governing ideal, the loss of an expected narrative trajectory of freedom as a global entitlement, and the loss of moral certitude of one's virtuous desire for unconstrained agency in the wake of felt powerlessness and suffering. These losses are enormous and cannot be overstated. And yet the melodramatic failure of freedom can, even in the midst of those devastating losses, energize a form of critique that does not demand giving up the idea of freedom as a practice, ideal, or norm of political life and agency. Instead the melodramatic failure of freedom pries open a space to rethink how freedom can look in a world of waning individual and state sovereignty, complex and unaccountable political powers, biopolitical governing strategies and neoliberal rationalities, and affectively overwhelming experiences of terrorism without then ceding the world to these conditions. I close the curtain on this study of melodrama with Technicolor performances of failed freedom, because they provide stronger support for reimagining freedom's possibility in our current moment than another empty promise of heroic sovereignty.

# NOTES

INTRODUCTION. MELODRAMA AND THE POLITICS OF FREEDOM

1. Linda Williams argues, "Melodrama is still the best, and most accurate, description of the serious narrative and iconic work performed by American mass culture, broadly conceived. . . . [Melodrama is] what most often typifies popular American narrative in literature, stage, film and television when it seeks to engage with moral questions." Jameson writes that the melodramatic plot is "the staple of mass culture" and that the end of melodrama would be "the end of mass culture itself." Linda Williams, *Playing the Race Card: Melodramas of Black and White from Uncle Tom to O. J. Simpson* (Princeton, NJ: Princeton University Press, 2001), 12, 17; and Fredric Jameson, "Realism and Utopia in *The Wire*," *Criticism* 52, nos. 3–4 (Summer / Fall 2010), 367–68. See also Christine Gledhill, "The Melodramatic Field: An Investigation," in *Home Is Where the Heart Is: Studies in Melodrama and the Woman's Film* (London: British Film Institute, 1987); David Grimsted, *Melodrama Unveiled: American Theater and Culture, 1800–1850* (Berkeley: University of California Press, 1988); and Jeffrey Mason, *Melodrama and the Myth of America* (Bloomington: Indiana University Press, 1993).

2. Lauren Berlant examines melodrama in order to analyze what she calls "national sentimentality"—a form of national belonging organized around shared experiences of empathic suffering with other injured Americans. In Berlant's pathbreaking analysis, melodramatic cultural products such as *Uncle Tom's Cabin*, *The King and I*, and *Now, Voyager* cultivate national sentimentality through fantasies of inclusive citizenship in which citizens' empathy with the suffering of the less fortunate indicates their own virtue and seems to correspond to the amelioration of injustice. The suffering that underpins national sentiment is produced by structural inequalities within the nation, and melodrama suggests that this suffering can mainly be redressed outside the political sphere, often in consumer products that locate remediation through the

consolations of intimate relationships. Berlant writes that national sentimentality is "a liberal rhetoric of promise historically entitled to the United States, which avows that a nation can best be built across fields of social difference through channels of affective identification and empathy." The suffering that binds the nation in melodramatic political discourse is different; it is caused by a villain outside the proper national body, rather than different allocations of privilege within the nation, and can best be redressed by vengeful declarations of state power. Melodramatic political discourse also aims to elide difference within the nation, rather than emphasize it (which I discuss more in chapter 1). Lauren Berlant, "The Subject of True Feeling," in *Cultural Studies and Political Theory*, ed. Jodi Dean (Ithaca, NY: Cornell University Press, 2002), 44. See also Lauren Berlant, *The Female Complaint: The Unfinished Business of Sentimentality in American Culture* (Durham, NC: Duke University Press, 2008). Other scholars who address the relationship between melodrama and national identity include Jeffrey Mason, Bruce McConachie, and Linda Williams.

3. In many of its manifestations from the eighteenth century onward, melodramas demonstrate a way of acting outward into the world. See Thomas Elsaesser, "Tales of Sound and Fury: Observations of the Family Melodrama," in *Home Is Where the Heart Is: Studies in Melodrama and the Woman's Film*, ed. Christine Gledhill (London: British Film Institute, 2002), 54–55; and Nicholas Vardac, *From Stage to Screen: Theatrical Method from Garrick to Griffith* (Cambridge, MA: Harvard University Press, 1949).

4. See Lindsey Green-Simms, "Occult Melodrama: Spectral Affect and West African Video-Film," *Camera Obscura* 27, no. 2 (2012); Kathleen McHugh and Nancy Abelmann, eds., *South Korean Golden Age Melodrama: Gender, Genre, and National Cinema* (Detroit, MI: Wayne State University Press, 2005); Louise McReynolds and Joan Neuberger, eds., *Imitations of Life: Two Centuries of Melodrama in Russia* (Durham, NC: Duke University Press, 2002); and Darlene Sadlier, ed., *Latin American Melodrama: Passion, Pathos, and Entertainment* (Urbana: University of Illinois Press, 2009).

5. George W. Bush, "President Pays Tribute at Pentagon Memorial," remarks at the Department of Defense Service of Remembrance, the Pentagon, Arlington, VA, October 11, 2001, State Department archives, accessed September 29, 2011, http://2001–2009.state.gov/coalition/cr/rm/2001/5338.htm.

6. On masculinist protection in post-9/11 rhetoric, see Iris Marion Young, "The Logic of *Masculinist Protection*: Reflections on the Current Security State," *Signs: A Journal of Women in Culture and Society* 29, no. 1 (Fall 2003).

7. Simon Stow's work on public mourning makes a similar point; he connects Bush's use of the Gettysburg Address at the first 9/11 anniversary to Thucydides's representation of Pericles's funeral oration to show how it promotes the glorification of the nation and a refusal of self-critique that generates an unthinking patriotism. By focusing on the Gettysburg Address, Stow finds tragedy in the patriotic discourse of post-9/11 politics. Melodrama works similarly, though its refusal of fate and promise

of mastering contingency makes it the more popular genre form that post-9/11 political discourse takes in its promotion of national virtue and righteousness. See Simon Stow, "Pericles at Gettysburg and Ground Zero: Tragedy, Patriotism, and Public Mourning," *American Political Science Review* 101, no. 2 (May 2007).

8. Steven Johnston argues that a willingness to sacrifice becomes a key component of membership in U.S. national identity grounded in patriotism, as willingness to be killed for one's nation becomes the final proof of one's love of country. Steven Johnston, *The Truth about Patriotism* (Durham, NC: Duke University Press, 2007).

9. Its widespread use may have also contributed to the widely reported feeling that watching the 9/11 events was similar to watching a movie. Kara Keeling explores the cinematic organization of perception by writing that "cinematic perception is not confined to interaction with moving-image media such as film and television. Involved in the production and reproduction of social reality itself, these perceptual and cognitive processes work to order, orchestrate, produce, and reproduce social reality and sociality." Kara Keeling, *The Witch's Flight: The Cinematic, the Black Femme, and the Image of Common Sense* (Durham, NC: Duke University Press, 2007), 11. Similarly, Davide Panagia argues for rethinking cinematic perception for its democratic possibility. Davide Panagia, *The Political Life of Sensation* (Durham, NC: Duke University Press, 2009).

10. See Judith Butler, *Precarious Life: The Powers of Mourning and Violence* (London: Verso, 2004); Jasbir Puar, *Terrorist Assemblages: Homonationalism in Queer Times* (Durham, NC: Duke University Press, 2007); and Leti Volpp, "The Citizen and the Terrorist," *UCLA Law Review* 49 (2002).

11. A sampling of early examples in U.S. scholarship includes Bill Chaloupka et al., eds., "Reflections on 11 September," special issue, *Theory and Event* 5, no. 4 (2001); Stanley Hauerwas and Frank Lentricchia, eds., "Dissent from the Homeland: Essays after September 11," special issue, *South Atlantic Quarterly* 101, no. 2 (Spring 2002); Ella Shohat, Brent Hayes Edwards, Stefano Harney, Randy Martin, Timothy Mitchell, and Fred Moten, eds., "9–11—A Public Emergency?," *Social Text* no. 72 (Fall 2002); and Austin Sarat, ed., *Dissent in Dangerous Times* (Ann Arbor: University of Michigan Press, 2005). In the news media, see *The Nation*, among other media sources.

12. Peter Brooks, *The Melodramatic Imagination: Balzac, Henry James, Melodrama, and the Mode of Excess* (New Haven, CT: Yale University Press, 1995), 52.

13. Gilles Deleuze, "Postscript on the Societies of Control," *October* 59 (Winter 1992): 3–7.

14. Sheldon Wolin, *The Presence of the Past: Essays on the State and the Constitution* (Baltimore, MD: Johns Hopkins University Press, 1989), 151–79.

15. On the increase of securitized state power that accompanies neoliberal deregulations, see Michel Foucault, *Birth of Biopolitics: Lectures at the Collège de France, 1978–1979*, trans. Graham Burchell (New York: Picador, 2008); David Garland, *Culture of Control: Crime and Social Order in Contemporary Society* (Chicago: Uni-

versity of Chicago Press, 2002); and Loïc Waquant, *Punishing the Poor: The Neoliberal Government of Social Insecurity* (Durham, NC: Duke University Press, 2009).

16. George W. Bush, "Bush: 'Freedom Will Be Defended,'" *Los Angeles Times*, September 12, 2001, accessed October 10, 2012, http://articles.latimes.com/2001/sep/11/news/ss-44622. Bush similarly explains in his 2002 State of the Union address: "It is both our responsibility and our privilege to fight freedom's fight. . . . We have known freedom's price. We have shown freedom's power. And in this great conflict, my fellow Americans, we will see freedom's victory." George W. Bush, "President Delivers State of the Union Address," the U.S. Capitol, Washington, DC, January 29, 2002, accessed October 10, 2012, White House Archives, http://georgewbush-whitehouse.archives.gov/news/releases/2002/01/20020129-11.html.

17. For key analyses of these topics, see Talal Asad, *On Suicide Bombing* (New York: Columbia University Press, 2007); Judith Butler, "Explanation and Exoneration; or, What We Can Hear," *Theory and Event* 5, no. 4 (2001); Judith Butler, *Frames of War: When Is Life Grievable?* (London: Verso, 2009); Alyson Cole, "9-1-1: The Nation as Victim," in *The Culture of True Victimhood: From the War on Welfare to the War on Terror* (Stanford, CA: Stanford University Press, 2007); William Connolly, "The Evangelical-Capitalist Resonance Machine," *Political Theory* 33, no. 6 (2005); Richard Grusin, *Premediation: Affect and Mediality after 9/11* (New York: Palgrave Macmillan, 2010); Mahmood Mamdami, *Good Muslim, Bad Muslim: America, the Cold War, and the Roots of Terror* (New York: Random House, 2005); and Marc Redfield, *The Rhetoric of Terror: Reflections on 9/11 and the War on Terror* (New York: Fordham University Press, 2009).

18. Saba Mahmood, *The Politics of Piety: Islamic Revival and the Feminist Subject* (Princeton, NJ: Princeton University Press, 2005), 20.

19. Mahmood, *The Politics of Piety*, 33.

20. Butler, *Precarious Life*, 39. She writes, "What kind of loss is this? It is the loss of the prerogative, only and always, to be the one who transgresses the sovereign boundaries of other states, but never to be in the position of having one's own boundaries transgressed. The United States was supposed to be the place that could not be attacked, where life was safe from violence initiated abroad, where the only violence we knew was the kind we had inflicted on ourselves."

21. Retort, "Afflicted Powers: The State, the Spectacle, and September 11," *New Left Review* 27 (May–June 2004): 14.

22. Max Weber, "Politics as a Vocation," in *On Max Weber: Essays in Sociology*, ed. H. H. Gerth and C. Wright Mills (Oxford: Oxford University Press, 1958).

23. John Ashcroft, the attorney general, narrated the derailment of the freedom story that entwines states and subjects when he said on September 11: "These heinous acts of violence are an assault on the security of our nation; they are an assault on the security and freedom of every American citizen." John Ashcroft, "Text: U.S. Attorney General John Ashcroft," news conference, Washingtonpost.com, September 11, 2001, accessed October 20, 2012, http://www.washingtonpost.com/wp-srv/onpolitics/transcripts/ashcrofttext_091101.htm.

24. Sharon Krause, "On Non-sovereign Responsibility: Agency, Inequality and Democratic Citizenship," paper presented at the annual meeting of the Association for Political Theory, University of Notre Dame, Notre Dame, Indiana, October 14, 2011, 1.

25. Butler, *Precarious Life*, 20.

26. On sovereignty in these iterations, see Giorgio Agamben, *Homo Sacer: Sovereign Power and Bare Life*, trans. Daniel Heller-Roazen (Stanford, CA: Stanford University Press, 1998); Jean Bodin, *On Sovereignty*, trans and ed. Julian Franklin (Cambridge, UK: Cambridge University Press, 1992); Thomas Hobbes, *Leviathan; or, The Matter, Forme and Power of a Commonwealth Ecclesiasticall and Civil*, ed. Michael Oakeshott (New York: Collier, 1968); Jean-Jacques Rousseau, *The Social Contract*, trans. G. D. H. Cole (New York: Penguin Classics, 1968); and Carl Schmitt, *Political Theology: Four Concepts on the Concept of Sovereignty*, trans. George Schwab (Chicago: University of Chicago Press, 2006).

27. Bonnie Honig, *Antigone, Interrupted* (Cambridge, UK: Cambridge University Press, 2013), 77.

28. Dick Cheney, "Vice President Dick Cheney Receives 2001 Freedom Award," transcript, CNN.com, October 23, 2001, accessed October 20, 2012, http://transcripts.cnn.com/TRANSCRIPTS/0110/23/se.22.html.

29. See, among many others, David L. Altheide, *Terrorism and the Politics of Fear* (Lanham, MD: AltaMira Press, 2006); Mark Barkun, *Chasing Phantoms: Reality, Imagination, and Homeland Security since 9/11* (Chapel Hill: University of North Carolina Press, 2011); Darrin Davis, *Negative Liberty: Public Opinion and the Terrorist Attacks on America* (New York: Russell Sage Foundation, 2007); Thomas Frank, *What's the Matter with Kansas?* (New York: Metropolitan Books, 2004); Hank Jenkins-Smith, "Rock and a Hard Place: Public Willingness to Trade Civil Rights and Liberties for Greater Security," *Politics and Policy* 37, no. 5 (October 2009); Jeffery J. Mondak, "Examining the Terror Exception: Terrorism and Commitments to Civil Liberties," *Public Opinion Quarterly* 76, no. 2 (January 2012); John Mueller and Mark Stewart, "The Terrorism Delusion: America's Overwrought Response to September 11," *International Security* 37, no. 1 (Summer 2012); Trevor Thrall and Jane Cramer, eds., *American Foreign Policy and the Politics of Fear: Threat Inflation since 9/11* (London: Routledge, 2011); and Sheldon Wolin, *Democracy Incorporated: Managed Democracy and the Specter of Inverted Totalitarianism* (Princeton, NJ: Princeton University Press, 2008).

30. Wendy Brown, *Edgework: Critical Essays in Knowledge and Politics* (Princeton, NJ: Princeton University Press, 2005), 100; and Wendy Brown, *Walled States, Waning Sovereignty* (New York: Zone Books, 2010).

31. Friedrich Nietzsche, *On the Genealogy of Morals and Ecce Homo*, trans. Walter Kauffman (New York: Vintage, 1989), 139–43.

32. Raymond Williams, "Social Environment and Theatrical Environment: The Case of English Naturalism," in *English Drama: Forms and Development*, ed. Raymond Williams (Cambridge, UK: Cambridge University Press, 1977).

33. Berlant writes of the scene of the impasse: "[In] a condition of being worn out by the activity of reproducing life, agency can be an activity of maintenance, not making; fantasy, without grandiosity." Lauren Berlant, *Cruel Optimism* (Durham, NC: Duke University Press, 2012), 100. Berlant describes the contemporary conditions of vulnerability and powerlessness that the impasse works through using the shorthand *precarity*, and I describe similar conditions through the shorthand *unfreedom*, a difference attributed in part because of the responses to these conditions we each examine, responses that circulate in different social and political fields.

34. Part of the differences between the impasse of lateral agency and the melodrama of orgies of feeling might be found in the fantasies they manage: the impasse and lateral agency work to manage fraying fantasies of the good life, while melodramatic politics works to manage to fraying fantasies of unburdened agency understood as freedom. To be sure, freedom is part of the good-life fantasy that Berlant tracks, and for Berlant the waning of sovereignty is part of what motivates lateral agency, but these fantasies do not exhaust each other.

35. Berlant, *Cruel Optimism*, 6.

36. Berlant, *Cruel Optimism*, 14.

37. Berlant, *Cruel Optimism*, 117.

38. Brown, *Walled States, Waning Sovereignty*, 104. Brown argues that border walls reveal the waning relevance of state sovereignty, as walls are a failed attempt to control, monitor, and govern what they simply cannot control: flows of people, goods, ideas, and capital: "The new walls thus dissimulate need and dependency as they resurrect myths of national autonomy and purity in a globalized world." Brown, *Walled States, Waning Sovereignty*, 103.

39. This mode of critique is found from Karl Marx's "On the Jewish Question," in *The Marx-Engels Reader*, ed. Robert Tucker (New York: W. W. Norton, 1978) to Theodor Adorno and Max Horkheimer's *Dialectic of Enlightenment: Philosophical Fragments*, trans. Edmund Jephcott (Stanford, CA: Stanford University Press, 2002) and onto more recent scholarship, including Stuart Hall's *The Hard Road to Renewal: Thatcherism and the Crisis of the Left* (London: Verso, 1988) and Wendy Brown's *States of Injury: Power and Freedom in Late Modernity* (Princeton, NJ: Princeton University Press, 1995).

40. Sheldon Wolin writes that collective identities are produced and perpetuated by public discourse, providing the vocabulary, ideologies, memories, myths, and values through which we think and talk about political life, even as these identities are unstable, multiple, shifting, and in competition with each other. Sheldon Wolin, *The Presence of Past: Essays on the State and the Constitution* (Baltimore, MD: Johns Hopkins University Press, 1989), 9. On genres of politics, see Bonnie Honig, *Democracy and the Foreigner* (Princeton, NJ: Princeton University Press, 2001); George Shulman, *American Prophecy: Race and Redemption in American Political Culture* (Minneapolis: University of Minnesota Press, 2008); and Elizabeth Wingrove, *Rousseau's Republican Romance* (Princeton, NJ: Princeton University Press, 2000).

41. See Daniel Dayan and Elihu Katz, *Media Events: The Live Broadcasting of History* (Cambridge, MA: Harvard University Press, 1992); Samuel Kernell, *Going Public: New Strategies of Presidential Leadership* (Washington, DC: CQ Press, 2006); Michael Schudson, *The Power of News* (Cambridge, MA: Harvard University Press, 1996); Matthew Seeger et al., "Media Use, Information Seeking, and Reported Needs in Post-crisis Contexts," in *Communication and Terrorism: Public and Media Responses to 9/11*, ed. Bradley Greenberg (Creeskill, NJ: Hampton Press, 2002); and Jeffrey Tulis, *The Rhetorical Presidency* (Princeton, NJ: Princeton University Press, 1988).

42. On the use of the jeremiad in American political discourse, see Elizabeth Castelli, "Persecution Complexes: Identity Politics and the 'War on Christians,'" *differences: A Journal of Feminist Cultural Studies* 18, no. 3 (2007); David Gutterman, *Prophetic Politics: Christian Social Movements and American Democracy* (Ithaca, NY: Cornell University Press, 2006); Andrew Murphy, *Prodigal Nation: Moral Decline and Divine Punishment from New England to 9/11* (New York: Oxford University Press, 2009); Vibeke Pederson, "In Search of Monsters to Destroy: The American Liberal Security Paradox and a Republican Way Out," *International Relations* 17 (June 2003); and Shulman, *American Prophecy*.

43. Noam Chomsky, interview from September 20, 2001, reprinted in Noam Chomsky, *9-11* (New York: Seven Stories Press, 2002), 23.

44. Jerry Falwell quoted in "Falwell Apologizes to Gays, Feminists, Lesbians," CNN .com, September 14, 2001, accessed October 20, 2012, http://europe.cnn.com/2001 /US/09/14/Falwell.apology/index.html. See also Murphy, *Prodigal Nation*, 4–5.

45. Robert Heilman, *Tragedy and Melodrama: Versions of Experience* (Seattle: University of Washington Press, 1968), 35, 85.

46. For Huntington's original argument, see Samuel Huntington, *The Clash of Civilizations and the Remaking of the World Order* (New York: Simon and Schuster, 1997). On its popular deployment after September 11, see Richard Bonney, *False Prophets: The Clash of Civilizations and the War on Terror* (London: Peter Lang, 2008).

47. Michael Rogin, *Ronald Reagan the Movie: And Other Episodes in Political Demonology* (Berkeley: University of California Press, 1988).

48. Huntington, *The Clash of Civilizations and the Remaking of the World Order*, 36.

49. Thomas Friedman, "9-11 Lesson Plan," *New York Times*, September 4, 2002, a21.

50. See Wendy Brown, *Regulating Aversion: Tolerance in the Age of Identity and Empire* (Princeton, NJ: Princeton University Press, 2006); Mamdani, *Good Muslim, Bad Muslim*.

51. See Berlant, *The Female Complaint*; Mary Anne Doane, *The Desire to Desire* (Bloomington: Indiana University Press, 1986); Christine Gledhill, ed., *Home Is Where the Heart Is: Studies in Melodrama and the Woman's Film* (London: British Film Institute, 1987); Lynne Joyrich, *Re-viewing Reception: Television, Gender, and Postmodern Culture* (Bloomington: Indiana University Press, 1996); E. Ann Kaplan, *Motherhood and Representation* (New York: Routledge, 1992); Barbara Klinger, *Melodrama and Meaning: History, Culture, and the Films of Douglas Sirk*

(Bloomington: Indiana University Press, 1994); Marcia Landy, ed., *Imitations of Life: A Reader on Film and Television Melodrama* (Detroit, MI: Wayne State University Press, 1991); Robert Lang, *American Film Melodrama: Griffith, Vidor, Minnelli* (Princeton, NJ: Princeton University Press, 1989); Laura Mulvey, *Visual and Other Pleasures* (New York: Palgrave MacMillan, 2009); and Linda Williams, "'Something Else Besides a Mother': Stella Dallas and the Maternal Melodrama," in *Imitations of Life: A Reader on Film and Television Melodrama*, ed. Marcia Landy (Detroit, MI: Wayne State University Press, 1991).

52. Steve Neale's research in the film industry showed how melodrama, in the trade press, was a category limited to action-oriented spectacles; domestic dramas and the woman's film were called adult films instead of melodrama. Melodrama's conceptual ambiguity powers reams of scholarship that draw and redraw melodrama's boundaries. See Rick Altman, "Reusable Packaging: Generic Products and the Recycling Process," in *Refiguring American Film Genres: History and Theory*, ed. Nick Browne (Berkeley: University of California Press, 1998); and Steve Neale, "Melo Talk: On the Meaning and Use of the Term 'Melodrama' in the American Trade Press," *The Velvet Light Trap*, no. 32 (1993). On melodrama and action, see Daniel Gerould, "Melodrama and Revolution," in *Melodrama: Stage, Picture, Screen*, ed. Jacky Bratton, Jim Cook, and Christine Gledhill (London: British Film Institute, 1994); Grimsted, *Melodrama Unveiled*; Tom Gunning, "The Cinema of Attraction: Early Film, Its Spectator and the Avant-Garde," *Wide Angle* 8, nos. 3–4 (1986); Heilman, *Tragedy and Melodrama*; Scott Higgins, "Suspenseful Situations: Melodramatic Narrative and the Contemporary Action Film," *Cinema Journal* 47, no. 2 (2008); Ben Singer, *Melodrama and Modernity: Early Cinema and Its Contexts* (New York: Columbia University Press, 2002); and Nicholas Vardac, *From Stage to Screen*.

53. Walter Benjamin, "Left-Wing Melancholy," in *Walter Benjamin: Selected Writings*, vol. 2, part 1, ed. Michael Jennings (Cambridge, MA: Harvard University Press, 2005), 423–27.

## 1. THE VENOMOUS EYE

1. Linda Williams and Christine Gledhill argue that melodrama is less a genre than a "mode"—a cultural worldview that shapes many other genres, including the woman's film, the action thriller, and the western. Yet for the purposes of this book, *genre* conveys more of the way that cultural conventions of storytelling invest in political policies, rather than the more nebulous and broad term *mode*. I thus retain the term *genre* for the purposes of melodramatic political discourse, because it better conveys how cultural conventions shape political knowledge. Christine Gledhill, "The Melodramatic Field: An Investigation," in *Home Is Where the Heart Is: Studies in Melodrama and the Woman's Film* (London: British Film Institute, 2002); and Linda Williams, "Melodrama Revised," in *Refiguring Film Genres*, ed. Nick Browne (Berkeley: University of California Press, 1998).

2. Louise McReynolds and Joan Neuberger, eds., *Imitations of Life: Two Centuries of Melodrama in Russia* (Durham, NC: Duke University Press, 2002), 4.

3. Peter Brooks, *The Melodramatic Imagination: Balzac, Henry James, Melodrama, and the Mode of Excess* (New Haven, CT: Yale University Press, 1995), 44.

4. Friedrich Nietzsche, *On the Genealogy of Morals and Ecce Homo*, trans. Walter Kauffman (New York: Vintage, 1989), 39.

5. Nietzsche, *On the Genealogy of Morals and Ecce Homo*, 37.

6. In melodramatic film and literature, innocence (and the virtue that attaches to innocence) is staged in establishing scenes that Linda Williams calls "fragile and fleeting spaces of innocence and freedom." In political discourse, however, innocence, like goodness, is recognizable only retrospectively, after it is besieged. Linda Williams, *Playing the Race Card: Melodramas of Black and White from Uncle Tom to O. J. Simpson* (Princeton, NJ: Princeton University Press, 2001), 28.

7. Brooks, *The Melodramatic Imagination*; Thomas Elsaesser, "Tales of Sound and Fury: Observations of the Family Melodrama," in *Home Is Where the Heart Is: Melodrama and the Woman's Film*, ed. Christine Gledhill (London: British Film Institute, 1987). For more on melodrama's theological inheritances, see chapter 2.

8. Arthur Kleinman, Veena Das, and Margaret Lock, eds., *Social Suffering* (Berkeley: University of California Press, 1997).

9. Lauren Berlant, "Poor Eliza," in *The Female Complaint: The Unfinished Business of Sentimentality in American Culture* (Durham, NC: Duke University Press, 2008).

10. Linda Williams suggests that melodramas contain cycles of pathos and action that energize the spectator, creating a roller coaster of empathic pain and vicarious thrills in the "tension between the paroxysm of pathos and the exhilaration of action." L. Williams, "Melodrama Revised," 69.

11. Rousseau writes, "I have devised a genre of drama in which the words and the Music, instead of proceeding together, are made to be heard in succession, and in which the spoken phrase is in a way announced and prepared by the musical phrase. The scene 'Pygmalion' is an example of this genre of composition, and it has not had imitators. By perfecting this method, one would bring together the double advantage of relieving the actor through frequent rests and of offering to the French spectator a type of *melodrame* most suited to his language." Jean-Jacques Rousseau, "Letter to M. Burney and Fragments of Observations on Gluck's 'Alceste,'" in *Essay on the Origin of Languages and Writings Related to Music*, trans. and ed. John T. Scott (Hanover, NH: Dartmouth College Press, 1998), 497.

12. Aristotle writes, "There is persuasion through the hearers when they are led to feel emotion (pathos) by the speech." It is "wakening emotion (pathos) in the audience so as to induce them to make the judgment desired." Aristotle, *On Rhetoric: A Theory of Civic Discourse*, trans. George Kennedy (Oxford: Oxford University Press, 1991), 38, 119. Amelie Rorty writes that for Aristotle, pathos is "whatever so changes us as to affect our judgment and is also attended by pain and pleasure." Amelie Rorty, *Essays on Aristotle's Ethics* (Princeton, NJ: Princeton University Press, 1992), 295. See also L. Williams, "Melodrama Revised."

13. Ben Singer, *Melodrama and Modernity: Early Cinema and Its Contexts* (New York: Columbia University Press, 2002), 44. Tom Gunning highlights this sensationalist

aspect of the melodrama as its primary quality. Railroad-track rescues, exploding machinery, lavish parties, fistfights, car chases, animal actors, and national festivals are forms of sensationalism and spectacle that aim to create visceral responses to the narrative and instigate highly charged emotion in the spectator, as a sensitization to the shocks of modernity, as visceral confirmation of the morality underpinning lived experience, and a pleasure in its own right. Tom Gunning, "The Horror of Opacity: The Melodrama of Sensation in the Plays of André de Lorde," in *Melodrama: Stage, Picture, Screen*, ed. Jacky Bratton, Jim Cook, and Christine Gledhill (London: British Film Institute, 1994), 50–61.

14. Gledhill remarks that melodrama's "sentimental dramaturgy demands a new kind of spectatorial response of recognition and identification with familiar characters in affecting circumstances." Gledhill, "The Melodramatic Field," 17. See also Mary Ann Doane, "The Woman's Film: Possession and Address," in *Re-vision: Essays in Feminist Film Criticism*, ed. Mary Ann Doane and Patricia Mellencamp (Frederick, MD: University Publications of America, 1984); E. Ann Kaplan, "Ann Kaplan Replies to Linda Williams's 'Something Else Besides a Mother': *Stella Dallas* and the Maternal Melodrama' (*Cinema Journal*, Fall 1984)," *Cinema Journal* 24, no. 2 (Winter 1985); and Laura Mulvey, "Notes on Sirk and Melodrama," in *Home Is Where the Heart Is: Melodrama and the Woman's Film*, ed. Christine Gledhill (London: British Film Institute, 1987).

15. For more on this point, see Elisabeth Anker, "Heroic Identifications; or, 'You Can Love Me Too—I Am So like the State,'" *Theory and Event* 15, no. 1 (2012).

16. Martha Vicinus, "Helpless and Unfriended: Nineteenth-Century Domestic Melodrama," *New Literary History* 13, no. 1 (Autumn 1991): 130.

17. On left melodrama, also see Elisabeth Anker, "Left Melodrama," *Contemporary Political Theory* 11, no. 2 (May 2012).

18. Nietzsche, *On the Genealogy of Morals and Ecce Homo*, 34.

19. Nietzsche refers to the venomous eye of ressentiment as an "imaginary revenge," and yet he also argues that this venomous eye has "triumphed again and again," overthrowing the hostile forces it holds responsible for injuring the self. The venomous eye of ressentiment demonstrates, in one sense, "the instinct for freedom forcibly made latent." But in another sense, and in melodramatic political discourse, its latent instinct is revived and redirected outward through the violent pursuit of agents responsible for injury. Nietzsche, *On the Genealogy of Morals and Ecce Homo*, 35, 87.

20. Marcia Landy, "Introduction," in *Imitations of Life: A Reader on Film and Television Melodrama*, ed. Marcia Landy (Detroit, MI: Wayne State University Press, 1991), 14.

21. Looking at the film-industry trade press, Steve Neale notes that women's films are rarely described as melodrama; melodrama's action form often ends in the spectacle of triumph for the unjustly persecuted or the heroes who rescue them. Steve Neale, "Melo Talk: On the Meaning and Use of the Term 'Melodrama' in the American Trade Press," *The Velvet Light Trap*, no. 32 (1993). See also Singer, *Melodrama and Modernity*.

22. See J. Peter Euben, *The Tragedy of Political Theory: The Road Not Taken* (Princeton, NJ: Princeton University Press, 1990); Steven Johnston, *Encountering Tragedy: Rousseau and the Project of Democratic Order* (Ithaca, NY: Cornell University Press, 1999); and David Scott, *Conscripts of Modernity: The Tragedy of Colonial Enlightenment* (Durham, NC: Duke University Press, 2004).

23. Melodrama's production of a virtuous and vengeful national identity defined by victimization is, at one level, akin to a *wounded attachment*—Wendy Brown's seminal term for political identities defined by the wounds that call them into being, but that also require their continued victimization for their stability as identities; these identities suffer a bind in which they are injured by the very state powers they depend on for redress, and can only make claims for power "by entrenching, restating, dramatizing, and inscribing [their] pain in politics." Wendy Brown, *States of Injury: Power and Freedom in Late Modernity* (Princeton, NJ: Princeton University Press, 1995), 49. Wounded attachments, in Brown's reading, describes the bind of minoritized identity groups, yet in melodramatic political discourse wounded attachments play out differently, in a national identity that affects not a minoritized population but the general public at large—a nation of wounded subjects. And this shifts both the experience of injury and its relationship to state power. In U.S. melodramatic political discourse, the wound is experienced not by those conventionally excluded from national identity but as the very substance of national identity. The state power deployed to redress the wound is then unproblematically coupled to this identity as a necessary counter to the injuring agent. This expansion shifts the content of an injured political subjectivity framed within and against the state to an identity that is injured by forces presumably external to it, and it thus encompasses state power wholeheartedly and uncritically, investing state power with moral authority and with the heroic capacity to heal the national wound through its own acts of domination.

24. Francesco Casetti, *The Eye of the Century: Film, Experience, Modernity*, trans. Erin Larkin and Jennifer Pranolo (New York: Columbia University Press, 2010).

25. Bernhard Debatin writes that 9 / 11 was "a worldwide synchronization of attention." "'Plane Wreck with Spectators': Terrorism and Media Attention," in *Communication and Terrorism: Public and Media Responses to 9 / 11*, ed. Bradley S. Greenberg (Cresskill, NJ: Hampton Press, 2002), 164–65.

26. John Carey, "The Functions and Uses of Media during the September 11 Crisis and Its Aftermath," in *Crisis Communications Lessons from September 11*, ed. Michael Noll (Lantham, MD: Rowman and Littlefield, 2003).

27. Michael Schudson, *The Power of News* (Cambridge, MA: Harvard University Press, 1996), 54.

28. Annamarie Oliverio argues that "incidents defined as terrorism often provide the script for historical interpretations of national identity and political sovereignty," and melodramatic depictions of the 9 / 11 attacks as an incident of terrorism worked in this way as a compelling nation-building discourse that rearticulated national identity and state legitimacy in relation to terror. Annamarie Oliverio, *The State of Terror* (New York: SUNY Press, 1998), 6.

29. Laura Frost, "Black Screens, Lost Bodies: The Cinematic Apparatus of 9/11 Horror," in *Horror after 9/11*, ed. Aviva Briefal and Sam Miller (Austin: University of Texas Press, 2011), 15.

30. Monahan sees melodrama in CNN and CBS (citing the earlier article form of this chapter) through he argues that the goal of the reporting was less vengeance than redemption. Brian Monahan, *The Shock of the News: Media Coverage and the Making of 9/11* (New York: New York University Press, 2010), 65, 80. See also Elisabeth Anker, "Villains, Victims and Heroes: Melodrama, Media, and September 11," *Journal of Communication* 55, no. 1 (March 2005).

31. While melodrama attaches to particular types of conservative and neoconservative politics, especially the xenophobic fear of others (in conservatism) and the moral imperative of U.S. global power (in neoconservatism), it is also found across the political spectrum—as shown in speeches and interviews during this hour—and in the political discourse of the radical Left, as I argue in chapter 6.

32. The author conducted all transcriptions of quotes from this hour of coverage.

33. Michel Chion, *Audio-Vision: Sound on Screen*, trans. and ed. Claudia Gorbman (New York: Columbia University Press, 1994), 63.

34. On the relationship between the close-up and identification, see Mary Anne Doane, "The Close-Up: Scale and Detail in the Cinema," *differences: A Journal of Feminist Cultural Studies* 14, no. 3 (Fall 2003).

35. Peter Brooks, "Melodrama, Body, Revolution," in *Melodrama: Stage, Picture, Screen*, ed. Jacky Bratton, Jim Cook, and Christine Gledhill (London: British Film Institute, 1994), 18.

36. And the eventual support for the legitimacy of the war on terror transcends racial divides, to a certain degree: A CBS poll in December 2001 that disaggregated support for the war on terror by race found that 75 percent of blacks supported the war on terror. This is a very high number. Yet it is not as high as the number of whites who supported it, which was at the breathtakingly high 90 percent. There are racial differences in who connects to this national identity that includes in its membership the uncritical support of state power, but both groups still provide high levels of support for the war on terror. "CBS News/New York Times Monthly Poll, December 2001 (ICPSR 3379)," available at Inter-university Consortium for Political and Social Research, accessed April 2, 2013, http://www.icpsr.umich.edu/icpsrweb /ICPSR/studies/3379#summary.

37. Melani McAlister, *Epic Encounters: Culture, Media, and U.S. Interests in the Middle East since 1945* (Berkeley: University of California Press, 2005), 304–6.

38. Jodi Melamed, "The Spirit of Neoliberalism: From Racial Liberalism to Neoliberal Multiculturalism," *Social Text* 24, no. 4 (Winter 2006): 6–7.

39. On this point, see, among others, Wendy Brown, *Regulating Aversion: Tolerance in the Age of Identity and Empire* (Princeton, NJ: Princeton University Press, 2006); Saba Mahmood and Charles Hirschkind, "Feminism, the Taliban, and Politics of Counter-insurgency," *Anthropological Quarterly* 75, no. 2 (Spring 2002); and Ann Norton, *On the Muslim Question* (Princeton, NJ: Princeton University Press, 2013);

and Chandan Reddy, *Freedom with Violence: Race, Sexuality, and the US State* (Durham, NC: Duke University Press, 2011).

40. In spatial montage, two disparate events share space rather than time. They are not sequential but are juxtaposed by space. Lev Manovich, *The Language of New Media* (Cambridge, MA: MIT Press, 2002).

41. Despina Kakoudaki captures the shift from confusion to war: "After a while, the incomprehensibility of terrorism is translated into the frightening but orderly demands of war, and the stunned silence of the first days is replaced by other emotions." Yet while Kakoudaki suggests that this shift took days, the coverage here on Fox News shows that it occurred within hours. Despina Kakoudaki, "Spectacles of History: Race Relations Melodrama and the Science Fiction / Disaster Film," *Camera Obscura* 17, no. 2 (2002): 110.

42. In this form of subjectivity, the hero and the victim are coconstitutive and mutually dependent. Neither can exist without the other, and each contain the other within themselves. L. Williams, "Melodrama Revised," 83n15.

43. As Susan Faludi shows, gendered norms often function in post-9/11 discourses to masculinize the first responders and feminize post-9/11 suffering through the valorization of the wives who lost husbands in the attack. Susan Faludi, *The Terror Dream: Fear and Fantasy in Post-9/11 America* (New York: Metropolitan, 2007).

44. As Scott Loren and Jörg Metelmann argue, melodramas use sentiment toward "the necessity of *making something visible*: namely, novel problems of social injustice and bourgeois morality." Scott Loren and Jörg Metelmann, *Irritation of Life: The Subversive Melodrama of Michael Haneke, David Lynch and Lars Von Trier* (Marburg, Germany: Shüren, 2013), 4.

45. Nietzsche describes the identity production of ressentiment as "an inversion of the value-positing eye—this need to direct one's view outward instead of back to oneself"—as a new mode of seeing. For Nietzsche, the venomous eye makes and marks values through what it chooses to view and how it chooses to see. Its subjectivity is designated through ocular metaphors: the nobles did "too much looking away" to practice the critical judgment involved in ressentiment. Now, after the revaluation, the evil man seen though ressentiment is the former good man now, "dyed in another color, interpreted in another fashion, *seen* in another way by *the venomous eye* of ressentiment." Nietzsche, *On the Genealogy of Morals and Ecce Homo*, 40.

46. The venomous eye of ressentiment generates a moral-visual nexus whereby the visual field of horrible suffering cements the moral judgment of the injured subject's own goodness. It works by "direct[ing] one's view outward instead of back to oneself." Nietzsche, *On the Genealogy of Morals and Ecce Homo*, 38.

47. This is different from the understanding of political-identity production and judgments in recent political theory, which views information gained from the visual realm with suspicion or distrust, interpreting political subjectivity in such a way that implies a curiously disembodied subject abstracted from its own materiality. The most obvious example is John Rawls's veil of ignorance, which literally exor-

cises the visual from the highest forms of decision making. Public deliberation about justice in Rawls's *A Theory of Justice* (Cambridge, MA: Harvard University Press, 1999) seems to require self-blinding in order to attain fair outcomes.

48. Frank Rahill, *The World of Melodrama* (University Park: Penn State University Press, 1967), 189.

49. Derrida quoted in Giovanna Borradori, Jürgen Habermas, and Jacques Derrida, *Philosophy in a Time of Terror: Dialogues with Jürgen Habermas and Jacques Derrida* (Chicago: University of Chicago Press, 2004), 108.

50. Robert Stam, "Television News and Its Spectator," in *Regarding Television*, ed. Ann Kaplan (Frederick, MD: American Film Institute, 1983), 102.

51. Mary Ann Doane, "Information, Crisis, and Catastrophe," in *The Historical Film: History and Memory in Media*, ed. Marcia Landy (New Brunswick, NJ: Rutgers University Press, 2001). See also Matthew Seeger et al., "Media Use, Information Seeking, and Reported Needs in Post-crisis Contexts," in *Communication and Terrorism: Public and Media Reponses to 9/11*, ed. Bradley Greenberg (Cresskill, NJ: Hampton Press, 2002).

52. Brooks, *The Melodramatic Imagination*, 9.

53. Neil Leach, "9/11," *diacritics* 33, nos. 3–4 (Winter 2003).

54. Brooks, "Melodrama, Body, Revolution," 18.

55. Eisenstein pioneered the use of associative montage in the 1920s and describes it: "The copulation . . . of two images is to be regarded not as their sum but as their product. . . . Each . . . separately corresponds to an object, to a fact, but their combination corresponds to a concept." Sergei Eisenstein, *Film Form: Essays in Film Theory* (New York: Harvest Books, 1995), 29–30.

56. As Sara Ahmed describes 9/11 discourses, the evil Other who causes our injury also produces our goodness. Sara Ahmed, *The Cultural Politics of Emotion* (London: Routledge, 2004), 42–61.

57. Gunning, "The Horror of Opacity," 54.

58. Lisa Wedeen, *Ambiguities of Domination: Politics, Rhetoric, and Symbols in Contemporary Syria* (Chicago: University of Chicago Press, 1999), 22.

59. Michael Ignatieff, *Blood and Belonging: Journeys into the New Nationalism* (New York: Farrar, Strauss, Giroux, 1994).

60. Volpp writes, "Despite Bush meeting with myriad Muslim leaders, . . . his statements have done little to disabuse people of their 'common sense' understanding as to who is the terrorist and who is the citizen. . . . The American people are being instructed that looking 'Muslim, Arab or Middle Eastern' equals 'potential terrorist.'" Leti Volpp, "Citizen and Terrorist," UCLA *Law Review* 49 (2002): 1576.

61. Volpp, "Citizen and Terrorist," 1576; my emphasis.

62. See Evelyn Alsultany, *Arabs and Muslims in the Media: Race and Representation after 9/11* (New York: New York University Press, 2012); Gargi Bhattacharyya, *Dangerous Brown Men: Exploiting Sex, Violence, and Feminism in the War on Terror* (London: Zed Books, 2008); Reddy, *Freedom with Violence*.

63. See Talal Asad, *On Suicide Bombing* (New York: Columbia University Press, 2007); Mahmood and Hirschkind, "Feminism, the Taliban, and Politics of Counter-insurgency"; Mahmood Mamdani, *Good Muslim, Bad Muslim: America, the Cold War, and the Roots of Terror* (New York: Random House, 2005); McAlister, *Epic Encounters*; and Norton, *On the Muslim Question*.

64. McAlister, *Epic Encounters*, 302.

65. Melamed, "The Spirit of Neoliberalism," 14.

66. See Judith Butler, *Precarious Life: The Powers of Mourning and Violence* (London: Verso, 2004).

67. On the varied cultural effects of an abstract U.S. national identity, see Sarah Banet-Wiser, *The Most Beautiful Girl in the World: Beauty Pageants and National Identity* (Berkeley: University of California Press, 1999).

68. In this way, the very format of news media, and particularly of catastrophic events, allies with the work of melodramatic discourse, especially in the coverage of 9 / 11. Both name doers for the deeds of social problems, turn the complications of public life into tidy story lines, imply that visuality conveys truth, work to make events morally legible, and create that legibility through the medium of visual spectacle.

69. Marc Lynch, "Al-Qaeda's Media Strategies," *The National Interest*, Spring 2006, 83.

70. Derrida and many others note that the media coverage of the attacks was crucial to the transformation of "September 11" into "9 / 11," and I would add that that melodrama was a part of that process. See Borradori, Habermas, and Derrida, *Philosophy in a Time of Terror*, 108.

71. Schudson responded to an earlier article form of this chapter: "[Anker] treats Al Qaeda's attacks [as] an entirely neutral or ambiguous event that Fox News prematurely turned to melodrama. . . . [But] it was a human act . . . generated by a profoundly Manichean world-view. Osama bin Laden takes the gold medal as the contemporary world's most successful purveyor and performer of melodrama." Michael Schudson, "The Anarchy of Events and the Anxiety of Story Telling," *Political Communication* 24 (2007): 255. See also Anker, "Villains, Victims and Heroes."

72. A second problem with the claim that the events were melodramatic because bin Laden is a melodramatist is that the events were not uniformly depicted through melodramatic genre conventions. As I argue in the introduction, other genres, including the jeremiad, narrated the attacks as a prophetic unraveling of U.S. society and an indicator of the evil lurking within American life.

## 2. THE MELODRAMATIC STYLE OF AMERICAN POLITICS

1. Bush quoted in Bob Woodward, *Plan of Attack: The Definitive Account of the Decision to Invade Iraq* (New York: Simon and Schuster, 2004), 24.

2. Peter Brooks, Linda Williams, and Christine Gledhill note melodrama's ability to perpetually modernize in relation to social, political, and technological change. As Williams states, melodrama "renew[s] itself with new objects of sympathy embedded within new social problems, new contexts for pathos and action, and new

media." Linda Williams, *Playing the Race Card: Melodramas of Black and White from Uncle Tom to O. J. Simpson* (Princeton, NJ: Princeton University Press, 2001), 16.

3. This chapter thus implicitly challenges the binary interpretation of the post-9/11 era either as a radical break from a pre-9/11 history or as simply more of the same policies of U.S. global power. The genealogy of melodramatic political discourse shows that the post-9/11 era is both; it is a turning point that introduces a qualitative shift in understandings of U.S. power through the intensification of preexisting modes of depicting state action.

4. Matthew Buckley argues that revolutionary drama was "a powerful language of social and political expression within a radically theatrical context of public action." Revolutionary drama became "a lingua franca in which the complexities of political ideas and intent could be captured in a single gesture, an inflection, a word." Matthew Buckley, *Tragedy Walks the Streets: The French Revolution in the Making of Modern Drama* (Baltimore, MD: Johns Hopkins University Press, 2006), 4.

5. See Jacky Bratton, Jim Cook, and Christine Gledhill, eds., *Melodrama: Stage, Picture, Screen* (London: British Film Institute, 1994).

6. Jean-Jacques Rousseau, "Letter to M. Burney and Fragments of Observations on Gluck's 'Alceste,'" in *Essay on the Origin of Languages and Writings Related to Music*, trans. and ed. John T. Scott (Hanover, NH: Dartmouth College Press, 1998), 497.

7. Christine Gledhill, "The Melodramatic Field: An Investigation," in *Home Is Where the Heart Is: Studies in Melodrama and the Woman's Film* (London: British Film Institute, 1987), 14–17.

8. Charles Nodier, "Introduction to Pixerecourt's *Theatre Choisi*," in Guilbert de Pixérécourt, *Pixérécourt: Four Melodramas*, trans. and ed. Daniel Gerould and Marvin Carlson (New York: Martin Segal Center Publications, 2002), ix.

9. Hunt sees melodrama as part of what she calls "revolutionary family romances." Lynn Hunt, *The Family Romance of the French Revolution* (Berkeley: University of California Press, 1993), xiv.

10. Charles Nodier, "Introduction to Pixérécourt's *Theatre Choisi*," xi; and James Lenning, *The Melodramatic Thread: Spectacle and Political Culture in Modern France* (Bloomington: Indiana University Press, 2007), 12.

11. Guilbert de Pixérécourt, *Coelina; or, The Child of Mystery*, in *Guilbert de Pixérécourt: French Melodrama in the Early Nineteenth Century*, trans. J. Paul Marcoux (New York: Pater Lang, 1992).

12. Hunt, *The Family Romance of the French Revolution*, 181–82.

13. Pixérécourt, *Coelina; or, The Child of Mystery*, 80.

14. Pixérécourt, *Coelina; or, The Child of Mystery*, 96.

15. David Grimsted, "Melodrama as Echo of the Historically Voiceless," in *Anonymous Americans*, ed. Tamara Harevan (Upper Saddle River, NJ: Prentice-Hall, 1971).

16. Guilbert de Pixérécourt, "Melodrama," in *Guilbert Pixérécourt: Four Melodramas*, trans. and ed. Marvin Carlson and Daniel Gerould (New York: Martin E. Segal Theater Center, 2002), 314; my emphasis.

17. Peter Brooks, *The Melodramatic Imagination: Balzac, Henry James, Melodrama, and the Mode of Excess* (New Haven, CT: Yale University Press, 1995), 15–16.

18. This dual function is what incites and revokes melodrama's critical potential.

19. Matthew Scherer, *Beyond Church and State: Democracy, Secularism, and Conversion* (Cambridge, UK: Cambridge University Press, 2013).

20. Hunt, *The Family Romance of the French Revolution*, 190.

21. John Cawelti, "The Evolution of Social Melodrama," in *Imitations of Life: A Reader of Film and Melodrama*, ed. Marcia Landy (Detroit, MI: Wayne State University Press, 1991), 34.

22. Guilbert de Pixérécourt, *Adeline, the Victim of Seduction: A Melo-dramatic Serious Drama in Three Acts*, trans. John Howard Payne (London: Theater Royal, Drury Lane, 1822), 7. The play's translator, Payne, was a successful melodramatist in his own right, and much of his work was in translating or adapting French melodramas for English-speaking audiences.

23. Pixérécourt, *Adeline, the Victim of Seduction*, 36.

24. Pixérécourt, *Adeline, the Victim of Seduction*, 37.

25. Pixérécourt, *Adeline, the Victim of Seduction*, 36.

26. Pixérécourt, *Adeline, the Victim of Seduction*, 38.

27. Pixérécourt, *Adeline, the Victim of Seduction*, 35.

28. Thomas Elsaesser, "Tales of Sound and Fury: Observations of the Family Melodrama," in *Home Is Where the Heart Is: Melodrama and the Woman's Film*, ed. Christine Gledhill (London: British Film Institute, 1987), 46.

29. For instance, Chuck Kleinans focuses on capitalism, Ben Singer examines melodrama's origins in urban modernity, and John Cawelti emphasizes the rise of bourgeois family structure. While each of these scholars, like Brooks, mentions changes in state formation and political ideas concurrent during melodrama's inception, none has adequately addressed melodrama's imbrications with the rise of liberalism and liberal theory's institutionalization in legal structures. See Cawelti, "The Evolution of Social Melodrama"; Chuck Kleinans, "Melodrama and the Family under Capitalism," in *Imitations of Life: A Reader on Film and Television Melodrama*, ed. Marcia Landy (Detroit, MI: Wayne State University Press, 1991); and Ben Singer, *Melodrama and Modernity: Early Cinema and Its Contexts* (New York: Columbia University Press, 2002).

30. Elaine Hadley's *Melodramatic Tactics: Theatricalized Dissent in the English Marketplace, 1800–1885* (Stanford, CA: Stanford University Press, 1995) on nineteenth-century Britain is an exception: it examines the way that melodramatic stage tactics shaped nineteenth-century British public discourses against England's New Poor Laws and other political issues. James Lehning's *The Melodramatic Thread: Spectacle and Political Culture in Modern France* (Bloomington: Indiana University Press, 2007) examines how melodrama was a partner in democratizing postrevolutionary French political culture that simplified national understandings of politics and citizenship.

31. John Locke, *The Second Treatise of Government* (New York: Macmillan, 1952), 12.

32. Herbert Marcuse serves as a reminder that at its outset, liberalism in political theory was intended as a radical critique against the specific conditions of monarchy and mercantilism, though as its tenets became institutionalized they developed into new forms of domination. Herbert Marcuse, *One-Dimensional Man: Studies in the Ideology of Advanced Industrial Society* (Boston: Beacon Press, 1991), 1–6.

33. Étienne Balibar, "Subjectivity and Subjectivation," in *Supposing the Subject*, ed. Joan Copjec (New York: Verso, 1994), 12.

34. Brooks, *The Melodramatic Imagination*, 67.

35. Jean-Jacques Rousseau, *The Social Contract*, trans. G. D. H. Cole (New York: Penguin Classics, 1968), 53.

36. Rousseau, *The Social Contract*, 50.

37. See Brooks, *The Melodramatic Imagination*; Daniel Gerould, "The Americanization of Melodrama," in *American Melodrama*, ed. Daniel Gerould (New York: Performing Arts Journal Publication, 2001); David Grimsted, *Melodrama Unveiled: American Theater and Culture, 1800–1850* (Berkeley: University of California Press, 1988); Singer, *Melodrama and Modernity*; Martha Vicinus, "Helpless and Unfriended: Nineteenth-Century Domestic Melodrama," *New Literary History* 13, no. 1 (Autumn 1991); and Linda Williams, "Melodrama Revised," in *Refiguring Film Genres*, ed. Nick Browne (Berkeley: University of California Press, 1998).

38. Gerould, "The Americanization of Melodrama," 7.

39. Grimsted, *Melodrama Unveiled*, xvii.

40. Grimsted, *Melodrama Unveiled*, xiii.

41. Gerould, "The Americanization of Melodrama," 7.

42. Lawrence Levine, "Foreword," in David Grimsted, *Melodrama Unveiled: American Theater and Culture, 1800–1850* (Berkeley: University of California Press, 1988), xiii.

43. Cited in Grimsted, *Melodrama Unveiled*, 67–68.

44. Grimsted, *Melodrama Unveiled*, 67–68.

45. Bruce McConachie, *Melodramatic Formations: American Theater and Society, 1820–1870* (Iowa City: University of Iowa Press, 1992), 68.

46. Dion Boucicoult, *The Poor of New York*, in *American Melodrama*, ed. Daniel Gerould (New York: Performing Arts Journal Publications, 2001).

47. Boucicoult, *The Poor of New York*, 48.

48. Boucicoult, *The Poor of New York*, 74.

49. On this shift of emphasis see Gerould, "The Americanization of Melodrama," 11.

50. Gerould, "The Americanization of Melodrama," 11.

51. For more analysis of the role of individualism in melodrama, see chapters 4 and 5.

52. McConachie calls melodramatic heroism the ideology of manly honor, republican independence, and hero worship. McConachie, *Melodramatic Formations*, 68.

53. Jeffrey Mason, *Melodrama and the Myth of America* (Bloomington: Indiana University Press, 1993).

54. Locke, *The Second Treatise of Government*, 15.

55. Grimsted, *Melodrama Unveiled*, 11.

56. One nineteenth-century American theater reviewer described melodramas as "such as they may everyday [*sic*] see in the families of others, and tremble for in their own." Quoted in Grimsted, *Melodrama Unveiled*, 10.

57. Augustin Daly, "Flash of Lightning," in *Plays by Augustin Daly*, ed. Don B. Wilmeth and Rosemary Cullen (Cambridge, UK: Cambridge University Press, 1984).

58. Augustin Daly, "Under the Gaslight," in *American Melodrama*, ed. Daniel Gerould (New York: PAJ Publications, 2001). More commonly, as in Daly's *Flash of Lightning*, victimization remains feminized and heroism is reserved for men.

59. John Stuart Mill, of course, is an exception to this. See John Stuart Mill, *On Liberty and the Subjection of Women* (New York: Penguin, 2006).

60. Feminist political theorists have long critiqued liberalism for its masculinity and paternalistic grounding. See Wendy Brown, *States of Injury: Power and Freedom in Late Modernity* (Princeton, NJ: Princeton University Press, 1995); Zillah Eisenstein, *Feminism and Sexual Equality: Crisis in Liberal America* (New York: Monthly Review Press, 1984); Catherine MacKinnon, *Toward a Feminist Theory of the State* (Cambridge, MA: Harvard University Press, 1991); Susan Okin, *Justice, Gender and Equality* (Boston: Basic Books, 1991); and Carole Pateman, *The Sexual Contract* (Stanford, CA: Stanford University Press, 1988).

61. Daly, "Under the Gaslight," 174–77.

62. Singer, *Melodrama and Modernity*, 221–62.

63. Sacvan Bercovitch, *The American Jeremiad* (Madison: University of Wisconsin Press, 1978). See also George Shulman, "American Political Culture, Prophetic Narration, and Toni Morrison's *Beloved*," *Political Theory* 24, no. 2 (May 1996).

64. Henry David Thoreau, *Civil Disobedience and Other Essays* (New York: Dover, 1993).

65. Harriet Beecher Stowe, *Uncle Tom's Cabin*, annotated ed., ed. Henry Louis Gates Jr. (New York: W. W. Norton, 2006).

66. Cawelti, "The Evolution of Social Melodrama," 31.

67. L. Williams, *Playing the Race Card*, 57.

68. James Baldwin, "Everybody's Protest Novel," in *Notes of a Native Son* (Boston: Beacon Press, 1984), 15.

69. As Lauren Berlant writes in her reading of *Uncle Tom's Cabin*, readers who empathize with the purity of Uncle Tom can also, through empathic identification, let his purity mark their own virtue. Lauren Berlant, "Poor Eliza," in *The Female Complaint: The Unfinished Business of Sentimentality in American Culture* (Durham, NC: Duke University Press, 2008).

70. Scott Loren and Jörg Metelmann, *Irritation of Life: The Subversive Melodrama of Michael Haneke, David Lynch and Lars Von Trier* (Marburg, Germany: Shüren, 2013), 32.

71. On racial melodrama, see Jane M. Gaines, *Fire and Desire: Mixed-Race Movies in the Silent Era* (Chicago: University of Chicago Press, 2001); and L. Williams, *Playing the Race Card*. On melodrama's travel from stage to screen, see Nicholas Vardac,

*From Stage to Screen: Theatrical Method from Garrick to Griffith* (Cambridge, MA: Harvard University Press, 1949).

72. Michael Rogin, *Ronald Reagan the Movie: And Other Episodes in Political Demonology* (Berkeley: University of California Press, 1988), 208.

73. L. Williams, *Playing the Race Card*, 113.

74. Karl Marx, "On the Jewish Question," in *The Marx-Engels Reader*, ed. Robert Tucker (New York: W. W. Norton, 1978).

75. In "The Little American," in *America First: Naming the Nation in US Film*, ed. Mandy Merck (London: Routledge, 2007), Kristen Whissel suggests that melodrama helped to generate new forms of political engagement during World War I. With the rise of melodramatic films about World War I, citizenship began to adapt to spectatorship: citizenship became a form of spectatorship, because political subjects are those who watch from a distance. The citizen became an astonished spectator converted to support America entering the war by films' scenes of its atrocities. See also the different mobilizations of good and evil to map out national morality (which often look a lot like melodramatic tactics) in James A. Morone, *Hellfire Nation: The Politics of Sin in American History* (New Haven, CT: Yale University Press, 2003).

76. John Baughman, *Republic of Mass Culture: Journalism, Filmmaking, and Broadcasting in America since 1945* (Baltimore, MD: Johns Hopkins University Press, 2005), 30–31.

77. Lynn Spigel, *Welcome to the Dreamhouse: Popular Media and Postwar Suburbs* (Durham, NC: Duke University Press, 2001), 2.

78. Michael Schudson, *The Power of News* (Cambridge, MA: Harvard University Press, 1996), 172.

79. Stephen Ambrose writes about the postwar moment: "Politicians looked for areas in which American influence could dominate, businessmen looked for profitable markets and new sources of cheap raw materials, and the military looked for overseas bases. All found what they wanted as America inaugurated a program of expansion that had no inherent limits." Stephen Ambrose, *Rise to Globalism: American Foreign Policy since 1938* (New York: Longman, 1998), xi.

80. Sheldon Wolin, "Democracy without the Citizen," in *The Presence of the Past: Essays on the State and the Constitution* (Baltimore, MD: Johns Hopkins University Press, 1989), 183. The immense national mobilization of industry during World War II perpetuated postwar expansion. Wolin explores how the momentum of wartime continued by systematic policies dramatically expanded the scope and penetration of state power, and Michael Rogin examines how a cold-war demonology of invisible communist agents spawned an enormous government bureaucracy engaged in surveillance and countersubversion. See Rogin, *Ronald Reagan the Movie*.

81. Douglas Stuart, *Creating the National Security State: A History of the Law That Changed America* (Princeton, NJ: Princeton University Press, 2008).

82. "Speech Broadcast throughout World," *New York Times*, March 13, 1947, 10.

83. Truman quoted in Ambrose, *Rise to Globalism*, 80–81.

84. Harry S. Truman, "President Harry S. Truman's Address before a Joint Session of Congress, March 12, 1947," March 12, 1947, accessed February 9, 2009, http://avalon.law.yale.edu/20th_century/trudoc.asp.

85. C. P. Trussel, "Congress Is Solemn: Prepares to Consider Bills after Hearing the President Gravely," *New York Times*, March 13, 1947, 1.

86. On post–World War II humanitarian discourse, see Robert Meister, *After Evil: A Politics of Human Rights* (New York: Columbia University Press, 2010); and Wendy Hesford, *Spectacular Rhetorics: Human Rights Visions, Recognitions, Feminisms* (Durham, NC: Duke University Press, 2011).

87. NSC-68 quoted in Ambrose, *Rise to Globalism*, 111.

88. Harry S. Truman, "Inaugural Address," January 20, 1949, accessed February 9, 2009, www.bartleby.com/124/pres53.html.

89. Gary Wills, *Bomb Power: The Modern Presidency and the National Security State* (New York: Penguin, 2010).

90. Singer argues that melodramatic spectacle is experienced viscerally as well as visually, generating agitation caused by seeing "vicious power victimizing the weak." Exotic locations, festivities, natural catastrophes, extreme violence, use of animals ("horstrionic dramas"), crowd and battle scenes, mobile ships on stage, optical illusions, and elaborate machinery all became central parts of the attraction and entrenched melodrama's moral lessons. Singer, *Melodrama and Modernity*, 40, 149–50.

91. Samuel Kernell, *Going Public* (Washington, DC: CQ Press, 2006).

92. Dwight Eisenhower "First Inaugural Address," January 20, 1953, accessed May 28, 2012, www.americanrhetoric.com/speeches/dwighteisenhowerfirstinaugural.htm.

93. Jodi Dean, "Evil's Political Habitats," *Theory and Event* 8, no. 2 (2005). Examining the use of the term *evil* in postwar American political discourse, Dean argues that evil has functioned as a foundational premise for the organization of American politics. Evil becomes an intransigent national problem, and each American president's ability to name and diagnose evil becomes symbolic of his moral goodness: "Under conditions of ontological evil, failing to recognize evil becomes moral weakness while naming it becomes a key signifier of moral strength, courage and will." For Dean, the deployment of evil primarily signifies the moral conviction of the speaker; in other words, the president who condemns a regime or leader as evil becomes a signifier of goodness. Dean's analysis points to the tight dialectic between naming evil and becoming good, yet her focus on the figure of the president diminishes the generative effect that *evil* has as it circulates. The power of evil rapidly exceeds the president who utters its name. Evil serves to mark not only the morality of the president but the morality of the entire nation.

94. In 1955 Eisenhower asked Congress for extraordinary measures to employ the armed forces in various places around the globe without asking Congress for authority; this is something that one of the drafters of the resolution remarked "never before in our history had anything been done like that." Only six members

of Congress voted against Eisenhower's blank check to expand military conflict and national-security measures without consulting Congress. Ambrose, *Rise to Globalism*, 142.

95. On this expansion, see Ira Katznelson, *Fear Itself: The New Deal and the Origins of Our Time* (New York: Liveright, 2013), 467–85.

96. Robert W. Johannsen et al., *Manifest Destiny and Empire: American Antebellum Expansionism*, ed. Sam W. Haynes and Christopher Morris (College Station: Texas A&M Univerity Press, 1997).

97. Rogin, *Ronald Reagan the Movie*.

98. Rogin, *Ronald Reagan the Movie*, 231.

99. Richard Nixon, "The Checkers Speech," in *Great Speeches*, vol. 2, The Great Speeches Video Series (Greenwood, IN: Educational Video Group Inc., 1988), VHS. For transcription see "American Rhetoric: Richard M. Nixon—'Checkers Speech,'" AmericanRhetoric.com, accessed January 18, 2011, http://www.americanrhetoric .com/speeches/richardnixoncheckers.html.

100. On the differences between melodrama and prophetic discourses in the jeremiad, see the introduction. On the use of the jeremiad in the latter part of the twentieth century, see Andrew Murphy, *Prodigal Nation: Moral Decline and Divine Punishment from New England to 9/11* (New York: Oxford University Press, 2009); and George Shulman, *American Prophecy: Race and Redemption in American Political Culture* (Minneapolis: University of Minnesota Press, 2008).

101. Ronald Reagan, "First Inaugural Address," *Great Speeches*, vol. 4, The Great Speeches Video Series (Greenwood, IN: Educational Video Group Inc., 1988), VHS. Quotes from this recording are my transcription.

102. Dean, "Evil's Political Habitats."

103. Francis Fukuyama, "The End of History," *The National Interest*, no. 16 (Summer 1989).

104. Francis Fukuyama, "The End of History," 18.

## 3. FELT LEGITIMACY

1. National polls reveal this support. Here is a small sample of polls in the weeks and months during and after these decisions. All polls cited in this note were last accessed November 1, 2013. On October 3, 2001, 90 percent of Americans supported military action as retaliation for 9/11: "Retaliation," Gallup, http://www.gallup .com/poll/4948/Retaliation.aspx. On October 7, 2001, 90 percent of Americans supported the war in Afghanistan and 92 percent of Americans approved of the way that President Bush was handling the war against terrorism: "Public Overwhelmingly Backs Bush in Attacks on Afghanistan," Gallup, http://www.gallup .com/poll/4966/Public-Overwhelmingly-Backs-Bush-Attacks-Afghanistan.aspx. On November 16, 2001, the poll described in "High Approval for Most People/Institutions Handling War on Terrorism" shows extraordinarily high approval ratings for most top governing officials, including President George W. Bush (89 percent), Congress (77 percent), Secretary of Defense Donald Rumsfeld (80 percent),

Attorney General John Ashcroft (77 percent), newly appointed Homeland Security Secretary Tom Ridge (60 percent, which would have been higher but was lowered because many people had not heard of him), and many others: Gallup, http://www .gallup.com/poll/5062/High-Approval-Most-PeopleInstitutions-Handling-War -Terrorism.aspx. In addition, on June 10, 2002, 72 percent supported the establishment of the Department of Homeland Security, which Bush called "the most sweeping proposal for the reorganization of government since Harry Truman proposed a new Department of Defense after World War II": "Americans Approve of Proposed Department of Homeland Security," Gallup, http://www.gallup.com/poll /6163/Americans-Approve-Proposed-Department-Homeland-Security.aspx. On December 18, 2001, 67 percent of American believed that the United States should actively use military force in other countries that harbor terrorists besides Afghanistan, even if Osama bin Laden is captured or killed: "Attack on America: Key Trends and Indicators," Gallup, http://www.gallup.com/poll/5011/Attack-America -Key-Trends-Indicators.aspx. On December 13, 2001, 90 percent of American approved of the way that the "American people" were handling the war on terror: "Government Leaders Still Get High Marks for Handling War," Gallup, http://www .gallup.com/poll/5116/Government-Leaders-Still-Get-High-Marks-Handling-War .aspx. On December 18, 2001, 69 percent of people were "very satisfied" with the war on Afghanistan: "Attack on America: Key Trends and Indicators," Gallup, http://www.gallup.com/poll/5011/Attack-America-Key-Trends-Indicators.aspx. See also "Bush Soars into State of the Union with Exceptional Public Backing," Gallup, January 29, 2002, http://www.gallup.com/poll/5251/Bush-Soars-into-State -Union-Exceptional-Public-Backing.aspx; "Public Little Concerned about Patriot Act," Gallup, September 9, 2003, http://www.gallup.com/poll/9205/public-little -concerned-about-patriot-act.aspx; and "Bush Job Approval Based on General Feelings, Not Specific Achievements," Gallup, May 30, 2002, http://www.gallup .com/poll/6109/Bush-Job-Approval-Based-General-Feelings-Specific-Achievements .aspx.

2. Hannah Arendt, *On Revolution* (New York: Penguin Press, 1990).

3. Bernard Manin, "On Legitimacy and Deliberation," trans. Elly Stein and Jane Mansbridge, *Political Theory* 15, no. 3 (August 1987): 352.

4. The categories of procedural and deliberative legitimacy frequently overlap, though I am separating them here for the purpose of pulling out their different emphases. For central work on procedural forms of legitimacy, see John Rawls, *The Law of Peoples* (Cambridge, MA: Harvard University Press, 1999); and John Rawls, *Political Liberalism* (New York: Columbia University Press, 1993). On deliberative legitimacy, see Seyla Benhabib, "Toward a Deliberative Model of Democratic Legitimacy," in *Democracy and Difference: Contesting the Boundaries of the Political* (Princeton, NJ: Princeton University Press, 1996); Joshua Cohen, "Deliberation and Democratic Legitimacy," in *The Good Polity*, ed. Alan Hamlin and Phillip Pettit (Oxford: Basil Blackwell, 1989); Pierre Rosanvallon, *Democratic Legitimacy: Impartiality, Reflexivity, Proximity* (Princeton, NJ: Princeton University Press, 2011); and John

Dryzek, "Legitimacy and Economy in Deliberative Democracy," *Political Theory* 29, no. 5 (October 2001). For work that brings both deliberative and procedural models together, see David Estlund, *Democratic Authority: A Philosophical Framework* (Princeton, NJ: Princeton University Press, 2008); and Jürgen Habermas, *Between Facts and Norms* (Cambridge, MA: MIT Press, 1998).

5. Max Weber, *Economy and Society: An Outline of Interpretive Sociology*, ed. Guenther Roth and Claus Wittich (Berkeley: University of California Press, 1978); Michel Foucault, *"Society Must Be Defended": Lectures at the Collège de France, 1975–1976*, trans. David Macey (New York: Picador, 2003).

6. Sharon Krause, *Civil Passions: Moral Sentiment and Democratic Deliberation* (Princeton, NJ: Princeton University Press, 2008).

7. Karl Marx, "On the Jewish Question," in *The Marx-Engels Reader*, ed. Robert Tucker (New York: W. W. Norton, 1978); and Foucault, *"Society Must Be Defended."*

8. Sheldon Wolin writes that democracy means participation, but it is not about voting or holding office; it is "originating or initiating cooperative action with others. . . . Democracy [is] political action in the most fundamental sense of using power to constitute a collaborative world." Sheldon Wolin, *The Presence of the Past: Essays on the State and the Constitution* (Baltimore, MD: Johns Hopkins University Press, 1989), 150, 154.

9. Deborah Gould, *Moving Politics: Emotion and ACT UP's Fight against AIDS* (Chicago: University of Chicago Press, 2009), 30.

10. Jürgen Habermas and William Rehg, "Constitutional Democracy: A Paradoxical Union of Contradictory Principles," *Political Theory* 29, no. 6 (Fall 2001): 779.

11. Examples include David L. Deephouse and Mark C. Suchman, "Legitimacy in Organizational Institutionalism," in *The SAGE Handbook of Organizational Institutionalism*, ed. Royston Greenwood, Christine Oliver, Roy Suddaby, and Kerstin Sahlin-Andersson (Thousand Oaks, CA: Sage, 2008); Cathryn Johnson, ed., *Legitimation Processes in Organizations* (Boston: Elsevier, 2004); and John Jost and Brenda Major, eds., *The Psychology of Legitimacy: Emerging Perspectives on Ideology, Justice, and Intergroup Relations* (Cambridge, UK: Cambridge University Press, 2001).

12. Weber, *Economy and Society*, 33.

13. Max Weber, "Politics as a Vocation," in *On Max Weber: Essays in Sociology*, trans. and ed. H. H. Gerth and C. Wright Mills (Oxford: Oxford University Press, 1958), 78; my emphasis.

14. Weber, *Economy and Society*, 35.

15. Weber, *Economy and Society*, 213.

16. Seymour Martin Lipset, *Political Man: The Social Basis of Politics* (Baltimore, MD: Johns Hopkins University Press, 1981). Lisa Wedeen aptly captures this aspect of Lipset's account, in which widespread belief in legitimacy is thus a sign of liberal pluralism, by referring to it as the state's popularity contest. See Lisa Wedeen, *Ambiguities of Domination: Politics, Rhetoric, and Symbols in Contemporary Syria* (Chicago: University of Chicago Press, 1999), 9. For a collection of essays on this

dynamic, see William E. Connolly, ed., *Legitimacy and the State* (New York: New York University Press, 1984).

17. Foucault, *"Society Must Be Defended"*, 26–27.

18. Wendy Brown argues that Foucault's refusal to conceptualize the state outside models of right ignores the ways that the state is a visible referent for power that relies on a discursive production of legitimacy to authorize its actions. For Brown, state power is not superseded by governmentality but extends its reach through governmentalizing functions. She offers her account as a Foucauldian corrective to Foucault's eschewal of studying the state, writing: "A full account of governmentality, then, would attend not only to the production, organization, and mobilization of subjects by a variety of powers but also to the problem of legitimizing these operations by the singularly accountable object in the field of political power: the state." Wendy Brown, *Regulating Aversion: Tolerance in the Age of Identity and Empire* (Princeton, NJ: Princeton University Press, 2006), 83.

19. Weber, *Economy and Society*, 25.

20. Deborah Gould writes, "Affect is a body's processing of social conditions, of its context." Affect is conditioned but not determined by social conventions and practices. Gould, *Moving Politics*, 31. See also Sara Ahmed, *The Cultural Politics of Emotion* (London: Routledge, 2004); and Patricia Clough, ed., *The Affective Turn: Theorizing the Social* (Durham, NC: Duke University Press, 2007).

21. Sianne Ngai, *Ugly Feelings* (Cambridge, MA: Harvard University Press, 2008), 25, 5.

22. Scholars of affect theory often piece apart affect from emotion and use the term *affect* to denote preconscious or what Brian Massumi calls the "prepersonal intensity" of feelings—and *emotion* to denote the conscious display of those feelings; *feeling* flows between them. In this project I use the terms *affect* and *feeling* interchangeably because I am less interested in piecing apart the conscious or preconscious origin of feelings than in drawing from affect's acknowledgment that feelings are public, resonant, and often originate in the environment and thus outside the body that feels them as its own. Brian Massumi, *Parables of the Virtual: Movement, Affect, Sensation* (Durham, NC: Duke University Press, 2002).

23. See Robert Ivie, "The Rhetoric of Bush's War on Evil," KB *Journal* 1, no. 1 (Fall 2004).

24. See chapter 1 for this argument.

25. George W. Bush, "Freedom at War with Fear," September 20, 2001, accessed June 1, 2011, http://georgewbush-whitehouse.archives.gov/news/releases/2001/09/20010920-8.html.

26. Christine Gledhill, "The Melodramatic Field: An Investigation," in *Home Is Where the Heart Is: Studies in Melodrama and the Woman's Film* (London: British Film Institute, 1987), 30.

27. George W. Bush, "Transcript of President Bush's Prayer Service Remarks," Washington National Cathedral, September 14, 2001, accessed September 11, 2011, http://www.opm.gov/guidance/09-14-01gwb.htm.

28. Judith Butler, *Precarious Life: The Powers of Mourning and Violence* (London: Verso, 2004), 4.

29. George W. Bush, "President Pays Tribute at Pentagon Memorial," October 11, 2001, accessed September 11, 2011, http://georgewbush-whitehouse.archives.gov/news /releases/2001/10/20011011–1.html.

30. Lauren Berlant, "The Epistemology of State Emotion," in *Dissent in Dangerous Times*, ed. Austin Sarat (Ann Arbor: University of Michigan Press, 2005), 54.

31. Gledhill, "The Melodramatic Field," 24.

32. On the liberal narrative of progress, see Wendy Brown, *Politics out of History* (Princeton, NJ: Princeton University Press, 2001); on melodrama's theological inheritance, see Peter Brooks, *The Melodramatic Imagination: Balzac, Henry James, Melodrama, and the Mode of Excess* (New Haven, CT: Yale University Press, 1995).

33. Bush, "Freedom at War with Fear."

34. Wendy Brown writes, "[Civilizational discourses] sanction illiberal aggression toward that which is marked as intolerable without tarring the 'civilized' status of the aggressor. . . . An opposition of civilization and barbarism . . . provides the mantle of civilization, progress, and peace as cover for imperialistic military adventures." Brown argues that the claim of tolerance implies that what is to be "tolerated" is inferior, and that the goal to extend tolerance to those who don't yet share its values is often an imperialistic one. W. Brown, *Regulating Aversion*, 179.

35. On this point see Uday Mehta, *Liberalism and Empire: A Study in Nineteenth-Century British Liberal Thought* (Chicago: University of Chicago Press, 1999).

36. To name a few: Brooks, *The Melodramatic Imagination*; Daniel Gerould, "The Americanization of Melodrama," in *American Melodrama*, ed. Daniel Gerould (New York: Performing Arts Journal Publication, 1983); and Robert Heilman, *Tragedy and Melodrama: Versions of Experience* (Seattle: University of Washington Press, 1968).

37. Peter Brown, *Augustine of Hippo* (Berkeley: University of California Press, 2000), 35–49.

38. Perhaps evil operates here like the king's two bodies, in which the office persists beyond the body of the individual office keeper; a mortal evil can be destroyed, but the larger category of evil is always populated by invasive and irrational power. See Ernst Kantorowitz, *The King's Two Bodies: A Study in Medieval Political Theology* (Princeton, NJ: Princeton University Press, 1997).

39. Martin J. Alperen, *Foundations of Homeland Security: Law and Policy* (Hoboken, NJ: Wiley, 2011), 4.

40. Melodramatic uses of *god*, *good*, and *evil* draw partly from Christian religious traditions but are not only religious phenomena. Brooks notes the origin of melodrama in the downfall of the French church as it became a new form of moral order, or what he calls the "moral occult." See chapter 2 for a discussion of Brooks's argument, as well as Brooks, *The Melodramatic Imagination*. Yet while it is commonplace to ascribe a theological frame to Bush's rhetoric, a focus only on its religious significance can diminish analysis of its concurrent melodramatic shapings

and political work. Indeed, most evangelical Christian responses to 9/11 that entered public discourse aligned more with prophetic or jeremiadic genre forms, rather than melodramatic ones. See William E. Connolly, *Capitalism and Christianity, American Style* (Durham, NC: Duke University Press, 2008); Melani McAlister, "Prophecy, Politics, and the Popular: The Left Behind Series and Christian Fundamentalism's New World Order," *The South Atlantic Quarterly* 102, no. 4 (Fall 2003); and George Shulman, *American Prophecy: Race and Redemption in American Political Culture* (Minneapolis: University of Minnesota Press, 2008).

41. See note 1 for these statistics, especially "High Approval for Most People/Institutions Handling War on Terrorism" from November 16, 2001, which shows extraordinarily high approval ratings for most of the top governing officials.

42. Michael Ignatieff, "The Year of Living Dangerously: A Liberal Supporter of the War Looks Back," *New York Times Magazine*, March 14, 2004, 13–14.

43. Foucault, *"Society Must Be Defended,"* 26–27.

44. Habermas explains, "Administrative planning has unintentional effects of disquieting and publicizing. These effects weaken the justification potential of traditions that have been forced out of their natural condition. Once they are no longer indisputable, their demands for validity can be stabilized only by way of discourse. Thus, the forcible shift of things that have been culturally taken for granted further politicizes areas of life that previously could be assigned to the private domain." Jürgen Habermas, *Legitimation Crisis*, trans. Thomas McCarthy (Boston: Beacon Press, 1973), 147.

45. In addition to Habermas's claims about capitalism, I would argue that this process also troubles political discourses that cultivate belief in state legitimacy by proclaiming its formally limited and neutral scope.

46. "Text: President Bush's Acceptance Speech to the Republican National Convention," September 2, 2004, accessed October 24, 2013, http://www.washingtonpost.com/wp-dyn/articles/A57466-2004Sep2.html; my emphasis.

47. These words were used repeatedly in Bush's speeches throughout October 2004 as well as in his nationally televised Republican National Convention speech in September of the same year. George W. Bush, "Remarks in Gainesville, Florida, October 31, 2004," accessed October 24, 2013, http://www.gpo.gov/fdsys/pkg/PPP-2004-book3/pdf/PPP-2004-book3-doc-pg2883.pdf.

48. See Ivo Daalder's *America Unbound: The Bush Revolution in Foreign Policy* (Washington, DC: Brookings Institution Press, 2004) for a detailed analysis of post-9/11 foreign policy that operates under the assumption that America performs God's work.

49. See M. H. Pham, "The Right to Fashion in an Age of Terrorism," *Signs* 36, no. 2 (Winter 2011).

50. Melodrama's moral economy overlaps with and cultivates what Sara Ahmed calls an "affective economy." Ahmed writes, "In such affective economies, emotions *do things*, and they align individuals with communities—or bodily space with social space—through the very intensity of their attachments . . . between the individual

and the collective." Sara Ahmed, "Affective Economies," *Social Text* 22, no. 22 (Summer 2004): 119.

51. Berlant, "The Epistemology of State Emotion," 48. For Berlant, "state emotion" is a public feeling that works as a strategy of social binding to set the terms for inclusion into nationhood: social belonging in U.S. citizenship is predicated on one's capacity to feel the pain caused by other Americans' subordination to power as well as the "visceral performance of moral clarity, which then may be supported by argument, but not of the sort traditionally taught involving hypothesis and ordered proof."

52. Berlant, "The Epistemology of State Emotion," 48.

53. Mary Anne Doane, "The Moving Image: Pathos and the Maternal," in *Imitations of Life: A Reader on Film and Television Melodrama*, ed. Marcia Landy (Detroit, MI: Wayne State University Press, 1991); and Linda Williams, "Film Bodies: Gender, Genre and Excess," *Film Quarterly* 44, no. 4 (1991).

54. Linda Williams, "Melodrama Revised," in *Refiguring Film Genres*, ed. Nick Browne (Berkeley: University of California Press, 1998), 62.

55. Berlant writes, "Not only is the political spectator deemed already to have consented to the priorities of the now hegemonic event, but she is also solicited to feel the impact that provides evidence that she belongs to a public constituted as a mass of spectators who see what she sees and feels what she feels. . . . The collective experience of social belonging privatizes her at the same time as it produces a subjective experience of participation in publicness." Berlant, "The Epistemology of State Emotion," 49.

56. Raymond Williams, "Structures of Feeling," in *Marxism and Literature* (Oxford: Oxford University Press, 1978).

57. Krause, *Civil Passions*.

58. Brian Massumi, "Potential Politics and the Primacy of Pre-emption," *Theory and Event* 10, no. 2 (Spring 2007).

59. Wolin, *The Presence of the Past*, 11–12.

60. Michael Hardt, "What Affects Are Good For," in *The Affective Turn*, ed. Patricia Clough (Durham, NC: Duke University Press, 2007), ix; my emphasis.

61. One wartime advisor in the Department of State revealed that "the startling mismanagement of planning for the postwar did not result from a sudden emergency and a lack of time to plan"; instead, the administration's certitude about "the inevitability and speed of America's triumph" led to its dismissal of reports detailing the enormous management and challenge a postwar Iraq would require. Larry Diamond, *Squandered Victory* (New York: Times Books, 2005), 291.

62. David Western describes Obama's lack of melodrama: "When he wants to be, the president is a brilliant and moving speaker, but his stories virtually always lack one element: the villain who caused the problem, who is always left out, described in impersonal terms, or described in passive voice, as if the cause of others' misery has no agency and hence no culpability." David Western, "What Happened to Obama's Passion?," *New York Times*, August 6, 2011, SR1.

63. Perhaps this is partly an effect of the very language that inaugurates it: if its mission is both nebulous and world historic, as protecting against evil and safeguarding civilization, with a moral absolute as its goal, it is no wonder it extends so far into the smallest crannies of individual lives. Dana Priest and William Arkin, "Top Secret America: A Washington Post Investigation," *Washington Post*, July 19–21, 2010, and December 10, 2010, accessed December 10, 2010, http://projects.washingtonpost .com/top-secret-america/.

64. Priest and Arkin, "Top Secret America."

## 4. ORGIES OF FEELING

1. Janet Staiger, "Introduction: Political Emotions and Public Feelings," in *Political Emotions*, ed. Janet Staiger, Ann Cvetcovich, and Ann Reynolds (New York: Routledge, 2010), 3–4.

2. Friedrich Nietzsche, *On the Genealogy of Morals and Ecce Homo*, trans. Walter Kauffman (New York: Vintage 1989), 136.

3. Nietzsche, *On the Genealogy of Morals and Ecce Homo*, 139.

4. Nietzsche, *On the Genealogy of Morals and Ecce Homo*, 60.

5. The term *orgies of feeling* is the English translation of the German *Gefühls-Ausschweifung* in Walter Kaufmann's translation of Nietzsche's *On the Genealogy of Morals and Ecce Homo* (139). Keith Ansell Pearson's edition translates it as "excess of feeling" in his renamed *Genealogy of Morality*. *Excess*, I would argue, implies a boundary of appropriate feeling that one is crossing—and that, if these emotions were less "excessive," would make these feelings more fitting to describe the experiences they attach to. This sense of inappropriateness is not, in my reading, what Nietzsche aims to convey with the term. It thus makes *excess* a less accurate translation than *orgies*, which links more with the "overflowing life" Nietzsche uses *orgies* to describe in this and in other books. On "excess of feeling," see Friedrich Nietzsche, *On the Genealogy of Morality*, ed. Keith Ansell Pearson and trans. Carol Diethe (Cambridge, UK: Cambridge University Press, 1994), 101. I thank Jörg Mettelman and Stephen White for conversations on this point.

6. Nietzsche, *On the Genealogy of Morals and Ecce Homo*, 127.

7. On the critical power of victimhood, see Alyson Cole, *The Cult of True Victimhood: From the War on Welfare to the War on Terror* (Stanford, CA: Stanford University Press, 2007).

8. Nietzsche, *On the Genealogy of Morals and Ecce Homo*, 162.

9. Nietzsche, *On the Genealogy of Morals and Ecce Homo*, 127.

10. Nietzsche, *On the Genealogy of Morals and Ecce Homo*, 128.

11. Friedrich Nietzsche, *The Birth of Tragedy and the Case of Wagner*, trans. Walter Kauffman (New York: Vintage, 1967).

12. Friedrich Nietzsche, *Twilight of the Idols*, in *Nietzsche: The Antichrist, Ecce Homo, Twilight of the Idols; And Other Writings*, trans. Judith Norman (Cambridge, UK: Cambridge University Press, 2005), 228. Also see chapter 1, "The Venomous Eye."

13. Nietzsche, *On the Genealogy of Morals and Ecce Homo*, 140.

14. Nietzsche, *On the Genealogy of Morals and Ecce Homo*, 162.
15. Nietzsche writes, "Every animal . . . instinctively strives for an optimum of favorable conditions under which it can expend all its strength and achieve its maximal feeling of power. . . . I am not speaking of its path to happiness, but its path to power, to action." Nietzsche, *On the Genealogy of Morals and Ecce Homo*, 107.
16. Nietzsche, *On the Genealogy of Morals and Ecce Homo*, 140.
17. Friedrich Nietzsche, *The Will to Power*, trans. Walter Kaufmann and R. J. Hollingdale (New York: Vintage, 1968), section 643.
18. Nietzsche, *On the Genealogy of Morals and Ecce Homo*, 120–21.
19. Suzanne Evans, "Dispatches from a Day of Terror and Shock: Darkness at Noon," letter to the editor, *New York Times*, September 12, 2001, A26.
20. Melodrama contributed to the circulation of heightened affects in the news media and political discourse, as its conventions infused the words and interviews of public officials—from, as I discuss in earlier chapters, Charles Schumer's response of "we feel your pain" to George W. Bush's identification of victims as "moms and dads, friends and neighbors" to the speeches defining the post-9/11 moment through affective states such as "Freedom at War with Fear." Melodramatic political discourse further contributed to this intensity when the news media employed melodramatic conventions in its live coverage of the attacks, including close-up shots of individuals suffering as they are pulled out of the debris, extradiegetic music (*melos*) borrowed from Hollywood tropes usually associated with dramatic excitement and danger, and newscasters' constant descriptions in a melodramatic narrative of injury, pathos, and vengeful redemption of the nation's horrified response.
21. N. R. Kleinfeld, "Buildings Burn and Fall as Onlookers Search for Elusive Safety," *New York Times*, September 12, 2001, A1. Also consider the news anchor Katie Couric's very first words upon watching live on NBC's *The Today Show* as an airplane hit the second tower: "This is so shocking, of course, to everybody watching." Rather than describe what she is seeing or articulate her own experience watching the events, Couric informs her viewers what *they* are experiencing. Her words cultivate the very affective charge they ascribe to others; indeed these words already normalize (through the *of course*) what a proper response should entail at the moment it occurs. The pathos and suffering melodrama cultivates in its readers continues in the *New York Times*'s coverage of the terrorist attacks and their aftermath, culminating in the Portraits of Grief series, which catalogued in a personal paragraph and picture many of the individuals who had died in the terrorist attacks. As David Simpson argues, the standard narrative accorded to so many individuals in Portraits of Grief both cultivated and homogenized the horrible suffering involved in their deaths, making each person a tragic stand-in for a lost American dream. David Simpson, *9/11: Culture of Commemoration* (Chicago: University of Chicago Press, 2005).
22. This frenzy has been illustrated and complicated in Art Spiegelman's vivid images of the visceral post-9/11 experience, which elaborate how national subjects were

both shaped by and fearful of various forms of dominating powers, and at the same time felt powerless to resist both. Art Spiegelman, *In the Shadow of No Towers* (New York: Hill and Wang, 2005). See also Elisabeth Anker, "The Only Thing We Have to Fear . . . ," *Theory and Event* 8, no. 3 (2005).

23. See, among many others, Wendy Brown, "Rights and Losses," in *States of Injury: Power and Freedom in Late Modernity* (Princeton, NJ: Princeton University Press, 1995); Manuel Castells, "Materials for an Explanatory Theory of the Network Society," *British Journal of Sociology* 51, no. 1 (January–March 2000); Gilles Deleuze, "Postscript on the Societies of Control," *October* 59 (Winter 1992); Jürgen Habermas, *Legitimation Crisis*, trans. Thomas McCarthy (Boston: Beacon Press, 1973); and Neil Smith, "Contours of a Spatialized Politics," *Social Text*, no. 33 (1992).

24. Theresa Brennan, *Globalization and Its Terrors* (London: Routledge: 2003), 1.

25. Timothy Melley, *Empire of Conspiracy: The Culture of Paranoia in Postwar America* (Ithaca, NY: Cornell University Press, 2000), 9.

26. In one very early and particularly provocative example of this unarticulated awareness, the postwar psychoanalyst Edward Bibring found that rising rates of depression were linked to societal-wide feelings of powerlessness over the postwar conditions of public life and the dramatic increases of global power that attended to them. Edward Bibring, "The Mechanism of Depression," in *The Meaning of Despair*, ed. Willard Gaylin (New York: Science House, 1968).

27. Michel Foucault, "The Subject and Power," in Hubert Dreyfus and Paul Rabinow, *Michel Foucault: Beyond Structuralism and Hermeneutics* (Chicago: University of Chicago Press, 1982), 212.

28. Jeffrey Nealon, *Foucault beyond Foucault: Power and Its Intensifications since 1984* (Stanford, CA: Stanford University Press, 2008).

29. Christine Gledhill, "The Melodramatic Field: An Investigation," in *Home Is Where the Heart Is: Studies in Melodrama and the Woman's Film* (London: British Film Institute, 1987), 31.

30. Christine Gledhill, "Rethinking Genre," in *Reinventing Film Studies*, ed. Christine Gledhill and Linda Williams (London: Arnold, 2000), 228–29.

31. Gledhill, "The Melodramatic Field," 27.

32. Nietzsche, *On the Genealogy of Morals and Ecce Homo*, 127.

33. Nietzsche, *On the Genealogy of Morals and Ecce Homo*, 127.

34. George W. Bush, "Address to a Joint Session of Congress and the American People," September 20, 2001, accessed June 1, 2011, http://georgewbush-whitehouse.archives .gov/news/releases/2001/09/20010920-8.html.

35. Nietzsche, *On the Genealogy of Morals and Ecce Homo*, 139.

36. Nietzsche writes that in order to drive pain out of consciousness even for a moment, "one requires an affect, . . . and, in order to incite that, any pretext at all. . . . The suffering are one and all dreadfully eager and inventive in discovering occasions for painful affects." He also argues, "Thinking through this single question— 'how can one produce an orgy of feeling'—has been virtually inexhaustible." Nietzsche, *On the Genealogy of Morals and Ecce Homo*, 127, 136.

37. Marc Redfield, *The Rhetoric of Terror: Reflections on 9/11 and the War on Terror* (New York: Fordham University Press, 2009).

38. Nietzsche, *Twilight of the Idols*, 179.

39. Nietzsche, *On the Genealogy of Morals and Ecce Homo*, 129–30.

40. Nietzsche, *On the Genealogy of Morals and Ecce Homo*, 87.

41. Melley, *Empire of Conspiracy*, 9.

42. For a detailed categorization of the prominent forms of American individualism, see Robert Bellah et al., *Habits of the Heart: Individualism and Commitment in American Life* (Berkeley: University of California Press, 2007).

43. Ontological narcissism presumes that the individual is an unencumbered subject, able to make the law that he or she follows, to choose freely, to calculate wisely, to help steer the state, to participate in the free market. William E. Connolly, *Identity/Difference* (Ithaca, NY: Cornell University Press, 1991), 30.

44. Étienne Balibar, "Subject and Subjectivation," in *Supposing the Subject*, ed. Joan Copjec (New York: Verso, 1994), 11. See also Immanuel Kant, *Groundwork of the Metaphysics of Morals*, trans. H. J. Patton (New York: Harper Torchbooks, 1956).

45. The state has a somewhat contradictory function within this version of American liberal individualism: as something to distrust, yet also as something that, by the fact of making the law, one helps to organize and master. Generated out of laws formally made by all, the state is democratically accountable to the people, steered toward their vision of the good life, and is an expression of the national destiny.

46. While Emerson's original formulation of these terms leads less toward mastery and more toward self-cultivation, their popularization in American political life turned autonomous individual freedom from an ontology into a moral norm. Ralph Waldo Emerson, "Heroism" and "Self-Reliance," in *The Essential Writings of Ralph Waldo Emerson* (New York: Modern Library, 2000).

47. Dana Nelson, *National Manhood: Capitalist Citizenship and the Imagined Fraternity of White Men* (Durham, NC: Duke University Press, 1998), 28.

48. See Wendy Brown, "Neo-liberalism and the End of Liberal Democracy," *Theory and Event* 7, no. 1 (2003); Michel Feher, "Self-Appreciation; or, The Aspirations of Human Capital," *Public Culture* 21, no. 1 (2009); and Michel Foucault, *Birth of Biopolitics: Lectures at the Collège de France, 1978–1979*, trans. Graham Burchell (New York: Picador, 2008).

49. W. Brown, *States of Injury*, 66.

50. Neoliberal legitimations of certain forms of state power reveal how neoliberalism has never been about the uniform retrenchment of all state power; it is about the retrenchment of only certain state powers embodied in social services, and the defense of other forms, including the state subsidization of corporate power. As I argue in the introduction and chapter 5, neoliberal policies often mobilize individualism to promote corporate-state power through uneven claims of deregulation. Stuart Hall gives one example of the assertion that neoliberalism is only about the retreat of the state, rather than the retreat of the state in its capacity to be a support to the citizenry: "[Neoliberalism] sees the state as tyrannical and oppres-

sive. The state must never govern society, dictate to free individuals how to dispose of their property, regulate a free-market economy or interfere with the God-given right to make profits and amass personal wealth." Stuart Hall, "The Neoliberal Revolution," *Cultural Studies* 25, no. 6 (November 2011): 706.

51. Jean Laplanche, Judith Butler, Kaja Silverman, and others working in the fields of feminist poststructuralism or relationality examine autonomy by highlighting the interdependence of humans with other humans, a condition that can neither be willed away nor mastered and overcome. Some theorists draw upon both Freudian psychoanalysis and Hegelian theory to suggest that humans are born into conditions of interdependence and are constituted by relations with others. For these thinkers, the individual is not merely socially mediated but socially constituted, what Butler calls "the constitutive sociality of the self." Judith Butler, *Undoing Gender* (New York: Routledge, 2004), 22. See also Jean Laplanche, *Life and Death in Psychoanalysis* (Baltimore, MD: Johns Hopkins University Press, 1985); and Kaja Silverman, *Flesh of My Flesh* (Stanford, CA: Stanford University Press, 2009).

52. Hannah Arendt, "What Is Freedom?," in *Between Past and Future: Eight Exercises in Political Thought* (New York: Penguin, 2006); Patchen Markell, *Bound by Recognition* (Princeton, NJ: Princeton University Press, 2003); and Linda Zerilli, *Feminism and the Abyss of Freedom* (Chicago: University of Chicago Press, 2005).

53. Zygmunt Bauman, *Liquid Modernity* (Cambridge, UK: Polity Press); Saskia Sassen, *Cities in World Economy* (Thousand Oaks, CA: Sage, 2011); and Saskia Sassen, *Sociology of Globalization* (New York: W. W. Norton, 2007).

54. The suffering produced by and alongside liberal individualism is thus threefold: the suffering of increasing impingements of power, the suffering generated out of the felt experience of failed sovereignty, and the suffering caused by the disavowal of these formations of suffering—a suffering that is experienced yet must be negated or displaced in order to continue one's identity as a sovereign subject.

55. As I argue in chapter 5, analogous with the individual, state agency is understood to be both sovereign and bound by its own laws.

56. This construction similarly operates in a broader context of subject production: see Judith Butler, *Bodies That Matter: On the Discursive Limits of "Sex"* (New York: Routledge, 1993), 3.

57. Nietzsche, *On the Genealogy of Morals*, 117–18.

58. Nietzsche explicitly states Emerson's influence on his thought in *Twilight of the Idols* (198–99) and "Schopenhauer as Educator," in *Untimely Meditations*, trans. R. J. Hollingdale (Cambridge, UK: Cambridge University Press, 1997), 193.

## 5. HEROIC IDENTIFICATIONS

1. This reading of widespread support for state power helps to explain the Gallup polls taken between 2001 and 2004 that show "an extraordinary increase in the faith and confidence that Americans have in their federal government," such that more than 68 percent had a "high" level of trust in government, levels not seen for forty years; 63–70 percent of Americans said that they were "*extremely* proud" to

be an American, a rise of 30 percentage points over the same polling question asked before the 9/11 attacks; support for the War in Afghanistan leveled at 80–92 percent of the U.S. population; 89–75 percent of the U.S. population had a "very favorable" view of the military throughout this time and more confidence in the military than in any other societal institution; between 53 and 64 percent of Americans favored military action in Iraq to remove Saddam Hussein from power. See Frank Newport, "Trust in Government Increases Sharply in Wake of Terrorist Attacks: Americans Also More Likely to Say That Government Should Do More to Help Solve the Nation's Problems," Gallup, October 12, 2001, accessed June 14, 2011, http://www.gallup.com/poll/4984/Trust-Government-Increases-Sharply-Wake -Terrorist-Attacks.aspx; Joseph Carroll, "Post-9/11 Patriotism Remains Steadfast: Nonwhites Least Likely to Feel Highly Patriotic," Gallup, July 19, 2005, accessed June 14, 2011, http://www.gallup.com/poll/17401/Post911-Patriotism-Remains -Steadfast.aspx; David W. Moore, "Public Overwhelmingly Backs Bush in Attacks on Afghanistan: Expects New Terrorist Attacks," Gallup, October 8, 2001, accessed June 14, 2011, http://www.gallup.com/poll/4966/Public-Overwhelmingly-Backs -Bush-Attacks-Afghanistan.aspx. See also David W. Moore, "Public Overwhelmingly Backs Bush in Attacks on Afghanistan: Expects New Terrorist Attacks," Gallup, October 8, 2001, accessed May 2, 2013, http://www.gallup.com/poll/4966 /Public-Overwhelmingly-Backs-Bush-Attacks-Afghanistan.aspx; Frank Newport, "Americans Approve of Proposed Department of Homeland Security: But Only One in Five Say It Will Be 'Very' Effective in Preventing Future Acts of Terrorism," Gallup, June 10, 2002, accessed May 2, 2013, http://www.gallup.com/poll /6163/Americans-Approve-Proposed-Department-Homeland-Security.aspx; and Lydia Saad, "Americans Generally Comfortable with Patriot Act: Few Believe It Goes Too Far in Restricting Civil Liberties," Gallup, March 2, 2004, accessed May 2, 2013, http://www.gallup.com/poll/10858/Americans-Generally-Comfortable -Patriot-Act.aspx.

2. The reading is commonplace. For a small sampling of political theorists who support it, see Raymond Guess, *Politics and the Imagination* (Princeton, NJ: Princeton University Press, 2010); Timothy Kaufman-Osborn, "We Are All Torturers Now: Accountability after Abu Ghraib," *Theory and Event* 11, no. 2 (2008); Sheldon Wolin, *Democracy Incorporated: Managed Democracy and the Specter of Inverted Totalitarianism* (Princeton, NJ: Princeton University Press, 2008); and Slavoj Žižek, *Iraq: The Borrowed Kettle* (New York: Verso, 2004). Also see popular magazine and newspaper articles by Thomas Friedman and George Packer, including Thomas Friedman, "Restoring Our Honor," *New York Times*, May 6, 2004; and George Packer, "The Political War," *New Yorker*, September 27, 2004.

3. There is another account of this support too: that the Bush administration deceived guileless Americans into supporting its programs, and it harbors sole responsibility for the violent and constricting effects of post-9/11 policy. This second answer interprets popular support for war and securitization as a product of only manipulation rather than informed consent, and thus erases the discomforting

implications of a citizenry that legitimates its own unfreedom. It reassures citizens that they bear no responsibility because they were deceived, while it furthers the pervasive distrust of the people as easy pawns of political leaders. For key texts on this topic, see Thomas Frank, *What's the Matter with Kansas* (New York: Metropolitan Books, 2004); Michael Ignatieff, "Getting Iraq Wrong," *New York Times Magazine*, August 5, 2007; and Thomas Ricks, *Fiasco: The American Military Adventure in Iraq* (New York: Penguin, 2006).

4. George W. Bush, "Securing Freedom's Triumph," editorial, *New York Times*, September 11, 2002.

5. The erosion of economic security and access to political power over the last few decades, while the state remains the primary site of accountability for power, creates conditions whereby people reinvest in state power perhaps because they feel they have no where else to turn. Melodrama helps to reinvest the capacity for protection and strength back into state power, perhaps because otherwise people would feel unbearably unprotected, exposed, and isolated from any support. For an aligned argument that looks at the conviviality between melodramatic films and neoliberalism, see Diane Negra and Yvonne Tasker, "Neoliberal Frames and Genres of Inequality: Recession-Era Chick Flicks and Male-Centered Corporate Melodrama," *European Journal of Cultural Studies* 16, no. 3 (June 2013).

6. Together, orgies of feeling and heroic identifications challenge confusing experiences of injury and powerlessness by affectively overwhelming them, displacing them onto a narrative of singular villainy, and then promising that they can be overcome by identifying with, and thus legitimating, dramatic and sovereign state power that will restore sovereignty to both the state and its citizens.

7. Diana Fuss, *Identification Papers: Readings on Psychoanalysis, Sexuality, and Culture* (New York: Routledge, 1995), 14.

8. Sigmund Freud, *The Ego and the Id*, trans. James Strachey (New York: Norton, 1962), 22–36.

9. Sigmund Freud, *Group Psychology and Analysis of the Ego*, trans. James Strachey (New York: W. W. Norton, 1990), 48.

10. Sigmund Freud, *An Outline of Psychoanalysis*, trans. James Strachey (New York: Norton, 1973), 193.

11. Freud, *The Ego and the Id*, 24.

12. Freud extends the relationship between loss and identification in his writings on melancholy. See Sigmund Freud, "Mourning and Melancholia," in *Collected Papers*, vol. 4, trans. Joan Riviere (New York: Basic Books, 1959). For analyses of these texts in conjunction with questions of subjectivity, see Judith Butler, *The Psychic Life of Power: Essays in Subjection* (Stanford, CA: Stanford University Press, 1997).

13. Jodi Dean, *Democracy and Other Neoliberal Fantasies* (Durham, NC: Duke University Press, 2009), 169.

14. See Giovanna Borradori, Jürgen Habermas, and Jacques Derrida, *Philosophy in a Time of Terror: Dialogues with Jürgen Habermas and Jacques Derrida* (Chicago: University of Chicago Press, 2004); Judith Butler, *Precarious Life: The Powers of*

*Mourning and Violence* (London: Verso, 2004); and Marc Redfield, "Virtual Trauma: The Idiom of 9 / 11," *diacritics* 37, no. 1 (Spring 2007).

15. Nancy Gibbs, "If You Want to Humble an Empire," *Time*, September 14, 2001.

16. "Nancy Siegrist, a 33-year-old physician's assistant with green scrubs and a thousand-yard stare, walked shakily down the riverside promenade. It was not the horror she had seen. It was the impotence." Barton Gellman, "In a Mountain of Dust, Fire, 'We Didn't Even Find People,'" *Washington Post*, September 12, 2001, A1.

17. Wendy Brown, "Political Idealization and Its Discontents," in *Edgework: Critical Essays on Knowledge and Politics* (Princeton, NJ: Princeton University Press, 2006).

18. Brown, "Political Idealization and Its Discontents," 29–30.

19. See my examination of William Connolly's concept of ontological narcissism in chapter 4.

20. See the collection of polls at Gallup.com from 2001 to 2004 on the wars in Afghanistan and Iraq.

21. Kim Schepple calls U.S. power to dictate other states' internal security measures the Global Patriot Act. Kim Schepple, "The Global Patriot Act," *The American Prospect*, August 29, 2011, accessed October 26, 2013, http://prospect.org/article /global-patriot-act.

22. Bush's approval rating after 9 / 11 was at 92 percent—the highest level of any president at any time in the sixty-plus years that Gallup has recorded public opinion. This number is particularly shocking considering that the 9 / 11 attacks were partly the product of the Bush administration's inability to focus on terrorism threats before September 11, 2001. It is less shocking when interpreted as a nationwide identification with Bush's belligerent post-9 / 11 stance, especially given his aggressive demands for executive power, the War in Afghanistan, the Patriot Act, and the creation of the Department of Homeland Security. See Frank Newport, "The American Public Reacts," Gallup, September 24, 2001, accessed June 14, 2011, http://www.gallup.com/poll/4927/American-Public-Reacts.aspx.

23. Michael Rogin, *Ronald Reagan the Movie: And Other Episodes in Political Demonology* (Berkeley: University of California Press, 1988).

24. Many people read the Iraq War as an oedipal tragic drama, in which Bush forcefully takes a nation to war in order to complete the elder George Bush's smaller incursion into Iraq. Yet this reading individuates and displaces the widespread national support for the war, as opposed to the interpretation that melodrama enables, which positions Bush as an easily identifiable American hero, fulfilling not simply his own fantasies but that of the nation that legitimates and identifies with his actions. To interpret the Iraq War as an oedipal tragedy is to refuse the investment of the majority of U.S. citizens who sanctioned and supported the push for war.

25. Lauren Berlant, *Cruel Optimism* (Durham, NC: Duke University Press, 2012).

26. Geuss, *Politics and the Imagination*, 22.

27. On entrepreneurial subjectivity, see Michel Foucault, *Birth of Biopolitics: Lectures at the Collège de France, 1978–1979*, trans. Graham Burchell (New York: Picador, 2008).

28. See Wendy Brown, *States of Injury: Power and Freedom in Late Modernity* (Princeton, NJ: Princeton University Press, 1995); Drucilla Cornell, *At the Heart of Freedom: Feminism, Sex, and Equality* (Princeton, NJ: Princeton University Press, 1998); Carole Pateman, *The Sexual Contract* (Stanford, CA: Stanford University Press, 1988); Sheldon Wolin, *The Presence of the Past: Essays on the State and the Constitution* (Baltimore, MD: Johns Hopkins University Press, 1989); and Linda Zerilli, *Feminism and the Abyss of Freedom* (Chicago: University of Chicago Press, 2005).

29. See Michel Foucault, *Security, Territory, Population: Lectures at the Collège de France, 1977–1978*, trans. Graham Burchell (New York: Picador, 2007); Michel Foucault, *"Society Must Be Defended": Lectures at the Collège de France, 1975–1976*, trans. David Macey (New York: Picador, 2003); and C. B. MacPherson, *The Political Theory of Possessive Individualism: Hobbes to Locke* (Oxford: Oxford University Press, 2011).

30. See chapter 2 for the argument that individualism was nationalized in the political discourses that postulated that international politics could be controlled and molded to America's needs.

31. Murray Edelman, *The Symbolic Uses of Politics* (Urbana: University of Illinois Press, 1965), 1.

32. Paul Passavant, "The Strong Neoliberal State: Crime, Consumption, Governance," *Theory and Event* 8, no. 3 (2005).

33. As Brown argues, the state continues to be "the singularly accountable object in the field of political power" even though it is not the only source of political power. Wendy Brown, *Regulating Aversion: Tolerance in the Age of Identity and Empire* (Princeton, NJ: Princeton University Press, 2006), 83.

34. See "Students Swarm White House after Death of Osama bin Laden," *GW Hatchet*, May 2, 2011, accessed October 26, 2013, http://blogs.gwhatchet.com/news-room/2011/05/02/photos-students-swarm-white-house-after-death-of-osama-bin-laden/.

35. Steven Johnston, *The Truth about Patriotism* (Durham, NC: Duke University Press, 2007), 65–66. Raymond Guess similarly argues that 9/11 was "a deep *narcissistic* wound on the American psyche." Guess, *Politics and the Imagination*, 15.

36. Johnston, *The Truth about Patriotism*, 37, 35.

37. Sigmund Freud, "On Narcissism: An Introduction," in *Collected Papers*, vol. 4, trans. Joan Riviere (New York: Basic Books, 1959), 30–59.

38. See Mikkel Borch-Jacobson, *The Freudian Subject*, trans. Catherine Porter (Stanford, CA: Stanford University Press, 1991); Judith Butler, *Bodies That Matter: On the Discursive Limits of "Sex"* (New York: Routledge, 1993); Butler, *The Psychic Life of Power*; Jacques Lacan, "The Mirror State as Formative of the *I* Function as Revealed in Psychoanalytic Experience," in *Ecrits*, trans. Bruce Fink (New York: W. W. Norton,

2000); and Kaja Silverman, *The Threshold of the Visible World* (New York: Routledge, 1995).

39. In Fuss's words, "Identification operates for the subject as the primary means for gaining control over the objects outside itself; identification is a form of mastery modeled directly on the nutritional instinct [incorporation as destruction and mastery]." Fuss, *Identification Papers*, 35.

40. The question as to the nature of this acknowledgment, of how the loss is acknowledged, remains a contentious topic in psychoanalytic literature. The acknowledgment of loss occurs in the unconscious to a certain degree; it centers in the ego, and involves the ego's attempt to broker loss by convincing the id that the ego itself is a substitute for the object that the id still desires. Yet loss can also function on a conscious level, as Freud seems to explain when marking the difference between mourning and melancholia. Mourning occurs when the desire for the lost object transforms into identification with it through a conscious working through of loss. Melancholia, by contrast, is a refusal to recognize loss, a process in which the loss remains disavowed. Part of the problem is that Freud provides different configurations of identification in different texts, and thus exactly how this acknowledgment happens remains unclear. Yet what remains constant is his insistence that some form of acknowledgment of loss and difference must predicate the process of identification.

41. Freud, *The Ego and the Id*, 20.

42. Lacan, "The Mirror State as Formative of the *I* Function as Revealed in Psychoanalytic Experience."

43. Another source of confusion is the distinction Freud continually draws between desire and identification—between wanting to "have" and to "be" a love object—distinctions that, as Fuss demonstrates, are constantly blurred. Identification with the state—wanting to be "like" the state—seems to operate as both something one wants to be (autonomous and master) and also what one wants to have (control over the powers that govern one's existence). I follow Fuss in refusing to falsely tidy those muddy distinctions: the distinction between wanting to "be" autonomous and to "have" or possess control over what is autonomous is very slippery, and I would suggest that both are part of the desire for mastery. Fuss, *Identification Papers*.

44. See Hannah Arendt, "What Is Freedom?," in *Between Past and Future: Eight Exercises in Political Thought* (New York: Penguin, 2006); and Zerilli, *Feminism and the Abyss of Freedom*.

45. Peter Fitzpatrick, "Enduring Freedom," *Theory and Event* 5, no. 4 (2001).

46. Jill Bennett, "The Limits of Empathy and the Global Politics of Belonging," in *Trauma at Home: After 9/11*, ed. Judith Greenberg (Lincoln: University of Nebraska Press, 2003); and Butler, "Violence Mourning, Politics," in *Precarious Life*.

6. LEFT MELODRAMA

1. Christine Gledhill quoted in Linda Williams, "Mega-Melodrama: Vertical and Horizontal Suspensions of the Classical," *Modern Drama* 55, no. 4 (Winter 2012): 524.

2. Walter Benjamin, "Left-Wing Melancholy," in *Walter Benjamin: Selected Writings*, vol. 2, part 1, ed. Michael Jennings (Cambridge, MA: Harvard University Press, 2005), 423–27.

3. Benjamin "Left-Wing Melancholy," 423–24.

4. Benjamin "Left-Wing Melancholy," 424.

5. Benjamin "Left-Wing Melancholy," 425.

6. Walter Benjamin, *The Origin of German Tragic Drama*, trans. John Osborne (London: Verso, 2003), 140.

7. Bertolt Brecht, *Brecht on Theater: The Development of an Aesthetic*, trans. and ed. John Willett (New York: Hill and Wang, 1964), 91–99.

8. Benjamin, *The Origin of German Tragic Drama*, 140.

9. Melancholy, for Benjamin, is always a product of the historical moment it inhabits. Its operations and source of sadness are temporally shifty; indeed, it is one aim of the *Origins of German Tragic Drama* to investigate the constellation of interpretations for how melancholy has been differently understood. Benjamin connects left melancholy to the work in *The Origins of German Tragic Drama* when writing that left melancholy is the latest development of two thousand years of melancholia. Left melancholy's deadening of revolutionary reflexes is inescapably situated in, and a product of, its time period. Perhaps, then, the making dead of live things provides an accurate reflection of the historical moment Benjamin analyzes: it is the work of commodification and alienation, of capital's turning the world and its inhabitants into dead objects. Left melancholy, possibly, encapsulates this turn, revealing the true story of the violence in which it is situated, of a life lived through processes that turn all living things into commodities and numbers, that render live things dead for efficiency and profit.

10. Benjamin, "Left-Wing Melancholy," 424.

11. Wendy Brown, "Resisting Left Melancholy," *boundary 2* 26, no. 3 (Fall 1999): 22.

12. Stuart Hall, *The Hard Road to Renewal: Thatcherism and Crisis of the Left* (London: Verso, 1988), 4.

13. I retain Freud's term *object* to describe what has been lost in left melodrama because the term attends to the psychic dimension of the losses I examine. I therefore use *object* as specific reference to the psychoanalytic valence of melancholy, and do not intend to mark a broad or quotidian use of the term.

14. See also Judith Butler, *The Psychic Life of Power: Essays in Subjection* (Stanford, CA: Stanford University Press, 1997).

15. *The Communist Manifesto* did not function as a worldwide spark for radical social transformation until years after its initial publication, yet its eventual influence makes it, perhaps, the most galvanizing work of political theory in Western modernity.

16. See Peter Brooks, *The Melodramatic Imagination: Balzac, Henry James, Melodrama, and the Mode of Excess* (New Haven, CT: Yale University Press, 1995); Matthew Buckley, *Tragedy Walks the Streets: The French Revolution in the Making of Modern Drama* (Baltimore, MD: Johns Hopkins University Press, 2006); and Thomas

Elsaesser, "Tales of Sound and Fury: Observations of the Family Melodrama," in *Home Is Where the Heart Is: Melodrama and the Woman's Film*, ed. Christine Gledhill (London: British Film Institute, 1987).

17. Christine Gledhill, "The Melodramatic Field: An Investigation," in *Home Is Where the Heart Is: Melodrama and the Woman's Film*, ed. Christine Gledhill (London: British Film Institute, 1987).

18. Daniel Gerould, "Melodrama and Revolution," in *Melodrama: Stage, Picture, Screen*, ed. Jacky Bratton, Jim Cook, and Christine Gledhill (London: British Film Institute, 1994), 185.

19. Elaine Hadley, *Melodramatic Tactics: Theatricalized Dissent in the English Marketplace, 1800–1885* (Stanford, CA: Stanford University Press, 1995).

20. Gerould, "Melodrama and Revolution," 186.

21. Daniel Gerould and Julia Przybos, "Melodrama in the Soviet Theater 1917–1928: An Annotated Chronology," in *Melodrama*, ed. Daniel Gerould (New York: New York Literary Forum, 1980), 75–92. Sergei Eisenstein's classic film *Battleship Potemkin* (1925) is a paradigmatic example of how melodrama quickly transitioned from Soviet theater to film.

22. Karl Marx and Friedrich Engels, *Manifesto of the Communist Party*, in *The Marx-Engels Reader*, ed. Robert Tucker (New York: W. W. Norton, 1978), 473–74. For the purpose of this chapter, I leave to one side ongoing and important debates about the different roles and attributions of Marx and Engels in crafting *The Communist Manifesto*. For a compelling analysis of Marx and Engels's various roles, see Terrell Carver, "The Engels-Marx Question," in *Engels after Marx*, ed. Manfred Steger and Terrell Carver (University Park: Penn State University Press, 1999), 22–23.

23. Carl Schmitt, *The Concept of the Political*, trans. George Schwab (Chicago: University of Chicago Press, 1996), 74.

24. Marx and Engels, *Manifesto of the Communist Party*, 474.

25. Linda Williams, *Playing the Race Card: Melodramas of Black and White from Uncle Tom to O. J. Simpson* (Princeton, NJ: Princeton University Press, 2001), 30.

26. Marx and Engels, *Manifesto of the Communist Party*, 490.

27. Marx and Engels, *Manifesto of the Communist Party*, 474.

28. On the concept and use of moralization, see Jane Bennett and Michael Shapiro, "Introduction," in *The Politics of Moralizing*, ed. Jane Bennett and Michael Shapiro (New York: Routledge, 2002), 1–10.

29. Steven Lukes argues as well for the moral reading of Marx; he writes, "It is not, I think, inaccurate to call [the manifesto] morally *inspirational*. . . . It conveys a Manichean vision of an intolerable world to be overcome and a truly human world to come, and a general call to action to hasten this transformation. It expresses in concentrated form the *moral* appeal of Marxism." Steven Lukes, "The Morals of the Manifesto," in *The Communist Manifesto by Karl Marx and Friedrich Engels*, ed. Jeffrey Isaac (New Haven, CT: Yale University Press, 2012), 120.

30. Wylie Sypher, "The Aesthetic of Revolution: The Marxist Melodrama," *Kenyon Review* 10, no. 3 (Summer 1948).

31. Marx and Engels, *Manifesto of the Communist Party*, 475–76.

32. Elsaesser, "Tales of Sound and Fury," 67.

33. Marx and Engels, *Manifesto of the Communist Party*, 479, 480.

34. Marx and Engels, *Manifesto of the Communist Party*, 482.

35. Karl Löwith, *Max Weber and Karl Marx* (London: Routledge, 1993), 110.

36. Marx and Engels, *Manifesto of the Communist Party*, 481.

37. Sheldon Wolin, *Politics and Vision* (Princeton, NJ: Princeton University Press, 2004), 434.

38. Jane M. Gaines, "The Melos of Marxist Theory," in *The Hidden Foundation: Cinema and the Question of Class*, ed. David E. James and Rick Berg (Minneapolis: University of Minnesota Press, 1996), 59–60; my emphasis.

39. Gaines, "The Melos of Marxist Theory," 60.

40. Brooks, *The Melodramatic Imagination*; Williams, *Playing the Race Card*.

41. Marx and Engels, *Manifesto of the Communist Party*, 500.

42. I am not suggesting that these books could be exclusively explained through recourse to melodrama, but instead I intend to show what can be illuminated when we read their projects as melodrama. See Giorgio Agamben, *Homo Sacer: Sovereign Power and Bare Life*, trans. Daniel Heller-Roazen (Stanford, CA: Stanford University Press, 1998); Giorgio Agamben, *States of Exception*, trans. Kevin Attell (Chicago: University of Chicago Press, 2005); Michael Hardt and Antonio Negri, *Empire* (Cambridge, MA: Harvard University Press, 2001); and Michael Hardt and Antonio Negri, *Multitude* (Cambridge, MA: Harvard University Press, 2004).

43. Agamben, *Homo Sacer*, 8.

44. Agamben, *Homo Sacer*, 27.

45. A similar question would be: is the Bush administration the main line of accountability for the state of emergency after 9 / 11? Agamben writes, "President Bush's decision to refer to himself constantly as the 'Commander in Chief' after September 11, 2001, must be considered in the context of this presidential claim to sovereign powers in emergency situations. If, as we have seen, the assumption of this title entails a direct reference to the state of exception, then Bush is attempting to produce a situation in which the emergency becomes the rule, and the very distinction between peace and war (and between foreign and civil war) becomes impossible." Agamben, *States of Exception*, 22.

46. Agamben, *Homo Sacer*, 123.

47. Agamben, *Homo Sacer*, 27.

48. Agamben, *Homo Sacer*, 115.

49. Slavoj Žižek, "Have Michael Hardt and Antonio Negri Rewritten the Communist Manifesto for the Twenty-First Century?," *Rethinking Marxism* 13, nos. 3–4 (2001).

50. Hardt and Negri, *Empire*, xi.

51. Hardt and Negri, *Empire*, 9.

52. Hardt and Negri, *Empire*, 66.

53. Hardt and Negri, *Empire*, 336, 9.

54. Timothy Brennan, *Wars of Position: Cultural Politics of Left and Right* (New York: Columbia University Press, 2005), 204.

55. Gledhill, "The Melodramatic Field," 21.

56. John Brenkman, *Cultural Contradictions of Democracy: Political Thought since September 11* (Princeton, NJ: Princeton University Press, 2007), 66.

57. On this point, see Christopher Nealon, "Reading on the Left," *Representations* 108 (2009): 41: "Though [Hardt and Negri] caution that this socialization does not mean that all struggles are alike, or that all exploitation is equally intense, their stance clearly makes room for the affect-workers of the northern literary academy to imagine themselves in alliance with the exploited of the global south."

58. See, for example, Jane Bennett, *Vibrant Matter: A Political Ecology of Things* (Durham, NC: Duke University Press, 2011); Wendy Brown, *Politics out of History* (Princeton, NJ: Princeton University Press, 2001); Butler, *The Psychic Life of Power*; William E. Connolly, *The Ethos of Pluralization* (Minneapolis: University of Minnesota Press, 1995); Jodi Dean, *The Communist Horizon* (London: Verso, 2012); Paul Gilroy, *Postcolonial Melancholia* (New York: Columbia University Press, 2005); Michael Hanchard, *Party/Politics: New Horizons in Black Political Thought* (New York: Oxford University Press, 2006); Timothy Kaufman-Osborn, "We Are All Torturers Now: Accountability after Abu Ghraib," *Theory and Event* 11, no. 2 (2008); David Scott, *Conscripts of Modernity: The Tragedy of Colonial Enlightenment* (Durham, NC: Duke University Press, 2004); Annika Thiem, *Unbecoming Subjects* (New York: Fordham University Press, 2008); and Roberto Mangabiera Unger, *The Left Alternative* (London: Verso, 2009).

## CONCLUSION. MELODRAMAS OF FAILED SOVEREIGNTY

1. On waning sovereignty, see the introduction and chapter 5 of this book, as well as Wendy Brown, *Walled States, Waning Sovereignty* (New York: Zone Books, 2010); and Saskia Sassen, *Sociology of Globalization* (New York: W. W. Norton, 2007).

2. For Hegel, the bird of wisdom "begins its flight only with the falling of dusk"; the conceptual understanding of the present order comes once that order is shifting to a new form. G. W. F. Hegel, *Outlines of the Philosophy of Right*, trans. T. M. Knox (Oxford: Oxford University Press, 2008), 16.

3. On the collaborative use of power toward the making of a shared world, see Sheldon Wolin, *The Presence of the Past: Essays on the State and the Constitution* (Baltimore, MD: Johns Hopkins University Press, 1989), 150–54.

4. Hayden White, "Anomalies of Genre," *New Literary History*, 34, no. 3 (Summer 2003): 609.

5. Jacques Rancière, *The Emancipated Spectator* (London: Verso, 2009), 12.

6. Rancière's argument is also limited in its usefulness for making this claim: it does not attend to the forms of power that encourage and legitimate some narrative genre forms over others, or to the affective attachments that collectives develop to certain narratives, or to the psychic work of disavowal that can contribute to policing what remains outside of popular genres of political discourse. Yet it is also a

useful provocation in its linkage between narration, translation, and collective practices of freedom; it suggests that even slightly refracted narrative trajectories within genre forms can undergird more emancipatory interpretations of politics and agency.

7. Hannah Arendt, "What Is Freedom?," in *Between Past and Future: Eight Exercises in Political Thought* (New York: Penguin, 2006), 165.

8. I thank Joel Schlosser for conversations on this point.

9. See, for example, Jean-François Lyotard, *The Postmodern Condition: A Report on Knowledge* (Manchester, UK: Manchester University Press, 1984); and Gianni Vattimo, *The End of Modernity: Nihilism and Hermeneutics in Post-modern Culture* (Baltimore, MD: Johns Hopkins University Press, 1991). For a critique of permanent inexplicability as a political stance, see Achille Mbembe and Janet Roitman, "Figures of the Subject in Times of Crisis," *Public Culture* 7 (1995).

10. Judith Halberstam, *The Queer Art of Failure* (Durham, NC: Duke University Press, 2011), 145.

11. As political theorists, including Steven Johnston and William E. Connolly, might be read to suggest, failure is part of the very constitutive practice of democracy, which always demands winners and losers, successes and failures from every agonistic decision.

12. Many pioneering feminist film theorists in the 1980s made this claim, most notably Ann Kaplan in *Motherhood and Representation* (New York: Routledge, 1992), but recent critics have claimed this as well. In an article on melodrama and political theory, Anna Siomopoulos argues that the domestic melodrama is a politically limited film genre that buttresses oppressive forms of liberal politics that perpetuate the disenfranchisement of politically oppressed subjects. Though I agree with her in certain respects, I hope here to pull out what makes the women's film a distinct site for imagining the failure of freedom, and for illustrating the incapacity of individualistic norms to redress political subordination. Anna Siomopoulos, "Political Theory and Melodrama Studies," *Camera Obscura* 21, no. 2 (2006). Also see Hamilton Carroll, *Affirmative Reaction: New Formations of White Masculinity* (Durham, NC: Duke University Press, 2012), for an argument that neoliberal ideology (via the film *Traffic*) manifests as a family melodrama.

13. Berlant argues that melodramas are part of a national sentimental project that "locate[s] real life in the affective capacity to bracket many kinds of structural and historical antagonisms on behalf of finding a way to reconnect with the feeling of belonging to a larger world . . . [that] holds tightly to some versions of the imaginable conventional good life in love . . . as an alleviation of what is hard to manage in the lived real—social antagonisms, exploitation, compromised intimacies, the attrition of life." Lauren Berlant, *The Female Complaint: The Unfinished Business of Sentimentality in American Culture* (Durham, NC: Duke University Press, 2008), 4–5.

14. Women's weepies were initially devalued in both academic and popular film criticism, considered too lowbrow to be worthy of scholarly critique. Yet melodrama

eventually became an object of study primarily through analysis of women's weepies, as Marxist film critics read the contradictions of capital into melodrama's formal and narrative qualities. Feminist film critics soon extended this line of interrogation, arguing that the weepies revealed the limitations of a life lived under a capitalist society shaped by gendered inequality and patriarchal domination.

15. Christine Gledhill, "The Melodramatic Field: An Investigation," in *Home Is Where the Heart Is: Studies in Melodrama and the Woman's Film* (London: British Film Institute, 1987), 7. My examination of Sirk does not aim, like left melodrama, to mimic the past in order to furnish visions of the future, nor does it aim to anachronistically repeat past melodramatic models. My intent is to show how these conventions are already lurking in popular discourse, and to show how melodramatic genre conventions deploy critical resources available to the present in new form.

16. Jackie Byars, *All That Hollywood Allows: Rereading Gender in 1950s Melodrama* (Bloomington: Indiana University Press, 1991), 64–66, 80–81. Jon Halliday writes that Sirk was often considered a master of the women's weepies. Jon Halliday, "All That Heaven Allows," in *Douglas Sirk*, ed. Laura Mulvey and Jon Halliday (Edinburgh: Edinburgh Film Festival, 1972), 59–66.

17. Byars writes that Sirk's melodrama "places motivation [for action] as structural rather than personal." Byars, *All That Hollywood Allows*, 11.

18. Thomas Elsaesser, "Tales of Sound and Fury: Observations of the Family Melodrama," in *Home Is Where the Heart Is: Melodrama and the Woman's Film*, ed. Christine Gledhill (London: British Film Institute, 1987), 55; my emphasis.

19. Rainer Werner Fassbinder, "Six Films by Douglas Sirk," in *Douglas Sirk*, ed. Jon Halliday and Laura Mulvey (Edinburgh: Edinburgh Film Festival, 1972), 97.

20. Elsaesser, "Tales of Sound and Fury," 56.

21. See Halliday, "All That Heaven Allows"; John Mercer and Martin Shingler, *Melodrama: Genre, Style, Sensibility* (New York: Wallfower Press, 2004), 60–68; Niall Richardson, "Poison in the Sirkian System: The Political Agenda of Todd Haynes's 'Far from Heaven,'" *Scope: International Journal of Film Studies*, no. 6 (October 2006); Salomé Aguilera Skvirsky, "The Price of Heaven: Remaking Politics in *All That Heaven Allows, Ali, Fear Eats the Soul*, and *Far from Heaven*," *Cinema Journal* 47, no. 3 (2008); and Michael Stern, "Patterns of Power and Potency, Repression and Violence: An Introduction to the Study of Douglas Sirk's Films of the 1950s," *The Velvet Light Trap* 16 (Fall 1976).

22. See Halliday, "All That Heaven Allows"; and Laura Mulvey, "Notes on Sirk and Melodrama," *in Home Is Where the Heart Is: Melodrama and the Woman's Film*, ed. Christine Gledhill (London: British Film Institute, 1987), 75–79. Mulvey, along with Mercer and Shingler in *Melodrama*, sees punishment and social messages for Cary alone at the end of the film; Ron is the backdrop against which her suffering is highlighted.

23. Berlant, *The Female Complaint*, 3, 10, 150.

24. She writes that the culture industry that produces melodramas "makes erotic, normal, and personal the risks and failures, the violence, the deferrals, and the impossible promises of democracy under capitalism." Berlant, *The Female Complaint*, 75.

25. For Mulvey, "their gratification is postponed by Ron's accident, . . . and a hidden shadow is cast implicitly over their perfect, joyful acceptance at love, although as the shutters are opened in the morning, the cold, hard light of repression is driven off the screen by the warm light of hope and satisfaction." Mulvey, "Notes on Sirk and Melodrama," 78.

26. Christine Gledhill describes melodrama as "taking its stand in the material world of everyday reality and lived experience, and acknowledging the limitations of the conventions of language and representation." Gledhill, "The Melodramatic Field," 33. The limitation of current norms is crucial to their critical potential—to their ability to gesture to the broad social transformation needed to rectify the problems they diagnose.

27. Marx examines situations of failed emancipatory efforts that show failure as well as the strategies of the exploited for gaining power over the very mechanisms that reentrenched their exploitation. Karl Marx, *The 18th Brumaire of Louis Bonaparte*, in *The Marx-Engels Reader*, ed. Robert Tucker (New York: W. W. Norton, 1978).

28. Marx, *The 18th Brumaire of Louis Bonaparte*, 598.

29. Halberstam is working in feminist and queer theory, and the model of sovereignty she attacks is drawn from the norms of a straight, white, male, individualist liberal subjectivity. Yet her argument does not delimit which subjects or bodies must necessarily be excluded from the experience of failure, even as that failure is differentiated across race, classed, sexual, and gendered bodies. I am drawing from her claims a way to think about failure in terms of individual sovereignty that is differentially experienced but that is violent to almost all people, even those who might seem to be situated squarely within its terms; no one, I am suggesting, can live up to them, even though the binds they produce are significantly tighter and more violent to people who do not match most or all of individual sovereignty's privileged positions. While Halberstam does not generally emphasize a language of "freedom" in her argument, her analysis of failure suggests that freedom can neither be conceived as an abstract norm nor apply in the same way at all times to all people. And yet most people fail at living up to the norms of individual sovereignty, which means, too, that the critical potential of failure is available to a wider range of people. Halberstam, *The Queer Art of Failure*.

30. Halberstam, *The Queer Art of Failure*, 88, 96.

31. For more on failures of sovereignty, see Elisabeth Anker, "Feminist Theory and the Failures of Post-9/11 Politics," *Politics and Gender* 8, no. 2 (June 2012).

32. Halberstam, *The Queer Art of Failure*, 88.

33. Stuart Hall, "The Problem of Ideology—Marxism without Guarantees," *Journal of Communication Inquiry* 10, no. 2 (June 1986).

34. We might liken it to Todd Haynes's 2004 remake of *All That Heaven Allows* into *Far from Heaven*, which draws on the aesthetics of the 1950s women's weepie to interrogate twenty-first-century formations of identity and power.

35. Byars, *All That Hollywood Allows*, 112.

36. Chris Matthews, interview on MSNBC's *Countdown with Keith Olbermann*, May 1, 2003.

37. "Bush Makes Historic Speech aboard Warship—May 1, 2003," CNN.com, May 1, 2003, accessed October 28, 2013, http://www.cnn.com/2003/US/05/01/bush.transcript/.

38. "President George W. Bush Lands on USS Lincoln in Navy Jet," NBC News, May 1, 2003, accessed October 28, 2013, http://archives.nbclearn.com/portal/site/k-12/flatview?cuecard=2701; the *Time* columnist Margaret Colson on CNN's *The Capital Gang*, May 3, 2003, quoted in "Mission Accomplished: A Look Back at the Media's Fawning Coverage of Bush's Premature Declaration of Victory in Iraq," Media Matters, April 27, 2006, accessed October 28, 2013, http://mediamatters.org/research/2006/04/27/mission-accomplished-a-look-back-at-the-medias/135513.

39. David Sanger, "In Full Flight Regalia, the President Enjoys a 'Top Gun' Moment," *New York Times*, May 2, 2003, A17.

40. Yes, this observation was made by the Watergate criminal G. Gordon Liddy on MSNBC's *Hardball* on May 7, 2003. Quoted in "Mission Accomplished," Media Matters.

41. Elsaesser, "Tales of Sound and Fury," 62.

42. "Bush to USS Lincoln: 'I Have the Balls,'" About.com, Netlore Archive, last updated July 4, 2003, accessed October 28, 2013, http://urbanlegends.about.com/library/bl_bush_uss_lincoln.htm.

43. John Mueller and Mark Stewart analyze polling data to show how "35–40 percent of the American people continue [up to mid-2012] since late 2001 to profess worry—even in the aftermath of the death of Osama bin Laden—that they or a family member might become a victim of terrorism. . . . If anything, respondents felt that the country was less safe in 2010 than it was in 2003 or 2004." John Mueller and Mark Stewart, "The Terrorism Delusion: America's Overwrought Response to September 11," *International Security* 37, no. 1 (Summer 2012): 107.

44. Here Cary is positioned differently from Ron, who is not asked to account for Cary's (less physical, though just as evident) suffering, and the gendered norms of the weepies play out as Cary is called to account for her complicity in social injustice while Ron is rendered unaccountable by his insentience. Yet it is still important to note how the film severs the typical melodramatic equation of injury and virtue in the figure of Cary.

45. On the moral work of Guantanamo in American media and political discourse, see Sasha Torres, "Televising Guantanamo," in *Political Emotions*, ed. Janet Staiger, Ann Cvetcovich, and Ann Reynolds (New York: Routledge, 2010), 49. She writes, "The mere existence of the camp and the practices that sustained it stymied so many of the ideals that formed the backdrop of everyday national life, at least for relatively privileged normative citizens."

46. See Timothy Kaufman-Osborn, "We Are All Torturers Now: Accountability after Abu Ghraib," *Theory and Event* 11, no. 2 (2008), on the complex ways this plays out.

47. Bonnie Honig, *Antigone, Interrupted* (Cambridge: Cambridge University Press, 2013), 80–82.

48. For Honig melodramatic depictions of overwhelming power enable the possibility for pursuing other options for political engagement, without exactly stating what those should be.

49. Geoffrey Nowell-Smith notes, "The importance of melodrama . . . lies precisely in its ideological failure. Because it cannot accommodate its problem, either in a real present or an ideal future, but lays them open in their shameless contradictoriness, it opens a space that most Hollywood forms have studiously closed off." Geoffrey Nowell-Smith, "Minnelli and Melodrama," in *Imitations of Life: A Reader of Film and Melodrama*, ed. Marcia Landy (Detroit, MI: Wayne State University Press, 1991), 118.

50. Linda Williams, "'Something Else Besides a Mother': Stella Dallas and the Maternal Melodrama," in *Imitations of Life: A Reader on Film and Television Melodrama*, ed. Marcia Landy (Detroit, MI: Wayne State University Press, 1991).

# BIBLIOGRAPHY

Adorno, Theodor, and Max Horkheimer. *Dialectic of Enlightenment: Philosophical Fragments*. Trans. Edmund Jephcott. Stanford, CA: Stanford University Press, 2002.

Agamben, Giorgio. *Homo Sacer: Sovereign Power and Bare Life*. Trans. Daniel Heller-Roazen. Stanford, CA: Stanford University Press, 1998.

———. *States of Exception*. Trans. Kevin Attell. Chicago: University of Chicago Press, 2005.

Ahmed, Sara. "Affective Economies." *Social Text* 22, no. 22 (Summer 2004): 117–39.

———. *The Cultural Politics of Emotion*. London: Routledge, 2004.

Alperen, Martin J. *Foundations of Homeland Security: Law and Policy*. Hoboken, NJ: Wiley, 2011.

Alsultany, Evelyn. *Arabs and Muslims in the Media: Race and Representation after 9/11*. New York: New York University Press, 2012.

Altheide, David L. *Terrorism and the Politics of Fear*. Lanham, MD: AltaMira Press, 2006.

Altman, Rick. "Reusable Packaging: Generic Products and the Recycling Process." In *Refiguring American Film Genres: History and Theory*, ed. Nick Browne, 1–41. Berkeley: University of California Press, 1998.

Ambrose, Stephen. *Rise to Globalism: American Foreign Policy since 1938*. New York: Longman, 1998.

Anker, Elisabeth. "Feminist Theory and the Failures of Post-9/11 Politics." *Politics and Gender* 8, no. 2 (June 2012): 208–15.

———. "Heroic Identifications; or, 'You Can Love Me Too—I Am So like the State.'" *Theory and Event* 15, no. 1 (2012).

———. "Left Melodrama." *Contemporary Political Theory* 11, no. 2 (May 2012): 130–52.

———. "The Only Thing We Have to Fear . . ." *Theory and Event* 8, no. 3 (2005).

———. "Villains, Victims and Heroes: Melodrama, Media, and September 11." *Journal of Communication* 55, no. 1 (March 2005): 22–37.

Arendt, Hannah. *On Revolution*. New York: Penguin Press, 1990.

———. "What Is Freedom?" In *Between Past and Future: Eight Exercises in Political Thought*, 143–72. New York: Penguin, 2006.

Aristotle. *On Rhetoric: A Theory of Civic Discourse*. Trans. George Kennedy. New York: Oxford University Press, 1991.

Asad, Talal. *On Suicide Bombing*. New York: Columbia University Press, 2007.

Baldwin, James. "Everybody's Protest Novel." In *Notes of a Native Son*, 13–23. Boston: Beacon Press, 1984.

Balibar, Étienne. "Subjectivity and Subjectivation." In *Supposing the Subject*, ed. Joan Copjec, 2–14. London: Verso, 1994.

Banet-Wiser, Sarah. *The Most Beautiful Girl in the World: Beauty Pageants and National Identity*. Berkeley: University of California Press, 1999.

Barkun, Mark. *Chasing Phantoms: Reality, Imagination, and Homeland Security since 9/11*. Chapel Hill: University of North Carolina Press, 2011.

Baughman, John. *Republic of Mass Culture: Journalism, Filmmaking, and Broadcasting in America since 1945*. Baltimore, MD: Johns Hopkins University Press, 2005.

Bauman, Zygmunt. *Liquid Modernity*. Cambridge, UK: Polity Press, 2000.

Bellah, Robert, Richard Madsen, William M. Sullivan, Ann Swidler, and Steven M. Tipton. *Habits of the Heart: Individualism and Commitment in American Life*. Berkeley: University of California Press, 2007.

Benhabib, Seyla. "Toward a Deliberative Model of Democratic Legitimacy." In *Democracy and Difference: Contesting the Boundaries of the Political*, ed. Seyla Benhabib, 67–94. Princeton, NJ: Princeton University Press, 1996.

Benjamin, Walter. "Left-Wing Melancholy." In *Walter Benjamin: Selected Writings*, vol. 2, part 1, ed. Michael Jennings, 423–27. Cambridge, MA: Harvard University Press, 2005.

———. *The Origin of German Tragic Drama*. Trans. John Osborne. London: Verso, 2003.

Bennett, Jane. *Vibrant Matter: A Political Ecology of Things*. Durham, NC: Duke University Press, 2011.

Bennett, Jane, and Michael Shapiro. "Introduction." In *The Politics of Moralizing*, ed. Jane Bennett and Michael Shapiro, 1–10. New York: Routledge, 2002.

Bennett, Jill. "The Limits of Empathy and the Global Politics of Belonging." In *Trauma at Home: After 9/11*, ed. Judith Greenberg, 132–38. Lincoln: University of Nebraska Press, 2003.

Bercovitch, Sacvan. *The American Jeremiad*. Madison: University of Wisconsin Press, 1978.

Berlant, Lauren. *Cruel Optimism*. Durham, NC: Duke University Press, 2012.

———. "The Epistemology of State Emotion." In *Dissent in Dangerous Times*, ed. Austin Sarat, 46–80. Ann Arbor: University of Michigan Press, 2005.

———. *The Female Complaint: The Unfinished Business of Sentimentality in American Culture*. Durham, NC: Duke University Press, 2008.

———. "The Subject of True Feeling." In *Cultural Studies and Political Theory*, ed. Jodi Dean, 42–62. Ithaca, NY: Cornell University Press, 2002.

Bhattacharyya, Gargi. *Dangerous Brown Men: Exploiting Sex, Violence, and Feminism in the War on Terror*. London: Zed Books, 2008.

Bibring, Edward. "The Mechanism of Depression." In *The Meaning of Despair*, ed. Willard Gaylin, 154–81. New York: Science House, 1968.

Bodin, Jean. *On Sovereignty*. Trans. and ed. Julian Franklin. Cambridge, UK: Cambridge University Press, 1992.

Bonney, Richard. *False Prophets: The Clash of Civilizations and the War on Terror*. Oxford: Peter Lang, 2008.

Borch-Jacobson, Mikkel. *The Freudian Subject*. Trans. Catherine Porter. Stanford, CA: Stanford University Press, 1991.

Borradori, Giovanna, Jürgen Habermas, and Jacques Derrida. *Philosophy in a Time of Terror: Dialogues with Jürgen Habermas and Jacques Derrida*. Chicago: University of Chicago Press, 2004.

Boucicoult, Dion. *The Poor of New York*. In *American Melodrama*, ed. Daniel Gerould, 31–74. New York: Performing Arts Journal Publications, 2001.

Bratton, Jacky, Jim Cook, and Christine Gledhill, eds. *Melodrama: Stage, Picture, Screen*. London: British Film Institute, 1994.

Brecht, Bertolt. *Brecht on Theater: The Development of an Aesthetic*. Trans. and ed. John Willett. New York: Hill and Wang, 1964.

Brenkman, John. *Cultural Contradictions of Democracy: Political Thought since September 11*. Princeton, NJ: Princeton University Press, 2007.

Brennan, Theresa. *Globalization and Its Terrors*. London: Routledge, 2003.

Brennan, Timothy. *Wars of Position: Cultural Politics of Left and Right*. New York: Columbia University Press, 2005.

Brooks, Peter. "Melodrama, Body, Revolution." In *Melodrama: Stage, Picture, Screen*, ed. Jacky Bratton, Jim Cook, and Christine Gledhill, 11–25. London: British Film Institute, 1994.

———. *The Melodramatic Imagination: Balzac, Henry James, Melodrama, and the Mode of Excess*. New Haven, CT: Yale University Press, 1995.

Brown, Peter. *Augustine of Hippo*. Berkeley: University of California Press, 2000.

Brown, Wendy. "Neo-liberalism and the End of Liberal Democracy." *Theory and Event* 7, no. 1 (2003).

———. "Political Idealization and Its Discontents." In *Edgework: Critical Essays on Knowledge and Politics*, 17–36. Princeton, NJ: Princeton University Press, 2006.

———. *Politics out of History*. Princeton, NJ: Princeton University Press, 2001.

———. *Regulating Aversion: Tolerance in the Age of Identity and Empire*. Princeton, NJ: Princeton University Press, 2006.

———. "Resisting Left Melancholy." *boundary 2* 26, no. 3 (Fall 1999): 19–27.

———. *States of Injury: Power and Freedom in Late Modernity*. Princeton, NJ: Princeton University Press, 1995.

———. *Walled States, Waning Sovereignty*. New York: Zone Books, 2010.

Buckley, Matthew. *Tragedy Walks the Streets: The French Revolution in the Making of Modern Drama*. Baltimore, MD: Johns Hopkins University Press, 2006.

Butler, Judith. *Bodies That Matter: On the Discursive Limits of "Sex."* New York: Routledge, 1993.

———. "Explanation and Exoneration; or, What We Can Hear." *Theory and Event* 5, no. 4 (2001).

———. *Frames of War: When Is Life Grievable?* London: Verso, 2009.

———. *Precarious Life: The Powers of Mourning and Violence*. London: Verso, 2004.

———. *The Psychic Life of Power: Essays in Subjection*. Stanford, CA: Stanford University Press, 1997.

———. *Undoing Gender*. New York: Routledge, 2004.

Byars, Jackie. *All That Hollywood Allows: Rereading Gender in 1950s Melodrama*. Bloomington: Indiana University Press, 1991.

Carey, John. "The Functions and Uses of Media during the September 11 Crisis and Its Aftermath." In *Crisis Communications Lessons from September 11*, ed. Michael Noll, 1–16. Lanham, MD: Rowman and Littlefield, 2003.

Carroll, Hamilton. *Affirmative Reaction: New Formations of White Masculinity*. Durham, NC: Duke University Press, 2012.

Carver, Terrell. "The Engels-Marx Question." In *Engels after Marx*, ed. Manfred Steger and Terrell Carver, 17–36. University Park: Penn State University Press, 1999.

Casetti, Francesco. *The Eye of the Century: Film, Experience, Modernity*. Trans. Erin Larkin and Jennifer Pranolo. New York: Columbia University Press, 2010.

Castelli, Elizabeth. "Persecution Complexes: Identity Politics and the 'War on Christians.'" *differences: A Journal of Feminist Cultural Studies* 18, no. 3 (2007): 152–80.

Castells, Manuel. "Materials for an Explanatory Theory of the Network Society." *British Journal of Sociology* 51, no. 1 (January–March 2000): 5–24.

Cawelti, John. "The Evolution of Social Melodrama." In *Imitations of Life: A Reader of Film and Melodrama*, ed. Marcia Landy, 33–49. Detroit, MI: Wayne State University Press, 1991.

Chaloupka, Bill, Thomas Dumm, Paul Patton, and Wendy Brown, eds. "Reflections on 11 September." Special issue, *Theory and Event* 5, no. 4 (2001).

Chion, Michel. *Audio-Vision: Sound on Screen*. Trans. and ed. Claudia Gorbman. New York: Columbia University Press, 1994.

Chomsky, Noam. *9–11*. New York: Seven Stories Press, 2002.

Clough, Patricia, ed. *The Affective Turn: Theorizing the Social*. Durham, NC: Duke University Press, 2007.

Cohen, Joshua. "Deliberation and Democratic Legitimacy." In *The Good Polity*, ed. Alan Hamlin and Phillip Pettit, 17–34. Oxford: Basil Blackwell, 1989.

Cole, Alyson. *The Cult of True Victimhood: From the War on Welfare to the War on Terror*. Stanford, CA: Stanford University Press, 2007.

Connolly, William E. *Capitalism and Christianity, American Style*. Durham, NC: Duke University Press, 2008.

———. *The Ethos of Pluralization*. Minneapolis: University of Minnesota Press, 1995.

———. "The Evangelical-Capitalist Resonance Machine." *Political Theory* 33, no. 6 (2005): 869–86.

———. *Identity/Difference*. Ithaca, NY: Cornell University Press, 1991.

———, ed. *Legitimacy and the State*. New York: New York University Press, 1984.

Cornell, Drucilla. *At the Heart of Freedom: Feminism, Sex, and Equality*. Princeton, NJ: Princeton University Press, 1998.

Daalder, Ivo. *America Unbound: The Bush Revolution in Foreign Policy*. Washington, DC: Brookings Institution Press, 2004.

Daly, Augustin, "Flash of Lightning." In *Plays by Augustin Daly*, ed. Don B. Wilmeth and Rosemary Cullen, 49–102. Cambridge, UK: Cambridge University Press, 1984.

———. "Under the Gaslight." In *American Melodrama*, ed. Daniel Gerould, 135–81. New York: PAJ Publications, 2001.

Davis, Darrin. *Negative Liberty: Public Opinion and the Terrorist Attacks on America*. New York: Russell Sage Foundation, 2007.

Dayan, Daniel, and Elihu Katz. *Media Events: The Live Broadcasting of History*. Cambridge, MA: Harvard University Press, 1992.

Dean, Jodi. *The Communist Horizon*. London: Verso, 2012.

———. *Democracy and Other Neoliberal Fantasies*. Durham, NC: Duke University Press, 2009.

———. "Evil's Political Habitats." *Theory and Event* 8, no. 2 (2005).

Debatin, Bernhard. "'Plane Wreck with Spectators': Terrorism and Media Attention." In *Communication and Terrorism: Public and Media Responses to 9/11*, ed. Bradley S. Greenberg, 163–74. Cresskill, NJ: Hampton Press, 2002.

Deephouse, David L., and Mark C. Suchman. "Legitimacy in Organizational Institutionalism." In *The SAGE Handbook of Organizational Institutionalism*, ed. Royston Greenwood, Christine Oliver, Roy Suddaby, and Kerstin Sahlin-Andersson, 49–77. Thousand Oaks, CA: Sage, 2008.

Deleuze, Gilles. "Postscript on the Societies of Control." *October* 59 (Winter 1992): 3–7.

Diamond, Larry. *Squandered Victory: The American Occupation and the Bungled Effort to Bring Democracy to Iraq*. New York: Times Books, 2005.

Doane, Mary Anne. "The Close-Up: Scale and Detail in the Cinema." *differences: A Journal of Feminist Cultural Studies* 14, no. 3 (Fall 2003): 89–111.

———. *The Desire to Desire*. Bloomington: Indiana University Press, 1986.

———. "Information, Crisis, and Catastrophe." In *The Historical Film: History and Memory in Media*, ed. Marcia Landy, 269–85. New Brunswick, NJ: Rutgers University Press, 2001.

———. "The Moving Image: Pathos and the Maternal." In *Imitations of Life: A Reader on Film and Television Melodrama*, ed. Marcia Landy, 283–306. Detroit, MI: Wayne State University Press, 1991.

———. "The Woman's Film: Possession and Address." In *Re-vision: Essays in Feminist Film Criticism*, ed. Mary Ann Doane and Patricia Mellencamp, 67–82. Frederick, MD: University Publications of America, 1984.

Dryzek, John. "Legitimacy and Economy in Deliberative Democracy." *Political Theory* 29, no. 5 (October 2001): 651–69.

Edelman, Murray. *The Symbolic Uses of Politics*. Urbana: University of Illinois Press, 1965.

Eisenstein, Sergei. *Film Form: Essays in Film Theory*. New York: Harvest Books, 1995.

Eisenstein, Zillah. *Feminism and Sexual Equality: Crisis in Liberal America*. New York: Monthly Review Press, 1984.

Elsaesser, Thomas. "Tales of Sound and Fury: Observations of the Family Melodrama." In *Home Is Where the Heart Is: Melodrama and the Woman's Film*, ed. Christine Gledhill, 43–69. London: British Film Institute, 1987.

Emerson, Ralph Waldo. "Heroism." In *The Essential Writings of Ralph Waldo Emerson*, 225–35. New York: Modern Library, 2000.

———. "Self-Reliance." In *The Essential Writings of Ralph Waldo Emerson*, 132–53. New York: Modern Library, 2000.

Estlund, David. *Democratic Authority: A Philosophical Framework*. Princeton, NJ: Princeton University Press, 2008.

Euben, J. Peter. *The Tragedy of Political Theory: The Road Not Taken*. Princeton, NJ: Princeton University Press, 1990.

Faludi, Susan. *The Terror Dream: Fear and Fantasy in Post-9/11 America*. New York: Metropolitan, 2007.

Fassbinder, Rainer Werner. "Six Films by Douglas Sirk." In *Douglas Sirk*, ed. Jon Halliday and Laura Mulvey, 95–107. Edinburgh: Edinburgh Film Festival, 1972.

Feher, Michel. "Self-Appreciation; or, The Aspirations of Human Capital." *Public Culture* 21, no. 1 (2009): 21–41.

Fitzpatrick, Peter. "Enduring Freedom." *Theory and Event* 5, no. 4 (2001).

Foucault, Michel. *Birth of Biopolitics: Lectures at the Collège de France, 1978–1979*. Trans. Graham Burchell. New York: Picador, 2008.

———. *Security, Territory, Population: Lectures at the Collège de France, 1977–1978*. Trans. Graham Burchell. New York: Picador, 2007.

———. *"Society Must Be Defended": Lectures at the Collège de France, 1975–1976*. Trans. David Macey. New York: Picador, 2003.

———. "The Subject and Power." In Hubert Dreyfus and Paul Rabinow, *Michel Foucault: Beyond Structuralism and Hermeneutics*. Chicago: University of Chicago Press, 1982.

Frank, Thomas. *What's the Matter with Kansas?* New York: Metropolitan Books, 2004.

Freud, Sigmund. *The Ego and the Id*. Trans. James Strachey. New York: W. W. Norton, 1962.

———. *Group Psychology and Analysis of the Ego*. Trans. James Strachey. New York: W. W. Norton, 1990.

———. "Mourning and Melancholia." In *Collected Papers*, vol. 4, trans. Joan Riviere, 152–70. New York: Basic Books, 1959.

———. "On Narcissism: An Introduction." In *Collected Papers*, vol. 4, trans. Joan Riviere, 30–59. New York: Basic Books, 1959.

———. *An Outline of Psychoanalysis*. Trans. James Strachey. New York: W. W. Norton, 1973.

Frost, Laura. "Black Screens, Lost Bodies: The Cinematic Apparatus of 9/11 Horror." In *Horror after 9/11*, ed. Aviva Briefel and Sam Miller, 13–39. Austin: University of Texas Press, 2011.

Fukuyama, Francis. "The End of History." *The National Interest*, no. 16 (Summer 1989): 3–18.

Fuss, Diana. *Identification Papers: Readings on Psychoanalysis, Sexuality, and Culture*. New York: Routledge, 1995.

Gaines, Jane M. *Fire and Desire: Mixed-Race Movies in the Silent Era*. Chicago: University of Chicago Press, 2001.

———. "The Melos of Marxist Theory." In *The Hidden Foundation: Cinema and the Question of Class*, ed. David E. James and Rick Berg, 56–71. Minneapolis: University of Minnesota Press, 1996.

Garland, David. *Culture of Control: Crime and Social Order in Contemporary Society*. Chicago: University of Chicago Press, 2002.

Gerould, Daniel. "The Americanization of Melodrama." In *American Melodrama*, ed. Daniel Gerould, 7–29. New York: Performing Arts Journal Publication, 2001.

———. "Melodrama and Revolution." In *Melodrama: Stage, Picture, Screen*, ed. Jacky Bratton, Jim Cook, and Christine Gledhill, 185–98. London: British Film Institute, 1994.

Gerould, Daniel, and Julia Przybos. "Melodrama in the Soviet Theater 1917–1928: An Annotated Chronology." In *Melodrama*, ed. Daniel Gerould, 75–92. New York: New York Literary Forum, 1980.

Gibbs, Nancy. "If You Want to Humble an Empire." *Time*, September 14, 2001, 34–50.

Gilroy, Paul. *Postcolonial Melancholia*. New York: Columbia University Press, 2005.

Gledhill, Christine. *Home Is Where the Heart Is: Studies in Melodrama and the Woman's Film*. London: British Film Institute, 1987.

———. "The Melodramatic Field: An Investigation." In *Home Is Where the Heart Is: Studies in Melodrama and the Woman's Film*, 5–39. London: British Film Institute, 2002.

———. "Rethinking Genre." In *Reinventing Film Studies*, ed. Christine Gledhill and Linda Williams, 221–43. London: Arnold, 2000.

Gould, Deborah. *Moving Politics: Emotion and ACT UP's Fight against AIDS*. Chicago: University of Chicago Press, 2009.

Green-Simms, Lindsey. "Occult Melodrama: Spectral Affect and West African Video-Film." *Camera Obscura* 27, no. 2 (2012): 25–59.

Grimsted, David. "Melodrama as Echo of the Historically Voiceless." In *Anonymous Americans: Explorations in Nineteenth-Century Social History*, ed. Tamara Harevan, 80–98. Englewood Cliffs, NJ: Prentice-Hall, 1971.

———. *Melodrama Unveiled: American Theater and Culture, 1800–1850*. Berkeley: University of California Press, 1988.

Grusin, Richard. *Premediation: Affect and Mediality after 9/11*. New York: Palgrave Macmillan, 2010.

Guess, Raymond. *Politics and the Imagination*. Princeton, NJ: Princeton University Press, 2010.

Gunning, Tom. "The Cinema of Attraction: Early Film, Its Spectator and the Avant-Garde." *Wide Angle* 8, nos. 3–4 (Fall 1986): 63–70.

———. "The Horror of Opacity: The Melodrama of Sensation in the Plays of André de Lorde." In *Melodrama: Stage, Picture, Screen*, ed. Jacky Bratton, Jim Cook, and Christine Gledhill, 50–61. London: British Film Institute, 1994.

Gutterman, David. *Prophetic Politics: Christian Social Movements and American Democracy*. Ithaca, NY: Cornell University Press, 2006.

Habermas, Jürgen. *Between Facts and Norms*. Cambridge, MA: MIT Press, 1998.

———. *Legitimation Crisis*. Trans. Thomas McCarthy. Boston: Beacon Press, 1973.

Habermas, Jürgen, and William Rehg. "Constitutional Democracy: A Paradoxical Union of Contradictory Principles." *Political Theory* 29, no. 6 (Fall 2001): 766–81.

Hadley, Elaine. *Melodramatic Tactics: Theatricalized Dissent in the English Marketplace, 1800–1885*. Stanford, CA: Stanford University Press, 1995.

Halberstam, Judith. *The Queer Art of Failure*. Durham, NC: Duke University Press, 2011.

Hall, Stuart. *The Hard Road to Renewal: Thatcherism and Crisis of the Left*. London: Verso, 1988.

———. "The Neoliberal Revolution." *Cultural Studies* 25, no. 6 (November 2011): 705–28.

———. "The Problem of Ideology—Marxism without Guarantees." *Journal of Communication Inquiry* 10, no. 2 (June 1986): 28–44.

Halliday, Jon. "All That Heaven Allows." In *Douglas Sirk*, ed. Laura Mulvey and Jon Halliday, 59–66. Edinburgh: Edinburgh Film Festival, 1972.

Hanchard, Michael. *Party/Politics: New Horizons in Black Political Thought*. New York: Oxford University Press, 2006.

Hardt, Michael. "What Affects Are Good For." In *The Affective Turn*, ed. Patricia Clough, ix–xiii. Durham, NC: Duke University Press, 2007.

Hardt, Michael, and Antonio Negri. *Empire*. Cambridge, MA: Harvard University Press, 2001.

———. *Multitude*. Cambridge, MA: Harvard University Press, 2004.

Hauerwas, Stanley, and Frank Lentricchia, eds. "Dissent from the Homeland: Essays after September 11." Special issue, *South Atlantic Quarterly* 101, no. 2 (Spring 2002).

Hegel, G. W. F. *Outlines of the Philosophy of Right*. Trans. T. M. Knox. Oxford: Oxford University Press, 2008.

Heilman, Robert. *Tragedy and Melodrama: Versions of Experience*. Seattle: University of Washington Press, 1968.

Hesford, Wendy. *Spectacular Rhetorics: Human Rights Visions, Recognitions, Feminisms*. Durham, NC: Duke University Press, 2011.

Higgins, Scott. "Suspenseful Situations: Melodramatic Narrative and the Contemporary Action Film." *Cinema Journal* 47, no. 2 (2008): 74–96.

Hobbes, Thomas. *Leviathan; or, The Matter, Forme and Power of a Commonwealth Ecclesiasticall and Civil*. Ed. Michael Oakeshott. New York: Collier, 1968.

Honig, Bonnie. *Antigone, Interrupted*. Cambridge, UK: Cambridge University Press, 2013.

——. *Democracy and the Foreigner*. Princeton, NJ: Princeton University Press, 2001.

——. *Emergency Politics: Paradox, Law, Sovereignty*. Princeton, NJ: Princeton University Press, 2010.

Hunt, Lynn. *The Family Romance of the French Revolution*. Berkeley: University of California Press, 1993.

Huntington, Samuel. *The Clash of Civilizations and the Remaking of the World Order*. New York: Simon and Schuster, 1997.

Ignatieff, Michael. *Blood and Belonging: Journeys into the New Nationalism*. New York: Farrar, Strauss, Giroux, 1994.

——. "Getting Iraq Wrong." *New York Times Magazine*, August 5, 2007, 26–29.

——. "The Year of Living Dangerously: A Liberal Supporter of the War Looks Back." *New York Times Magazine*, March 14, 2004, 13–18.

Ivie, Robert. "The Rhetoric of Bush's War on Evil." *KB Journal* 1, no. 1 (Fall 2004).

Jameson, Fredric. "Realism and Utopia in *The Wire*." *Criticism* 52, nos. 3–4 (Summer / Fall 2010): 359–72.

Jenkins-Smith, Hank. "Rock and a Hard Place: Public Willingness to Trade Civil Rights and Liberties for Greater Security." *Politics and Policy* 37, no. 5 (October 2009): 1095–129.

Johannsen, Robert W., John M. Belohlavek, Thomas R. Hietala, Samuel J. Watson, Sam W. Haynes, and Robert E. May. *Manifest Destiny and Empire: American Antebellum Expansionism* (Walter Prescott Webb Memorial Lectures), ed. Sam W. Haynes and Christopher Morris. College Station: Texas A&M University Press, 1997.

Johnson, Cathryn, ed. *Legitimacy Processes in Organizations*. Boston: Elsevier, 2004.

Johnston, Steven. *Encountering Tragedy: Rousseau and the Project of Democratic Order*. Ithaca, NY: Cornell University Press, 1999.

——. *The Truth about Patriotism*. Durham, NC: Duke University Press, 2007.

Jost, John, and Brenda Major, eds. *The Psychology of Legitimacy: Emerging Perspectives on Ideology, Justice, and Intergroup Relations*. Cambridge, UK: Cambridge University Press, 2001.

Joyrich, Lynne. *Re-viewing Reception: Television, Gender, and Postmodern Culture*. Bloomington: Indiana University Press, 1996.

Kakoudaki, Despina. "Spectacles of History: Race Relations, Melodrama, and the Science Fiction / Disaster Film." *Camera Obscura* 17, no. 2 (2002): 109–53.

Kant, Immanuel. *Groundwork of the Metaphysics of Morals*. Trans. H. J. Paton. New York: Harper Torchbooks, 1956.

Kantorowitz, Ernst. *The King's Two Bodies: A Study in Medieval Political Theology*. Princeton, NJ: Princeton University Press, 1997.

Kaplan, E. Ann. "Ann Kaplan Replies to Linda Williams's 'Something Else Besides a Mother: *Stella Dallas* and the Maternal Melodrama' (*Cinema Journal*, Fall 1984)." *Cinema Journal* 24, no. 2 (Winter 1985): 40–43.

——. *Motherhood and Representation*. New York: Routledge, 1992.

Katznelson, Ira. *Fear Itself: The New Deal and the Origins of Our Time*. New York: Liveright, 2013.

Kaufman-Osborn, Timothy. "We Are All Torturers Now: Accountability after Abu Ghraib." *Theory and Event* 11, no. 2 (2008).

Keeling, Kara. *The Witch's Flight: The Cinematic, the Black Femme, and the Image of Common Sense*. Durham, NC: Duke University Press, 2007.

Kernell, Samuel. *Going Public*. Washington, DC: CQ Press, 2006.

Kleinhans, Chuck. "Melodrama and the Family under Capitalism." In *Imitations of Life: A Reader on Film and Television Melodrama*, ed. Marcia Landy, 197–204. Detroit, MI: Wayne State University Press, 1991.

Kleinman, Arthur, Veena Das, and Margaret Lock, eds. *Social Suffering*. Berkeley: University of California Press, 1997.

Klinger, Barbara. *Melodrama and Meaning: History, Culture, and the Films of Douglas Sirk*. Bloomington: Indiana University Press, 1994.

Krause, Sharon. *Civil Passions: Moral Sentiment and Democratic Deliberation*. Princeton, NJ: Princeton University Press, 2008.

———. "On Non-sovereign Responsibility: Agency, Inequality and Democratic Citizenship." Paper presented at the annual meeting of the Association for Political Theory, University of Notre Dame, Notre Dame, Indiana, October 14, 2011.

Lacan, Jacques. "The Mirror State as Formative of the *I* Function as Revealed in Psychoanalytic Experience." In *Ecrits*, trans. Bruce Fink, 75–82. New York: W. W. Norton, 2000.

Landy, Marcia, ed. *Imitations of Life: A Reader on Film and Television Melodrama*. Detroit, MI: Wayne State University Press, 1991.

———. "Introduction." In *Imitations of Life: A Reader on Film and Television Melodrama*, ed. Marcia Landy, 13–30. Detroit, MI: Wayne State University Press, 1991.

Lang, Robert. *American Film Melodrama: Griffith, Vidor, Minnelli*. Princeton, NJ: Princeton University Press, 1989.

Laplanche, Jean. *Life and Death in Psychoanalysis*. Baltimore, MD: Johns Hopkins University Press, 1985.

Leach, Neil. "9/11." *diacritics* 33, nos. 3–4 (Winter 2003): 75–92.

Lehning, James. *The Melodramatic Thread: Spectacle and Political Culture in Modern France*. Bloomington: Indiana University Press, 2007.

Levine, Lawrence. "Foreword." In *Melodrama Unveiled: American Theater and Culture, 1800–1850*, ed. David Grimsted, xi–xiv. Berkeley: University of California Press, 1988.

Lipset, Seymour Martin. *Political Man: The Social Base of Politics*. Baltimore, MD: Johns Hopkins University Press, 1981.

Locke, John. *The Second Treatise of Government*. New York: Macmillan, 1952.

Loren, Scott, and Jörg Metelmann. *Irritation of Life: The Subversive Melodrama of Michael Haneke, David Lynch and Lars Von Trier*. Marburg, Germany: Shüren, 2013.

Löwith, Karl. *Max Weber and Karl Marx*. London: Routledge, 1993.

Lukes, Steven. "The Morals of the Manifesto." In *The Communist Manifesto by Karl Marx and Friedrich Engels*, ed. Jeffrey Isaac, 119–43. New Haven, CT: Yale University Press, 2012.

Lynch, Marc. "Al-Qaeda's Media Strategies." *The National Interest*, Spring 2006, 50–56.

Lyotard, Jean-François. *The Postmodern Condition: A Report on Knowledge*. Manchester, UK: Manchester University Press, 1984.

MacKinnon, Catherine. *Toward a Feminist Theory of the State*. Cambridge, MA: Harvard University Press, 1991.

MacPherson, C. B. *The Political Theory of Possessive Individualism: Hobbes to Locke*. Oxford: Oxford University Press, 2011.

Mahmood, Saba. *The Politics of Piety: Islamic Revival and the Feminist Subject*. Princeton, NJ: Princeton University Press, 2005.

Mahmood, Saba, and Charles Hirschkind. "Feminism, the Taliban, and Politics of Counter-insurgency." *Anthropological Quarterly* 75, no. 2 (Spring 2002): 339–54.

Mamdani, Mahmood. *Good Muslim, Bad Muslim: America, the Cold War, and the Roots of Terror*. New York: Random House, 2005.

Manin, Bernard. "On Legitimacy and Political Deliberation." Trans. Elly Stein and Jane Mansbridge. *Political Theory* 15, no. 3 (August 1987): 338–68.

Manovich, Lev. *The Language of New Media*. Cambridge, MA: MIT Press: 2002.

Marcuse, Herbert. *One-Dimensional Man: Studies in the Ideology of Advanced Industrial Society*. Boston: Beacon Press, 1991.

Markell, Patchen. *Bound by Recognition*. Princeton, NJ: Princeton University Press, 2003.

Marx, Karl. *The 18th Brumaire of Louis Bonaparte*. In *The Marx-Engels Reader*, ed. Robert Tucker, 594–617. New York: W. W. Norton, 1978.

———. "On the Jewish Question." In *The Marx-Engels Reader*, ed. Robert Tucker, 26–52. New York: W. W. Norton, 1978.

Marx, Karl, and Friedrich Engels. *Manifesto of the Communist Party*. In *The Marx-Engels Reader*, ed. Robert Tucker, 469–500. New York: W. W. Norton, 1978.

Mason, Jeffrey. *Melodrama and the Myth of America*. Bloomington: Indiana University Press, 1993.

Massumi, Brian. *Parables of the Virtual: Movement, Affect, Sensation*. Durham, NC: Duke University Press, 2002.

———. "Potential Politics and the Primacy of Pre-emption." *Theory and Event* 10, no. 2 (Spring 2007).

Mbembe, Achille, and Janet Roitman. "Figures of the Subject in Times of Crisis." *Public Culture* 7 (1995): 323–52.

McAlister, Melani. *Epic Encounters: Culture, Media, and U.S. Interests in the Middle East since 1945*. Berkeley: University of California Press, 2005.

———. "Prophecy, Politics, and the Popular: The Left Behind Series and Christian Fundamentalism's New World Order." *The South Atlantic Quarterly* 102, no. 4 (Fall 2003): 773–98.

McConachie, Bruce. *Melodramatic Formations: American Theater and Society, 1820–1870.* Iowa City: University of Iowa Press, 1992.

McHugh, Kathleen, and Nancy Abelmann, eds. *South Korean Golden Age Melodrama: Gender, Genre, and National Cinema.* Detroit, MI: Wayne State University Press, 2005.

McReynolds, Louise, and Joan Neuberger, eds. *Imitations of Life: Two Centuries of Melodrama in Russia.* Durham, NC: Duke University Press, 2002.

Mehta, Uday. *Liberalism and Empire: A Study in Nineteenth-Century British Liberal Thought.* Chicago: University of Chicago Press, 1999.

Meister, Robert. *After Evil: A Politics of Human Rights.* New York: Columbia University Press, 2010.

Melamed, Jodi. *Represent and Destroy: Rationalizing Violence in the New Racial Capitalism.* Minneapolis: University of Minnesota Press, 2011.

———. "The Spirit of Neoliberalism: From Racial Liberalism to Neoliberal Multiculturalism." *Social Text* 24, no. 4 (Winter 2006): 1–24.

Melley, Timothy. *Empire of Conspiracy: The Culture of Paranoia in Postwar America.* Ithaca, NY: Cornell University Press, 2000.

Mercer, John, and Martin Shingler. *Melodrama: Genre, Style, Sensibility.* New York: Wallflower Press, 2004.

Mill, John Stuart. *On Liberty and the Subjection of Women.* New York: Penguin, 2006.

Monahan, Brian. *The Shock of the News: Media Coverage and the Making of 9/11.* New York: New York University Press, 2010.

Mondak, Jeffery J. "Examining the Terror Exception: Terrorism and Commitments to Civil Liberties." *Public Opinion Quarterly* 76, no. 2 (January 2012): 193–213.

Morone, James A. *Hellfire Nation: The Politics of Sin in American History.* New Haven, CT: Yale University Press, 2003.

Mueller, John, and Mark Stewart. "The Terrorism Delusion: America's Overwrought Response to September 11." *International Security* 37, no. 1 (Summer 2012): 81–110.

Mulvey, Laura. "Notes on Sirk and Melodrama." In *Home Is Where the Heart Is: Melodrama and the Woman's Film,* ed. Christine Gledhill, 75–79. London: British Film Institute, 1987.

———. *Visual and Other Pleasures.* New York: Palgrave MacMillan, 2009.

Murphy, Andrew. *Prodigal Nation: Moral Decline and Divine Punishment from New England to 9/11.* New York: Oxford University Press, 2009.

Neale, Steve. "Melo Talk: On the Meaning and Use of the Term 'Melodrama' in the American Trade Press." *The Velvet Light Trap,* no. 32 (1993): 66–89.

Nealon, Christopher. "Reading on the Left." *Representations* 108 (2009): 22–50.

Nealon, Jeffrey. *Foucault beyond Foucault: Power and Its Intensifications since 1984.* Stanford, CA: Stanford University Press, 2008.

Negra, Diane, and Yvonne Tasker. "Neoliberal Frames and Genres of Inequality: Recession-Era Chick Flicks and Male-Centered Corporate Melodrama." *European Journal of Cultural Studies* 16, no. 3 (June 2013): 344–61.

Nelson, Dana. *National Manhood: Capitalist Citizenship and the Imagined Fraternity of White Men*. Durham, NC: Duke University Press, 1998.

Ngai, Sianne. *Ugly Feelings*. Cambridge, MA: Harvard University Press, 2008.

Nietzsche, Friedrich. *The Birth of Tragedy and the Case of Wagner*. Trans. Walter Kauffman. New York: Vintage, 1967.

———. *On the Genealogy of Morality*. Ed. Keith Ansell Pearson and trans. Carol Diethe. Cambridge, UK: Cambridge University Press, 1994.

———. *On the Genealogy of Morals and Ecce Homo*. Trans. Walter Kauffman. New York: Vintage, 1989.

———. "Schopenhauer as Educator." In *Untimely Meditations*, trans. R. J. Hollingdale, 125–94. Cambridge, UK: Cambridge University Press, 1997.

———. *Twilight of the Idols*. In *Nietzsche: The Antichrist, Ecce Homo, Twilight of the Idols; And Other Writings*, trans. Judith Norman, 153–230. Cambridge, UK: Cambridge University Press, 2005.

———. *The Will to Power*. Trans. Walter Kaufmann and R. J. Hollingdale. New York: Vintage, 1968.

Nodier, Charles. "Introduction to Pixérécourt's *Theatre Choisi*." In Guilbert de Pixérécourt, *Pixérécourt: Four Melodramas*, trans. and ed. Daniel Gerould and Marvin Carlson, 310–18. New York: Martin Segal Center Publications, 2002.

Nowell-Smith, Geoffrey. "Minnelli and Melodrama." In *Imitations of Life: A Reader of Film and Melodrama*, ed. Marcia Landy, 268–74. Detroit, MI: Wayne State University Press, 1991.

Okin, Susan. *Justice, Gender and Equality*. Boston: Basic Books, 1991.

Oliverio, Annamarie. *The State of Terror*. New York: SUNY Press, 1998.

Packer, George. "The Political War." *New Yorker*, September 27, 2004.

Panagia, Davide. *The Political Life of Sensation*. Durham, NC: Duke University Press, 2009.

Passavant, Paul. "The Strong Neoliberal State: Crime, Consumption, Governance." *Theory and Event* 8, no. 3 (2005).

Pateman, Carole. *The Sexual Contract*. Stanford, CA: Stanford University Press, 1988.

Pederson, Vibeke. "In Search of Monsters to Destroy: The American Liberal Security Paradox and a Republican Way Out." *International Relations* 17 (June 2003): 213–32.

Pham, M. H. "The Right to Fashion in an Age of Terrorism." *Signs* 36, no. 2 (Winter 2011): 385–410.

Pixérécourt, Guilbert de. *Adeline, the Victim of Seduction: A Melo-dramatic Serious Drama in Three Acts*. Trans. John Howard Payne. London: Theater Royal, Drury Lane, 1822.

———. *Coelina; or, The Child of Mystery*. In *Guilbert de Pixérécourt: French Melodrama in the Early Nineteenth Century*, trans. J. Paul Marcoux, 55–96. New York: Pater Lang, 1992.

———. "Melodrama." In *Guilbert Pixérécourt: Four Melodramas*, trans. and ed. Marvin Carlson and Daniel Gerould, 310–14. New York: Martin E. Segal Theater Center, 2002.

Puar, Jasbir. *Terrorist Assemblages: Homonationalism in Queer Times*. Durham, NC: Duke University Press, 2007.

Rahill, Frank. *The World of Melodrama*. University Park: Penn State University Press, 1967.

Rancière, Jacques. *The Emancipated Spectator*. London: Verso, 2009.

Rawls, John. *The Law of Peoples*. Cambridge, MA: Harvard University Press, 1999.

———. *Political Liberalism*. New York: Columbia University Press, 1993.

———. *A Theory of Justice*. Cambridge, MA: Harvard University Press, 1999.

Reddy, Chandan. *Freedom with Violence: Race, Sexuality, and the US State*. Durham, NC: Duke University Press, 2011.

Redfield, Marc. *The Rhetoric of Terror: Reflections on 9/11 and the War on Terror*. New York: Fordham University Press, 2009.

———. "Virtual Trauma: The Idiom of 9/11." *diacritics* 37, no. 1 (Spring 2007): 55–80.

Retort. "Afflicted Powers: The State, the Spectacle, and September 11." *New Left Review* 27 (May–June 2004).

Richardson, Niall. "Poison in the Sirkian System: The Political Agenda of Todd Haynes's 'Far from Heaven.'" *Scope: An Online Journal of Film Studies*, no. 6 (October 2006).

Ricks, Thomas. *Fiasco: The American Military Adventure in Iraq*. New York: Penguin, 2006.

Rogin, Michael. *Ronald Reagan the Movie: And Other Episodes in Political Demonology*. Berkeley: University of California Press, 1988.

Rorty, Amelie. *Essays on Aristotle's Ethics*. Princeton, NJ: Princeton University Press, 1992.

Rosanvallon, Pierre. *Democratic Legitimacy: Impartiality, Reflexivity, Proximity*. Princeton, NJ: Princeton University Press, 2011.

Rousseau, Jean-Jacques. "Letter to M. Burney and Fragments of Observations on Gluck's 'Alceste.'" In *Essay on the Origin of Languages and Writings Related to Music*, trans. and ed. John T. Scott, 486–505. Hanover, NH: Dartmouth College Press, 1998.

———. *The Social Contract*. Trans. G. D. H. Cole. New York: Penguin Classics, 1968.

Sadlier, Darlene, ed. *Latin American Melodrama: Passion, Pathos, and Entertainment*. Urbana: University of Illinois Press, 2009.

Sarat, Austin, ed. *Dissent in Dangerous Times*. Ann Arbor: University of Michigan Press, 2005.

Sassen, Saskia. *Cities in World Economy*. Thousand Oaks, CA: Sage, 2011.

———. *Sociology of Globalization*. New York: W. W. Norton, 2007.

Scherer, Matthew. *Beyond Church and State: Democracy, Secularism, and Conversion*. Cambridge, UK: Cambridge University Press, 2013.

Schmitt, Carl. *The Concept of the Political*. Trans. George Schwab. Chicago: University of Chicago Press, 1996.

———. *Political Theology: Four Concepts on the Concept of Sovereignty*. Trans. George Schwab. Chicago: University of Chicago Press, 2006.

Schudson, Michael. "The Anarchy of Events and the Anxiety of Story Telling." *Political Communication* 24 (2007): 253–57.

———. *The Power of News*. Cambridge, MA: Harvard University Press, 1996.

Scott, David. *Conscripts of Modernity: The Tragedy of Colonial Enlightenment*. Durham, NC: Duke University Press, 2004.

Seeger, Matthew, Steven Venette, Robert Ulmer, and Timothy Sellnow. "Media Use, Information Seeking, and Reported Needs in Post-crisis Contexts." In *Communication and Terrorism: Public and Media Reponses to 9/11*, ed. Bradley Greenberg, 53–63. Cresskill, NJ: Hampton Press, 2002.

Sennett, Richard. *The Fall of Public Man*. New York: W. W. Norton, 1992.

Shohat, Ella, Brent Hayes Edwards, Stefano Harney, Randy Martin, Timothy Mitchell, and Fred Moten, eds. "9-11—A Public Emergency?" Special issue, *Social Text* no. 72 (Fall 2002).

Shulman, George. "American Political Culture, Prophetic Narration, and Toni Morrison's *Beloved*." *Political Theory* 24, no. 2 (May 1996): 295–314.

———. *American Prophecy: Race and Redemption in American Political Culture*. Minneapolis: University of Minnesota Press, 2008.

Silverman, Kaja. *Flesh of My Flesh*. Stanford, CA: Stanford University Press, 2009.

———. *The Threshold of the Visible World*. New York: Routledge, 1995.

Simpson, David. *9/11: Culture of Commemoration*. Chicago: University of Chicago Press, 2005.

Singer, Ben. *Melodrama and Modernity: Early Cinema and Its Contexts*. New York: Columbia University Press, 2002.

Siomopoulos, Anna. "Political Theory and Melodrama Studies." *Camera Obscura* 21, no. 2 (2006): 179–83.

Skvirsky, Salomé Aguilera. "The Price of Heaven: Remaking Politics in *All That Heaven Allows*, *Ali*, *Fear Eats the Soul*, and *Far from Heaven*." *Cinema Journal* 47, no. 3 (2008): 90–121.

Smith, Neil. "Contours of a Spatialized Politics." *Social Text*, no. 33 (1992): 54–81.

Spiegelman, Art. *In the Shadow of No Towers*. New York: Hill and Wang, 2005.

Spigel, Lynn. *Welcome to the Dreamhouse: Popular Media and Postwar Suburbs*. Durham, NC: Duke University Press, 2001.

Staiger, Janet. "Introduction: Political Emotions and Public Feelings." In *Political Emotions*, ed. Janet Staiger, Ann Cvetcovich, and Ann Reynolds, 1–17. New York: Routledge, 2010.

Stam, Robert. "Television News and Its Spectator," In *Regarding Television*, ed. Ann Kaplan, 23–43. Frederick, MD: American Film Institute, 1983.

Stern, Michael. "Patterns of Power and Potency, Repression and Violence: An Introduction to the Study of Douglas Sirk's Films of the 1950s." *The Velvet Light Trap* 16 (Fall 1976): 1–21.

Stow, Simon. "Pericles at Gettysburg and Ground Zero: Tragedy, Patriotism, and Public Mourning." *American Political Science Review* 101, no. 2 (May 2007): 195–208.

Stowe, Harriet Beecher. *Uncle Tom's Cabin*. Annotated ed. Ed. Henry Louis Gates Jr. New York: W. W. Norton, 2006.

Stuart, Douglas. *Creating the National Security State: A History of the Law That Changed America*. Princeton, NJ: Princeton University Press, 2008.

Sypher, Wylie. "The Aesthetic of Revolution: The Marxist Melodrama." *Kenyon Review* 10, no. 3 (Summer 1948): 431–44.

Theim, Annika. *Unbecoming Subjects*. New York: Fordham University Press, 2008.

Thoreau, Henry David. *Civil Disobedience and Other Essays*. New York: Dover, 1993.

Thrall, Trevor, and Jane Cramer, eds. *American Foreign Policy and the Politics of Fear: Threat Inflation since 9/11*. London: Routledge, 2011.

Torres, Sasha. "Televising Guantanamo." In *Political Emotions*, ed. Janet Staiger, Ann Cvetcovich, and Ann Reynolds, 45–65. New York: Routledge, 2010.

Tulis, Jeffrey. *The Rhetorical Presidency*. Princeton, NJ: Princeton University Press, 1988.

Unger, Roberto Mangabiera. *The Left Alternative*. London: Verso, 2009.

Vardac, Nicholas. *From Stage to Screen: Theatrical Method from Garrick to Griffith*. Cambridge, MA: Harvard University Press, 1949.

Vattimo, Gianni. *The End of Modernity: Nihilism and Hermeneutics in Post-modern Culture*. Baltimore, MD: Johns Hopkins University Press, 1991.

Vicinus, Martha. "Helpless and Unfriended: Nineteenth-Century Domestic Melodrama." *New Literary History* 13, no. 1 (Autumn 1991): 127–43.

Volpp, Leti. "The Citizen and the Terrorist." *UCLA Law Review* 49 (2002): 1575–600.

Waldman, Amy. *The Submission*. New York: Picador, 2011.

Waquant, Loïc. *Punishing the Poor: The Neoliberal Government of Social Insecurity*. Durham, NC: Duke University Press, 2009.

Weber, Max. *Economy and Society: An Outline of Interpretive Sociology*. Trans. and ed. Guenther Roth and Claus Wittich. Berkeley: University of California Press, 1978.

———. "Politics as a Vocation." In *On Max Weber: Essays in Sociology*. Trans. and ed. H. H. Gerth and C. Wright Mills, 77–128. Oxford: Oxford University Press, 1958.

Wedeen, Lisa. *Ambiguities of Domination: Politics, Rhetoric, and Symbols in Contemporary Syria*. Chicago: University of Chicago Press, 1999.

Whissel, Kristen. "The Little American." In *America First: Naming the Nation in US Film*, ed. Mandy Merck, 23–43. London: Routledge, 2007.

White, Hayden. "Anomalies of Genre." *New Literary History* 34, no. 3 (Summer 2003): 597–615.

Williams, Linda. "Film Bodies: Gender, Genre and Excess." *Film Quarterly* 44, no. 4 (1991): 2–13.

———. "Mega-melodrama: Vertical and Horizontal Suspensions of the Classical." *Modern Drama* 55, no. 4 (Winter 2012): 523–43.

———. "Melodrama Revised." In *Refiguring Film Genres*, ed. Nick Browne, 42–88. Berkeley: University of California Press, 1998.

———. *Playing the Race Card: Melodramas of Black and White from Uncle Tom to O. J. Simpson*. Princeton, NJ: Princeton University Press, 2001.

———. "'Something Else Besides a Mother': *Stella Dallas* and the Maternal Melodrama." In *Imitations of Life: A Reader on Film and Television Melodrama*, ed. Marcia Landy, 307–30. Detroit, MI: Wayne State University Press, 1991.

Williams, Raymond. "Social Environment and Theatrical Environment: The Case of English Naturalism." In *English Drama: Forms and Development*, ed. Marie Axton and Raymond Williams, 203–23. Cambridge, UK: Cambridge University Press, 1977.

———. "Structures of Feeling," In *Marxism and Literature*, 128–35. Oxford: Oxford University Press, 1978.

Wills, Gary. *Bomb Power: The Modern Presidency and the National Security State*. New York: Penguin, 2010.

Wingrove, Elizabeth. *Rousseau's Republican Romance*. Princeton, NJ: Princeton University Press, 2000.

Wolin, Sheldon. *Democracy Incorporated: Managed Democracy and the Specter of Inverted Totalitarianism*. Princeton, NJ: Princeton University Press, 2008.

———. *Politics and Vision*. Princeton, NJ: Princeton University Press, 2004.

———. *The Presence of Past: Essays on the State and the Constitution*. Baltimore, MD: Johns Hopkins University Press, 1989.

Woodward, Bob. *Plan of Attack: The Definitive Account of the Decision to Invade Iraq*. New York: Simon and Schuster, 2004.

Young, Iris Marion. "The Logic of Masculinist Protection: Reflections on the Current Security State." *Signs: A Journal of Women in Culture and Society* 29, no. 1 (Fall 2003): 1–25.

Zerilli, Linda. *Feminism and the Abyss of Freedom*. Chicago: University of Chicago Press, 2005.

Žižek, Slavoj. "Have Michael Hardt and Antonio Negri Rewritten the Communist Manifesto for the Twenty-First Century?" *Rethinking Marxism* 13, nos. 3–4 (2001): 190–99.

———. *Iraq: The Borrowed Kettle*. New York: Verso, 2004.

# INDEX

NOTE: Page numbers followed by *f* indicate a figure.

anti-immigration discourse, 17, 18–19, 139, 264n38
anti-Islamic/Muslim/Arab discourse, 58–59, 126, 272n60
Arendt, Hannah, 111, 173, 229
Aristotle, 35, 267n12
Ashcroft, John, 126, 262n23
associative montage, 53–54, 272n55
Authorization for the Use of Military Force against Terrorists (AUMF), 110

Baker, James, 40–43, 60
Baldwin, James, 84–85
Balibar, Étienne, 170
Bauman, Zygmunt, 173–74
Benjamin, Walter, 24, 29, 205–9, 297n9
Bennett, Jill, 201–2
Bercovitch, Sacvan, 82
Berlant, Lauren, 259n2; on crisis ordinariness, 189–90; on the impasse, 17–18, 264nn33–34; on juxtapolitical spaces, 237–39; on spectacle of injury, 34; on state emotion, 131–32, 286n51, 286n55; on *Uncle Tom's Cabin*, 277n69; on the vernacular of the viscera, 122; on women's weepies, 230–31, 237, 301n13, 303n24
Bibring, Edward, 289n26
bin Laden, Osama: killing of, 164, 194–95, 250–52, 304n43; as melodramatist, 64, 273nn71–72; personification of villainy in, 53–55, 164
*The Birth of a Nation*, 2, 10, 84–87
*The Birth of Tragedy* (Nietzsche), 155
Borch-Jacobsen, Mikkel, 197
border walls, 18–19, 264n38
Boucicault, Dion, 78–79
Brecht, Bertolt, 206–7
Brennan, Teresa, 160
Brennan, Timothy, 220
British melodrama, 275n30
*Brokeback Mountain*, 10
Brooks, Peter, 8, 33, 284n40; on evil in melodrama, 32, 220; on making the

ordinary extraordinary, 103; on melodrama's modernization, 273n2; on the melodramatic body, 44; on melodramatic characters, 188; on revolutionary context of melodrama, 72–73, 74, 215
Brown, Wendy, 14; on civilizing discourse, 284n34; on the failure of the liberal individual, 173; on heroic identification with the state, 186, 295n33; on left melancholy, 207–9; on legitimacy of state power, 193; on proliferation of border walls, 18–19, 264n38; on wounded attachments, 38, 269n23
Buckley, Matthew, 274n4
Bush, George H. W., 294n24
Bush, George W., 4–7, 262n16; as action figure toy, 247; affective intensity of, 122, 288n20; as authoritative voice of the U.S., 57–58, 272n60; blurred distinction between war and peace of, 299n45; "Mission Accomplished" performance of, 30, 188–89, 200–201, 244–55, 294n24; performance of masculine heroism by, 245–50; public support for, 110, 126, 280n1, 291n1, 292n3, 294n22; speech at the Republican National Convention (2004) of, 128–30, 285n47; speeches on 9/11 of, 55–60, 66–67, 288n20; speech on "Freedom at War with Fear" of, 119–31, 133, 162, 288n20; speech on war in Afghanistan (October 2001) of, 4–6, 10; use of the Gettysburg Address by, 260n7. *See also* post-9/11 era
Butler, Judith: on individual exposure to violence, 12; on interdependence, 173, 197, 201–2, 291n51; on the losses of 9/11, 11–12, 262n20; on suffering and redress, 59, 120
Byars, Jackie, 243, 302n17

*Capital* (Marx), 213
capitalism, 7, 35–36, 213–15, 275n29

Cassetti, Francesco, 38
Catholic Church, 72–73, 275n18
Cawelti, John, 73, 84, 275n29
Central Intelligence Agency (CIA), 93
Checkers speech, 100–102
Cheney, Dick, 13
Chion, Michel, 41
Chomsky, Noam, 21–22
citizenship, 7–8, 25, 87, 260n8; America's
    conventional moral vision of, 73, 76–77,
    87; Bush's instructions on, 130–31; as
    consumers, 189; felt legitimacy and,
    134–37; melodramatic indicators of, 6,
    260n7; of Reagan's depoliticized
    neoliberal heroes, 105–7; as spectator-
    ship, 278n75; unified suffering and
    victimization in, 4–5, 34, 136–37, 260n8,
    270n36
Citizens United decision, 195
civic nationalism, 58
Civil Disobedience (Thoreau), 84
Civil Passions (Krause), 134
clash of civilizations thesis, 23–24
Clinton, Hillary Rodham, 48, 59
close-up, 43–45, 288n20
Coelina, ou l'enfant du mystère (Pixéré-
    court), 26, 70–73, 76–77, 80
cold war era, 3, 9, 64, 88–109, 278nn79–80;
    executive-branch power in, 98, 279n94;
    good-evil binary of, 29n93, 88, 89,
    95–100, 107; Nixon's Checkers speech,
    100–102; Reagan's neoliberal heroes in,
    102–7; Soviet demise in, 107–9; state
    power in, 98–99, 278nn79–80; Truman
    Doctrine, 89–95, 98; U.S. global power
    in, 89
communism, 7; promises of freedom from,
    9; Soviet demise and, 107–9; Truman
    Doctrine on, 89–95, 98; U.S. demoniza-
    tion of, 99–100. See also cold war era
The Communist Manifesto (Marx and
    Engels), 29–30, 205–6, 209–16, 222–23,
    239, 297n15; agency of heroic victims in,
    221–22; as lost object of melancholy,

209–10, 218, 221, 223; melodramatic
    narrative form of, 210–16; open-ended
    vision of the future in, 205–6, 222;
    victim-heroes of, 212–15; villainy of
    capital and capitalists in, 213–15
Connolly, William E., 169–70, 301n11
countermelodrama: left melodrama as,
    204, 206; of Three Kings, 141–48
Couric, Katie, 288n21
cowardice, 57–59

Daly, Augustin, 81–82
Dark Victory, 231
Dean, Jodi, 97, 185, 279n93
debilitated agency, 133, 140, 226; heroic
    identification with state power and,
    189–95; orgies of feeling and, 151–63,
    176–77, 288n15, 288nn20–22, 289n26; in
    women's weepies, 231–33, 237, 239, 250.
    See also unfreedom
Declaration of Independence, 170
Declaration of the Rights of Man and of the
    Citizen, 76
Deleuze, Gilles, 9
deliberative legitimacy, 110, 114–15, 281n4.
    See also legitimacy
demonization, 99–100
depoliticization: of the Iraq War, 126–28;
    in legitimation of the war on terror, 111,
    113, 127–31; of Reagan's neoliberal
    heroes, 105–7
Derrida, Jacques, 50, 64, 273n70
distanciation, 206–7
domestic melodrama. See women's
    weepies
domino theory, 89–95
drama (as term), 34, 69

economies of affect, 285n50
Edelman, Murray, 193
18th Brumaire of Louis Bonaparte (Marx),
    239
Eisenhower, Dwight D., 95–100, 107
Eisenstein, Sergei, 53–54, 272n55

Heilman, Robert, 22

helplessness. *See* unfreedom

heroes. *See* victim-heroes

heroic identification with state power, 180–202, 293nn5–6; contemporary motivations for, 189–95; desire for mastery in, 181–82, 186–201; electoral accountability and, 192–93; Freud on process of, 183–84, 196, 198–99, 296n40, 296n43; interdependence and, 195–97, 201–2; patriotism and trust in, 180, 185–87, 195–96, 291n1, 292n3; weakening of, 200–201, 243

historical development of melodrama, 7–8, 25–27, 65–109; American cultural articulations of, 26, 68, 77–87, 277n56; basis in liberalism of, 68–69, 75–77, 275nn29–30; Eisenhower's good-evil binary in, 29n93, 95–100, 107; French origins of, 26, 34, 67–78, 256n11, 274n4; Fukuyama's "End of History" in, 107–9; location of moral law in Man in, 72–73, 81; Nixon's Checkers speech, 100–102; post–World War II political discourse in, 88–109; Reagan's ordinary neoliberal heroes in, 102–7; rise of liberalism and, 68, 75–77; shifting and modernization in, 68, 273n2; televisual spectacle in, 26–27, 88–89, 95–96, 279n90; Truman Doctrine/domino theory in, 89–95, 98

Hobbes, Thomas, 112

homeland security. *See* security; U.S. Department of Homeland Security

*Homo Sacer* (Agamben), 216–19

Honig, Bonnie, 13, 254, 305n48

Hudson, Rock, 232, 233*f*, 236*f*, 238–39, 243. See also *All That Heaven Allows*

Hunt, Lynn, 69–70, 72–73, 274n9

Huntington, Samuel, 23–24

Hussein, Saddam, 127, 135

identification: Freud on the process of, 183–84, 196, 198–99, 201, 293n12, 296n40, 296n43; with state power,

180–202, 296n39; with victims, 34–35, 43–46, 149–53, 166, 288nn20–22

Ignatieff, Michael, 126–27

*Imitation of Life*, 232

immigration. *See* anti-immigration discourse

impasse (genre), 6, 17–18, 264nn33–34

individualism/individual sovereignty, 8–14, 37, 152–53; deterioration under globalization of, 226; of the enlightened political subject, 170–71, 191; expectations of freedom in, 8–14, 34, 36–37, 122–23, 149–50, 152–53, 170–71, 181, 189–92; failure under neoliberalism of, 172–77, 194, 199; heroic identification with state power in, 181–202, 293nn5–6; vs. interdependence, 173–75, 195–97, 201–2, 291n51, 291n54; liberalism's fostering of, 68, 75, 77–84, 168–71, 235–39, 290nn45–46; 9/11's challenge to, 175–79; ontological narcissism of, 169–70, 175–78, 290n43; orgies of feeling and, 152–53, 175–79; waning (unfreedom) of, 14–20, 151–52, 187–95. *See also* debilitated agency; freedom; self-reliance

infamy, use as term, 45–46, 65, 271n41

injury, 38, 52–53, 60, 151–52; link to freedom of, 56–57; in melodramas of failure, 30, 252–53, 304n44; spectacle of, 34; wounded attachment to, 38, 49, 269n23

interdependence, 173–75, 195–97, 201–2, 291n51, 291n54

Iraq War, 10–11; Abu Ghraib torture of, 137–38, 200–201, 253; affective fact of threat in, 135; depoliticization of, 126–27, 126–28; instability of felt legitimacy of, 137–38, 286–87nn61–63; left melodrama's responses to, 217–21; "Mission Accomplished" narrative of, 30, 188–89, 200–201, 244–55, 294n24; as oedipal tragedy, 294n24; violence and terror of, 190, 248–49

Islamophobia. *See* anti-Islamic/Muslim/ Arab discourse

Marshall Plan, 93

Marx, Karl, 204–6, 211; on failure and transformation, 230, 239–42, 303n27; on legitimating juridical procedures, 113; on liberal politics, 87; on material constraints of freedom, 172; on melancholy, 222; melodramatic tropes used by, 212–13, 298n29; trust in dialectics of, 240. See also *The Communist Manifesto*

Marxism: left melodrama in, 204–6, 212–13, 298n29, 301n14; revolutionary desire of, 29–30, 214–15. See also *The Communist Manifesto*

Massumi, Brian, 135, 283n22

Matthews, Chris, 245

McAlister, Melani, 45, 48, 58–59

McConachie, Bruce, 78, 276n52

media. *See* news media

Melamed, Jodi, 45, 59

melancholy: Freud on the lost object of, 206, 208, 209, 297n13; in leftist political theory, 29–30, 205–9, 220–24, 297n9

Melley, Timothy, 160

melodrama: action forms of, 24, 37, 63, 266n52; affective pull of, 133, 215; basis in liberalism of, 68–69, 75–77, 275nn29–30; challenges to unfreedom in, 19–20, 180, 226–27; conventional moral vision of, 73, 76–77, 87; countermelodramatic challenges of legitimacy and, 141–48; gender and, 24, 82, 268n21; genre conventions of, 2, 4–6, 266n1; historical trajectory of, 7–8, 65–109; innocence of the self in, 165; interruption of political resignation in, 254–57; moral legibility of, 8; origin as term of, 34, 69; otherness of evil in, 22–24, 83; pathos and tragedy in, 10, 149–50, 267–68nn12–14; popularity in mass culture of, 2, 7–8, 259n1

melodramas of failure, 30, 227–57; interruption of political resignation in, 254–57; the juxtapolitical realm of social

agency in, 237–39; killing of bin Laden and, 250–52; logic of failure and transformation in, 239–42, 303n27, 303n29; refracted melodramatic political discourse in, 228–42, 249–53, 300n6, 301n11; virtue and injury in, 30, 252–53, 304n44; war on terror as, 30, 136–37, 242–53; women's weepies as, 30, 37, 230–42, 268n21, 301nn12–14, 303n27

melodramatic political discourse, 1–8; alternative political forms of, 25; clash of civilizations thesis and, 23–24; felt legitimacy through, 27, 110–14, 130–37, 175–79; five conventions of, 31–38, 63–64, 266n1; forms of demonization of, 99–100; intensification of affect in, 34–35, 43–46, 149–53, 166, 288nn20–22; in leftist political theory, 25, 29, 203–5; marginalization of dissent through, 6–7; masculinized action orientation of, 24, 37, 266n52; moral economy of good and evil in, 1–3, 6–8, 32–33; nation-building role of, 3–6, 22, 34, 259n2, 260n8; orgies of feeling and unfreedom in, 15–20, 28, 35–36, 149–53, 264n34; political actors of, 2–8, 33–34; political spectrum of, 270n31; political work of, 24–27; production of expectations of freedom in, 8–14, 34, 36–37, 122–23, 149–50, 152–53, 181, 225–27; refraction in melodramas of failure of, 228–42, 249–53, 300n6, 301n11; on responsibility for violence, 22; temporalities of, 22–23; weakness and instability of, 137–41, 286–87nn61–63

melodramatic subjectivity, 8, 25; authorization of expanded state power and, 27–29, 180–83; heroic identification with state power of, 181–202, 293nn5–6; judgment of legitimacy and, 28–29, 113; orgies of feeling in, 28, 165–67; unfreedom and powerlessness in, 16–20, 27–28, 35–36, 182. *See also* felt legitimacy; individualism

9/11 attacks (continued)
11–14, 185–86, 262n20, 262n23, 294n22;
jeremiadic discourse on, 21–23, 284n40;
mediated personal experience of, 38–39;
news media coverage of, 25, 31–32,
38–63, 158, 164, 261n9, 270n30,
288nn20–22; as orgy of feeling, 157–67,
175–79; temporal discourses on, 22–23.
*See also* post-9/11 era
*9–11* (Chomsky), 21–22
"9/11 Lesson Plan" (Friedman), 23–24
Nixon, Richard, 100–102
Nodier, Charles, 69
*Now, Voyager*, 237, 259n2
Nowell-Smith, Geoffrey, 305n49
NSC-68 report, 93–94

Obama, Barack, 139–40, 251, 286n62
Office of Homeland Security. *See* U.S.
Department of Homeland Security
Oliverio, Annamarie, 269n28
"On Narcissism" (Freud), 196
*On the Genealogy of Morals* (Nietzsche),
153–57, 287n5
ontological narcissism, 169–70, 175–78,
290n43
Operation Enduring Freedom, 10–11, 123.
*See also* war in Afghanistan
orgies of feeling, 15–20, 28, 149–79,
264n34; ameliorative impact of blame
in, 154–55, 158, 161–67, 174–79, 291n54;
debilitated agency and, 150–63, 176–79,
288n15, 288nn20–22, 289n26; definition
of, 150, 165–66; the error of imaginary
causes in, 166–67, 174–75; expectations
of freedom in, 149–50, 152–53; ideal
of ontological narcissism in, 169–70,
175–78, 290n43; melodramatic
character of the victim in, 163;
Nietzsche's exploration of, 15, 28,
150, 152–57, 159, 162–63, 165–67, 174,
287n5; 9/11 attacks as, 157–67, 175–79;
overcoming of unfreedom with, 152–57,
163–66, 175–79

*The Origin of German Tragic Drama*
(Benjamin), 206, 297n9

pain and suffering. *See* victimization/
suffering
Passavant, Paul, 193
pathos, 10, 215; as identification with
suffering, 35, 149–50, 267–68nn12–14;
9/11 news coverage and, 43–45; proving
one's goodness with, 85
patriotic narcissism, 195–96, 295n35
patriotism, 185–87, 195–96, 260n7
*Les pauvres de Paris*, 79–80
Pearl Harbor attack, 46, 59–61, 65–67
Pearson, Keith Ansell, 287n5
Pentagon. *See* 9/11 attacks; U.S. Department of Defense
*The Perils of Pauline*, 82
Pixérécourt, Guilbert de, 70–76
political actors. *See* victim-heroes; villains
political discourse: genres of, 20–24,
264n40, 266n1; sites of, 20–21. *See also*
melodramatic political discourse
political work of melodrama, 24–27
*The Poor of New York* (Boucicault), 26,
78–79, 81, 83–84
popular legitimacy. *See* felt legitimacy;
legitimacy
Portraits of Grief series, 288n21
postcolonial studies, 208
post-9/11 era: binary interpretation of, 274n3;
blurred distinction between war and
peace, 299n45; Bush's legitimating
discourse of, 119–31; clarification of social
complexity in, 161–62; executive branch
power of, 110, 119; fear and depression
rates in, 289n26, 304n43; felt legitimacy
in, 110–14, 131–41, 175–79; heroic
identification with state power in,
180–202, 293nn5–6; interdependence of,
195–97, 201–2; leftist political theory of,
208–9; left melodrama of, 216–21; orgies
of feeling in, 165–67; patriotism of, 185–87,
195–96, 291n1, 292n3; refracted melodra-

matic political discourse of, 230, 237–42, 249–53; state emotion of, 131–34, 286n51, 286n55; trading of freedom for security in, 14–20, 98–99, 126–27, 139–41, 187–95; weakened identification with the state of, 200–201, 243–44. *See also* war on terror

post–World War II era. *See* cold war era

power. *See* Foucault, Michel; freedom; individualism; security; state sovereignty; unfreedom

powerlessness, 35–36, 86–87, 189–90, 289n26. *See also* unfreedom

procedural legitimacy, 110, 114–15, 281n4. *See also* legitimacy

queer studies, 208

race/racism, 59, 270n36; in American melodrama, 84–87, 277n69; in anti-immigration policies, 17, 18–19, 139, 264n38; in Bush's "Freedom at War . . ." speech, 123–24, 284n34; in homeland security discourses, 58–59, 126, 272n60

Rahill, Frank, 49–50

Rancière, Jacques, 228, 300n6

Rawls, John, 271n47

Reagan, Ronald, 26, 102–7

recession of 2008, 195

Redfield, Marc, 166

refraction, 228–42, 249–53, 300n6

renarrativization, 228, 300n6

Republican National Convention speech of 2004 (G. W. Bush), 128–30, 285n47

"Resisting Left Melancholy" (Brown), 207–9

response to melodrama. *See* melodramatic subjectivity

ressentiment. *See* venomous eye of ressentiment

revolutionary melodrama, 72–73, 74; in French melodramatic theater, 69, 72, 76, 210–11, 274n4, 274n18; of the left, 204, 210–11, 215

Ridge, Tom, 126

Rogin, Michael, 23, 99, 188, 278n80

Roosevelt, Franklin D., 46, 65–67

Rorty, Amelie, 267n12

Rousseau, Jean-Jacques, 69, 75–76, 256n11; on the enlightened political subject, 170; invention of term *mélodrame* by, 34, 210; revolutionary thought of, 76

Russell, David O., 141

sanctioned villainy, 33–34

Sassen, Saskia, 173–74

*Saving Private Ryan*, 10

Schmitt, Carl, 212

Schudson, Michael, 39, 88, 273n71

Schumer, Charles, 59–61, 288n20

security: discourse on legitimation of, 121, 123; heroic identification with state power and, 181–202, 293nn5–6; institutionalization of racism in, 58–59, 123–24, 126, 272n60; public support for, 180; trading of freedom for, 14–20, 98–99, 126–27, 139–41, 187–95. *See also* state sovereignty; unfreedom; U.S. Department of Homeland Security

self-reliance: depoliticized formulations of, 105–7; Emerson's influence on, 171, 177, 290n46, 291n58; as failed neoliberal premise, 12–13, 26–29, 104–7, 172–77, 191; vs. interdependence, 173–75, 195–97, 201–2, 291n51, 291n54; of the liberal subject, 68, 75, 77–84, 94–95, 168–71, 191, 235–39; in Thoreau's *Walden*, 233, 235. *See also* individualism

September 11, 2001 attacks. *See* 9/11 attacks

Sharon, Ariel, 45–46

Silverman, Kaja, 197, 291n51

Simpson, David, 288n21

Singer, Ben, 35, 82, 275n29, 279n90

Siomopoulos, Anna, 301n12

Sirk, Douglas: left melodrama of, 211, 218–19, 302n15; women's weepies of, 232–43, 250, 302nn16–17

U.S. Department of Homeland Security, 140; Bush's legitimating discourse for, 119–31; expanded state powers and, 126–27; procedural illegitimacy of, 110, 114–15, 281n4. *See also* war on terror

U.S. identity discourses, 99–100, 107–9. *See also* melodramatic political discourse

*Valentine, ou la séduction* (Pixérécourt), 26, 73–76

venomous eye of ressentiment, 25; basis in literal pain of, 48–49; moral justification of punishment in, 52; as strategy of identity production, 32–33; transformation of victimhood into power and, 36, 268n19; visuality in the production of identity and, 49–50, 271nn45–47

Vicinus, Martha, 35

victim-heroes, 2–8, 22–24, 33–34, 267n6; agency required of, 221–22, 226; in American melodrama, 80–84; Bush's naming of freedom as, 55–57; *The Communist Manifesto* on, 212–14; encoding anti-Muslim sentiment in, 58–59, 272n60; expectations of freedom for, 8–14, 34, 36–37, 122–23, 149–50, 152–53, 181, 189–92, 225–27; gender stereotypes of, 48, 82, 271n43, 276n52, 277n57, 277n60; heroic identification with state power of, 180–202, 293nn5–6; moral authorization for heroism of, 36–38, 46–50, 52, 59–61, 269n23, 271n42. *See also* unfreedom

victimization/suffering, 2, 4–5, 33–34; debilitated agency and, 150–63, 176–79, 226, 288n15, 288nn20–22, 289n26; impact of orgies of feeling on, 163–67, 174–75, 291n54; intensified affect through identification with, 10, 34–35, 46, 149–50, 166, 267–68nn12–14, 288nn20–22; of left melodrama's readers, 211–15, 221, 300n57; national unification through, 4–5, 34, 45–49, 120–21, 136–37, 270n36; racialized

portrayals of, 84–87, 277n69; role of injury in, 34, 38, 52–53, 60–61. *See also* unfreedom

Vietnam era, 102

villains, 33–34, 73, 227; accepted definitions of, 34; in *The Communist Manifesto*, 213–15; forms of demonization of, 99–100; manicheistic portrayal of, 64, 124–25, 273nn71–72, 284n38, 284n40; Nietzsche on location of blame in, 153–55, 164, 165–67, 174–75, 177; as outside of the self, 165; visual personification of bin Laden as, 53–55, 64. *See also* communism

virtue, 8; of felt legitimacy, 136–37; in melodrama of failure, 30, 252–53, 304n44; in moral economy of goodness and evil, 8, 30, 252–53, 304n44; in 9/11 sequencing of images, 42–44, 51; racialized images of, 84–87, 277n69

Volpp, Leti, 58, 272n60

Wahlberg, Mark, 145

*Walden* (Thoreau), 233, 235

war in Afghanistan, 27; Bush's legitimating discourse for, 4–6, 10, 119–31; felt legitimacy of, 110–11; left melodrama's responses to, 217–21; official title of, 10–11, 123; outcomes of, 125–26, 140–41; procedural illegitimacy of, 110, 114–15, 281n4; public opinion on, 110, 126, 280n1; torture and violence used in, 137–38

war on terror, 1–8; black support for, 270n36; Bush's legitimating discourse for, 4–6, 10, 119–31; failure of, 140–41; felt legitimacy of, 110–14, 131–37, 175–79; Guantánamo prison of, 137–38, 253, 304n45; heroic identification with state power of, 180–202, 293nn5–6; killing of bin Laden in, 164, 194–95, 250–52; left melodrama's responses to, 217–21; limitless power required in, 125–26, 141; "Mission Accomplished" narrative of,

war on terror (continued)
30, 188–89, 200–201, 244–55, 294n24; public opinion on, 110, 126, 180, 280n1, 291n1, 292n3, 294n22; pursuit of sovereign freedom in, 8–14, 225–57; torture used in, 137–38, 200–201; trading of freedom for security in, 14–20, 98–99, 126–27, 139–41, 181, 187–202; weakened state identification in, 137–41, 200–201, 243–44, 286–87nn61–63; as women's weepie, 30, 136–37, 242–55. *See also* Iraq War; post-9/11 era; war in Afghanistan

Watergate era, 102

Weber, Max, 12, 24, 25, 112–18

Wedeen, Lisa, 55, 282n16

Western, David, 286n62

White, Hayden, 228

Williams, Linda, 2, 259n1; on *The Birth of a Nation*, 86; on feeling of righteousness, 133; on identification with victims, 35, 256n10; on melodrama as mode, 212, 215, 266n1; on melodrama's modernization, 273n2; on moral authorization for heroism, 46–47, 271n42; on victim innocence, 267n6; on women's weepies, 255

Williams, Raymond, 16, 133–34

*Will to Power* (Nietzsche), 156–57

Wilson, Woodrow, 86

Wolin, Sheldon, 89, 215, 264n40, 278n80, 282n8

women's weepies, 30, 37, 229–57, 268n21; delinking of virtue and injury in, 252–53, 304n44; feminist critique of, 230–31, 237, 255, 301nn12–14, 303n24; gendered norms of, 304n44; lived unfreedom in, 235–39; refracted melodramatic political discourse in, 228–42, 249–53, 300n6, 303n27; sites of agency in, 231, 237–39, 250; war on terror and "Mission Accomplished" as, 30, 136–37, 242–55. See also *All That Heaven Allows*; melodramas of failure

World Trade Center. *See* 9/11 attacks

World War I, 88, 278n75

World War II, 3–4, 26–27; Pearl Harbor attack of, 46, 59–61, 65–67; political discourse of, 65–67. *See also* cold war era

wounded attachment, 38, 49, 269n23

*Written on the Wind*, 232

Wyman, Jane, 232, 234f, 236f. See also *All That Heaven Allows*

"The Year of Living Dangerously: A Liberal Supporter of the War Looks Back" (Ignatieff), 126–27

Zerilli, Linda, 173

*Zero Dark Thirty*, 251–52